Food, Agriculture, and Development in the Pacific Basin

About the Book and Editors

This book is concerned with the management of food production and the distribution of food in the Pacific Basin, exploring food's potential for engendering both increased conflict and cooperation in the region. The authors begin by discussing the role of food and agriculture in the international economy and the implications of two contrasting approaches to food security: international trade and self-sufficiency. They also consider the problem of international migration of labor in the region and look at how agriculture can contribute to the development of the economy in individual countries. The book concludes with a discussion of the prospects for international collaboration in dealing with the domestic and international adjustments required to enhance overall growth and equity in food supply and distribution.

Dr. G. Edward Schuh is director of agriculture and rural development at the World Bank. He is coeditor (with Gale Johnson) of *The Role of Markets in the World Food Economy* (Westview, 1983). Dr. Jennifer L. McCoy is assistant professor of political science at Georgia State University.

Published in cooperation with
The Hubert H. Humphrey Institute of Public Affairs
University of Minnesota, Minneapolis, Minnesota

Pacific Basin Project, Publication #3

Other Titles in This Series

The Management of Pacific Marine Resources: Present Problems and Future Trends, John P. Craven

The Industrial Future of the Pacific Basin, Roger Benjamin and Robert T. Kudrle

Food, Agriculture, and Development in the Pacific Basin

Prospects for International Collaboration in a Dynamic Economy

edited by G. Edward Schuh and Jennifer L. McCoy

Foreword by Harlan Cleveland

LONDON AND NEW YORK

First published 1986 by Westview Press

Published 2018 by Routledge
52 Vanderbilt Avenue, New York, NY 10017
2 Park Square, Milton Park, Abingdon, Oxon OX14 4RN

Routledge is an imprint of the Taylor & Francis Group, an informa business

Copyright © 1986 by Hubert H. Humphrey Institute of Public Affairs

All rights reserved. No part of this book may be reprinted or reproduced or utilised in any form or by any electronic, mechanical, or other means, now known or hereafter invented, including photocopying and recording, or in any information storage or retrieval system, without permission in writing from the publishers.

Notice:
Product or corporate names may be trademarks or registered trademarks, and are used only for identification and explanation without intent to infringe.

Library of Congress Cataloging-in-Publication Data
Main entry under title:
Food, agriculture, and development in the Pacific Basin.

(Pacific basin project ; publication 3)
"Published in cooperation with the Hubert H. Humphrey Institute of Public Affairs, University of Minnesota, Minneapolis, Minnesota."
Papers resulting from an international workshop held in June 1982 in Mexico City and sponsored by Sistema Alimentario Mexicano, a special organization in the office of the President of Mexico.
Bibliography: p.
Includes index.
1. Food supply—Pacific Area—Congresses.
2. Agriculture—Economic aspects—Pacific Area—Congresses. I. Schuh, George Edward, 1930-
II. McCoy, Jennifer L. III. Hubert H. Humphrey Institute of Public Affairs. IV. Series.
HD9018.P16F66   1986   338.1'099   86-1301

ISBN 13: 978-0-367-00605-1 (hbk)
ISBN 13: 978-0-367-15592-6 (pbk)

Contents

List of Tables and Figures ix
Foreword, *Harlan Cleveland* xiii
Acknowledgments xvii

    Introduction, *Jennifer L. McCoy and G. Edward Schuh* 1

Part 1
The Setting: Development, Food, and the International Economy

1 Food and Agriculture in the Pacific Basin: An Overview,
    G. Edward Schuh and Jennifer L. McCoy 11

2 Economic Growth, Comparative Advantage, and
    Agricultural Trade of Pacific Basin Countries,
    Kym Anderson 22

Part 2
International Trade and Self-Sufficiency: Contrasting Approaches to Food Security

3 The Trade Approach to Food Security, *Ralph Lattimore* 45

4 The SAM Approach to Food Security, *Cassio Luiselli
    and Alejandro Cruz-Serrano* 56

Part 3
Case Studies in Domestic Policy and International Trade

5 Food Policy and the Rice Trade in the Pacific
    Basin Region, *Chung H. Lee and James Roumasset* 73

6 Agricultural-Industrial Interactions,
    Byung-joon Ahn 90

7 Agricultural Development and Policy in the
   People's Republic of China, *Wu Daxin* 105

Part 4
The International Migration of Labor

8 The U.S.-Mexican Labor Market, *Wallace E. Huffman* 121

9 International Migration Within the Pacific Basin:
   Characteristics, Causes, and Consequences,
   Michael J. Greenwood and P. Lynn Stuart 144

Part 5
Technological and Research Capacity, Exchange, and Diffusion

10 Resources for the Production of Agricultural
   Growth in the Pacific Basin Region,
   M. Ann Judd and Robert E. Evenson 161

11 Development of Agricultural Research Capacity:
   Some Perspectives from Asian Experience,
   Vernon W. Ruttan 206

12 The Changing Institutional Nature of Technology
   Diffusion in Latin America: Policy Implications,
   Martin E. Piñeiro and E. J. Trigo 223

Part 6
Conclusions

13 Future Issues and Prospects for International Collaboration
   in the Pacific Basin, *G. Edward Schuh* 255

About the Contributors 275
Index 277

Tables and Figures

Tables

1.1 Wheat imports by world regions for selected periods
from 1934 to 1979......................................13
1.2 Trend of share of food in total imports for 132 developing
countries, 1961-1978 14

2.1 Population, gross national product, land endowment, and
agricultural trade in Pacific Basin countries for 1981 or
earlier selected years 28
2.2 Changing structure of production and employment
in Pacific Basin countries, 1960 to 1981..................30
2.3 Changing export structure and "revealed" comparative
advantage in Pacific Basin countries, 1960 to 1979..........32
2.4 Major commodity shares of agricultural exports for
Pacific Basin countries, 1977-1979.......................36
2.5 Commodity composition and self-sufficiency ratios for
agricultural production in Japan, Korea, and Taiwan,
1955 to 1979..37
2.6 Estimated nominal rates of agricultural protection
in Japan, Korea, and Taiwan, 1955 to 1982...............38
2.7 Changing ratio of farm household incomes to urban
wage and salary earners' household incomes
in Japan and Korea, 1955 to 1979........................41

3.1 Sample distributions of domestic price levels for selected
commodities and countries, 1978.........................52

4.1 Food structure in the Pacific Basin countries 64
4.2 Food imports, food aid, and reserve stocks suggested
by the World Food Council for the least-developed
countries in the Pacific Basin, 1980-1982..................68

4.3	Some food-security indicators in the Pacific Basin countries	68
5.1	Summary rice statistics, world and Pacific Basin area, 1970-1979	74
5.2	Rice trade among selected countries, 1978	76
5.3	Breakdown of Pacific Basin countries by domestic pricing policy and trade position in rice	78
5.4	Effect of domestic pricing policies on international rice trade and prices	78
6.1	Average annual growth rates of economic sectors of selected Pacific Basin countries, 1960-1979	97
6.2	Percentage of GNP by industrial group in the Republic of Korea, selected years from 1956 to 1981	98
6.3	Projected growth rates of economic sectors in national economic plans of the Republic of Korea, 1962-1981	98
6.4	Food production in the Republic of Korea, 1976-1980	100
7.1	Output comparisons of some major farm products and livestock, People's Republic of China, 1949 and 1981	107
7.2	Output of major farm products and number of livestock, People's Republic of China, 1981	107
7.3	Output of major farm products and number of livestock, People's Republic of China, 1982 and 1983	107
8.1	U.S. immigration by country of origin, for selected periods from 1820 to 1977	123
8.2	A summary of macroeconomic indicators—real output, investment, population, labor force, wage rates, and price levels—for the United States, 1950-1980	126
8.3	A summary of macroeconomic indicators—real output, investment, population, labor force, wage rates, and price levels—for Mexico, 1950-1980	128
10.1	Agricultural research expenditures and manpower for Pacific Basin countries by industrial class, 1959-1980	164
10.2	Agricultural research expenditures and manpower by world region (Pacific Basin or other) and by industrial class, 1959-1980	168
10.3	Agricultural research expenditures per scientist man-year by world region (Pacific Basin or other) and by industrial class, 1959-1980	173
10.4	Agricultural extension service expenditures per scientist man-year by world region (Pacific Basin or other) and by industrial class, 1959-1980	174

10.5	Average number of publications on selected agricultural commodities for Pacific Basin and other countries by industrial class, 1972 and 1976	175
10.6	Ratio of number of publications to value of agricultural output (thousands in constant 1980 US $) for Pacific Basin and other countries by industrial class, 1972 and 1976	176
10.7	Private-sector agricultural research activity in selected countries for selected years	179
10.8	Patent activity as reflected by number of patents for agricultural technology fields, United States, 1800s and 1900s	182
10.9	Industrial design patents and trademarks granted in selected countries (grouped by level of economy), 1975 and 1980	184
10.10	Utility models (petty patents) granted in selected countries, 1967, 1975, and 1980	186
10.11	Average annual distribution of patents granted in selected countries (by industrial sector), according to the International Patent Classification, 1970–1974	188
10.12	Comparison of "LAARC" research developments and inventions with availability of patent or variety protection in various Latin American countries and the United States	192
10.13	Patents granted in relation to agricultural production, selected countries, 1965–1972	196
10.14	Patents granted in relation to agricultural production, by level of per capita income in the countries involved, 1965–1972	197
11.1	U.S. multilateral and bilateral assistance to developing countries for selected fiscal years from 1970 to 1979	208
11.2	Illustration of a funding model for agricultural research support	219
12.1	Funding for agricultural research in Latin America and the Caribbean for selected years from 1960 to 1980	230
12.2	Personnel entering agriculturally related postgraduate studies at INTA (Argentina), ICA (Colombia), and La Molina Agrarian University (Peru), 1965–1978	231
12.3	Total staff with postgraduate training (MS or PhD) at INTA (Argentina), ICA (Colombia), and La Molina Agrarian University (Peru), 1965–1978	232
12.4	Latin America: Average annual percentage yield increases of thirteen products in eighteen countries, 1958–1978	233
12.5	Average annual percentage rates of increase in production and yields of eight products in different world regions, 1958–1978	234

12.6 Nitrogen and phosphorus consumption per hectare of arable land or land under permanent crops in Latin America, 1961-1965 and 1977-1978 238

Figures

1.1 U.S. trade weighted exchange rate versus U.S. agricultural exports. 18
3.1 A classification of food price policies 49
5.1 Domestic supply and demand curves for the major exporter of rice. 80
5.2 Domestic supply and demand curves for the major importer of rice 80
5.3 World supply and demand curves in an international rice market affected by policies of a major exporter and a major importer 81
5.4 World supply and demand curves in a simplified model of the international rice market 81
8.1 An isocost, isoquant relationship in a three-factor (U, S, K), two-commodity (A, M) trade model............ 132
8.2 A three-factor (U, S, K), two-commodity (A, M) general equilibrium model 133

Foreword

In the late 1970s a sudden wave of organizational enthusiasm crested for various projects concerning the Pacific. Japan's Prime Minister (1979-1980) Masayoshi Ohira initially envisioned the concept of a "Pacific Community" and discovered a mutually interested party in Australia's Prime Minister Malcolm Fraser. In fact, Australia sponsored the first in a series of seminars about a Pacific Community of nations. Meanwhile, in the United States, congressional committees compiled reports and held hearings on Ohira's Pacific Community idea.

In the structure of world order the technologically strong are usually the first to demand and establish organization and institutions. The technologically weak—the developing nations—customarily react with apprehension, fearing that the strong want to freeze their comparative strength. So it was with the Pacific Community. A Korean described the concept as "a prematurely born child." Voices from ASEAN (the Association of Southeast Asian Nations), protective of their newly valued subregional cooperation, were fiercely cautious about what one of their spokesmen called "promoting a generalized Community."

In the Western Pacific and East Asia, wartime Japan's greater East Asian Co-Prosperity Sphere still lives in memory. Forty years later, another co-prosperity sphere, even if promoted by certifiably democratic politicians in Japan, Australia, and the United States, still evokes too many disturbing overtones. Just now, it seems every U.S., Japanese, or Australian drumbeat for new Pacific-wide political institutions intensifies the polite but firm, passive resistance of the Pacific's "South"—ASEAN, the Pacific islands, the Republic of Korea, and the two parts of a still divided China.

Meanwhile, two independent institutes in the United States that are engaged in policy research have remained deeply interested in the future

---

The first few paragraphs of this foreword (relating the history of the Pacific Basin Project) and the last few paragraphs (about the future of this exciting region) are adapted from the first volume in this Pacific Basin Series, referred to in the text below.

of the Pacific—the Aspen Institute for Humanistic Studies and the University of Minnesota's newly expanded Hubert H. Humphrey Institute of Public Affairs. Together they envisioned a new approach to the Pacific Community, namely, to set aside for the time being the issue of political organization in the Pacific Basin and begin instead with the underlying questions: What concrete problems need to be tackled, what functions need to be performed that might require new forms of international consultation, cooperation, coordination, parallel national action, or common action by concerned communities in the Pacific Basin?

Until there is some consensus about what has to be done and by whom, the questions raised by "Pacific Community" in its generalized form are indeed unanswerable because prematurely political. A political question like "Which countries should be 'members' of a Pacific Community?" can be addressed only in the context of the functional questions: What action is required, and which countries are in a position to do what about it?

To answer these questions, the Pacific Basin Project was born, a joint venture of the Aspen and Humphrey Institutes. After a time, the Aspen Institute was unable to continue as a sponsor, but the University of Pittsburgh (whose new provost, Dr. Roger Benjamin, had as a member of the University of Minnesota faculty been a prime mover in the project) became the Humphrey Institute's main U.S. partner in carrying the project to completion.

The key strategy of the project was to assemble an international "core group," persons from different nations and economic systems who were willing to suspend, for the project's purpose, their natural biases of nation and culture and ideology. The core group has remained glued together for this purpose during a five-year period. It includes a businessman from New Zealand (Michael Hirschfeld), a journalist from Indonesia (Mochtar Lubis), a research institute director from Singapore (K. S. Sandhu), an economist from Japan (first Saburo Okita, then Seizaburo Sato), a political economist from Mexico (Jorge Lozoya, now an undersecretary of state), and three participants from the United States (sociologist Herbert Passin of Columbia University, political scientist Roger Benjamin of Pittsburgh, and myself).

In its first meeting, at Baca Grande in Colorado during the summer of 1980, the core group developed a clear-headed plan of attack. We would first consider, in a series of multinational but nongovernmental workshops, four functional fields in which a thicker web of Pacific-wide cooperation might turn out to be needed: (1) the management of the Pacific Ocean itself, (2) the changing industrial geography of the Pacific Basin, (3) the prospects for food and development, and (4) the Pacific impact of the communications/information revolution. Thereafter we would tackle the most difficult puzzle: to derive from these functional studies some feel for (5) the political and institutional futures in the Pacific Basin.

The first workshop, on marine resources, was held in Tokyo in June 1981, cosponsored and hosted by the International House of Japan. The program was organized by Dr. John P. Craven, Dean of Marine Programs at the University of Hawaii and director of the international Law of the

Sea Institute. The resulting book, *The Management of Pacific Marine Resources*, by John P. Craven, was published by Westview Press as Volume 1 in our Pacific Basin Series.

Volume 2, also published by Westview Press, was *The Industrial Future of the Pacific Basin*, edited by Roger Benjamin and Robert T. Kudrle. It was the product of a second international workshop, held in August 1981 in Seoul, Republic of Korea, on the changing industrial structure of the world's most dynamic region. That workshop was hosted by the Korean-U.S. Economic Council (KUSEC) and the Korean Development Institute (KDI), and cosponsored by the East-West Center in Honolulu.

This book is the third in the Pacific Basin Series. It began as a collection of commissioned papers for a project workshop in Mexico City in June 1982, cosponsored and hosted by SAM (*Sistema Alimentario Mexicano*), a special organization in the office of the president of Mexico for the promotion of agricultural development. That workshop was organized by Dr. G. Edward Schuh, then chairman of the University of Minnesota's Department of Agricultural and Applied Economics and now a senior official of the World Bank, who with Jennifer McCoy has edited the present volume.

Since that time the Pacific Basin Project has carried through its original mandate. A fourth functional workshop on "Pacific Communications: The Passing of Remoteness," was held in Singapore in December 1984, with the assistance of the East-West Center and hosted by the Institute for Southeast Asian Studies and the Asian Mass Communication Research and Information Center. The integrating session of the core group, an effort to think through the "Political and Institutional Futures in the Pacific Basin," was hosted by the East-West Center in Honolulu in August 1985.

* * *

In ancient Greece people traveled from afar to consult the oracle at Delphi. In reply to the questions they posed, they got paradoxes that left them, baffled but still intrigued, with the task of deciphering their own destinies.

In modern times we need only consult the oracles on the world food problem (it's not yet organized enough to call it a "system") to find paradoxes that are comparably baffling and intriguing. How do we rescue the weakest consumers yet set the strongest producers free? How do we reconcile two equally legitimate ambitions—high prices with restricted output and high yields to increase volume? How do we marry the U.S. (and Canadian and Australian) drive to export food and feed with the imperative impulse to develop agriculture in the developing world? Why, even though we understand food *needs*, do we focus public policy on the *demand* for food by the affluent hungry? What does it mean to advocate both *free* and *fair* (which is to say managed) trade in agricultural commodities? The Delphic oracle would have been charmed by the food policy debates of the 1980s.

But in one part of the world a combination of education, agricultural research, and comparatively stable governance may make it possible to avoid that cruelest of modern dilemmas, famine in the midst of plenty. If governments don't manage by policy to deny the promise, the Pacific Basin may be the world's first major region both to produce enough food *and* to spread it around more or less fairly to those who need to eat it.

Futurists have been forecasting a "Pacific century." To participants in our Tokyo workshop, the long-run prospects for the Pacific Basin were hard to be pessimistic about if we were willing to look a generation ahead.

The central problem for the Pacific region today is all too obvious: its great dependence on Middle East oil and Atlantic products, squeezing through the narrow choke points of Malacca and Panama. With modern technologies and a generation of time, the Pacific Basin contains sufficient resources to erase the region's energy deficit. Meanwhile more and more Pacific nations will be moving—they already are moving—from the periphery to the center of communications and information flows. The rapid development of educated peoples and rural enterprise already points to an era of food adequacy without undue dependence on the great world granaries, which also rim the Pacific. The message of overpopulation has gotten through, including to China. In one generation, without war, there should be no "poor nations" lapped by the Pacific Ocean.

Harlan Cleveland, Dean
Hubert H. Humphrey Institute of Public Affairs
University of Minnesota

Acknowledgments

This volume is a product of an international workshop and thus would not have been possible without considerable institutional and personal support from several sources. Our host in Mexico City, where the workshop was held, was the *Sistema Alimentario Mexicano* (SAM). Cassio Luiselli and Alejandro Cruz-Serrano of SAM made all the local arrangements and provided invaluable assistance in organizing and leading the conference. Roger Benjamin, as director of the Pacific Basin Project, was responsible for the conference from its earliest planning stages through to its realization. Of course, the workshop would not have been the success it was without the participants who provided the expertise, the stimulating discussions, and the ideas about potential international collaboration in the issues of food and agriculture in the Pacific Basin.

Several people contributed to the actual compilation of the published volume. Howard Lehman, Roger Marietta, and Bruce Posey provided much appreciated editorial assistance. Kim Holschuh very capably entered the manuscript and its many revisions into the word processor.

G. Edward Schuh
Jennifer L. McCoy

Food, Agriculture, and Development in the Pacific Basin

Introduction

Jennifer L. McCoy
G. Edward Schuh

We are facing today in the global political economy the frustration and cruelty of starvation in a world of plenty. While ten years ago the specter of food scarcity seemed very real, in the 1980s there is no *aggregate* shortage of food supplies. Instead, the problem lies in the distribution of that food— and in broader terms in underdevelopment, poverty, and international and national inequality of incomes.

Among the countries that rim the Pacific Ocean are some of the world's largest food exporters and importers. How to manage the growth in worldwide agricultural production and trade becomes, then, a central issue for the Pacific Basin nations. How can the agricultural sector contribute to overall national and global economic development and improve the welfare of individuals within the international community? What are the prospects for international cooperation, rather than competition and conflict, to emerge as nation-states strive to ensure a secure food supply for their own citizens? In what specific areas should we look for potential international collaboration and cooperation in resolving the cruel dilemma of hunger amidst plenty?

This volume is the product of an international workshop where scholars and practitioners from countries of the Pacific Basin addressed the issues raised above. Meeting in Mexico City in 1982, the authors first presented the papers included here, later revising them specifically for this volume. Approaching the food issue as related to underdevelopment and structural discrimination against the poor, the workshop focused on four more specific sets of questions. First, what is the potential for international cooperation and conflict in the area of food security as nations pursue different self-sufficiency strategies and trade options? Second, how can national policies regarding the interaction between agricultural development and industrial development be better formulated as a means of addressing the general development problem and improved food distribution capacities? Third, what are the causes and consequences of the international migration of labor within the Pacific Basin? Finally, what are the possibilities for cooperation in the area of technology development and transfer, and thus increased productivity?

The organization of the volume follows these themes, with Part 1 providing the setting of development and agriculture in the Pacific Basin. In Chapter 1, Schuh and McCoy provide an overview of the trends in food production and agricultural trade over the past two decades. There we argue that the central food problem today is not a Malthusian population crisis of food scarcity, but rather a problem of distribution in a world of relative food abundance. The challenge that lies ahead, therefore, is not one of how to increase world agricultural production. Instead, it is one requiring a resolution of the difficult problems of poverty and income distribution. We need to consider how agriculture can contribute to the development of the general economy in individual countries, and how international trade can be managed to improve the welfare of all peoples in the Pacific Basin.

In the second chapter, Kym Anderson analyzes the relationships between economic development, changing comparative advantage, and food trade. Asking what happens to the agricultural trade situation of a country as its economy grows, Anderson answers his question both theoretically and empirically by analyzing the actual changes that have occurred in the Pacific Basin countries over the past two decades. Concluding that the agricultural sector of each country will decline in relative and possibly absolute terms, and that comparative advantage in agricultural trade will follow suit for most countries, he discusses some possible policy responses to those changes and their implications for closer economic integration in the region.

Food Security: International Trade or Self-Sufficiency?

The issue of food security is a politically sensitive one. Indeed, the definition of food security itself is open to debate. The link between food security and national strategic security, the concern with national autonomy, and the desire for stability in price and supply bring the debate over the best approach to food security into the political arena as well as the economic. The ability to ensure an adequate supply of food for a population on a regular basis can be achieved through a variety of strategies. Internal measures include stockpiling food or pursuing self-sufficiency strategies. International measures include collective stockpiling, international food-security schemes, and relying on trade to make up for any shortfalls in production. Part 2 of this volume presents two contrasting approaches to the achievement of food security. In the first, economic arguments based on the gains from trade support the achievement of food security through international trade. This perspective is challenged, however, primarily on the part of Third World countries, by the second argument for food security through self-sufficiency.

Ralph Lattimore analyzes the gains from trade for food security and concludes that international trade can indeed provide a reliable source of food to enable a country to meet food consumption needs. Even more, though, exposure to international trade contributes significantly to efficient development of both agriculture and industry in the underdeveloped countries of the region. The challenge lies in improving the rules of international food trade to help offset extreme variations in world markets and assure an equitable distribution of food while still making the most efficient use of global agricultural resources.

A contrasting approach to food security is the Mexican Food System (SAM), which emphasizes self-sufficiency. A primary motivation for food self-sufficiency is the reduction of dependence on food imports, based on national security needs, and the corollary issue of the availability of food as a political weapon. The actual use of grain embargoes as a foreign policy instrument by the United States gives grounds for concern to many countries striving to reduce their dependence on food imports, and thereby decrease vulnerability. Cassio Luiselli and Alejandro Cruz-Serrano define food security in a broad sense to include not only assured access to essential foodstuffs necessary for national consumption, but such issues as technology transfers, equitable trade flows, distribution mechanisms, transfer of financial resources, and permanent reserves. They argue that food security can be achieved through increased self-sufficiency in food production, and that such a strategy contributes both to broader economic and social development goals and to enhanced national sovereignty. For larger industrializing countries with sufficient arable land, they suggest that the SAM approach to food production, initiated in Mexico in 1980, can provide a model for achieving these goals. Finally, they make recommendations for new international and regional cooperative efforts in food production, trade, and distribution.

Domestic Policy and International Trade

In addition to the motivations for self-sufficiency, another set of factors affecting free trade in agriculture involves the domestic policy interventions of individual nation-states. Policy interventions include not only trade barriers and exchange rate interventions, but also agricultural price supports, credits, subsidies, and storage policies. It may be possible for increasing internal intervention to coexist with increasing liberalization of international trade. Nevertheless, the enormous impact of domestic policies, particularly in the food-exporting nations, on the stability of the world food market must be recognized. For example, while the food exporters of the region (the United States, Canada, Australia, and New Zealand) were able to relax their interventionist policies in the 1970s because of past price supports, the lower world food prices of the 1980s have contributed to movements back toward policies of large reserve holdings in which these countries, and the United States in particular, may again function as international stockholder and central banker.

At the same time, the high-income and newly industrializing importing countries have become trapped in policies protecting high agricultural prices in the domestic economy due to such factors as the previously high international prices and the political clout of farmers. Low-income countries, meanwhile, are penalizing their agricultural sectors through such policy interventions as import-substitution strategies and artificially low food prices.

In Part 3 of this volume, Chung Lee and James Roumasset address these issues in their analysis of domestic rice policies in the Pacific Basin countries and the effect of these policies on international trade, prices of rice, and world price stability. From a perspective emphasizing the pursuit of a more efficient allocation of resources in accordance with comparative advantage as one means of increasing world rice production, the authors compare the effect of provisionist, protectionist, and self-sufficiency national rice policies on trade. They conclude by assessing the possibilities for the removal of many of the distorting policies without significantly reducing food security.

The interaction between agricultural development policies and industrial development policies is a crucial theme running throughout the volume. Certainly agricultural development policies must be incorporated in overall development strategies, but unfortunately, these policies have often been generated in a vacuum, virtually divorced from industrial policies. A focus on either the agricultural sector or the industrial sector alone can lead to unbalanced growth processes. This kind of focus has been particularly problematic for some of the newly industrializing countries (NICs) in East Asia, with their emphasis on export-led industrial growth necessitating large agricultural imports. In South Korea, for example, the development of technical capacity and research efforts at first focused almost exclusively on industry, with investment in agricultural research equalling only one-fourth to one-fifth of that spent in other developing countries in the region.

Byung-joon Ahn analyzes such agricultural-industrial interactions both theoretically and in a case study of South Korea. He describes the transformation from a subsistence agriculture economy to a newly industrializing one based on an outward-looking, export-led growth strategy in South Korea. The subsequent stagnation of the agricultural sector caused a policy change in the 1970s, however, as a new attempt to redress the imbalance was initiated. The South Korean government instituted new agricultural price support policies and launched the Saemaul Movement, or New Community Movement, aimed at promoting the physical environment of the rural villages and at raising rural incomes through self-help, cooperative programs. The debate over food security through trade or through self-sufficiency continues in South Korea.

The example of the South Korean self-help programs and mobilization of peasant farmers raises broader questions concerning the methods for social innovation, such as how to motivate the peasants and small farmers to participate in these self-help programs. Traditional patterns and attitudes may serve as constraints on social change. In this case, education of the peasants, decentralization of the administrative structure, and examples set by the government become crucial to developing the peasant and small farmer agricultural sector. It is in this context that the social aspects of development must be taken into account, not as derivatives, but as primary forces of social and economic change. Development processes have tremendous impact on traditional social structures because they involve vast movements of people and they affect values and cultural identity. This social dimension has been far too often neglected in assessments and proposals for agricultural development strategies.

The interaction of agricultural and industrial policies and the relative priorities given to each sector in the overall development strategies are also rooted in security and political issues. South Korea today is an example of an attempt to achieve a balanced economy through both outward-looking strategies of industrial exports and inward-looking strategies of food production to reduce dependence on imported food. Mexico attempted an outward-looking strategy, but returned to an inward strategy in part to reduce the undesirable dependence on imports. The People's Republic of China is striving for food self-sufficiency and the development of a strong agricultural base for the economy, in part for security reasons.

Wu Daxin discusses recent changes in Chinese agricultural policy in his chapter on agricultural development in China. After discussing the achievements in agricultural production since 1949, Wu describes a major series of agricultural policies and rural economic measures formulated since 1978 to correct existing problems and increase agricultural production. These new policies include measures to respect the self-management of production teams in the countryside; the relaxation of restrictions on private plots, livestock, and sideline occupations; and the diversification of the rural economy. The success of Chinese agriculture these last three years, with successive annual increases of 10 percent per year, illustrate what can happen when policy provides appropriate incentives to producers.

The International Labor Market

International migration affects agriculture through both a "brain drain" of skilled labor and the loss of unskilled workers. Incentives for migration arise out of a number of factors, such as barriers to trade, barriers to international capital flow, and political repression. Furthermore, even though migration and the tolerance of migration by governments on both sides may result in second-best policies that inhibit growth for each, political considerations make difficult such solutions as opening up the economies to freer trade and capital flows.

Part 4 deals with the issue of international labor migration. Wallace Huffman analyzes the largest labor market in the Pacific Basin: the U.S.-Mexican labor market. After reviewing the history of Mexican emigration to the United States, Huffman presents a model of immigration and trade to predict the long-term effects of significant U.S. immigration. He concludes with recommendations for a coordinated migrant labor policy among Pacific Basin countries.

Michael Greenwood and Lynn Stuart present a more general analysis of international migration within the Pacific Basin. Focusing on migration to the United States from a variety of countries, the authors identify the dominant migratory flow patterns and the motivations for migration in the region, present a descriptive profile of the demographic and labor-force characteristics of migrants, and discuss the probable effects of migration on both the receiving and sending countries.

Technology and Research in Agriculture

Agricultural research and technology transfer may prove to be the most feasible area for international cooperation, at least in the near future. Existing international research institutes and the somewhat less politically sensitive motives of technology provide a useful base from which to initiate cooperative efforts. Although National Research Institutes have been established since the 1950s in most Pacific Basin countries, their capacity has been eroding in more recent years along with the decline of international aid. In their place, the international agricultural research systems now appear to be the bright spot in technical advances, with the big advances achieved in the past now being institutionalized and developed by these centers.

One of the most crucial issues today for technical advance in agricultural productivity is the capacity of individual countries to adapt technology developed abroad or in the international centers to local conditions and requirements. Particularly for underdeveloped countries (for which the adopted technology is biased toward the needs of the industrially advanced countries in which it was created), suitable adaptive capacity is critical if the imported technology is to increase local productivity.

A second issue in the development of national research capacity in many of the Pacific Basin countries is the lack of advanced training at the national level. In many of these countries, the National Research Institutes have followed the U.S. model but have failed to connect the research with the teaching. As a result, the universities do little or no applied agricultural research and so do not have a demand for postgraduate research programs.

Part 5 addresses these issues in the development and exchange of technological and research capacity. Ann Judd and Robert Evenson assess the capacity to achieve agricultural growth through technology in the region as a whole. The discussion includes both the public-sector programs of support for agricultural research and extension programs, and the private-sector contribution with emphasis on the role of legal systems in encouraging invention. The authors conclude that the legal systems in place in most developing and semiindustrialized economies of the region do very little to encourage technology production in the private sector and stimulate indigenous invention.

Vernon Ruttan discusses the development of agricultural research capacity from an Asian perspective. In his chapter, Ruttan first discusses international assistance for national agricultural research systems. He then goes on to compare several of the major Asian research systems. Finally, he discusses some of the crucial challenges present today, pointing out such factors as the relative neglect of development of scientific staff, excessive administrative burdens, lack of congruence between research budgets and the economic importance of major commodities for the economy, and the cycles of development and erosion of capacity that have characterized a number of national agricultural research systems. Ruttan concludes with a proposal for reform of the system of international support for agricultural research.

Martin Piñeiro and E. J. Trigo analyze the changing institutional nature of technology diffusion from a Latin American perspective. They trace technological change in Latin American agriculture through three historical periods: the pre-World War II era, the post-World War II era of strong participation by the public sector through the National Research Institutes, and the third phase beginning in the mid-1970s in which the private sector has become increasingly predominant, especially through transnational firms producing the capital goods and inputs required for technological innovation. The authors conclude that the process of technical change in Latin America is increasingly determined by developments that take place in the industrialized world and the existence of certain institutional mechanisms. New institutional developments themselves present difficult policy issues concerning the role of public-sector institutions and the nature of technical change in a context in which the private sector becomes increasingly important in the generation of knowledge.

The last part of the book provides a discussion of the issues facing the Pacific Basin in the decade ahead. G. Edward Schuh lays out the crucial issues and challenges in food and agricultural development, then discusses the prospects for international cooperation and collaboration to deal with these challenges in the years ahead.

Part 1

The Setting: Development, Food, and the International Economy

1
Food and Agriculture in the Pacific Basin: An Overview

G. Edward Schuh
Jennifer L. McCoy

Events of the 1970s gave the world a rather severe scarcity syndrome with respect to its ability to feed itself. This perspective arose, in part, out of the rapid rise in agricultural prices in the United States in the early 1970s, which came after a relatively long period of stable and, in real terms, downward drifting commodity prices. After twenty years of dealing with a problem of chronic excess production, U.S. citizens and policymakers suddenly experienced food and agricultural prices that were rising at a dramatic rate. After almost twenty years of implicit and explicit export subsidies, the world witnessed the United States placing an embargo on soybean exports in order to assure domestic supplies.

These events coincided—fortunately or unfortunately—with the publication of *The Limits to Growth*[1] and other reports of the Club of Rome, and with the rapid escalation of petroleum prices as OPEC (the Organization of Petroleum Exporting Countries) gained control of the price of petroleum. All of these developments reinforced the notion that something drastic had occurred on the world scene and that despite the previous extended period of prosperity the world was now truly facing a Malthusian crisis.

Trade in agricultural products grew rapidly during the 1970s. Given that much of the expansion of imports during this period came from the less-developed countries where population was growing rapidly, the image of a Malthusian crisis was further reinforced. The Soviet Union changed its policies so that consumer diets were not affected by domestic shortfalls. Moreover, it made a concerted effort to upgrade the quality of diet it provided its citizens. The periodic surges in imports which this policy elicited brought Soviet shortfalls to world attention. When this excess demand came on world markets that were already relatively tight for other reasons, the image of a world unable to feed itself was brought into sharp focus.

But the image is not the reality. Contrary to a world of scarcity, what we have really been experiencing is a world of relative abundance—if taken in the aggregate. This is not to say that there are not many hungry people around the world. But it is important to recognize the causes of that hunger. Proper diagnosis is the road to devising proper policies to deal with this problem.

Indeed, our challenge for the decades ahead is how to deal with the potential abundance we may well have. This will require that we devise means to use the agricultural sector and its considerable resources to contribute to the more general development of the international economy. Devising ways to cooperate in raising per capita incomes on a broad basis in the Pacific Basin is quite a different matter than devising ways to deal with a Malthusian crisis. Rather than focusing on increasing agricultural production, it requires that we examine the role of agriculture in the larger economy, that we consider the rural-urban labor adjustment problem that many countries will face, that we consider how agriculture can contribute to the development of the general economy in individual countries, and that we devise means so that international trade and an international division of labor can lead to an increase in the welfare of all peoples in the Pacific Basin.

Background on the International Food and Agricultural Economy

A useful starting point in developing a background on the international food and agricultural economy is to recognize that total trade in all goods and services has grown at a faster rate than has world GNP (gross national product) almost throughout the post–World War II period. That should not have been a surprise in light of the rapid technological progress made in the communication and transportation sectors of the world economy. But it did surprise many observers who had witnessed the collapse of the international trading system in the 1930s and who observed the spread of autarchic policies at the end of World War II. Overall, most of us probably underestimated the progress made in this period in lowering trade barriers by a series of multilateral trade negotiations.

The increased interdependence that this growth in total trade represented is important, for it serves as an important backdrop for the increased interdependence in food and agricultural products that eventually followed. It is interesting that the growth in trade in nonagricultural goods and services was generally viewed positively. When trade in food and agricultural products suddenly expanded at a rapid rate, it did not elicit the same positive views.

This pattern of world trade in food products has changed markedly over time.[2] Wheat is a major element in world food trade, and changes in its pattern can be used to typify the changing overall food trade patterns. Prior to World War II almost three-quarters of the world wheat trade was

TABLE 1.1
Wheat Imports by World Regions for Selected Periods from 1934 to 1979 (Percentages of World Totals)

Period	Europe, USSR, Japan	Latin America, Asia (except Japan), Africa
1934-1938	73	27
1959-1963	52	48
1969-1971	32	68
1978-1979	31	69

Source: FAO (Food and Agriculture Organization) Trade Yearbooks, various issues, as reported in Grant M. Scobie, Government Policy and Food Imports: The Case of Wheat in Egypt (Washington, D.C.: International Food Policy Research Institute, 1981).

composed of the imports of Europe, the USSR, and Japan. By 1978-1979 this position relative to the developing regions of the world had been exactly reversed. In that year almost three-quarters of world wheat trade was composed of the imports of Latin America, Asia (excluding Japan), and Africa (see Table 1.1).

The total trade in cereals has evolved in much this same direction. From 1971 to 1979, for example, net grain imports by the less-developed countries increased over sixfold, from 8.9 million to 54.5 million metric tons, and imports by the centrally planned (socialist) economies increased over sevenfold, from 6.5 million to 54.6 million metric tons. During this same period, exports to major traditional markets, including Japan, the European Community, and other Western European countries increased only 40 percent, from 27.4 million to 38.3 million metric tons. Most of this latter increase was accounted for by Japan; imports by the European Community actually declined by 68 percent, from 13 million to 4.2 million metric tons in this period. Since 1980, the European Community—aided by sizable export subsidies—has actually become a net exporter of wheat.

It would be a mistake to conclude from the above data that the low-income countries are becoming more dependent on trade for food supply, however. Clearly, for the less-developed countries as a whole the absolute imports of cereals are increasing. Moreover, for the group as a whole, the share of imports in total consumption is higher now than in the postwar years. But much of the growth in food trade (and especially in cereals) has been accounted for by middle-income countries, with the predominant features being the rise in their imports of livestock feed and livestock products. In the 1950s less than 20 percent of the international trade in grains was used as feed for animals. Today, over 40 percent is so used. The increased demand for livestock products is associated with increases in per capita incomes. Hence, the increase in cereal trade is motivated at least in part by increases in per capita income, not by Malthusian conditions.

TABLE 1.2
Trend of Share of Food in Total Imports for 132 Developing Countries, 1961-1978

Per Capita Income (US $)	Number of Countries in Which Share of Food:[a]			
	Fell	Remained Unchanged	Rose	Total
Low ($400)	17	11	19	47
Middle ($400-$800)	30	4	7	41
High ($800)	26	10	8	44
Total	73	25	34	132

[a] Includes beverages, cereals, sugar, meats and meat products, fruits and vegetables, oils, and oilseeds.

Source: FAO data types, as reported in Grant M. Scobie, Government Policy and Food Imports: The Case of Wheat in Egypt (Washington, D.C.: International Food Policy Research Institute, 1981).

Another way to view this issue is to ask whether imports of food are, over time, taking a larger or smaller share of the total claims of the developing countries in foreign goods and services. Grant Scobie, in the IFPRI study cited in note 2, asked just such a question. What he found was that during the last two decades imported food has become a *smaller* share of the claims of these countries on foreign goods and services. In fact, he found that whereas food imports in 1960 represented almost 20 percent of the import bills (excluding fuels) of these countries, that proportion had fallen to 10 percent by 1980.

There is considerable diversity among countries on such an issue. Scobie examined the record for 132 developing countries, and the results are presented in Table 1.2. What he found was that the share of food imports in the total claims against foreign goods and services had fallen in over half (seventy-three) of the 132 countries and that it had remained unchanged in another twenty-five. This share increased in only one-fourth of the countries, or thirty-four. Of these thirty-four, only nineteen were classified as low-income countries. Although thirty-four countries is obviously a significant number, the trend is still a different matter from the general perception that the less-developed countries in toto are facing a growing import burden for food.

Clearly, the share of food imported can rise rapidly in a particular country in a particular year or years. However, that is a rather different problem to deal with by policy or institutional means than a secular problem, if it existed, that was becoming increasingly serious.

It is useful to remind ourselves of the various factors that can lead to increases in food imports. The population problem has tended to dominate the debate during the last decade—a debate with heavy Malthusian overtones.

However, increases in per capita income can also lead to increases in import demand even if the supply side of agriculture is doing reasonably well. An example was given above in terms of the increased demand for livestock feed and livestock products as a component of total import demand. It should be noted in this regard that an important component of the demand for feed grains is the rapid spread around the world of the new production technology for the poultry industry. This technology to date has been low in location specificity. Moreover, poultry are relatively efficient converters of grains into livestock products. Overall, there appear to be rather significant efficiency gains from the diffusion of this technology, if the comparison is made to other livestock products. Moreover, there are significant income and welfare gains because the new technology leads to a significant decline in the real prices of these protein sources.

Another factor leading to increased food imports is rapidly growing foreign exchange earnings. With flexible exchange rates this growth leads to a rise in the value of the home country's currency and with that rise a decline in the real price of imports. Outstanding examples of countries experiencing such changes are the petroleum exporters such as Nigeria, Indonesia, Mexico, Venezuela, and the Middle East nations. We should note that such exchange rate realignments often shift the domestic terms of trade against agriculture, damping domestic agricultural supply and leading to an increased dependence on food imports.

Real exchange rates are often implicitly altered when countries cling to a fixed exchange rate even though their domestic rate of inflation is outpacing that of their trading partners. When this situation occurs, the real value of the country's currency is forced to rise artificially. Such a rise constitutes an implicit import subsidy and/or an implicit export tax. It may cause a country to export less or to import more, and in some cases to shift from being a net exporter of agricultural products to being a net importer.

Such distortions of the exchange rate have been typical of Mexico in recent years and help to explain in part why Mexico's dependence on imported food is growing so rapidly. It would be useful to know to what extent the growing imports of the nineteen low-income countries referred to above were due to such distortions in the exchange-rate policy. Burgeoning import bills for petroleum have forced many countries to adopt more restrictive exchange rate policies in recent years. This move will obviously force more favorable domestic terms of trade for agriculture in those countries.

Finally, we should recognize that changes in real commodity prices themselves may affect food imports. If the real prices facing importing countries were to fall, food imports could be expected to increase even if there was considerable progress in home-country agriculture. Similarly, imports could be expected to decline even if progress in home-country agriculture was slow, if the real prices facing the importing countries were to rise.

What in fact has been happening to real commodity prices? The scarcity syndrome would lead us to believe that they were rising over this past decade. That increase really is the economic content and implication of a Malthusian world.

But is that increase what is happening? Corn and wheat are two widely traded and widely consumed food cereals. In 1982 the real prices of these two commodities were at their lowest levels since 1932, at the pit of the Great Depression. D. Gale Johnson noted that in the latter half of the 1970s the real prices of wheat and maize were as low as at any time since the last century.[3] These low prices were the case in spite of the significant expansion in demand and the significant increase in trade during the 1970s—hardly a picture of a scarcity situation.

The same picture emerges if one considers a broader set of data. Scobie constructed a simple average of the real price indices of ten commodities that constitute principal foodstuffs.[4] Expressing 1965-1969 as 100, the pattern of real prices, calculated as unit export prices in constant 1979 dollars, is:

1950-1954	$127	
1955-1959	$104	
1960-1964	$101	
1965-1969	$100	
1970-1974	$116	($103 excluding 1974)
1975-1979	$84	

Given that there have not been many changes in the quality of these commodities over time, the unit price is a reasonable representation of the cost per unit. Similarly, export prices represent supply availability. If countries put a tariff on these imports or otherwise charge their domestic consumers higher prices, that is another matter. The representative supply price is the export price.

In any case, what one sees is anything but a rise in the real price of the principal food commodities. The data for the early 1950s were influenced by the commodity boom associated with the Korean War—an episodic event. Under more normal conditions the prices would probably not have been that high. Historically, we will increasingly look back at the 1970s as the monetary event that it primarily was—associated with two successive devaluations of the dollar, the shift to flexible exchange rates, and an astounding increase in international monetary reserves.[5] The price data in 1974, incidentally, were strongly influenced by an unusual price hike for sugar—a hike of only temporary duration and caused as much by policy errors and autarchic policies as by anything else. Only two countries—Japan and the United States—let the world price of sugar be transmitted to their domestic consumers and producers in that year. Hence, there was little incentive for adjustment on the part of consumers or producers, and the large increase and subsequent collapse in price were almost inevitable.

Historically, we may come to realize that the low prices of the late 1970s were due in part to the considerable weakness of the dollar in that period, a phenomenon very much associated with inappropriate energy policies on the part of the United States (see Figure 1.1). Although the short-term consequence of the devaluation of the dollar in the early 1970s was an increase in the dollar prices of U.S. commodities—of which there are five in Scobie's unweighted index—the import prices in terms of other currencies declined significantly. That import price decline is what gave the large short-term stimulus to the commodity markets. But the large increase in dollar prices elicited a large supply response from U.S. agriculture, which fed the burgeoning trade in grain in response to the decline in prices as viewed by importers. As the adjustment worked itself out, the result was an extended decline in real dollar export prices.

Since 1980 the world has been adjusting to another major exchange rate realignment, plus a major slump in economic activity—the most severe slump since the Great Depression of the 1930s. From mid-1980 through approximately the end of 1984 the U.S. dollar experienced an unprecedented rise, which was the result of a combination of four factors. First, starting in October 1979, the U.S. Federal Reserve declined to monetize the large and growing federal deficit in the United States. This refusal led to unprecedented high interest rates, a consequent shift into dollar assets worldwide (a flow of capital into the United States), and in turn to a rise in the value of the dollar. Second, the deficit in the federal budget has burgeoned, as indicated. Third, U.S. monetary policy has been based largely on U.S. economic considerations rather than on world economic conditions that would be consistent with the role the United States plays as central broker for the world (given that the world is essentially on a dollar standard). And fourth, a change has been made in U.S. energy policy. One of the first things President Ronald Reagan did upon taking office was to deregulate the U.S. petroleum industry. The virtual elimination of import subsidies that were involved in the previous period caused the U.S. import bill for petroleum to decline dramatically. This decline contributed significantly to the strength of the U.S. dollar.

U.S. commodity programs complicated the adjustments that follow such a large exchange rate realignment. As the dollar rose in value, U.S. grain prices declined in dollar terms (and rose in terms of other currencies). As the dollar prices fell, they essentially came to rest on the loan levels of these commodities. When dollar prices could decline no further, additional rises in the value of the dollar produced higher prices in the currencies of other countries. This result not only choked off foreign demand for U.S. exports but stimulated grain prices (and production) elsewhere. The increasing output is causing world prices to decline.

Now, let's take a step back from these data and try to understand them in terms of the longer term sweep of history. From 1955 through 1974 the data are broadly consistent with a perfectly elastic long-run supply of foodstuffs to the world economy. Trade grew even more rapidly in the late 1970s than it had in the previous twenty-year period, probably due to a significant exchange-rate realignment. Clearly, during this period the opportunity cost of acquiring imported food relative to a bundle of manufacturing exports to developing countries had declined.

FIGURE 1.1
U.S. Trade Weighted Exchange Rate Versus U.S. Agricultural Exports

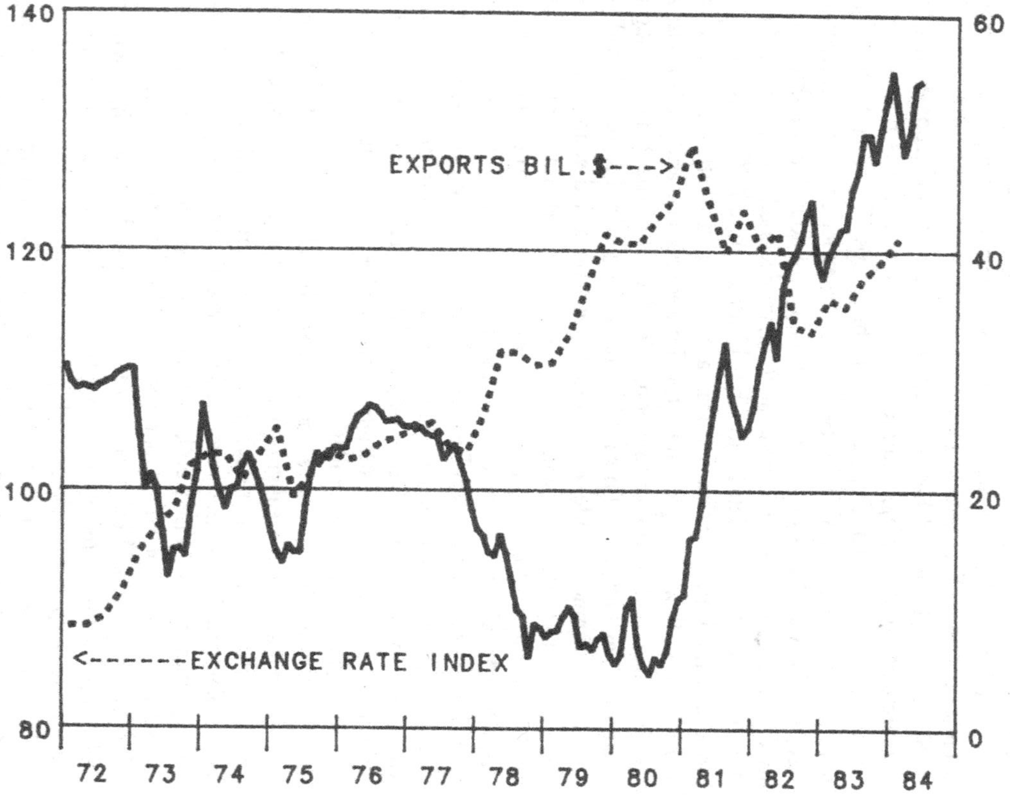

But suppose we interpret both the experience of the early 1950s and those of the late 1970s as episodic events. Then, the data are broadly consistent with a perfectly elastic long-run supply curve for agricultural output.[6] Moreover, we can use this assumption with a reasonable degree of confidence as we extrapolate into the future.

On this interpretation, the secular expansion of agricultural trade throughout the post–World War II period has been largely demand motivated by population growth and increases in per capita income. The production side of agriculture has been able to accommodate this growth in demand with no rise in supply price in secular terms. That is not to say that there have been no short-term fluctuations in commodity prices in response to episodic events or that relative prices within the food and agriculture sector have not changed. Moreover, the exchange rate realignments of the 1970s led to a significant supply response by the United States, and this supply response may have had more of an impact in the markets than did demand considerations.

As we look to the future, what degree of confidence can we have that the world economy will continue as it has in the past? Those who recall that many less-developed countries expanded their agricultural output during the 1950s and the 1960s by bringing additional land into production, and that easily cultivable reserves of land are no longer readily available, may have cause for concern. But two factors must be considered as we look to the future. First, despite the considerable progress in reducing the taxation of agriculture in many countries this past decade, a large number of countries still discriminate against their agriculture to a significant degree. Rising food prices provide strong incentives to reduce this taxation and to release the productive capacity of their agricultural sectors.

Second, the world is already investing heavily to develop the productive technology that will ease the constraints imposed by rising supply prices of land. Beginning in the mid-1960s, investments have been made in a system of international agricultural research centers.[7] These centers are now producing a steady flow of new production technology. In addition, many Third World countries are investing heavily in developing their own production technologies. Some twenty years ago investments in agricultural research were made largely in the developed countries. That is no longer the case. Trained cadres have been built up, and ambitious research programs are now underway.

Could one expect the real supply price of agricultural commodities to decline in the future, as has occurred with commodities as disparate as maize, wheat, and poultry in the United States? It could occur, but probably at a slower rate as we move into the decades ahead. The inevitable population growth for the next decade will be considerable. If low-income countries can replicate the success of the now middle-income countries, there will be further impetus to demand. It will take unusual technological breakthroughs to lead to a general decline in the supply price of food and agricultural products in the future. Even if individual countries should make unusual progress in extending their technological frontiers, such progress would probably be reflected in scarcity rents to their fixed factors such as land; supply prices would be bid up even as technical change proceeded. As we look to the decade ahead, the more conservative projection is for a perfectly elastic long-term supply of agricultural output.

Before concluding this background section, we need to make two additional points. First, most countries and protectorates are only marginally dependent on imports for their food supplies. (The exceptions are notable: Japan, Hong Kong, Singapore, and Norway.) We saw one dimension of this low dependence earlier when we said that in 1980 only 10 percent *of the import bill* (excluding fuels) of the developing countries was for food. Put more directly, most countries seldom depend on imports for more than 5-8 percent of their total food supply. This low dependence on trade for food supplies has important implications for trade and trade policy.

The second point is that the rather optimistic food and agricultural situation we have outlined above refers to the world at large; important exceptions are Africa as a whole and the centrally planned economies. The countries making up the Pacific Basin, however, are in general consistent with the overall pattern.

Concluding Remarks

The central argument of the previous section is that the world does not face a Malthusian crisis in the decade ahead if past trends continue into the future. And there is no obvious reason why those trends cannot continue. In fact, one can be mildly optimistic that the world will be able to deal with its food production problems and promote a widely shared growth in per capita incomes and well-being.

This perspective changes significantly the way we need to think about the food and agriculture sector in the future. Hunger and malnutrition emerge as a problem of distribution and of poverty and low incomes—both within countries and among countries. The general issue then is to understand agriculture in the context of maximizing its contribution to overall economic development. This understanding, in turn, requires that we make maximum use of the world's agricultural resources, realizing the comparative advantage of individual countries and regions. It also requires that we deal with the problem of poverty and low incomes. And finally, it requires that we find ways of dealing with short-term instability and food-security issues.

Notes

1. Donella Meadows, Dennis Meadows, Jørgen Randers, and William Behrens III, *The Limits to Growth*, a report for the Club of Rome's Project on the Predicament of Mankind (New York: Universe Books, 1972, 1974).

2. Unless otherwise noted, the data in this section are taken from Grant M. Scobie, *Government Policy and Food Imports: The Case of Wheat in Egypt* (Washington, D.C.: International Food Policy Research Institute, Research Report No. 29, 1981).

3. D. Gale Johnson, "The World Food Situation: Developments During the 1970's and Prospects for the 1980's," in *Contemporary Economic Problems*, edited by W. Fellner (Washington, D.C.: American Enterprise Institute for Public Policy Research, 1980), p. 311.

4. See Scobie, note 2. The commodities are rice, maize, wheat, soybeans, sugar, beef, bananas, copra and coconut oil, palm oil, and soybean oil. The data are from *Commodity Trade and Price Trends*, International Bank of Reconstruction and Development, August 1980.

5. See G. Edward Schuh, "The Exchange Rate and U.S. Agriculture," *American Journal of Agricultural Economics* 56 (February 1974):1-13. From 1969 through 1972 total international reserves, less gold, and measured in SDRs (special drawing rights), increased 134 percent.

6. This interpretation is different from Scobie's for his own data.

7. Annual expenditures by this system are currently running at about US $180 million per year.

2
Economic Growth, Comparative Advantage, and Agricultural Trade of Pacific Basin Countries

Kym Anderson

What happens to the agricultural trade situation of a country as its economy grows? As with all interesting economic questions, the answer is: It depends. Agriculture's contributions to employment and output tend to decline with economic growth. However, the correlation between per capita income and agriculture's contribution to exports is considerably weaker, with numerous high-income countries continuing to dominate world agricultural markets.[1] The purpose of the first section of this chapter is to give a brief nontechnical guide to the determinants of a growing country's changing agricultural trade situation. The second and main section discusses the actual changes that have taken place over the past two decades in the major countries on both sides of the Pacific Ocean. The final section points to some implications of these developments, and of possible policy responses to them, for closer economic integration among countries of the Pacific Basin.

Determinants of a Country's Agricultural Trade Situation

According to neoclassical trade theory, a country's comparative advantage is determined primarily by its resource endowment ratios relative to those ratios in the rest of the world.[2] For present purposes it is helpful to think initially of two productive sectors, agriculture and manufacturing, and three sets of resources, labor, agricultural land, and capital (defined broadly to include human skills and technological knowledge). The agricultural sector

---

An earlier version of this paper appeared in the December 1983 issue of the *Review of Marketing and Agricultural Economics*, published by the New South Wales Department of Agriculture.

requires labor and land, and the manufacturing sector requires labor and capital. (See below for the important case where farmers also use capital.) In this model, at a given set of international prices, the wage rate is determined by the overall per worker endowment of land (adjusted for quality differences) and capital, with labor being allocated between the two sectors according to the ratio of land to capital.

A country with little capital relative to land will export agricultural products in exchange for manufactures. As capital is accumulated or flows in from abroad, labor will tend to be attracted to the manufacturing sector, which will expand relative to the agricultural sector. Hence, the country will gradually switch from exporting agricultural goods to exporting manufactures if international prices remain unchanged. This transformation will begin at a lower level of capital per worker, and the manufactures initially produced will be more labor intensive, the lower the country's land endowment per worker. Over time, with further increases in the per worker endowment of capital, comparative advantage within the agricultural and manufacturing sectors will shift toward more capital-intensive industries unless it is possible for industries initially using labor-intensive techniques to switch to more capital-intensive techniques.

The conclusion that a country well endowed with land per worker will begin manufacturing at a later stage of capital accumulation per worker, and will specialize in manufacturing less than densely populated countries, is strengthened if a mining sector is added to the model. However, comparative advantage in agriculture will be less in this expanded model, to an extent that will depend on the country's mineral reserves relative to agricultural land.

The above conclusion is further strengthened if allowance is made for the fact that primary production also requires capital. It is strengthened partly because as capital becomes available some of it will be used in primary production rather than manufacturing, but also because the possibility of substituting capital for land and/or labor in rural production increases the scope for slowing the rate of decline in comparative advantage in agriculture. The latter is important in some countries, especially in North America and Australia. Recall that capital is defined broadly to include human skills and technological knowledge. Thus the possibility exists for farmers to improve their managerial skills and for researchers to produce new land-augmenting and/or labor-saving agricultural technologies sufficiently rapidly for an economy not to reduce its agricultural comparative advantage as it grows.

In addition, the conclusion that countries tend to switch from being net primary exporters to net exporters of manufactures as capital accumulates is stronger when the model recognizes that many primary products are inputs into manufacturing so that domestic demand for them expands with manufacturing output.

A further necessary complication to the model is the addition of a nontradables sector that can be called services. As incomes rise, the demand for services also rises, so that labor and capital are drawn out of tradable sectors. When agriculture is the major employer of labor, as in early stages of development, most of the labor needed in service industries will come from farms. This farm labor loss will add to the tendency for agriculture's output and employment shares to decline with economic growth. In advanced industrialized countries where manufacturing is the major employer for the tradable sector, extra resources for services will be drawn predominantly from manufacturing. Thus, for high-income countries the industrial as well as agricultural shares of output and employment are likely to decline with further domestic income growth.

As domestic economic growth, capital accumulation, and industrialization tend to weaken a developing country's specialization in primary products, similar changes in the rest of the world tend to have the opposite effect on the same country, insofar as they result in an increased demand, and hence terms of trade improvement, for primary products (contrary to the pessimistic conclusion for primary exports of the Prebisch model of world development). The extent of improvement in prices of primary products relative to manufactures will be greater, the more overseas growth is concentrated in large and/or resource-poor countries. Should the growth be concentrated in higher-wage countries, it would also improve the relative price of labor-intensive manufactures. Similarly with technological improvements: If farm production technologies improve more slowly at home than abroad, for example, domestic comparative advantage in agriculture will decline, as it will if manufacturing technologies improve more rapidly at home than abroad, ceteris paribus.

The above economic forces are often modified by government policies, particularly trade policy. There seems to be a community preference in a number of countries for a more "balanced," less specialized economy than would occur under free market conditions, particularly in countries with extreme factor endowment ratios. Thus, countries at an early stage of development, and even resource-rich, high-income countries, often tax primary exports and/or provide import restrictions to protect the import-competing manufacturing sector. On the other hand, densely populated industrializing countries may, for food-security reasons, have a community preference for steadily raising assistance to the declining agricultural sector so as to slow the pace of decline in food self-sufficiency. Lobbying pressure from rural groups adds to the government's incentive to provide such assistance. Similar vested-interest group pressures exist for protection of declining labor-intensive manufacturing industries in advanced industrialized countries.[3] The resulting distortions to incentives will tend to reduce the extent of, but usually not alter the directions of, trade specialization discussed above.[4] It is politically easier to assist import-competing industries than export industries, because import and export taxes raise government revenue whereas export subsidies drain the treasury. Therefore the structure of imports is likely to be less revealing of a country's comparative advantage than the structure of exports. For this reason, the empirical discussion in the next section will concentrate mainly on export trade.

To sum up, the preceding discussion suggests that at a point in time, a country's comparative advantage in agriculture will tend to be less, the lower its per worker endowment of agricultural land relative to mineral reserves and capital—compared with the rest of the world. Over time, in the course of economic growth in this and other countries, this country's comparative advantage (and shares of output and employment) in agriculture will decline faster, the faster its increase in capital per worker and its mineral extraction, and the slower its rate of agriculture relative to other technological change, again compared with these rates in other countries.

Experience of Pacific Basin Countries

How well can the above discussion shed light on recent changes in comparative advantage and agricultural trade of Pacific Basin countries? For the present purposes the Pacific Basin is defined to include the Americas, East Asia, and Australasia. To keep the number of countries manageable, data are presented for only the eight largest Latin American countries. Also excluded are the Communist states of Vietnam, Cambodia, Laos, and North Korea, as well as the many Pacific island economies, because of their very minor participation in world trade. The Pacific Basin countries currently account for half the world's agricultural exports and almost a third of the world's agricultural imports.

Table 2.1 provides some crude proxies for relative resource endowments of Pacific Basin countries. Gross national product (GNP) per capita can probably serve as an index of capital per worker. A rough index of natural resource endowments (especially agricultural land) per worker is given by land area per capita. It is clear from the column on total land endowment per capita in the table that most of East Asia is extremely densely populated compared with the rest of the world (which has an average of more than three hectares per person)—and especially compared with North and South America and Australasia. These data suggest that East Asia, especially Japan and the four Asian NICs (the newly industrializing countries and protectorates of South Korea, Taiwan, Singapore, and Hong Kong), can be expected to have a strong comparative disadvantage in agriculture relative to other countries with similar per capita income levels. The opposite would be expected of Australia and most of North and South America.

The column on percent of real growth rate annually in Table 2.1 suggests that East Asia is also distinguished by extremely rapid growth in incomes over the past two decades and hence also in capital:labor ratios. By contrast, incomes in Australasia and the Americas (except Brazil and Ecuador) have grown at well below the average of 4.0 percent per year for middle- and high-income countries.[5] The other major area of rapid postwar economic growth, namely Western Europe, is also extremely densely populated. Thus the resource-rich countries of the Pacific Basin would have experienced a slower decline in comparative advantage in primary products, while the resource-poor, newly industrializing countries would have enjoyed a rapid growth of comparative advantage in labor-intensive manufactures. The emergence of OPEC-induced energy price rises in the 1970s would have reduced the comparative advantage in agriculture in those countries well endowed with energy reserves per capita, but increased it in those countries not so well endowed with energy.

Table 2.2 confirms that agriculture's share of production and employment have declined over the past two decades in Pacific Basin countries, with industry's share growing in the low- and middle-income countries but falling in the high-income countries. The extent of intersectoral change is especially rapid in the fastest growing East Asian economies.

Table 2.3 shows the changing export structure of each country as well as its "revealed" comparative advantage. The latter is defined as the ratio of a particular commodity group's share in a country's exports to that commodity group's share of world exports. The more a ratio exceeds unity, the stronger a country's apparent comparative advantage in that commodity group; the more a ratio falls below unity, the stronger a country's apparent comparative disadvantage in that commodity group.[6] The ratios in the three columns on "revealed" comparative advantage in Table 2.3 confirm the major expectations discussed above. Japan clearly has a strong and increasing comparative disadvantage in food vis-à-vis manufacturing, whereas the resource-rich developed countries have maintained a strong comparative advantage in food despite increases (from a low base) in their manufacturing comparative advantage. The four Asian NICs, like Japan, have also rapidly increased their comparative disadvantage in food vis-à-vis manufacturing. The picture is mixed for other Southeast Asian countries: Thailand and the Philippines have retained their strong comparative advantage in food; Malaysia has increased its comparative advantage in food at the expense of fuels, minerals, and metals (although since 1977 the comparative advantage in food may have declined again with the expansion in fuel and timber exports from East Malaysia); and Indonesia has reduced its comparative advantage in food as petroleum exports have expanded. Among the East Asian countries, only Thailand and the Philippines enjoy a greater comparative advantage in food than developing countries as a whole. Conversely, all except Indonesia and Malaysia currently enjoy a greater comparative advantage in manufactures than developing countries as a whole, and all have experienced rapid rises in manufacturing export shares.

By contrast, all the large Latin American countries except Chile and Venezuela have a strong comparative advantage in food; the latter two have a very strong comparative advantage in fuels, minerals, and metals. Mexico's moderate comparative advantage in food and greater-than-average (for developing countries) comparative advantage in manufactures is to be expected, given its relatively high population density by Latin American standards. Latin American comparative advantage in manufacturing has apparently increased in the 1970s only in Argentina, Brazil, and Colombia, but from a low base and at a much slower pace than in the resource-poor Asian NICs.

There are also marked differences between Pacific Basin countries in their structures of comparative advantage within agriculture. Cereals, for example, are major primary export items for Australia, Canada, and the United States among the high-income countries, but are of export significance only to Thailand and Argentina among the region's major developing countries. Livestock exports are even more highly concentrated, primarily from Australia, New Zealand, and Argentina. This picture is what might be expected given the extreme per capita endowments of arable and pasture land in these countries, as shown in the columns on land endowments per capita in Table 2.1. Many food-surplus countries of the region are net cereal importers because much of their arable land is used for apparently more profitable cash crops. Table 2.4 shows that coffee is the prime agricultural export of six of the eight large Latin American countries, while timber, rubber, and sugar, rather than food staples, feature prominently in Southeast Asian agricultural exports. This pattern persists despite the fact that in many of these countries the export-oriented cash crops are subject to considerably more taxation than food staples.

As incomes rise in developing countries, the demand for livestock products and fruits and vegetables tends to rise by at least the same proportion, whereas the demand for staples rises much more slowly. Fruit and vegetable production and intensive livestock production (pork, chicken, eggs) require relatively little land per dollar of output. Fresh fruits and vegetables, in addition, often enjoy natural protection from foreign competition because of their perishable nature, as does fluid milk.[7] Thus, countries facing a declining comparative advantage in agriculture in general may nonetheless be able to profitably switch some farm resources into these activities. Although this move would reduce the need to import these items, it is likely that a large-scale expansion in intensive livestock production would necessitate increased dependence on imported feedgrains. In Northeast Asia, for example, exactly these types of changes have occurred, as is clear from Table 2.5, which shows that the shares of livestock products and fruits and vegetables in the gross value of agricultural production have increased substantially at the expense of cereals over the past twenty-five years. Self-sufficiency of intensive livestock products has been maintained at close to 100 percent, while the self-sufficiency ratios of feedstuffs, especially corn (maize) and soybean, have fallen dramatically (and for wheat and beef to a lesser extent). Similar trends have also occurred in other countries. Mexico, in particular, has expanded its production of fruits and vegetables to satisfy not only domestic demand growth, but also growing United States import demand. In this case production is occurring close to the Mexico-U.S. border and the lower labor costs in Mexico provide it with a considerable comparative advantage over the United States in producing these relatively labor-intensive foods.

Future Prospects for Pacific Economic Integration and Food Trade

Overall, the trade trends in Pacific Basin countries are consistent with the theory of changing comparative advantage, despite the fact that numerous

TABLE 2.1
Population, Gross National Product, Land Endowment, and Agricultural Trade in Pacific Basin Countries for 1981 or Earlier selected Years

	Population (millions) 1981	GNP (US $ billions), 1981	GNP Per Capita US $, 1981	Real Growth Rate (% annually), 1960-1981	Ratio of Exports to GNP (%) 1960	1981
Developed Pacific countries						
Australia	15	165	11,100	2.5	15	15
Canada	24	276	11,450	3.3	18	28
Japan	118	1,085	10,100	6.3	11	15
New Zealand	3	25	7,310	1.5	23	29
United States	230	2,946	12,800	2.3	5	10
Developing East Asia						
China	991	297	300	5.0	4	9
Hong Kong	5	17	5,100	6.9	82	111
Indonesia	150	79	530	4.1	13	28
Korea, Rep.	39	66	1,700	6.9	30	39
Malaysia	14	26	1,800	4.3	54	53
Philippines	50	39	800	2.8	11	19
Singapore	2	13	5,200	7.4	163	164
Taiwan	18	46	2,500	6.8	11	49
Thailand	48	37	800	4.6	17	25
Developing Latin America						
Argentina	28	72	2,600	1.9	7	13
Brazil	121	267	2,200	5.1	9	7
Chile	11	29	2,600	0.7	18	23
Colombia	26	36	1,400	3.2	12	18
Ecuador	9	10	1,200	4.3	22	24
Mexico	71	160	2,300	3.8	13	12
Peru	17	20	1,200	1.0	17	27
Venezuela	15	65	4,200	2.4	30	31

na = not available.

Sources: World Bank, World Development Report (New York: Oxford University Press, 1983) and World Bank Atlas (Washington, D.C.: World Bank, 1983); FAO Production Yearbook and Trade Yearbook (Rome: Food and Agriculture Organization, 1984); Key Indicators of Developing Member Countries of ADB (Manila: Asian Development Bank, 1983).

TABLE 2.1 (cont.)

	Land Endowment Per Capita (ha)		World Agricultural Export (Import) Share (%), 1977-1979	Net Agricultural Exports (US $ millions annually), 1977-1979	Net Food Exports Per Capita (US $ annually), 1976-1978
Total, 1981	Arable and Permanent Crop, 1981	Permanent Pasture, 1981			
53.51	2.97	31.09	3.5 (0.4)	5,409	224
42.12	1.87	1.00	2.8 (0.2)	1,073	28
0.32	0.08	0.00	0.3 (7.4)	-13,533	-62
8.31	0.14	4.25	1.4 (0.1)	2,181	352
4.26	0.87	1.10	17.5 (8.3)	14,631	26
0.99	0.10	0.23	1.5 (2.4)	-1,930	0
0.02	0.00	0.00	0.3 (1.2)	-1,898	-248
1.37	0.12	0.09	1.1 (0.6)	743	0
0.26	0.06	0.00	0.3 (1.1)	-1,608	-19
2.41	0.48	0.00	1.7 (0.5)	2,012	-30
0.64	0.17	0.02	0.9 (0.2)	1,152	10
0.02	0.00	0.00	0.6 (0.7)	-366	-15
0.21	0.05	0.00	0.9 (1.1)	-900	na
1.13	0.38	0.01	1.4 (0.2)	2,057	35
10.35	1.31	5.36	2.7 (0.2)	4,376	102
6.93	0.33	1.17	4.0 (0.8)	5,395	36
6.94	0.53	1.09	0.1 (0.2)	-226	-14
4.36	0.21	0.67	1.3 (0.2)	2,004	62
3.51	0.32	0.32	0.4 (0.1)	574	63
2.91	0.34	1.10	0.9 (0.5)	591	10
7.43	0.20	1.57	0.2 (0.2)	77	0
6.33	0.37	1.17	0.1 (0.7)	-1,194	-52

TABLE 2.2
Changing Structure of Production and Employment in Pacific Basin Countries, 1960 to 1981

	Distribution of GDP (%)						Distribution of Labor Force (%)	
	Agriculture		Industry		Services		Agriculture	
	1960	1981	1960	1981	1960	1981	1960	1980
Developed Pacific countries								
Australia	12	5	37	na	51	na	11	6
Canada	6	4	34	32	60	64	13	5
Japan	13	4	45	43	42	53	33	12
New Zealand	na	11	na	31	na	58	15	9
United States	4	3	38	34	58	63	7	2
Developing East Asia								
China	47	35	33	46	20	20	na	69
Hong Kong	4	1	39	na	57	na	8	3
Indonesia	50	24	25	42	25	54	75	55
Korea, Rep.	37	17	20	39	43	44	66	34
Malaysia	36	23	18	36	46	41	63	50
Philippines	26	23	28	37	46	40	61	46
Singapore	4	1	18	41	78	58	8	2
Taiwan	28	8	29	51	43	41	56	19
Thailand	40	24	19	28	41	48	84	76
Developing Latin America								
Argentina	16	9	38	38	46	53	20	13
Brazil	16	13	35	34	49	53	52	30
Chile	9	7	35	35	56	58	31	19
Colombia	34	27	26	31	40	42	51	26
Ecuador	26	12	20	38	54	50	57	52
Mexico	16	8	29	37	55	55	55	36
Peru	18	9	33	41	49	50	52	39
Venezuela	6	6	22	45	72	49	35	18
All industrial market economies	6	3	40	36	54	61	12	6
All middle-income countries	24	14	30	38	46	48	62	45
All low-income countries	48	37	25	34	27	29	77	70

na = not available.

Sources: World bank, **World Development Report** (New York: Oxford University Press, 1983); **Key Indicators of the Developing Member Countries of ADB** (Manila: Asian Development Bank, 1983).

TABLE 2.2 (cont.)

Industry 1960	Industry 1980	Services 1960	Services 1980	Agriculture 1960-1970	Agriculture 1970-1981	Industry 1960-1970	Industry 1970-1981	Services 1960-1970	Services 1970-1981
40	33	49	61	2.0	na	5.9	na	4.0	na
34	29	52	66	2.5	1.3	6.3	2.9	5.5	4.3
30	39	37	49	2.1	0.2	13.0	5.6	10.2	4.2
37	35	48	56	na	na	na	na	na	na
36	32	57	66	0.5	1.6	4.6	2.3	4.4	3.3
na	19	na	12	1.6	2.8	11.2	8.3	5.7	4.4
52	57	40	40	na	na	na	na	na	na
8	15	17	30	2.7	3.8	5.2	11.2	4.8	9.5
0	29	25	37	4.4	3.0	17.2	14.4	8.9	8.2
12	16	25	34	na	5.2	na	9.3	na	8.5
15	17	24	37	4.3	4.9	6.0	8.4	5.2	5.3
23	39	69	59	5.0	1.7	12.5	9.0	7.7	8.5
11	40	33	41	3.4	1.4	16.4	11.3	7.8	7.4
4	9	12	15	5.6	4.5	11.9	9.9	9.1	7.5
36	28	44	59	1.8	2.5	5.8	1.4	3.8	2.2
15	24	33	46	na	5.2	na	9.1	na	8.3
20	19	50	62	3.1	3.0	4.4	0.7	4.6	2.9
19	21	30	53	2.0	4.1	8.2	9.3	4.5	7.5
19	17	24	31	na	2.9	na	12.5	na	8.7
20	26	25	39	4.5	3.4	9.4	7.4	7.3	6.6
20	19	28	43	3.7	0.3	5.0	3.4	5.3	3.5
22	27	43	55	5.8	3.4	4.6	2.7	7.3	5.9
38	38	44	56	1.4	1.6	5.7	2.9	4.6	3.6
15	21	23	34	3.4	3.0	7.4	6.8	5.5	6.1
9	15	14	15	2.2	2.3	6.6	3.6	4.2	4.6

TABLE 2.3
Changing Export Structure and "Revealed" Comparative Advantage in Pacific Basin Countries, 1960 to 1979

	Year	Sectoral Share of Total Merchandise Exports (percent)						"Revealed" Comparative Advantage[a]		
		Cereals (incl. feeds)[b]	Live-stock Products[c]	Total Food[d]	Nonfood Agriculture[e]	Fuels, Minerals, and Metals[f]	Manu-factures[g]	Food[d]	Fuels, Minerals,[f] and Metals	Manu-factures[g]
Developed Pacific countries										
Australia	1960	12	13	39	40	10	11	2.2	0.5	0.2
	1970	11	13	33	18	27	21	2.3	1.7	0.3
	1979	13	14	33	13	28	26	2.8	1.1	0.4
Canada	1960	11	2	21	16	30	33	1.2	1.5	0.6
	1970	6	1	12	10	26	51	0.8	1.6	0.8
	1979	5	1	11	12	25	52	0.9	1.0	0.9
Japan	1960	0	0	7	3	1	88	0.4	0.1	1.6
	1970	1	0	4	2	2	93	0.3	0.1	1.5
	1979	0	0	1	1	1	97	0.1	0.0	1.6
New Zealand	1960	0	52	55	42	0	3	3.2	0.0	0.1
	1970	1	53	58	28	1	12	4.0	0.1	0.2
	1979	1	38	46	28	6	20	3.9	0.2	0.3
United States	1960	10	1	21	6	8	65	1.2	0.4	1.2
	1970	8	1	16	5	9	70	1.1	0.6	1.1
	1979	12	1	19	5	7	69	1.6	0.3	1.2
Developing East Asia										
China	1968			91	9	0	0			
	1978		38			13	49			
Hong Kong	1960	1	0	11	4	2	83	0.6	0.1	1.5
	1970	0	0	4	2	2	93	0.3	0.1	1.5
	1979	0	0	3	2	2	93	0.3	0.1	1.6
Indonesia	1960	1	0	17	46	37	0	1.0	1.8	0.0
	1970	2	0	20	35	44	1	1.4	2.7	0.0
	1979	1	0	10	18	69	3	0.8	2.8	0.1

TABLE 2.3 (cont.)

	Year	Sectoral Share of Total Merchandise Exports (percent)						"Revealed" Comparative Advantage[a]		
		Cereals (incl. feeds)[b]	Live-stock Products[c]	Total Food[d]	Nonfood Agriculture[e]	Fuels, Minerals, and Metals[f]	Manu-factures[g]	Food[d]	Fuels, Minerals,[f] and Metals	Manu-factures[g]
Developing East Asia (cont.)										
Korea, Rep.	1960	12	2	40	16	24	19	2.3	1.2	0.4
	1970	0	0	0	7	7	77	0.7	0.4	1.2
	1979	0	0	8	2	1	89	0.7	0.0	1.5
Malaysia	1960	0	0	10	54	30	5	0.6	1.5	0.1
	1970	0	1	13	48	29	10	0.9	1.8	0.2
	1979	0	0	19	39	27	15	1.5	1.1	0.3
Philippines	1960	0	0	60	26	10	5	3.4	0.5	0.1
	1970	6	0	44	26	23	8	3.0	1.4	0.1
	1979	3	0	44	8	14	34	3.5	0.7	0.5
Singapore	1960			18	34	18	30	1.0	0.9	0.6
	1970	3	1	16	28	25	31	1.1	1.5	0.5
	1979	1	0	8	14	26	52	0.7	1.1	0.9
Taiwan	1960			45	6	3	46	2.6	0.2	0.9
	1970			19	3	2	76	1.3	0.1	1.2
	1979			12	1	2	85	1.0	0.1	1.4
Thailand	1960	38	3	53	34	9	4	3.0	0.5	0.1
	1970	31	1	51	24	15	11	3.5	0.9	0.2
	1979	20	1	51	12	11	26	4.1	0.5	0.4
Developing Latin America										
Argentina	1960	29	26	72	23	2	3	4.1	0.1	0.1
	1970	36	25	74	11	1	14	5.1	0.1	0.2
	1977	25	13	65	7	1	27	5.2	0.0	0.4

33

TABLE 2.3 (cont.)

	Year	Sectoral Share of Total Merchandise Exports (percent)						"Revealed" Comparative Advantage[a]		
		Cereals (incl. feeds)[b]	Live-stock Products[c]	Total Food[d]	Nonfood Agriculture[e]	Fuels, Minerals, and Metals[f]	Manu-factures[g]	Food	Fuels, Minerals, and Metals[f]	Manu-factures[g]
Developing Latin America (cont.)										
Brazil	1960	0	0	71	16	9	3	4.1	0.5	0.1
	1970	8	4	63	12	11	14	4.3	0.7	0.2
	1979	9	2	47	42	11	36	3.9	0.5	0.6
Chile	1960	0	0	7	3	87	3	0.4	4.4	0.1
	1970	0	0	5	3	88	4	0.3	5.4	0.1
	1977	5	0	14	8	67	6	1.1	2.8	0.1
Colombia	1960	0	0	77	4	15	3	4.4	0.8	0.1
	1970	1	6	75	6	11	8	5.1	0.7	0.1
	1977	1	4	71	6	4	19	5.6	0.2	0.3
Ecuador	1960	3	0	96	1	0	2	5.5	0.0	0.0
	1970	37	0	94	3	1	2	6.4	0.1	0.0
	1977	35	0	46	2	50	2	3.7	2.1	0.0
Mexico	1960	3	5	36	24	24	16	2.1	1.2	0.3
	1970	14	9	40	9	19	32	2.7	1.2	0.5
	1977	0	3	33	6	32	29	2.6	1.3	0.5
Peru	1960	0	0	38	21	41	1	2.2	2.1	0.0
	1970	0	0	44	6	49	1	3.0	3.0	0.0
	1977	0	0	37	8	47	9	2.9	2.0	0.1
Venezuela	1960	0	0	1	0	93	6	0.1	4.7	0.1
	1970	0	0	2	0	97	1	0.1	6.0	0.0
	1977	0	0	1	0	97	2	0.1	4.1	0.0

TABLE 2.3 (cont.)

		Sectoral Share of Total Merchandise Exports (percent)					"Revealed" Comparative Advantage[a]		
Year	Cereals (incl. feeds)[b]	Live-stock Products[c]	Total Food[d]	Nonfood Agriculture[e]	Fuels, Minerals, and Metals[f]	Manu-factures[g]	Food	Fuels, Minerals, and Metals	Manu-factures[g]

Industrial market economies

Year	Cereals	Livestock	Total Food	Nonfood Agr.	Fuels, Min.	Manuf.	Food	Fuels, Min.	Manuf.
1960			15	8	10	68	0.9	0.5	1.3
1970	3		12	5	9	74	0.8	0.6	1.2
1978	3		12	4	8	76	0.9	0.4	1.2

Developing countries

1960			36	18	31	15	2.1	1.6	0.3
1970	3		26	10	44	17	1.8	2.7	0.3
1978	2		16	5	57	22	1.3	2.7	0.4

World

1960			17	9	20	54	1.0	1.0	1.0
1970	2		15	6	16	63	1.0	1.0	1.0
1977	2		12	4	24	60	1.0	1.0	1.0
1978	2		13	4	21	62	1.0	1.0	1.0
1979	2		12	4	24	60	1.0	1.0	1.0

a. Defined as ratio of share of commodity group in a country's exports to that commodity group's share of world exports.
b. Standard International Trade Classification (SITC) 04, 081, 221.4.
c. SITC 00 to 02 (excludes inedible products).
d. SITC 0, 1, 22, 4.
e. SITC 2 excluding 22, 27, 28.
f. SITC 27, 28, 3, 68.
g. SITC 5 to 9 excluding 68.

Sources: World Tables (Washington, D.C.: World Bank, 1980) and World Development Report (Washington, D.C.: World Bank, 1981); UN, Yearbook of International Trade Statistics (New York: United Nations, various issues); FAO, Trade Yearbook (Rome: Food and Agriculture Organization, various issues).

TABLE 2.4
Major Commodity Shares of Agricultural[a] Exports for Pacific Basin Countries, 1977-1979

	Agricultural Share of Total Trade (%)		Share of Agricultural Exports from:
	Exports	Imports	
Developed Pacific countries			
Australia	42	10	Wool 26%, Beef 20%, Wheat 20%
Canada	28	10	Timber 21%, Oils and fats 17%, Wheat 13%
Japan	2	27	—
New Zealand	71	8	Wool 26%, Dairy products 19%, Sheepmeat 17%
United States	24	14	Maize 16%, Soybean 15%, Wheat 12%
Developing East Asia			
Hong Kong	5	21	—
Indonesia	25	20	Timber 40%, Rubber 24%, Coffee 18%
Korea, Rep.	11	19	Fish products 41%, Fruit and vegetables 8%
Malaysia	52	19	Rubber 36%, Timber 23%, Oil palm 16%
Philippines	51	9	Coconut product 39%, Sugar 16%, Timber 14%
Singapore	13	13	—
Taiwan	11	16	Fish products 20%, Canned food 17%, Sugar 7%
Thailand	63	8	Rice 24%, Rubber 16%, Sugar 10%
Developing Latin America			
Argentina	73	10	Maize 12%, Beef 10%, Wheat 9%
Brazil	55	12	Coffee 28%, Cocao 6%, Sugar 6%,
Chile	22	16	Fish meal 18%, Timber 13%
Colombia	80	12	Coffee 79%, Cotton 4%, Bananas 3%
Ecuador	48	10	Coffee 31%, Bananas 22%, Cocoa 6%
Mexico	32	16	Coffee 24%, Fruit and vegetables 23%, Cotton 14%
Peru	27	16	Coffee 33%, Fish meal 30%, Sugar 9%
Venezuela	1	14	Coffee 35%, Cocoa 34%

a. SITC 0, 1, 2, 4 excluding 27, 28 (that is, including forestry and fishery products).

Sources: *Commodity Trade and Price Trends* (Washington, D.C.: World Bank, 1981); UN, *Yearbook of International Trade Statistics* (New York: United Nations, 1980); FAO, *Trade Yearbook* (Rome: Food and Agriculture Organization, 1979).

TABLE 2.5
Commodity Composition and Self-Sufficiency Ratios for Agricultural Production in Japan, Korea, and Taiwan, 1955 to 1979

	Share of Gross Value of Agricultural Production[a] (%)				Self-sufficiency Ratios[b] (%)							
	Cereals	Livestock Products	Fruit and Vegetables	Other	Wheat	Maize	Soybean	Beef	Pork	Chicken	Eggs	Milk Products
Japan												
1955-1959	58	12	17	13	37	15	34	95	100	100	100	91
1960-1964	50	18	20	12	33	4	20	97	99	99	100	87
1965-1969	46	20	21	13	20	1	8	94	98	96	99	85
1970-1974	37	25	26	12	7	0	4	77	93	96	98	86
1975-1979	38	26	26	10	5	0	4	73	87	95	97	85
Korea, Rep.												
1955-1959	na	na	na	na	38	54	82	100	100	100	100	100
1960-1964	78	7	6	9	28	22	89	100	100	100	100	100
1965-1969	60	13	13	14	21	40	94	100	100	100	100	100
1970-1974	57	14	15	14	9	15	81	99	102	100	100	100
1975-1979	53	16	22	11	3	6	66	78	99	100	100	95
Taiwan												
1955-1959	56	20	7	17	13	60	29	100	100	100	100	23
1960-1964	55	22	9	14	11	83	29	100	102	100	100	20
1965-1969	46	26	13	15	6	24	20	100	101	100	100	18
1970-1974	39	33	18	10	0	5	9	88	104	100	101	17
1975-1979	34	36	20	10	0	5	5	45	105	100	101	11

a. Valued at current domestic prices.
b. Production divided by production plus net imports minus change in stocks, expressed as a percentage.
na = not available.

Source: K. Anderson, "Growth of Agricultural Production in East Asia," Food Policy 8(4), November 1983: 327-336.

TABLE 2.6
Estimated Nominal Rates of Agricultural Protection[a] in Japan, Korea, and Taiwan, 1955 to 1982 (percentage)

	1955-1959	1960-1964	1965-1969	1970-1974	1975-1979	1980-1982
Japan	44	68	87	110	147	151
Korea, Rep.	-15	-5	9	55	129	166
Taiwan	-21	2	2	17	36	55

a. The nominal rate is the percentage by which the domestic price exceeds the border price. The above estimates are the weighted averages for grains, soybean, and meats. Weights are based on domestic production valued at border prices. The producer price rather than wholesale price was used as the domestic price for grains and soybean (to compute the producer price subsidies), which underestimates the rate of protection by the producer-to-wholesale marketing margin.

Source: K. Anderson, "Growth of Agricultural Production in East Asia," Food Policy 8(4), November, 1983 :327-336.

price and trade policies in various countries tend to distort the patterns of production and trade from those that would emerge if free market prices operated. Northeast Asia, for example, has had a dramatic transformation of its food trade situation in spite of extremely large increases in farm price supports and protection from food imports (see Table 2.6). Other developing countries, especially those relying increasingly on imports of food staples, are also raising incentives to domestic producers of the staples, relative to other agricultural products.[8] Thus many of the recent trends in food and production and trade in the region might be expected to continue over the next decade or so, assuming that relative economic growth rates continue as in the recent past. Japan and the four Asian NICs will become ever-larger importers of wheat and feedgrains as well as tropical agricultural products. The extent of increase in their imports of rice, beef, and dairy products, however, will hinge crucially on the rate of increase in protection of domestic producers of these commodities. The continuing industrial growth in Southeast Asia and parts of Latin America is likely to further reduce these countries' comparative advantage in agriculture. The expansion in resource exports expected in a number of resource-rich Pacific Basin countries, once the world economy comes out of recession, may weaken agricultural comparative advantage in these countries. The extent to which North America and Australasia can retain their strong comparative advantage in agriculture will also depend on their rates of farm relative to nonfarm technological advance compared with those rates in the rest of the world. In all countries, including those able to maintain their comparative advantage in agriculture, agriculture's share of national production and employment is likely to continue to decline as incomes rise, because of the required expansion of the service sector. However, the decline will be more marked in the newly industrializing countries where the relative importance of the manufacturing sector is still expanding.

In the light of the conclusions that the agricultural sector of each economy will decline in relative and possibly absolute terms and that, for most countries, comparative advantage in agricultural trade will also decline, what policy responses might be forthcoming? It is clear that Northeast Asia has chosen a defensive policy approach, increasingly raising the degree of agricultural protection to slow the decline in food self-sufficiency and the pace of adjustment that would be required if free market prices operated. The prime objectives of this approach are to maintain farm family incomes at levels close to the rapidly rising incomes of urban families and to slow the deterioration in perceived food security.[9] Other rapidly industrializing countries may well take a similar approach as their farmers lose competitiveness, following the examples not just of Northeast Asia but of the majority of advanced industrialized countries.[10] There may well be politico-economic reasons why such a trend, from taxing to subsidizing agriculture in the course of economic development, is inevitable. Even so, it may be possible to reduce the extent of increase in agricultural protectionism by adopting more positive policy approaches. Many countries underinvest in rural education and in agricultural research. Future public expenditure in these areas may not only boost economic growth but also facilitate adjustment by farmers to changing economic circumstances: better education will help those farmers leving the land to obtain jobs in the nonfarm sector, and together with appropriate production and diffusion of new farm technologies, it will help the remaining farmers to profitably alter their farm input and output mixes.

The underlying political forces that tend to lead to increases in agricultural protection as an economy grows are not well understood. They may simply be narrowly focused, vested rural-interest group pressures aimed at preserving the status quo for farmers. But insofar as there is also a genuine concern by society that food security is important and is synonymous with food self-sufficiency, there may be scope for reducing this source of protectionist pressure if societies can be convinced that the two are *not* synonymous. A change of attitude may require a greater use of institutional arrangements to decrease the risk associated with depending more on food imports. Arrangements that come to mind are long-term contracts, futures markets, and the possibility of borrowing from the International Monetary Fund in times of high world prices or low domestic yields. In addition, restraint by major food exporters in the use of food trade as a foreign policy instrument would reduce the insecurity of depending on imports.

Finally, scope may also exist for reducing agricultural protection in a context of Pacific regional trade liberalization negotiations. Regional trade bargaining would be facilitated by the high regional shares of each Pacific Basin country's trade.[11] Negotiation could aim to liberalize trade, or to seek assurances that there would be no further increases in protection, not only for food items, but also for those processed primary products and manufactures in which Pacific Basin countries are the major suppliers to the region. Concessions could then be given on a most-favored-nation basis but with the selection of commodities ensuring that the opportunities provided for export expansion would be available mainly to participants in the regional trade negotiations. In this way each country's vested interests in export expansion would be brought into conflict with, and so help to offset, vested interests in protection. And an international agreement involving reciprocal assurances on market access and supply would reduce concerns in each country that trade-dependent growth and food security might be undermined at some future time by changes in trade policy abroad. The formation of a Pacific community organization aimed at building trust and sharing perspectives on international economic policy issues among the countries of the region might be an important first step in moving toward such negotiations.[12]

Notes

1. In 1977, the correlation coefficients between per capita income (a rough index of stage of economic development) and agriculture's contributions to employment, national product, and exports were -0.71, -0.69 and -0.52, respectively, using a sample of seventy-two countries for which data were available. The value of agricultural exports from developing countries in 1977-1979 was about half that from industrial countries. More than one-quarter of the world's agricultural exports in those years came from the four high-income countries of Australasia and North America.

2. This brief, nontechnical section is based on a number of more detailed analyses, including Anne O. Krueger, *Growth Distortions and Patterns of Trade Among Many Countries* (Princeton: Princeton University, International Finance Section, 1977); K. Anderson, "Changing Agricultural Comparative Advantage in the Pacific Basin," in *Australian Agriculture and Newly Industrialising Asia: Issues for Research*, ed. K. Anderson and A. George (Canberra: Australia-Japan Research Centre, 1980), Ch. 2; R. Garnaut and K. Anderson, "ASEAN Export Specialization and the Evolution of Comparative Advantage in the Western Pacific Region," in *ASEAN in a Changing Pacific and World Economy*, ed. R. Garnaut (Canberra: Australian National University Press, 1980), Ch. 13; and K. Anderson and B. Smith, "Changing Economic Relations Between Asian ADC's and Resource-Exporting Developed Countries," in *Trade and Growth of the Advanced Developing Countries in the Pacific Basin*, ed. W. Hong and L. Krause (Seoul: Korea Development Institute Press, 1981), pp. 243-338.

3. For a discussion of the politico-economic reasons for expecting these pressures to influence policy outcomes, see K. Anderson and R. E. Baldwin, "The Political Market for Protection in Industrial Countries: Empirical Evidence," Staff Working Paper No. 492 (Washington, D.C.: World Bank, 1981).

4. Nonetheless, government policy may affect comparative advantage to some extent through public investments in technology production and diffusion. Expenditure on agricultural research and extension, for example, may be given low political priority in poor, food-surplus countries but given prominence in wealthier, food-deficit countries seeking to reduce the growth in food import dependence. As a result, farmers in the latter type of country are likely to be closer to the frontier of available technologies than those in countries neglecting such public expenditure.

5. Many economists would argue that the high economic growth in East Asia as compared with Latin America or South Asia can be attributed in part to the relatively high degree of openness of these economies, as shown in the columns on ratio of exports to GNP in Table 2.1. See, for example, Anne O. Krueger,

Foreign Trade Regions and Economic Development: Liberalization Attempts and Consequences (Cambridge, U.K.: Ballinger for the National Bureau of Economic Research [NBER], 1978) and Bela Balassa, Development Strategies in Semi-Industrial Countries (Baltimore: Johns Hopkins University Press, 1982).

6. This concept of comparative advantage is incomplete because it does not capture the extent to which a country is an importer of particular commodities. However, since the structure of imports is often distorted because of intersectoral differences in import restrictions, a misleading impression would be given if imports were also to be considered. The concept of "revealed" comparative advantage was developed by Bela Balassa, "Trade Liberalization and 'Revealed' Comparative Advantage," *Manchester School of Economic and Social Studies* 33(2), May 1965:99–124.

7. Canned, dried, and frozen fruit and vegetables and powdered and UHT (ultra-high-temperature) vacuum-packed fluid milk are of course close substitutes for the fresh product and can be traded internationally. The c.i.f. price (cost, insurance, and freight) of imports of such substitutes would thus determine the ceiling on domestic prices of the fresh products in the absence of import restrictions.

8. Three examples discussed in recent papers are Colombia (J. Garcia, *The Effects of Exchange Rates and Commercial Policy on Agricultural Incentives in Colombia: 1953–1978* [Washington, D.C.: International Food Policy Research Institute, Research Report No. 24, June 1981]); Malaysia (R.J.G. Wells and S. Meyanathan, "Malaysian Economic Development and Food Trade," paper presented to the Second Western Pacific Food Trade Workshop, Jakarta, 22–23 August 1982); and Mexico (F. Meissner, "The Mexican Food System [SAM]: A Strategy for Sowing Petroleum," *Food Policy* 6[4], November 1981:219–230).

9. Japan and Korea appear to have more than succeeded in the first of these objectives. According to official statistics, the ratio of farm household incomes to urban wage and salary earners' household incomes has moved as in Table 2.7 during the past twenty-five years.

TABLE 2.7
Changing Ratio of Farm Household Incomes to Urban Wage and Salary Earners' Household Incomes in Japan and Korea, 1955 to 1979

	1955–1959	1960–1964	1965–1969	1970–1974	1975–1979
Japan	0.90	0.86	1.00	1.10	1.17
Korea, Rep.	0.77	0.90	0.74	0.84	0.97

Source: *Japan Statistical Yearbook* (Tokyo: Bureau of Statistics, various issues); *Handbook of Korean Economy* (Seoul: Economic Planning Board, 1980).

10. For cross-sectional evidence on the extent of agricultural protection in developed countries, see M. D. Bale and E. Lutz, "Price Distortions in Agriculture and Their Effects: An International Comparison," *American Journal of Agricultural Economics* 63(1), February 1981:8–22. Time series evidence is provided in O. Gulbrandsen and A. Lindbeck, *The Economics of the Agricultural Sector* (Stockholm: Almquist and Wicksell, 1973) and A. Yeats, "Agricultural Protectionism: An Analysis of its International Economic Effects and Options for Institutional Reform," *Trade and Development* (UNCTAD) 3 (Winter 1981):1–30.

11. K. Anderson, "Prospects for Trade Growth Among Pacific Basin Countries," *The Developing Economies* 21 (December 1983):376–385.

12. One set of recent high-level discussions about such an organization is reported in J. G. Crawford, ed., *Pacific Economic Cooperation: Suggestions for Action* (Hong Kong: Heinemann, 1981).

Part 2

International Trade and Self-Sufficiency: Contrasting Approaches to Food Security

Part 2

Intonational Tone
and Self-Sufficiency
Columbus is Approaches
to Food Security

3
The Trade Approach to Food Security

Ralph Lattimore

The Pacific Basin contains a high proportion of the world's population. It also includes countries that are among the world's major agricultural and food product importers and exporters. The region is extremely diverse in terms of agricultural resources ratios, tastes and preferences in food, and institutional and political structures. As a result, policies and programs implemented to promote food security in the region are equally diverse. In recent years, they have included programs at the national level to establish grain buffer stocks in the ASEAN group; administered pricing programs to promote self-sufficiency in dairy products and/or meat production in Australia, Canada, Indonesia, Japan, South Korea, and the United States; long-term trade agreements between grain exporters and the People's Republic of China; and explicit grain reserve stocks in the United States.

The need to improve food security, particularly in the developing countries, is one of those ideas whose time has come. In fact, it has been a major issue now for almost a decade. Like "the basic needs approach," "Keynesian economics," and the "New International Economic Order," which addressed concerns in other domains, "food security" has become a convenient banner to orient private- and public-sector actions toward a higher priority for food at a time when the world food system continues to be buffeted by shocks that exacerbate the problems of the hungry consumer and the small farmer alike. Food security may be defined, following Siamwalla and Valdés, as "the ability of food deficit countries, or regions or households within these countries, to meet target levels of consumption on a yearly basis."[1]

The political environment that surrounds the food-security issue at the present time is rich in its diversity. In large part this diversity stems from frustrations with our inability to deal with international trade and aid concerns. Streeten has noted three concerns of less developed countries.[2] They are the perceived inadequate quantity and quality of development assistance, increasing political independence juxtaposed with decreasing economic independence (increasing interdependence), and the success of

OPEC, until very recently, and a few other mineral exporters that "offer an alternative to appealing to the conscience of the rich."

The last two concerns in particular are also perceived to be causes for concern in international relations between the developed countries. In the field of agricultural trade relations, these concerns are compounded by continuing difficulties in dealing with protection arising from domestic policies.

A wide literature has developed in this area. Much of this work is well summarized in Siamwalla and Valdés.[3] Indeed, the International Food Policy Research Institute (IFPRI) has contributed much important work in the area. The study by McIntire for the Sahel is a good example.[4]

At the same time, it is important to recognize that the technical and economic factors that surround the food-security issue are little different from those that have always faced agriculturalists, economists, and policy-makers. Given the possibilities for the specialization of labor and other resources, fundamental trade-offs exist between growth and equity at the level of the individual (producer and consumer), the firm, and the nation. There is no "free lunch" in allocating agricultural resources.

Trade is an important ingredient in the set of food-policy choices that have to be made at all levels of productive activity, particularly in the Pacific Basin countries. Trade is an important source of economic gains; it aids the specialization process and contributes to both growth and equity objectives. In all but the most primitive societies, trade is an essential ingredient in achieving food security. Trade permits the division of labor in the rural community to pursue production specialization with its attendant higher productivity and standard of living. Regional trading permits the same productive specialization to occur between rural and urban centers. International trade performs this function between nations. The trade-off involved in this process is vulnerability. Hence, the real question becomes one of deciding upon the appropriate long-term growth strategy (including gain from trade) in a risky environment.

The second important benefit from trade arises from multiple sourcing possibilities, an extension of the previous topic. Specialization (and trade) permits economic gains at the expense of exposure to trade risks. However, multiple sourcing of requirements by the household or the nation minimizes the attendant risks.

The absence of trading opportunities, conversely, is often a constraint to growth. In less developed countries perhaps the greatest marketing (trade) constraint to meeting food security is the lack of efficient interregional trading opportunities between food-surplus and food-deficit regions. Problems of infrastructure, transportation, and market information often result in a lack of domestic supply responsiveness to market requirements. A broad discussion of trade in general and its relevance for food security is beyond the scope of this paper. This discussion will focus only on aspects of international trade as they impinge on food security.

The Setting

Any discussion of food security in the current world agricultural setting is complicated by a variety of factors that are having an impact on national agricultural and food-policy settings. These policies are, in turn, influencing the probability of attaining food security at home and also abroad.

World food production has tended to increase faster than demand, with the result that per capita consumption is rising in the aggregate. However, the world totals mask a deteriorating situation for many countries in selected regions like Africa. Furthermore, food-deficit countries overall have become increasingly dependent on imported supplies over the past two decades. In many countries domestic supplies have failed to increase at the same rate as domestic market requirements. This problem has occurred for staples like wheat and food corn, but the trend is even more pronounced for livestock products and feedgrains.

At the same time, food exports have tended to become more concentrated in the hands of the few major exporters. Of particular importance here is the world wheat trade, where the export market share of the United States, Canada, Australia, and Argentina has increased significantly over the past thirty years. This situation has political and economic implications in the face of the increased politicization of trade in food. On a number of occasions in the past decade, economic sanctions, trade embargoes, and prohibitions on food exports have been used for political and economic purposes by a number of countries. These restrictions have seldom been of long duration and their impact has never been as great as expected. For example, the partial grain embargo imposed on the Soviet Union resulted in purchase limitations for that country of only a fraction of the intended limitation. The market tended to circumvent the restrictions, opening up price differentials of around 10 percent in the dichotomized grain market in the weeks following the embargo's announcement.

As far as less-developed countries are concerned, the impact of other restrictions on commercial trade appears to have been much less. Siamwalla and Valdés[5] were unable to find an example of a country in which wheat was unavailable at any price. However, the Thailand export embargo on rice in 1973 did apparently cause major problems in many Asian importing countries according to the same authors.

Finally, the last decade has been strewn with external shocks that tripled grain prices in 1973, caused two major surges in oil prices, caused persistent balance-of-payments problems, inflation, recessions, and now 5-10 percent (and greater) real interest rates for an extended period. The response to these pressures has been reinforced efforts to insulate producers and consumers from international food-market influences. The sum of these responses has been continuing high levels of intervention in world markets with concomitant effects on countries that remain exposed to them. In contrast to trade in manufactures, very little success has been achieved in reducing the overall level of protection against trade in food and agricultural products. In this environment it is extremely difficult for policymakers to resist domestic pressures to insulate the domestic food and agricultural sector by employing unilateral measures. Part of this problem is the crisis in international institutions referred to by Schuh and Streeten.[6]

International Trade and Food Security

Two fundamental components of the food-security issue are addressed in the remainder of this paper.[7] The first is whether "to trade or not to trade" in food. This question quickly reduces to the familiar self-sufficiency argument. If the answer to this question is in the affirmative, the question of how best to conduct trade in food arises. Both issues—to trade or not to trade—are taken up in this section.

The Case for Self-Sufficiency

The question addressed in this section is the familiar one faced by a country unable to alter the external terms of trade and considering the range of national policy settings in terms of the resulting contribution of the agricultural sector to various goals. Food-security goals are important in many cases, but there are others, including regional development objectives and the contribution to growth and export earnings, which are likewise often important.

The starting point for such analysis is a baseline. Any baseline would do; its role is merely to serve as a point of reference. The range of alternative policy settings will be evaluated as differences from this base. Unfortunately, in far too many instances, the base case is described in normative terms with almost mystical properties associated with it. However, the baseline has no such status in objective analysis.

By tradition economists have often used the so-called free trade case as the baseline. There are good reasons for this choice. Deadweight losses in efficiency terms are often associated with food and agricultural policy intervention both in terms of private resource allocation and public administration costs. It is important to know what these losses are in evaluating alternative policies. The free trade baseline is an excellent way of highlighting them.

It is possible to generally describe particular policy settings vis-à-vis a free trade baseline for individual food commodities in a simple classification system. In Figure 3.1, the effects of national food price policies (as composites comprised usually of numerous instruments) are classified according to whether the commodity *would be* an importable or an exportable commodity at border (or world) prices. The policies are also classified according to whether existing policy results in a domestic price that is higher or lower than the border price.

One word of caution is necessary before proceeding. It is frequently the case that private costs and returns (for labor, capital, foreign exchange, and land) differ from social values. Distortions in the domestic market require

FIGURE 3.1
A Classification of Food Price Policies

LOW PRICE POLICY

1. Negative Effective Protection
2. Few Producer Incentives
3. Overvalued Effective Exchange Rate

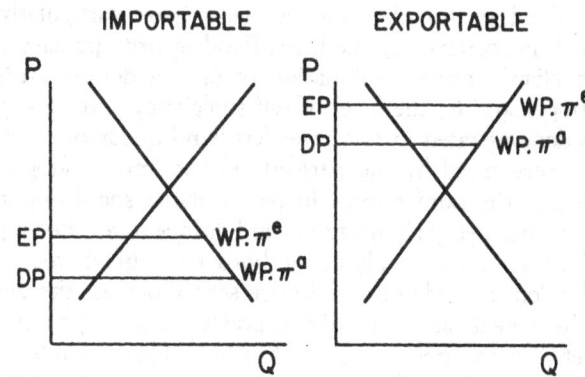

HIGH PRICE POLICY

1. Positive Effective Protection
2. Many Producer Incentives
3. Undervalued Effective Exchange Rate

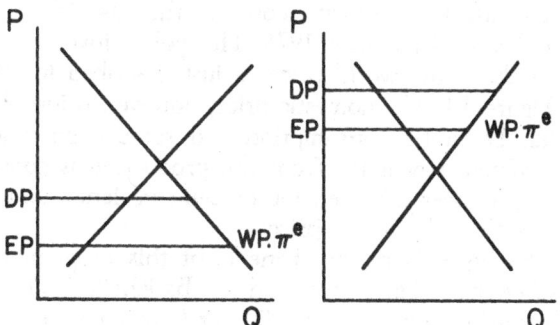

LEGEND   DP: domestic price
EP: equilibrium price
WP: world price
π: exchange rate (superscript a denotes actual and e denotes real effective)

careful consideration in this context. It is common to find that production regions in less developed countries would significantly increase output if the incentive package was raised close to border price levels. High domestic marketing costs, for instance, frequently place domestic producers at a severe competitive disadvantage with regard to imports.

It is also common to find a complex set of incentives and disincentives operating for a particular food commodity. For purposes of analysis, these multiple incentives must be collapsed into a single indicator so that their net effect can be ascertained. Such adjustments are important because it is not uncommon to find that a food item that is being imported would, in the absence of policy intervention, be an exportable product.

Food security becomes a major issue particularly, but not exclusively, with importable commodities. Food-security policies are designed in general to change some combination of (a) the domestic price level, (b) domestic supply, and (c) the level of self-sufficiency and imports. This type of action is demonstrated in the lower left-hand quadrant of Figure 3.1. The baseline is represented by the perfectly elastic import supply schedule (EP), which defines the border price in terms of the social opportunity cost of foreign exchange net of all incentives and disincentives affecting the product (whether the instruments apply at the border or elsewhere). The line DP represents the domestic administered price set to increase the degree of self-sufficiency. The benefits and costs of this policy are measured in terms of the difference between the policy and the baseline. They include a higher degree of self-sufficiency, lower foreign exchange requirements for imports, insulation from world market instability, higher returns to producers and production regions, higher consumer prices, and lower production of competing crops.

As an example of the impact of a policy in the Pacific Basin designed to increase food security, consider the case of the Canadian dairy policy as it has evolved since 1974. The policy involves setting an administered price above the world price as just described for the lower left quadrant of Figure 3.1. The domestic price, however, is just above the self-sufficiency point. Domestic consumption and some exports are subsidized through government payments. Domestic production is constrained by quotas to a level just over 100 percent of self-sufficiency and consumers pay prices higher than the world price.

The broad costs and benefits of this program relative to a free trade baseline have been estimated by Barichello.[8] The policy increases dairy incomes by around US $7,000 per farmer per year, and the degree of self-sufficiency in milk and dairy products is increased from 75 percent ot 105 percent. On the cost side, consumers pay US $25 per capita per year more than they would under baseline conditions, and taxpayers pay an additional US $10 per year on a per capita basis. In addition, production, farm cash receipts, and export earnings (or import savings) from hogs, corn, soybeans, and horticultural crops are lower as a result of the policy. Differences between private and social values do not appear to have been used in this analysis, but in this case they differ by five percent or less, and their exclusion is not expected to bias the results markedly.

Overall, it costs US $1.30 to deliver US $1.00 in program benefits to producers. The program is currently supported because it is seen to contribute to rural settlement and regional development objectives with acceptable efficiency costs. Direct program costs are less than 0.5 percent of government expenditures and the weight of dairy products in the consumer price index is 3.2 percent. At the same time, however, there is very little recognition of the indirect and long-term effects of the policy on the adoption of technology, economic efficiency, impact on the next generation of dairy farmers, and constraints on other agricultural production.

This example has two interesting corollaries. First, under a baseline policy Canada would be a small participant in the world market (3-5 percent of world aid and trade). Hence the small-country framework might appear to be appropriate. However, the world export supply schedule is inelastic (with respect to the world price) and a change in Canada's self-sufficiency ratio of 30 percent would be expected to have a measurable effect on world prices. Second, because world market prices are so strongly affected by domestic policies, the definition of a "small country" ought to be examined in terms of its foreign policy leverage or the leverage of bargaining groups to which the country belongs, as well as its degree of participation in actual trade. In the current fluid international situation, the two concepts need not coincide.

The foregoing discussion is highly simplified and in actual practice the framework often has to cope with wider ramifications and probabilistic elements. South Korea, for example, has introduced administered prices for beef at three times the world price. This policy has increased the degree of self-sufficiency in beef, but at the same time increased considerably the degree of dependence on imported feedgrains. Given the magnitudes involved, this is hardly consistent with the stated aim to improve food security. Overall, there has been little if any reduction in the degree of foreign dependence of the agricultural sector.

The Case for Stability

If policymakers are persuaded that the national interest is served by trading in a particular food commodity, there is no guarantee that unregulated exposure to the world market will prove to be optimal. With an adequate commodity intelligence system, foreign representation, and commodity purchasing program, timely supplies can be assured. World prices, on the other hand, are inherently unstable and extremely difficult to forecast from one year to the next.

Administered pricing is often used as a means of insulating the domestic agricultural sector from what is perceived to be an undesirable degree of instability in the world market. It has been shown by Jabara and Thompson that such a policy used in conjunction with variable levies and export taxes may indeed be optimal from a resource allocation standpoint.[9] Furthermore, the use of this rationale is unlikely to result in domestic prices that are more than a few percentage points above world prices on average. The above recommendation, however, begs the question of comparative administrative costs of administered versus market pricing systems. That is to say, optimal policy recommendations strictly ought to include possible differences in the costs of regulation. Casual observation would suggest that (world) market pricing schemes using ad valorem or specific taxes or subsidies collected at the border might require fewer resources than administered pricing schemes. The latter usually involve considerable regulatory action domestically by a government in addition to border controls (usually quotas).

TABLE 3.1
Sample Distributions of Domestic Price Levels for Selected Commodities and Countries, 1978

Domestic Price Level	Wheat Price	No. of Countries	Corn Price	No. of Countries	Milk Price[a]	No. of Countries
Low	$100/ton[b]	1	$75/ton	1	$150/ton	5
Medium	$100–$150/ton	15	$75–$125/ton	17	$150–$250/ton	16
High	$150–$200/ton	16	$125–$175/ton	--	$250–$350/ton	--
Very high	$200/ton	17	$175/ton	19	$350/ton	2
Representative export price	$112/ton		$83/ton		$100/ton	

a. Milk prices are expressed in terms of milk equivalent.
b. All prices are given in metric tons.

Sources: USDA, Foreign Agricultural Circular (Washington, D.C.: U.S. Department of Agriculture, FG-6-79, 18 April 1979) and R.G. Lattimore and S. Weedle, The "World Price" Impact of Multilateral Free Trade in Dairy Products (Ottawa: Agriculture Canada, working paper, August 1981).

Other forms of stabilization policy may be sufficient in particular circumstances to protect producers or consumers from extreme variation in world market conditions. Deficiency payments and two-price systems, for example, are both used by some countries for this purpose. With any of these instruments, it is important to ensure that the support levels are responsive to the long-term trend in world market conditions unless there are overwhelming reasons to diverge from this trend.

International Market Considerations

Attitudes toward international trade in food and agricultural products are strongly conditioned by the structure, behavior, and performance of world markets in these products. Hence, an understanding of the major forces at work is important if a country is going to make the best use of them.

First, world food markets are volatile in part due to supply variations in large producing countries. Second, these markets are highly distorted by policies and programs designed to insulate national agricultural sectors from the discipline and "natural" instability associated with market exposure (many of these programs are so-called food-security policies).[10]

Some appreciation for the size of these distortions can be gained by examining the sample price distributions in Table 3.1. The table shows the distribution of domestic (supply) prices for selected countries in 1978 for wheat, corn, and milk. These distributions are compared with a representative export price. Fifty major coarse grain producers were surveyed for the data in Table 3.1. Thirty-two countries had domestic corn prices more than 50 percent above the world price in that year.[11] It is important to recognize that policy-induced insulation by national governments imposes an externality on other participants in the world trading system. This externality can take the form of lower levels of food security in countries exposed to world market conditions and can limit export opportunities in others.

The more that countries intervene to induce high domestic prices, the lower the world price level is likely to be in response to lower demand (and the more unstable it is likely to become). Conversely, as more of these interventionist policies are removed, the higher the world price is likely to be. It has been estimated elsewhere that multilateral free trade in dairy products would raise the price of these products on the world market over 100 percent, to a level close to the current support levels in the European Economic Community (EEC) and North America.[12]

The policies and programs that induce these distortions have been implemented by both exporting and importing countries. Importers do not have a monopoly on world trade and price distortions. The programs are paid for directly by taxpayers and consumers and indirectly by foreign producers and taxpayers. The cost of agricultural and food programs in developed countries is typically in the range of 20-30 percent of value added in primary agriculture. Many of the expenditures involved have trade diversion effects of one type or another.[13]

What are the implications of this situation for food policy in less-developed countries? First, the sum effect of these interventionist policies is to drive down the world market (border) price of food commodities toward the minimum supply price of the least-cost exporter. This tendency is stronger the more highly distorted the world market. (Sugar and dairy products provide examples of highly distorted markets.) The more distorted these markets become, the greater must be the level of intervention for a small country participant to maintain the relative size of its food industry. However, it may not be optimal for a country to pursue this course of action because, fundamentally, it involves attempting to match treasury expenditures from much larger countries. Where important wage goods are the focus of food policy in less developed countries, such an approach would have serious general equilibrium impacts not only on the agricultural sector, but on the manufacturing and tertiary sectors as well.

An alternative approach is to maintain pressure to reform existing international arrangements to produce equitable "rule-based" trade laws snd guidelines on a multilateral basis. The point of the analysis above is that by using trade intervention, individual countries are imposing negative externalities on each other in the form of unstable prices. Agreeing to forego these situations would eliminate the externalities.

Second, it has been suggested that the increasing concentration of food trade on the import side, coupled with extensive intervention, may have completely offset the oligopolistic power that used to exist in world grain trade (and probably also existed in the meat, dairy, and sugar markets).[14] World food markets are characterized by a few dominant sellers and buyers, which suggests that significant premiums for market information may occur, having implications for market intelligence and research work in trading countries.

Market structure considerations have given rise over the years to a debate (still unsettled) as to the balance of power, particularly in the cereal market. However, the polar positions in the grain debate may be even more valid in other food markets. On the one hand is the argument formalized by McCalla and by Alaouse et al. that world cereal markets tend to be oligopolistic, with the major exporters implicitly extracting a rent from importers through supply and pricing behavior.[15] This theory has a certian popular appeal and is often used as an argument for import substitution, on the one hand, and the potential for cartels on the other.

At the other end of the spectrum lie the arguments that major importers have in effect applied optimum tariffs in world cereals markets and that these markets actually tend to be oligopsonistic rather than oligopolistic.[16] The economic forces and use of policy instruments that could potentially give rise to either or both frameworks certainly exist in the marketplace for most livestock products and feedstuffs. The small market participant is unable to influence the situation (by definition), but the elements do imply that such a country can make gains from improved market information and contingency planning. The market situation does not imply that importers should necessarily minimize dependence on these markets, but rather use them intelligently.

Conclusions

International trade can provide a reliable source of food to marginally supplement domestic supplies and ensure that a country is able "to meet target levels of food consumption on a yearly basis."[17] More than that, however, exposure to international trade (properly tailored to national needs) provides perhaps the cheapest and most effective market discipline system on the food sector. This discipline is crucial for efficient development of both the industrial and agricultural sectors in less-developed countries of the Pacific Basin. However, in many circumstances it may prove necessary to offset extreme variations in world markets. The challenge is to find ways to do this that do not sacrifice resource efficiency and thus economic development, and that do not impose larger externalities on other countries.

In any event, all countries have a vested interest in trying to improve the rules under which food and agricultural trade is conducted, in order to make the most efficient use of the world's agricultural resources and to assure that food is made available to all consumers in an equitable fashion. It will not be a simple task to reach agreement on such rules, but the potential benefits to consumers in food-deficit countries, to producers in exporting countries, and to taxpayers everywhere dictate that a major effort to this end be made.

Notes

1. Ammar Siamwalla and Alberto Valdés, "Food Insecurity in Developing Countries," *Food Policy* 5(4), November 1980.
2. Paul Streeten, "Approaches to a New International Economic Order," *World Development* 10(1), January 1982:1-17.
3. Siamwalla and Valdés, "Food Insecurity in Developing Countries."
4. John McIntire, "Food Security in the Sahel: Variable Import Levy, Grain Reserves and Foreign Exchange Assistance" (Washington, D.C.: International Food Policy Research Institute, Research Report No. 26, September 1981).
5. Siamwalla and Valdés, "Food Insecurity in Developing Countries."
6. G. Edward Schuh, "Towards Reform of our International Monetary and Trade Institutions," in *Issues in Third World Development*, ed. K. C. Nobe and R. K. Sampath (Boulder: Westview Press, 1983); Streeten, "Approaches to a New International Economic Order."
7. There are other major issues in this context not dealt with here. The role of food aid is a case in point. One body of opinion argues that, other than the case of emergency relief measures, food aid is not a useful tool for increasing food security for a variety of reasons. Others would argue that in spite of the negative elements, food aid can still contribute to food security.
8. Richard R. Barichello, "The Economics of Canadian Dairy Industry Regulation" (Ottawa: Economics Council of Canada, Technical Report E/12, 1981).
9. Cathy Jabara and Robert L. Thompson, "Agricultural Comparative Advantage under International Price Uncertainty: The Case of Senegal," *American Journal of Agricultural Economics* 62(2), May 1980:188-198.
10. D. Gale Johnson, "World Agriculture, Commodity Policy and Price Variability," *American Journal of Agricultural Economics* 57(4), December 1975:823-828.
11. The comparison was made at official exchange rates, not at equilibrium exchange rates.
12. Ralph Lattimore and S. Weedle, *The "World Price" Impact of Multilateral Free Trade in Dairy Products* (Ottawa: Agriculture Canada, working paper, August 1981).
13. Trade Consortium, "Report of the U.S./Canada Agricultural Trade Consortium," U.S. Department of Agriculture, ERS, December 1982.
14. Colin Carter and Andrew Schmitz, "Import Tariffs and Price Formation in the World Wheat Market," *American Journal of Agricultural Economics* 61(3), August 1979:517-522.
15. Alex F. McCalla, "A Duopoly Model of World Wheat Pricing," *Journal of Farm Economics* 48(3), August 1966:711-727; Chris M. Alaouze, A. S. Watson, and N. H. Sturges, "Oligopoly Pricing in the World Wheat Market," *American Journal of Agricultural Economics* 60(2), May 1978:173-185.
16. Carter and Schmitz, "Import Tariffs and Price Formulation in the World Wheat Market."
17. Siamwalla and Valdés, "Food Insecurity in Developing Countries."

4
The SAM Approach to Food Security

Cassio Luiselli
Alejandro Cruz-Serrano

The subject of international or regional food security has been widely discussed, but the possibilities and interrelations of a food-security scheme or system for the Pacific Basin countries have never been adequately explored. The aim of this chapter is to examine and demonstrate a convergence of interests in the so-called "Transpacific Community" for the possible establishment of a food-security system for the Pacific countries, based on the fundamentals and the strategic approach of the Mexican Food System (SAM).[1]

The first step is to clarify the concept and definition of food security. The Mexican Food System considers food security as the possibility of continuous access to foodstuffs essential for the development and normal functioning of the individuals in a society. The food-security system is also understood as an integration of efforts in different areas, such as an adequate transfer of technology, sufficient and equitable flows of trade, fluid systems and mechanisms of distribution, a transfer of financial resources to cope effectively with the development of autonomous technologies, and, of course, the formation and maintenance of reserves as a permanent activity. Food security also implies the means to ensure that the present world fluctuations in basic foodstuffs will not affect adversely the continuity of basic consumption.

These features seem quite obvious but have not been accepted by many countries as yet, countries that think it is enough from the point of view of food security to be able to count on an adequate availability of reserves. Thus, there is no internationally accredited world food system, but a combination of policies of national production, reserves, commerce, and consumption that do not pursue a common objective. The cornerstone of world food security, as visualized by the World Food Conference in 1974, consisted of internationally agreed-upon measures on supply and stabilization of prices of basic grains, but this limited concept did not take root in practice.

For most countries, world food security is related to an international availability of foodstuffs, especially cereals, on a continuous and secure basis. World or regional food-security objectives have, however, remained a manifest desire still far from reality. Various international organizations of food aid, technical institutions, financial circles, discussion forums, and political forums have constituted a disarticulate machinery with bureaucratic interests that have not allowed the development of either a food strategy on a worldwide basis or a food-security system.

The second step of an exploration that should be carried out is to determine not only who are the real participants of such projected food cooperation, but what their food systems are all about, understood as socioeconomic structures that carry out in an integrated manner consecutive processes of production, marketing, transformation, distribution, and consumption. In the analysis it would also be necessary to resort to the traditional classification of developed and developing countries, but above all, to a classification that would show which countries are of a complementary nature and which are competitive, based on existing trade patterns and production potential.

Among the Pacific Basin countries, several have food strategies, but many do not. Hunger and malnutrition are present even in countries rich in food. Several countries of this region have planned for self-sufficiency in foodstuffs, other have already achieved it, and others do not even consider it a high priority. Several countries are exporters of basic and secondary foodstuffs, but others are more and more dangerously and increasingly net importers. The possibilities of complementation and the opportunities for bilateral and multilateral cooperation, based on the diversity of natural, human, financial, and technological resources, justify a cooperative effort to explore the possibilities of a food-security system in the Pacific Basin.

A third step would require a clear statement of objectives. In agreement with the integrated approach of the Mexican Food System, the participating countries could adopt as their basic objectives:

1. An increase in the production, productivity, and trade of all farming, livestock, and fishing activities in a realistic and feasible complementary manner.
2. The establishment of a food-security scheme or system for the Pacific Basin that would allow the elimination of hunger and malnutrition from the area and would guarantee sufficient reserves and adequate distribution mechanisms for the future.
3. A substantial increase in the levels of commercial, technological, and financial exchange through this cooperation scheme, with not only the industrialized countries benefiting, as has been the case traditionally, but also the developing nations of the area. The redistribution of the benefits derived from the increases in production and trade for the developing countries of the Pacific Basin naturally does not imply that the industrialized countries of the area will not obtain benefits.

Cooperation in this new effort should be explored not only in relation to trade, but also in the relatively unexplored fields of food technology transfer, the financing of projects, coinvestments, and scientific cooperation. Attention must be paid to all the stages of the food chain from production to consumption in farming and livestock production, as well as in fisheries. The limited material produced to date on the food question in the Pacific Basin area has examined almost exclusively the agriculture of some of the Pacific countries, with special attention to foreign agricultural trade. This approach would again lead to a very partial and misleading vision, not only of the problems but also of the possibilities and perspectives, in particular confirming the orientation of bigger benefits once again toward the developed or industrialized countries.

The most reasonable food-policy recommendations for the region would have to evaluate, for example, the natural resources of one country, the financial and technological resources of another, and the human resources of still another, in order to be able to construct an efficient set of structures whose processes and actions are oriented toward the common objective of food security, with the possibility of a real benefit for all. This initiative includes all the potential to be realized in a common effort of twenty-one or more countries with a minimum population of 2 billion human beings. Taking into consideration the economic dynamism of the countries of the Pacific Basin, a cooperative effort should find a way to take optimum advantage of all this potential and dynamism.

The objective of food security requires solutions that involve not only technical aspects, but also political actions on both a national scale and bilateral, subregional, and regional scales. Such solutions are variable and are highly dependent on the nature of the problem and on its dimensions. These solutions are closely related to the critical condition of the international economic system and to what has been called the "international food system."

Such solutions should not, however, be sought in the traditional and obsolete arguments of exportation, comparative advantage, growing importation of food on the part of developing countries, food aid, the role of the industrialized countries as granaries or world suppliers, and the increasingly important participation of transnational companies in the control of production, productivity, transformation, distribution, and consumption of the basic foodstuffs. This pattern of arguments would continue to show the international food system incapable of satisfying the needs of nourishment for the majority of the world's population. Obviously, this road would not lead to the achievement of regional food security in the Pacific Basin area.

Protectionism, oligopolization of trade in foodstuffs, and disloyal practices (manipulation of prices, embargoes, etc.) make the "international food system" highly vulnerable. The political use of surplus food is a permanent possibility on the part of some countries that at present not only direct the organization of the world market but also concentrate the export capacity of foodstuffs.

The Mexican Food System

Given the points of view that have been presented in previous forums of the Pacific Basin Project in relation with the thesis of comparative advantage, it becomes necessary to explain the SAM philosophy (shared essentially by Japan) concerning food.

It is highly risky to base an entire development strategy on a scheme of comparative advantages. This practice means employment of cheap labor and very fast increases of income in the short run, but later on a decrease in the agricultural production. In addition, a rapidly growing demand for food and purchasing power (abroad) dependent on the pace of industrial investment are variables over which a country has little control or power of decision. For cases like Singapore or Hong Kong perhaps there is no alternative to the practice described, but for countries with a larger population and arable land, experience has shown that development based on assembly plants has come at the cost of neglecting food production. Several of those countries have set out on the known and dangerous course of importing food *first* because it is apparently cheaper abroad (which discourages domestic production) and *later* because it is not produced in the country.

The standpoint and the experience of SAM regarding the concept of comparative advantage can be firmly sustained with empirical evidence from countries that have chosen a development strategy based on such grounds. Aside from these observable examples, there exist only the expected phenomena such as growing oligopolistic control of the world grain market, the crisis of 1973-1974, and a rising tendency in the prices of cereals until a few years ago. In addition to warning against the fragility of the model of industrial growth followed by many countries and the inoperativeness of the theory of comparative advantage, the strategy adopted by Mexico also implies caution against an agricultural growth pattern that is too capital and energy intensive. The attempts to generalize such a pattern are difficult due to the implications for foreign exchange expenditure, ecological damage, and unemployment. Aside from the fact that the world prospect in energy sources is uncertain and that it will be increasingly difficult to obtain hydrocarbons, it is necessary to emphasize the fact that one of the underlying characteristics of such a model is the concentration of income and benefits.

The problems of interest to the developing countries of the Pacific Basin are totally compatible with the fundamental principles upon which SAM is based. That is to say, we would try to discuss possible solutions to the problem of promotion of industrial growth as a road to modernization without neglecting or leaving to one side the concomitant development of the countryside to emphasize self-sufficiency in food and increases in the peasants' income. The concepts of self-sufficiency in food and nutritional security, developed by SAM as its basic thesis and closely related to the objective of food security, can be conceived as the Mexican answer to the need for integrating food policy into the policy of economic and social development.

In the framework of the transformations manifested, to a lesser or higher degree, by the countries of the Pacific Basin as a consequence of industrial growth, it seems appropriate to focus the analysis of the food question around the models of industrialization ("export led" and "substitution of imports"). This focus relates to the need for self-sufficiency as a vital aspect of national sovereignty. Food and nutritional security are objectives that the developing countries have fruitlessly tried to reach and are closely related to existing development patterns and food systems, as well as to the various strategic options to cope with the food problem as a whole.

Food security depends on external factors (available exportable offers, variations in international prices, and the degree of vulnerability of the "international food system"), which have a direct bearing on the real income of a country. The degree of vulnerability of national food systems can increase or decrease according to the efficiency of their strategies. The achievement of food security based on the execution of a strategy includes the concepts of self-sufficiency in food, independence in food, and national sovereignty.

The SAM approach, in short, is based on the following fundamental principles:

1. SAM should be understood as a strategy of rural development providing an alternative to the model that directs the different rural sectors toward certain specialization as a function of their "comparative advantage." That is, the objectives of SAM were outlined against the powerful argument of specialization of agriculture based on comparative advantage, i.e., importing cheap grains and exporting fruits and vegetables.
2. Adopting the agricultural specialization development model implied both economic and political risks in choosing comparative advantage in the presence of an oligopolistic market dominated by a few transnational companies, a market far from being perfectly competitive or (therefore) cheapest and safest.
3. SAM was designed to reactivate the rural economy by means of production of basic foodstuffs and by increasing general consumption through a distribution of income and highly selective subsidies. In this context, an integral and integrated solution of the problems along the food chain in farming, livestock production, and fishing would imply an automatic tendency toward food security.
4. Because SAM is an integrated strategy of production-income-consumption, social and economic development takes place, making easier the attainment of food and nutritional security.

Recommendations

The strategic model of the Mexican Food System permits the application and adaptation of its approach, its fundamentals, its objectives, and its mechanisms to the realities and possibilities of action and cooperation among the Pacific Basin countries. On this basis we wish to point out a number of considerations and suggest some political measures:

1. The profound differences in the levels of development present in the Pacific Basin countries are in their turn currently reflected in differences in the evolution of their food sectors. Thus, the United States of America, Canada, Australia, and New Zealand as food-exporting countries (the first two are the principal sellers of grain in the world) coexist with nations that have had or still have deficits in food —nations such as Japan, China, the Philippines, Peru, Ecuador, Chile, Mexico, Malaysia, the Democratic People's Republic of Korea, the Republic of Korea, and the protectorates of Singapore and Hong Kong.

2. One situation that should not be forgotten, for being too obvious, is the clear correlation between a higher level of development and a surplus of farming and livestock balance evident in the Pacific Basin, with the exception of Japan. Among these nations there has been a tendency in recent decades for the developed countries to obtain self-sufficiency in food and to become exporters of grains, while the developing countries have become dependent on food imports.

The pattern of industrial development followed by several of the Asian countries and protectorates (significantly South Korea, Singapore, Hong Kong, and Taiwan), specializing in providing parts, components, and assembly of products that are finished in Japan and the United States, implies a subsidiary relation with these latter two economies and the international market for industrial goods. The degree of exterior vulnerability of these countries and protectorates is extremely high.

3. Regarding food consumption, a warning should be given on the risks implied in the changes of protein pattern that accompany modernization. Due to the large number of inhabitants in several Asian countries, an increase in the intake of animal protein (due to the increase in income and an imitation of patterns such as those of the United States) has had unavoidable repercussions on the availability and prices of grains on an international level. For example, a greater need for corn for fattening pigs in China would mean larger profits for U.S. farmers and a rise in the price of corn in the international market, resulting in difficulties in its acquisition by poor countries.

It is also important to point out that the policy of promoting U.S. agricultural exports, whether to get rid of a surplus or to maintain prices at a certain high level, plays a very important part in fomenting habits of animal protein consumption. That is, habits that in the future become an effective demand for U.S. wheat and corn are deliberately encouraged. Several Asian countries, due to their high demographic density, have to practice intensive farming in order to satisfy demands for animal protein. This situation has serious consequences for their system of agricultural and livestock production, as well as for the world agricultural and food economy.

4. Due to the fact that almost all the countries in the Pacific Basin have enormous coastal areas, fishing is the resource that has the greatest potential

in the future to satisfy human and animal nutrition and is an incomparable source of proteins. The international obstacles of enormous distances and the corresponding communications problems can be diminished if a rational and joint exploitation of the sea through equitable projects is expanded and emphasized.

5. The distance between the countries of the Pacific Basin, and consequently of their markets, provides a motive to find more feasible subregional and bilateral understandings. Through these efforts a net of interactions should be established for the achievement of food security in the region, which is essential for the developing countries. However, before proposing concrete measures for a large program of bilateral, subregional, and regional cooperation, it is imperative that the developing countries of the area implement or execute national food strategies of an integral nature. These strategies should give priority to basic foods and point out the instruments and the political will that are indispensable for the achievement of food security.

6. The developing countries of the region, when forming and putting into practice their food strategy aimed at increasing the degree of self-sufficiency and at reaching the goal of food security, would be responding to agreements and mandates of the Food and Agriculture Organization, (FAO), the World Food Council, and the United Nations itself. At the same time, however, they would be contributing in a coordinated way to achieving the goals of the international strategy of development and of the New International Economic Order.

7. The differences in resource endowments make complementation and a convergence of interests in the different areas of cooperation possible. For example, according to Table 4.1, possibilities for developing countries to take advantage of include the experiences and advances of China in aquaculture, preparation of soil, and organization of small production units. Nations such as Mexico, Peru, Colombia, Ecuador, and Chile could consider the different technologies of Canada, Australia, New Zealand, and the two Koreas. The United States and Japan could share diverse techniques and technologies in the fields of food processing, fertilizers, pesticides, biotechnology, storage nets, and so on. Japan has made great advances in exploiting fisheries and in researching chemical fertilizers, optimum exploitation of soil, and future foodstuffs. The organization of production and consumption cooperatives in South Korea is worth taking advantage of by many developing countries of the area. Mexico has started to share with other Latin American and even African countries its experiences in the fields of strategy and food planning.

8. Foreign trade in food in the Pacific Basin area presents wide prospects because, again, the differences make complementation feasible. Commercial ties that have developed are due more to geographic proximity than to economic rationality. The latter possibilities should be explored to provide technological trade, as well as trade of products, with a long-term vision.

9. Without ignoring or underestimating the importance the above-mentioned aspects have for the achievement of food security in the Pacific

Basin area, it is undoubtedly the financial factor that is the most relevant one. Even though national food strategies can be formulated or promoted by each government, their execution requires solid financial backing. If such backing is important in the national framework, in the international arena it is crucial.

A new cooperation scheme, especially in the fields of food production, processing and distribution, must include an adequate infrastructure for marketing and distribution, sufficient inputs, economic and technological opportunities on the part of the producers, and the absence of high risks in investment. It must be established on a strong enough foundation to guarantee the benefits expected by all the participating countries. The need for financing is not doubted, but when dealing with a new scheme, no funds or credit are available from regional banks like the Inter-American Development Bank (IDB), the Asian Development Bank (ADB), or the World Bank.

For this reason a development bank of the Pacific Basin or a similar financial institution is particularly needed to act as an economic support for the actions taken in the framework of cooperative efforts to promote regional food security. The proposed bank would give credits to projects and programs, preferential rates to the developing countries of the region, resources to top priority products and fields in basic foodstuffs, and would promote foreign trade in the area. This bank would utilize a shared-risk mechanism based on subregional technological packages, support for modernization, and coinvestment in agricultural industries of the developing countries.

It is important to point out, however, that credit in itself has a limited effect. In order to be effective in increasing the small producer's productivity, credit must be accompanied by available information inputs on new proven technologies and by a guaranteed supply of inputs for the long term. Questions arising out of issues such as flexibility in the criteria of the loan, the selectivity, the control, the continuity, and group responsibility would acquire a great importance in the design of such a financial institution.

A final thought must be added for food security, reserves, and stability of the international market. In the most recent report of the World Food Council's executive director of food security,[2] great emphasis has been placed on three facts: the stocks in the five main exporting countries will never reach the level registered in the 1960s due to the increasing cost in storage and the high interest rates; the international market stability affects all countries, both exporters and importers, although the rich may protect their farmers and their consumers; and there is an imperative need to establish reserves for each developing country (see Tables 4.2 and 4.3). The report also pointed out that the concentration of cereal supplies originating in North America has continued to increase, that cereals consumed by cattle and monogastrics showed the most active global increase in demand during recent years, and that financing plays a fundamental role through the financial facilities of the International Monetary Fund (IMF).

TABLE 4.1
Food Structure in the Pacific Basin Countries

Country	Main Crops	Main Livestock and Fishing Products	Main Food Exports	Main Food Imports	Advanced Technologies
Low-income countries and China					
1. China	rice, barley, soy, wheat, sweet potato, millet, tea	pigs, aviculture, aquaculture	canned food, fruits and vegetables, rice, live animals and meat	wheat, processed foods	aquaculture, treatment of soil organization
2. Indonesia	rice, sweet potato, corn, peanut, manioc	goats, beef cattle, buffaloes, shrimp & fresh fish	seeds, almonds, oil crops, nuts, coffee, tea, shrimp	rice, cereals, processed foods	
Medium-income countries					
3. Thailand	rice, sugar cane, manioc, corn, bananas	aviculture, buffaloes, beef cattle, pigs, aquaculture	rice, oily seeds, fishing products	cereals, processed foods, edible oils	
4. Philippines	sugar cane, rice, corn, tubers, fruits, nuts	barnyard fowl, carabaos, shrimps, sardines, shad	sugar, fruits, vegetables, seeds, nuts, oil, almonds	rice, wheat, corn, other cereals, dairy products	
5. Papua New Guinea	coconuts, cocao, coffee, palm tree	barnyard fowl, fishing products	coconut oil, coffee, cocoa	food in general, live animals	
6. Peru	potatoes, corn, meat, sugar cane, fruits	beef cattle, fishing products	fish flour, canned and frozen fish and fruits	wheat, corn, oil products, dairy products	fishing industry

TABLE 4.1 (cont.)

Country	Main Crops	Main Livestock and Fishing Products	Main Food Exports	Main Food Imports	Advanced Technologies
Medium-income countries (cont.)					
7. Colombia	coffee rice corn bananas potatoes sorghum	beef cattle sheep aviculture	coffee sugar bananas	wheat corn oil products dairy products	nutrition strategy
8. Ecuador	bananas sugar cane rice corn potato	beef cattle sheep fishing products	bananas sugar cane frozen and canned fish and fish flour	wheat corn oil products dairy products	
9. Korea, People's Dem. Rep.	rice corn soy tea	pigs beef cattle fishing products			organization
10. Malaysia	rice palm oil yucca	aviculture pigs fishing products	palm oil	cereals meat processed foods	
11. Korea, Rep.	rice sweet potatoes barley potato soy	aviculture beef pigs fishing products	fresh and dry fish	rice corn wheat processed foods	fishing industry organization of cooperatives
12. Taiwan	sweet potatoes rice sugar cane manioc bananas	pigs fishing	sugar canned pineapple and mushrooms bananas	soy wheat rice processed foods	organization

TABLE 4.1 (cont.)

Country	Main Crops	Main Livestock and Fishing Products	Main Food Exports	Main Food Imports	Advanced Technologies
Medium-income countries (cont.)					
13. Mexico	corn beans wheat soy rice sorghum fruits and vegetables	beef cattle pigs goats aviculture shrimp and tunafish	fruits and vegetables coffee tomato shrimp	corn sorghum, soy beans wheat sugar dried milk	fixation of nitrogen fermentation exploitation of secondary farm products enrichment, packing, and baling of foods
14. Chile	sugar beets wheat potato corn beans barley	sheep beef cattle anchovies caranx sardines other seafood	fish flour frozen fish fruits	wheat corn dairy products meat processed foods	
15. Hong Kong	rice sweet potatoes	aviculture pigs	sugar canned food	rice sugar forages processed foods	marketing techniques
16. Singapore	sweet potatoes manioc	aviculture pigs	sugar fish flour canned food	rice cereals fish dairy products	
Industrialized countries					
17. New Zealand	wheat barley corn tea potatoes artificial grass	beef cattle sheep	meat and processed meat, milk, and dairy products	coffee cacao sugar fruits and vegetables	dairy products pastures handling of beef cattle and sheep

TABLE 4.1 (cont.)

Country	Main Crops	Main Livestock and Fishing Products	Main Food Exports	Main Food Imports	Advanced Technologies
Industrialized countries (cont.)					
18. Japan	rice oranges cabbages potatoes bananas sugar beets sweet potatoes	aviculture pigs beef cattle (milk) fishing products	frozen and canned fish and seafood fruits and other vegetables	wheat soy rice meat dairy products fruits tea	chemical fertilizers future foodstuffs sea exploitation optimum soil exploitation
19. Australia	wheat barley oats sorghum sugar cane citric fruits	beef cattle (milk and meat) sheep goats pigs	wheat secondary cereals meats dairy products	coffee tea cacao processed and canned food	development of arid and semi-arid areas preparation of soil tropical agriculture sheep raising
20. Canada	wheat barley corn oat colza linen potatoes fruits	beef cattle (milk and meat) pigs sheep codfish trout	wheat colza barley meats linen live cattle dairy products	fruits coffee tea sugar meats oil products	production of wheat raising milk cattle family-size units machinery or farm tools fishing and fishery storage nets (grains, cold storage)
21. United States	corn soybeans wheat oats fruits potatoes barley sorghum rye	beef cattle (milk and meat) sheep pigs aviculture herring codfish tunafish	wheat corn secondary cereals fruits and vegetables meats fish	coffee tea cacao sugar fish meats fruits and vegetables	scientific research fertilizers and pesticides processing of all kinds of foods production of corn, wheat, oil crops machinery and farm tools storage nets

Source: Office of International Affairs, Sistema Alimentaria Mexicano (SAM), based on FAO data and United Nations statistics.

TABLE 4.2
Food Imports, Food Aid, and Reserve Stocks Suggested by the World Food Council for the Least-Developed Countries in the Pacific Basin, 1980-1982 (thousands of metric tons)

	Wheat				Secondary Cereals			
	1980-1981		1981-1982		1980-1981		1981-1982	
	Total Imports	Food Aid	Total Needs	Reserve	Total Imports	Food Aid	Total Needs	Reserve
China	135,000	-	14,000	500	1,000	-	1,000	500
El Salvador	125	32	130	95	15	5	70	50
Indonesia	1,386	110	1,450	500	246	14	140	130
Nicaragua	103	-	40	40	34	-	5	5
Philippines	936	34	950	500	368	34	400	360
Thailand	200	-	230	200	-	-	-	-

Source: World Food Security and the Market Stability: A Reserve Owned by Each Developing Country (Rome: World Food Council, Report by the Executive Director, 1982).

TABLE 4.3
Some Food-Security Indicators in the Pacific Basin Countries

Country	Per Capita Food Production, Average Index 1977-1979 (1969-1971 = 100)	Annual Average Growth Rate of Agricultural Production (percentage)		Share of Agriculture in the GDP (percentage)	
		1960-1970	1970-1979	1960	1979
China	114	1.6	3.2	--	31
Indonesia	103	2.7	3.6	54	30
Thailand	126	5.5	5.4	40	26
Papua New Guinea	106	--	--	49	37
Philippines	115	4.3	4.9	26	24
Peru	88	3.7	0.1	13	10
Colombia	119	3.5	4.8	34	29
Ecuador	102	--	0.7	33	15
People's Democratic Republic of Korea	133	--	--	--	--
Malaysia	112	--	5.0	37	24
Republic of Korea	138	4.4	4.8	37	20
Mexico	194	3.8	2.2	16	10
Chile	95	2.6	3.5	11	8
Hong Kong	55	--	-11.0	4	1
Singapore	159	1.7	12.5	4	2
New Zealand	106	--	--	--	11
Japan	98	4.0	1.1	13	5
Australia	124	2.7	--	12	--
Canada	109	2.5	2.2	6	4
United States	116	0.3	0.9	4	3

Source: World Development Report 1981 (Washington, D.C.: World Bank, 1981).

TABLE 4.2 (cont.)

Rice				Total Cost of Reserve in US $ millions	IMF Quota in Millions of Special Drawing Rights
1980-1981		1981-1982			
Total Imports	Food Aid	Total Needs	Reserve		
185	5	150	--	147.5	1,800.0
7	4	7	3	24.2	64.5
1,213	81	1,150	50	126.0	720.0
16	10	--	5	9.9	51.0
--	--	--	--	131.4	315.0
--	--	--	--	36.0	271.5

TABLE 4.3 (cont.)

Share of Food and Agriculture in Value Added of Manufacturers (Percentage)	Share of Food Products in Total Imports (Percentage)		Percentage of Labor Force Devoted to Agriculture		Daily Provision of Calories per Capita	
						Percentage of Needs
1978	1960	1978	1960	1979	1977	1977
--	--	17	--	64	2,453	104
20	23	18	75	59	2,272	105
--	10	4	84	77	1,429	105
--	30	--	89	82	2,268	85
38	15	8	61	47	2,189	108
28	16	16	53	38	2,274	97
31	8	11	51	27	2,364	102
31	13	7	57	52	2,104	92
--	--	--	62	60	2,837	121
21	29	17	63	51	2,610	117
19	10	8	66	36	2,785	119
22	4	13	55	37	2,654	114
19	--	15	30	20	2,656	109
--	27	15	8	3	2,883	126
6	21	10	8	2	3,074	134
26	8	7	15	9	3,345	127
9	17	17	33	13	2,949	126
18	6	6	11	6	3,428	129
13	12	8	13	5	3,374	127
11	24	10	7	2	3,576	135

The new community we envisage cannot and should not be allowed to continue the mistakes, failures, and divorce of interest from past regional arrangements. The pioneering work should be historically successful.

Notes

1. Since this article was written, the Mexican Food System (SAM) program has been temporarily suspended for budgetary reasons.
2. *World Food Security and the Market Stability: A Reserve Owned by Each Developing Country* (Rome: World Food Council, Report by the Executive Director, 1982, vol. 5.

Part 3

Case Studies in Domestic Policy and International Trade

5
Food Policy and the Rice Trade in the Pacific Basin Region

Chung H. Lee
James Roumasset

Adequate provision of food for people has long been a major concern of governments. The biblical account (Genesis 41) of Pharaoh's dream of seven fat cows and seven skinny cows along the Nile bank suggests that food security has been one of officialdom's earliest preoccupations. Because of Joseph's interpretation of the dream, Pharaoh stored food grains during the seven years of bumper crops and sold them, presumably at a substantial profit, during the subsequent seven years of poor harvest. The problem of food security is still with us. Unfortunately, Joseph is not.

There is, however, one important difference between the world of Pharaoh and Joseph and the world in which we now live. Theirs was a world where international trade in grains was nil or virtually so, whereas ours is a world of interdependence in almost everything that we produce and consume. In the case of rice this interdependence among the countries in the Pacific Basin area (henceforth, the PBA) seems clearly recognized, as trade in rice is heavily concentrated in the region.

The purpose of this chapter is to investigate national rice policies of Australia, Canada, China, Hong Kong, Indonesia, Japan, South Korea, Mexico, the Philippines, Taiwan, Thailand, and the United States and their effect on trade in rice among these countries. The PBA will be identified with these countries.[1] Rice is a key food grain for a majority of people in the region. Because of its importance as a food grain and because of various national rice policies pursued in these countries, rice justifiably deserves our attention and focus.

In the first section some statistics on rice are presented to draw attention to its quantitative magnitude in production, consumption, and trade in the last ten or so years. In the second and third sections we discuss domestic rice policies pursued in the PBA countries and their effect on international trade, prices of rice, and world price stability. The final section summarizes

TABLE 5.1
Summary Rice Statistics, World and Pacific Basin Area, 1970-1979 (million metric tons)

	World Rice Production	PBA Rice Production	PBA's Share of World Rice Production (percentage)	PBA Rice Consumption[a]	PBA's Rice Exports to World[b]
1970	312	177	57	119	58
1971	318	183	57	124	59
	(1.9)[c]	(3.0)		(4.2)	(1.7)
1972	306	176	58	120	56
	(-3.9)	(-3.6)		(-3.4)	(-5.1)
1973	330	189	57	125	64
	(7.8)	(7.0)		(4.5)	(14.3)
1974	337	201	60	133	68
	(2.1)	(6.8)		(6.0)	(6.3)
1975	360	203	57	134	69
	(7.0)	(1.1)		(0.7)	(1.5)
1976	350	205	59	135	70
	(-2.8)	(0.7)		(0.8)	(1.4)
1977	371	208	56	137	71
	(6.1)	(1.5)		(1.4)	(1.4)
1978	385	220	57	143	77
	(3.8)	(6.0)		(4.9)	(8.5)
1979	369	222	60	147	75
	(-4.3)	(0.6)		(2.2)	(-2.6)
Average	(2.0)	(2.6)	58	(2.4)	(3.0)

a. Includes stock adjustment.
b. PBA production minus consumption, per preceding columns.
c. Figures in parentheses are percentage rates of growth.

Source: USDA, Foreign Agriculture Circular (Washington, D.C.: U.S. Department of Agriculture, December 1979).

the economic effects of existing policies and identifies directions of policy reform for further consideration.

Rice Production, Consumption, and Trade in the PBA

Table 5.1 presents rice production in million metric tons (mmt) for the world and for the PBA for the period from 1970 through 1979. The entire world produced 312 mmt of rice in 1970. The production of rice has increased since then at an annual average rate of 2 percent, reaching 369 mmt in 1979. For the PBA the figures for 1970 and 1979 are 177 mmt and 222 mmt, respectively, with an average annual growth rate of 2.6 percent. The PBA production of rice accounted for 56-60 percent of world production during the period; for the entire period its average share was 58 percent. The PBA consumed (including changes in stocks) 119 mmt of rice in 1970, increased its consumption at an average annual rate of 2.4 percent, and consumed 147 mmt in 1979.

The PBA had, therefore, a higher rate of growth in rice production than the world as a whole (2.6 percent versus 2 percent), while its consumption did not increase as rapidly as its own rice production (2.4 percent versus 2.6 percent). The figures in Table 5.1 thus indicate that the PBA was a major rice-producing area of the world and was also a net exporter of rice to the rest of the world during the 1970-1979 period. The last column in Table 5.1 presents the net trade position in rice of the PBA vis-à-vis the rest of the world for 1970 through 1979. The PBA had net exports of 58 mmt in 1970 and 75 mmt in 1979; its net exports grew at an average annual rate of 3 percent during the period.

Net PBA exporters are Thailand, the United States, Australia, China, and Taiwan. Net importers are Indonesia, Mexico, Hong Kong, and Canada. Japan was a net importer during the 1961-1968 period but since then has become a net exporter of rice. South Korea was a net exporter during the 1961-1966 period but since then has become a net importer. The Philippines also changed its status from a net importer to a net exporter in 1978.

Table 5.2 shows the trade matrix for rice for the major exporting and importing countries. In addition to the patterns among PBA countries, note that Pakistan is the third-largest exporter, selling primarily to non-PBA markets, and that three Mideast countries (Saudi Arabia, Iran, and Iraq) together constitute a major importer, especially from the United States.

How much trade in rice is there among the PBA countries? As a measure of this magnitude we calculated the share of U.S. rice exports that went to the PBA for the calendar years 1970 through 1979. In the early 1970s this share was approximately 50 percent, but since then it declined to about a quarter of total U.S. exports of rice to the world. These data indicate that the PBA has become a less important market for U.S. rice exports. Of the total rice exports of Thailand, 34 percent, 18 percent, and 30 percent went to other PBA countries in 1977, 1978, and 1979, respectively. Australia sent 33 percent and 17 percent of its total rice exports to other PBA countries in 1978 and 1979, respectively. Hence, a large share of trade in rice is made with countries outside the region. This fact should be kept in mind when considering any regional planning and coordination on rice, which may have both trade-creating and trade-diverting effects.

Food Policy in the PBA

As Falcon and Monke recently pointed out, international trade in rice is carried out in a world burdened with various national policies that have distorting effects on the production and consumption of rice.[2] Although there are probably very few things that are internationally traded without some intervention by government, trade in rice seems to be especially subject to government regulations. Given various national policies employed both in the exporting and in the importing countries, as will be discussed in

TABLE 5.2
Rice Trade Among Selected Countries, 1978 (metric tons)

Imports by	from...	United States	Thailand	Pakistan	Burma	Australia	China	Rest of World (residual)	Total
Indonesia[a]		391,377	193,830	95,019	120,443	42,546	68,947	929,418	1,841,580
Malaysia[a]								--	408,588
Saudi Arabia-Iran-Iraq		625,998[b]	149,665[b]	158,756[b]	n.d.[c]	1,563	--	148,097	1,084,069[bd]
Hong Kong		2,349	93,856	n.d.	407	58,270	--	3,737	343,638
Singapore		80	144,633	9,776	22,510	2,682	185,019	5,956	194,435
Sri Lanka		n.d.	--	23,178	142,379	n.d.	8,798	21,297	186,854
Korea, Rep.		--	1,864	n.d.	n.d.	n.d.	n.d.	--	1,864
Vietnam[a]								--	150,000[d]
USSR[a]								--	413,887[d]

a. No breakdown by sources of imports available.
b. Figures are for Iran and Iraq only.
c. The abbreviation n.d.(no data) signifies no trade reported.
d. Figures from FAO trade yearbook for 1978.

Source: UN Yearbook of International Trade Statistics (New York: United Nations, 1978), unless otherwise noted.

this section, the pattern and the volume of trade in rice that we have discussed in the first section do not accurately reflect comparative advantage in rice production among the PBA countries. Because one possible way to increase the quantity of world rice production is to utilize resources in accordance with comparative advantage, that is, to improve allocative efficiency, it is important to find out how national rice policies affect international trade in rice and what measures are consistent with a more efficient allocation of resources, while simultaneously remaining compatible with other objectives of governments.

For the purpose of analyzing the effect of national rice policies on trade, we may classify the PBA countries in terms of their net trade position in rice and domestic pricing policies. Tyers and Chisholm[3] label the countries that maintain average domestic food prices below those prevailing at the border as *provisionists*.[4] The effect of the provisionist policy is to suppress domestic supply and increase domestic demand and thus to place upward pressure on international trading prices. Alternatively, countries that maintain the producer price of rice above that at the border are labeled *protectionists*. The effect of the protectionist policy is to expand domestic supply, contract domestic demand, and thus to exert downward pressure on international trading prices of rice.

Estimates of various prices of rice by Falcon and Monke and by Tyers and Chisholm, and net trade positions reported in the USDA's *Foreign Agricultural Circular*, lead to the classification of the PBA countries presented in Table 5.3. There are two points of interest to note in the table. The first is the fact that both net exporters and importers can be either protectionists or provisionists. This observation implies that although the provisionist policy suppresses domestic supply and increases domestic demand, its effect can be either pro-trade or anti-trade. If the country is a net importer, the effect is pro-trade, expanding trade in rice and bringing about upward pressure on international trading prices of rice. However, if the country is a net exporter, the effect is anti-trade, contracting trade while causing upward pressure on prices.

The protectionist policy expands domestic supply and contracts domestic demand. If the country is a net importer, the effect of the policy is antitrade, contracting trade and bringing about downward pressure on international trading prices of rice. If the country is a net exporter and also a protectionist, it will be subsidizing its exports in order to make them competitive at the world price. The effect of the policy is therefore protrade, expanding trade by causing downward pressure on prices. These results are summarized in Table 5.4, where the arrow indicates the direction of change.

The second point of interest is that the status of some countries in terms of trade position and national policies has changed over time. For example, Japan changed from being a net importer to becoming a net exporter, while remaining a protectionist. The dynamics of this change and its relationship with economic development of the country deserve further

TABLE 5.3
Breakdown of Pacific Basin Countries by Domestic Pricing Policy and Trade Position in Rice

	Net Exporters	Net Importers
Protectionists	Japan (1969-) U.S. [a] Taiwan Australia Korea, Rep. (1961-1966)	Canada Japan (1961-1968) Korea, Rep. (1967-) Malaysia
Provisionists	Thailand [a] China [a] Philippines (1978-)	Indonesia [b] Philippines (1960-1977)

a. major exporters (more than one million metric tons of rice per year)
b. major importers (more than one million metric tons of rice per year)
Source: USDA, Foreign Agricultural Circular (Washington, D.C.: U.S. Department of Agriculture, December 1979).

TABLE 5.4
Effect of Domestic Pricing Policies on International Rice Trade and Prices

	Net Exporters	Net Importers
Protectionists	Q ↑ P ↓	Q ↓ P ↓
Provisionists	Q ↓ P ↑	Q ↑ P ↑

Q = the quantity traded.
P = international trading prices.
↑ = increase.
↓ = decrease.

investigation.[5] Other countries may not fit neatly into one of the four categories of Table 5.3. In particular, Hong Kong and Singapore are net importers but have neither protectionist nor provisionist food policies.

A common feature to be found in national rice policies of most of the importing countries of the PBA is the objective of "self-sufficiency."[6] Hong Kong seems to be the only place that has not made self-sufficiency a national policy objective. Even rice exporters such as Thailand and the United States regard the provision of adequate supply to meet domestic demand at "reasonable" prices to consumers as a policy objective.

Although it is often pointed out that the policy of self-sufficiency is simply another name for a protectionist policy, there are some differences between the two. The protectionist policy as defined here is the policy of maintaining the domestic price of rice above that prevailing at the border. For a net importer this policy will certainly lead to a decrease in the quantity imported. The policy of self-sufficiency, however, also includes measures that would shift the domestic demand curve of rice to the right (and in some cases those measures that would shift the domestic demand curve to the left). For our analytical purpose here we will regard the policy of self-sufficiency as comprising only those measures that would shift the supply (and the demand) curve, and the protectionist policy only as one of fixing the domestic price above that prevailing at the border. Some of the measures taken for the policy of self-sufficiency are, for example, subsidies to farmers, extension services provided to farmers at the public's expense, and public investment in agricultural research and infrastructure. Although these measures may not distort prices, they may still involve inefficient allocation of investment funds.

Impact of Food Policy on Trade, Prices, and Price Stability

What are the effects of these national rice policies—the protectionist/provisionist policies and the policy of self-sufficiency—on international trade in rice? The effect of the protectionist/provisionist policies is to turn the international market for rice into a "residual" market for domestic excess demand or supply. The effect of the policy of self-sufficiency is to inhibit the allocation of resources in accordance with comparative advantage. Furthermore, it makes the international market relatively *thin* in the sense that a relatively small portion of world production is traded. In fact, Falcon and Monke report that world trade in rice never exceeded more than 4 percent of total world production between 1961 and 1978.

Effects of the Protectionist/Provisionist Policies

The use of the international market by major exporters and importers as a residual market has an unfavorable effect on the stability of international trading prices of rice.[7] To see this effect, let us assume a world that consists of one major exporter of rice (a protectionist) such as the United States, and one major importer (a provisionist) such as Indonesia, with the rest of the world limited to many small exporters and importers. The first two maintain fixed domestic prices of rice; any excess demand and supply are satisfied in the international market.

Figures 5.1 and 5.2 describe the domestic rice market for the major exporting country and for the major importing country, respectively. The major exporter maintains a domestic price, P_d, higher than the international trading price (not shown) and in year 1 it has an excess supply of $e_1 - e_0$, which it disposes of in the world market at whatever price it may fetch.

FIGURE 5.1
Domestic Supply and Demand Curves for the Major Exporter of Rice

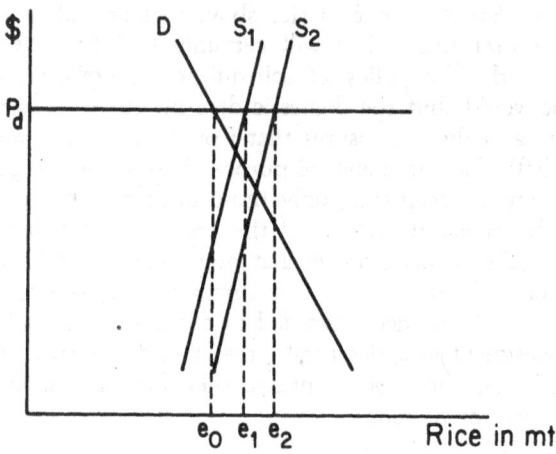

FIGURE 5.2
Domestic Supply and Demand Curves for the Major Importer of Rice

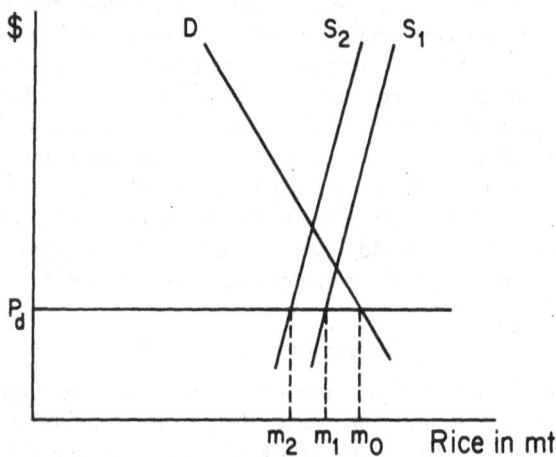

The major importer likewise maintains a domestic price, P_d, lower than the international trading price and in year 1 it purchases $m_0 - m_1$, whatever the price may be in the world market. Figure 5.3 depicts the international rice market where X_r and M_r are the export supply curve and the import demand curve of the rest of the world, respectively. Adding $(e_1 - e_0)$ to X_r, we obtain the export supply curve for the entire world in year 1. M_1 is likewise the import demand curve for the entire world; that is, $M_1 = M_r + (m_0 - m_1)$. In year 1 the international trading price of rice is thus P_1.

FIGURE 5.3
World Supply and Demand Curves in an International Rice Market Affected by Policies of a Major Exporter and a Major Importer

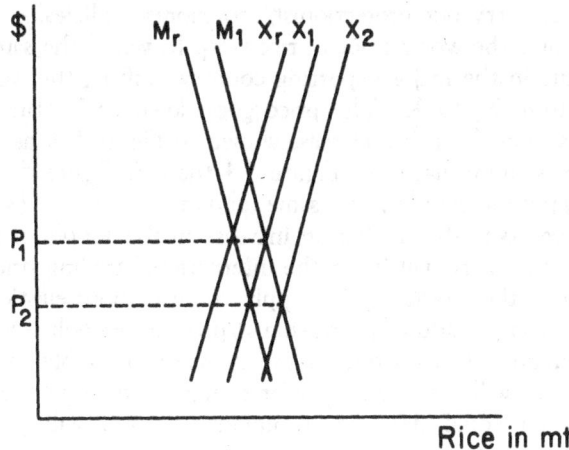

FIGURE 5.4
World Supply and Demand Curves in a Simplified Model of the International Rice Market

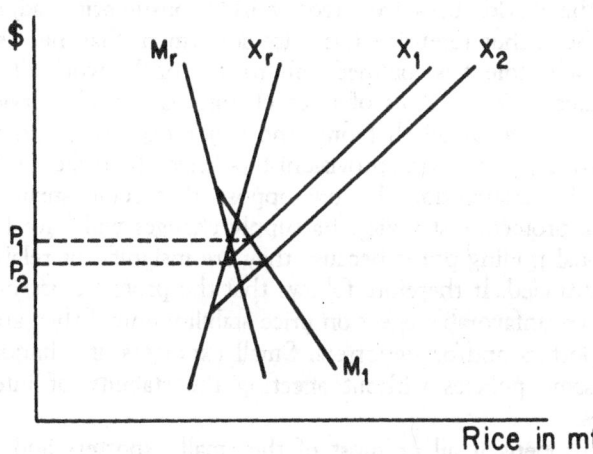

In year 2 the supply of rice in the major exporter country increases due to, say, better weather conditions (that is, supply shifts from S_1 to S_2 in Figure 5.1). The effect of this increase is to increase the world export supply (Figure 5.3) from X_1 to X_2, resulting in a price decrease from P_1 to P_2.

This price change is of course no surprise. But is this change more than what would be expected if there were no protectionist/provisionist policies? To answer this question we present Figure 5.4, where X_1 is the export supply curve of the entire world and M_1 is the import demand curve of the entire world. In Figure 5.4 the quantity exported by the major exporter is a positive function of price, and the quantity imported by the major importer is a negative function of price. These differences follow simply from the assumption that in Figure 5.4 the major exporter and the major importer do not carry out protectionist/provisionist policies.

Again, in year 1 the world price of rice is P_1. In year 2 the same increase in supply occurs in the major exporting country, shifting the world export supply curve from X_1 to X_2. The price goes down to P_2. But this price decrease is less than the price decrease shown in Figure 5.3, as the import demand curve is more elastic in Figure 5.4 than in Figure 5.3 (although the export supply increases by the same amount).

It can also be easily shown that an increase in the supply of rice in the major importing country will lower the international trading prices of rice. However, because the world export supply curve is more elastic in a free-trade world than in a world of protectionist/provisionist policies, a decrease in the world import demand due to the increase in supply in the major importing country will result in a smaller change in price in the free-trade situation than an equal decrease in import demand will cause under protectionist/provisionist policies.

The reason for this price stability is actually quite obvious. In a world of protectionist/provisionist policies for some countries, the only place where a consumption adjustment is made in response to a change in supply is the rest of the world. In a free-trade world, consumption adjustment is made everywhere, thus requiring less price adjustment than necessary when consumption adjustment is confined only to part of the world. That is, the burden of adjustment in terms of price changes is spread everywhere.

So far we have assumed that only the major exporting and importing countries invoke protectionist/provisionist policies. To make clear the significance of this assumption, let us suppose that some small exporting country has a protectionist policy. Its supply changes will have little effect on international trading prices because they are insignificant relative to the total quantity traded. It therefore follows that the protectionist/provisionist policies have an unfavorable effect on price stability only if they are pursued by major exporters and/or importers. Small exporters and importers may pursue the same policies without affecting the stability of international trading prices.

Yet what happens if all or most of the small exporters and importers pursue protectionist/provisionist policies? In the case where all countries, including major exporters and importers, carry out such policies it can be easily shown that either there is no market-clearing international price or there is no determinate price. In the case where a large number of small exporters and importers pursue the policies, their combined effect will be destabilizing only if supply changes in these countries are highly correlated. On the basis of casual observation we would severely discount this possibility.

Of we assume that the supply change in Figure 5.1 is due to, say, changes in weather conditions and that there is no additional cost due to the increase, we may carry out some simple welfare analysis. The welfare of the major exporter depends on whether $P_1 \times (e_1 - e_0)$, the revenue from its rice exports in year 1, is greater than or less than $P_2 \times (e_2 - e_0)$, the revenue from its rice exports in year 2. Obviously the answer depends on the elasticity of import demand of the rest of the world; if it is greater than one, an increase in supply leads to an increase in the export revenue, benefiting the major exporter. The major importer also gains, however, as it can now import $m_0 - m_1$ at P_2, which is less than P_1. The exporters in the rest of the world lose, and the importers in the rest of the world gain.

We can also easily see the effect of a crop failure in the major importing country. It will certainly lose as it now imports more at a higher price. The major exporter gains because it exports the same quantity at a higher price. In the rest of the world, exporters gain because they export more at a higher price, and importers lose because they import less at a higher price.

Effects of Self-Sufficiency Policies

As noted above, the policy of self-sufficiency reduces the volume of trade in rice. That is, a smaller quantity of rice is traded relative to total world production than if the policy is not pursued. What is the effect of this policy adopted by a country large enough to have more than a negligible effect on price stability in world trade? In order to answer this question, let us assume that the major exporter and importer pursue the protectionist/provisionist policies, and that the rest of the world does not pursue the policy of self-sufficiency.

Obviously, more rice will now be traded in the rest of the world. If there is an increase in supply, say, in the major exporting country, as depicted in Figure 5.1, the export supply curve of the entire world will shift to the right by the same amount. However, because the volume of trade is larger in a world without the policy of self-sufficiency, the same absolute change will bring about a smaller proportionate change in quantity traded than in a world with the policy of self-sufficiency. What actually happens to the price of rice depends on the price elasticities of the export supply and the import demand of the rest of the world. If the elasticities remain the same although more is traded in the world market, the percentage change in price will be less. If the export supply and the import demand become *more* elastic with the increase in trade volume, then the proportionate change in price will be smaller than if the elasticities remained the same. If they become *less* elastic, no definite answer can be obtained without numerical values for parameters and variables. In other words, if the policy of self-sufficiency, which reduces the volume of trade, does not increase the elasticities at the same time, it will definitely increase the percentage change in price due to a given supply shock.

To investigate the effect of the policy of self-sufficiency on international trading prices of rice we must therefore first find out how the policy affects the elasticities of the export supply and the import demand of the rest of the world. There are various measures that a country may take to bring about self-sufficiency in rice, and it is likely that their effects are varied. Some would increase the elasticities and others would decrease them. Clearly, further research is needed before we can answer the question of what effect the policy of self-sufficiency has on the stability of international trading prices of rice.

Our analysis in this section, however, allows us to reach the following conclusions:

1. The protectionist/provisionist policies pursued by major exporters and importers lead to greater price instability in the rest of the world.
2. The same policies pursued by small exporters and importers have little effect on price stability.
3. Combined with protectionist/provisionist policies by major exporters and importers, the policy of self-sufficiency in the rest of the world increases price instability unless the policy increases the price elasticities of the export supply and the import demand of the rest of the world.

Welfare Effects of Common Policy Distortions and Possible Policy Reforms

Industrialized countries tend to follow protectionist agricultural policies, regardless of whether they import or export grain. These policies either increase exports or decrease imports. In either case, protectionism depresses world prices to the benefit of food-importing countries. This kind of stabilization in industrialized countries also has the effect of exporting instability to developing countries. That is, a given supply shock in a regime of stabilized domestic prices has a greater impact on world prices than in a regime of free trade. The phenomenon of exporting instability derives from the inhibition of price-induced consumption adjustments.

Increased price instability is usually understood to transfer wealth from producers to consumers.[8] Consumers benefit proportionately more from low prices than they are hurt by high prices, because of their ability to adjust consumption after the price is known. Producers are generally thought to be made worse off by increased instability. If the price could be known before input decisions are made, then producers would gain more from high prices than they would lose from low prices. However, if input decisions are made in the face of price uncertainty, and if increased risk causes producers to be more conservative in input decisions, then farmers—the producers—may be made worse off. This latter effect is mitigated, however, by the inverse relationship between price and production, by risk-management options available to the farmer, and by mechanisms for risk-spreading in the economy.[9]

Because resource allocation under uncertainty may not be efficient in the absence of futures markets for all contingencies, an increase in price instability may increase the extent of excess burden. Even if government intervention in pricing is costless, however, the efficiency benefits of optimal distortions are likely to be small.[10] The market can accommodate price fluctuations in a variety of ways. Storage, diversification, credit, and financial portfolio management all facilitate the smoothing of consumption streams in the face of uncertainty about both prices and production. Thus, an increase in price instability will most likely have a negative but small effect on the economic welfare of importing LDCs (less-developed countries). This small negative effect is likely to be more than offset by a large welfare gain due to lower average prices to food-importing LDCs.

The biggest losers from the protectionist policies are the consumers in the protected countries. They face domestic prices substantially in excess of world prices. The higher domestic prices not only transfer wealth away from consumers but induce efficiency losses because the marginal social benefit of food in these countries exceeds the marginal social cost. This analysis suggests that it would be possible to dismantle protection, tax part of the resulting benefits conferred on consumers to compensate producers, and still be left with benefits to consumers. Alternatively, the surplus benefits could be used to compensate consumers in importing LDCs for the resulting increases in world prices.

How does the analysis change if protectionist policies in an importing country are combined with supply-shifting policies? The combination represents an aggressive pursuit of self-sufficiency. This case is particularly useful for interpreting the agricultural policies of Japan. Shifting the supply curve further decreases excess demand, thus augmenting the effects of protection. This move tends to decrease the size of the world market and further lower world prices. As noted in the previous section, investments in self-sufficiency will also tend to increase the variance of world prices.

Another effect of policies that suppress demand for imports is to lower the price of foreign exchange. It tends to discriminate against manufacturing exports. Given Japan's reliance on exports for maintaining employment, this may help explain Japan's aggressive export promotion policy. Of course, export promotion is not uniform and discriminates in turn against certain types of exports or potential export goods. The same argument may help to explain the persistence of nontariff barriers on certain imports.

Thus, relaxing protectionism in agriculture would not only benefit consumers and reduce excess burden in the food sector, it could potentially allow relaxation of distortions elsewhere in the economy. Again, liberalizing these distortions could be tied with some scheme of compensation or partial compensation for potential losers, especially farmers.

The last case we wish to analyze is the combination of provisionism and supply shifting, which can be said to characterize rice-importing LDCs such as Indonesia. Interestingly, this combination is often described as a program for promoting self-sufficiency. In fact, only the latter policy reduces the demand for imports. Provisionism raises consumption above its free-trade level and reduces the degree of self-sufficiency.

The combination of these contradictory policy instruments provides an example of the "patch-on/patch-up" nature of economic policy in many developing countries.[11] Provisionism is motivated by political pressures to maintain a relatively low ceiling on the price of rice. This policy causes foreign exchange difficulties[12] and motivates investments that shift the supply curve outward. However, some of the supply-increasing policies may be inefficient. Thus, although supply-increasing policies may neutralize the effect of provision on import demand, both policies misallocate resources. The excess burden of the two policies in this case is additive, not offsetting.

Specifically, supply may be increased by investing in productive capacity and by subsidizing inputs. Productive capacity can be increased by investing in research and development or in infrastructure development, especially irrigation. Inputs can be subsidized directly or in combination with extension and rural credit programs. Many of these policies may distort resource allocation.[13] If one were to hazard a generalization it would be that productive capacity, especially via agricultural research, represents a more efficient use of resources than extension, subsidized credit, and fertilizer subsidies. For present purposes, however, the important point is to recognize that both the quantity and the composition of supply-shifting investment can be a source of inefficiency. At the same time, one should be aware of systematic underinvestment in certain activities, notably agricultural research.[14]

The dilemma for policymakers is that following what may be the efficient policy of raising domestic prices may not be politically expedient. In fact, if rice consumption by a target group is regarded as a public good or a consumption externality, then cheap domestic prices are not necessarily inefficient. It may be possible, however, to raise domestic rice prices without lowering nutritional levels of poorer consumers. In market areas, this adjustment can be made by lowering the prices of "inferior" foods (wheat flour, corn, and inferior grades of rice) and by establishing limited-access, fair-price shops. In nonmarket areas, effective nutrition intervention may take the form of providing planting materials for high-yielding food crops (for example, rice, corn, and cassava in the Indonesian case).

Scope of International Conflict and Cooperation

The consumers in developing countries are natural allies of the producers in developed countries in the maintenance of agricultural protection. Lowering protection in the interests of the domestic consumers in industrialized countries and in the interests of overall efficiency will presumably require some compensation to those who would bear the costs of such reforms. One possibility along these lines is to finance compensation via commodity taxes, out of the gains of consumers in developed countries. A more efficient alternative is to lower protection of manufacturing industries in all countries. This move will benefit both agricultural producers and consumers.

There is also considerable scope for cooperative agreements in the area of food security. From the point of view of developing countries, the pursuit of less protectionism by industrialized countries would not be consistent with food security, even though those policies increase world price stability. However, food security in LDCs could be enhanced by changing the *form* of agricultural protection in MDCs (more-developed countries). In particular, support prices could be lowered to approximate, for example, average world prices. This minimum price guarantee could be supplemented by a program of export subsidies. These moves would maintain a degree of protection to food producers in industrialized countries without exporting instability.

Many government policies that have been justified on grounds of self-sufficiency and food security are costly for developing countries to undertake. Importing grain for domestic consumption at below world prices, government investment in buffer stocks, and supply-shifting investments with low or negative rates of return all have sizable welfare costs. Before recommending that these policies be abandoned in the name of efficiency, however, we need to seek alternative mechanisms for assuring food security. One such mechanism is for industrialized countries to provide assurances (contracts) that grain will be available at prices below some upper bound.

Much of the food-security problem stems from enforcement difficulties in long-term contracts. If developing countries could negotiate and rely on long- or medium-term contracts for rice and other grains, then much of their food-security problem would be solved. However, in a world where embargoes and other trade restrictions may prevent such contracts from being carried out, the utility of long-term contracting is diminished. In the absence of a world government, there is a need to explore alternative mechanisms for enhancing both negotiation and reliability of these contracts.[15]

The IMF has recently taken steps to enhance food security without resorting to subsidizing buffer stocks. In 1981, the IMF extended its compensatory financing facility for export earnings to cover excess cereal import bills as well. This "integrated financial facility for food imports" provides credit to cover the shortfall in export earnings plus cereal imports above trend.[16] This scheme is related to D. Gale Johnson's earlier proposals for grain insurance, which, like other insurance programs, is subject to moral hazard problems.

Much of the food-security problem of a developing country is, after all, a result of that country's own economic policy. Trying to maintain low consumer rice prices in the face of high and rising world prices, for example, will undoubtedly strain a country's foreign exchange resources. Extending credit to ease such difficulties clearly lowers the incentive to avoid them.

As noted earlier, LDCs can remove much of the distorting policy apparatus without substantially reducing food security. Removing protection of the manufacturing sector enhances domestic production of food. The effect of raising domestic rice prices toward world levels can be ameliorated by limited-access, fair-price stores and by the provision of rice substitutes. Part of the foreign exchange savings from lowering grain imports can be used to further increase a country's rice-producing capacity. International agreements and programs of donor agencies should be designed so as to increase the incentive for an LDC to rationalize its own economic policy, not to perpetuate existing distortions.

Acknowledgment

The authors wish to thank Ramon Clarete for research assistance.

Notes

1. We should note here that countries identified as belonging to the Pacific Basin vary from author to author. For example, according to Peter Drysdale in "An Organization for Pacific Trade, Aid and Development: Regional Arrangements and the Resource Trade," in *Mineral Resources in the Pacific Area*, ed. L. B. Krause and H. Patrick (San Francisco: Federal Reserve Bank of San Francisco, 1978), the Pacific Basin nations are the United States, Japan, Australia, New Zealand, and Canada plus the developing countries of East Asia, Southeast Asia, and the rest of the Western Pacific. K. Anderson in *Economic Development, Changing Comparative Advantage and Food Trade: Pacific Basin Experience* (Canberra: Research School of Pacific Studies, Australian National University, June 1982) also includes the Pacific rim countries of Latin America.

2. W. P. Falcon and E. A. Monke, "International Trade in Rice," *Food Research Institute Studies* (1979-1980):279-306.

3. R. Tyers and A. H. Chisholm, "Food Security and Agricultural Policy in Asia and the Pacific," (Honolulu: East-West Center, East-West Resource Systems Institute, Working Paper WP81-19, 1981).

4. The first taxonomy of grain policies in terms of provision policy (or low-price policy) and protection policy (or high-price policy) is attributed to Eli Heckscher in *Mercantilism*, 2nd ed., vols. 1 and 2, (London: George Allen and Unwin, 1955). For a historical account of grain policies, see Ch. 2 in T. Grennes, P. R. Johnson, and M. Thrusby, *The Economics of World Grain Trade* (New York: Praeger, 1978).

5. See, for example, K. Anderson, *Economic Development, Changing Comparative Advantage and Food Trade.*

6. FAO, *National Rice Policies 1970* (Rome: Food and Agriculture Organization, 1970).

7. Destabilizing effects of domestic pricing policies on international prices have been investigated recently by many writers. Their analyses are, in most cases, based on two-country models, and no distinction is made between the effects of domestic pricing policies pursued by large and small countries. See, for example, M. C. Bale and E. Lutz, "The Effects of Trade Intervention on International Price Instability," *American Journal of Agricultural Economics* 61(3), August 1979:512-516; S-Y Shei and R. L. Thompson, "The Impact of Trade Restrictions on Price Stability in the World Wheat Market," *American Journal of Agricultural Economics* 59(4), November 1977:628-638; and A. C. Zwart and K. D. Meilke, "The Influence of Domestic Pricing Policies and Buffer Stocks on Price Stability in the World Wheat Industry," *American Journal of Agricultural Economics* 61(3), August 1979:434-455.

8. See P.B.R. Hazell and P. L. Scandizzo, "Optimal Price Intervention Policies When Production is Risky," in *Risk, Uncertainty and Agricultural Development*, ed. J. Roumasset, J. M. Broussard, and I. Singh (Manila: Southeast Asian Research Council for Agriculture/Agricultural Development Council, 1979).

9. D.M.G. Newberry and J. E. Stiglitz, *Theory of Commodity Price Stabilization* (London: Oxford University Press, 1981).

10. J. A. Roumasset, "The Case Against Crop Insurance in Developing Countries," *Agricultural Development Council Teaching and Research Forum* reprint No. 20

(May 1979); D.M.G. Newberry and J. E. Stiglitz, "The Choice of Techniques and the Optimality of Market Equilibrium with Rational Expectations," *Journal of Political Economy* 90(2), April 1982:223-246.

11. R. Bautista, J. Power, and associates, *Industrial Promotion Policies in the Philippines* (Makati, The Philippines: Philippine Institute for Development Studies, 1979).

12. Vernon Ruttan characterized Indonesia's problem more poetically. Exporting oil to finance cheap rice consumption, he said, is "like burning down your house to keep warm." More recently, Indonesia has dramatically cut rice imports both by raising domestic prices and by stimulating production, especially by promoting high-yielding rice varieties and higher levels of inputs per hectare. One is tempted to apply Ruttan's simile to the Mexican case in recent years. See V. W. Ruttan, *Agricultural Research Policy* (Minneapolis: University of Minnesota Press, 1982).

13. See, for example, J. K. Boyce and R. E. Evenson, *National and International Agricultural Research and Extension Programs* (New York: Agricultural Development Council, 1975).

14. Ruttan, *Agricultural Research Policy*.

15. D. Gale Johnson expresses some pessimism about this course. Even if U.S. stocks are rebuilt and assurances of access to these stocks are given, "the probability is very small that the trade interference that contributed so significantly to international price stability will be modified in the reasonably near future." See D. G. Johnson, "Food Reserves and International Trade Policy," in *International Trade and Agriculture: Theory and Policy*, ed. J. S. Hillman and A. Schmitz (Boulder: Westview Press, 1979), p. 247.

16. B. Huddleston et al., "Financial Arrangements for Food Security," unpublished paper (October 1981).

6
Agricultural-Industrial Interactions

Byung-joon Ahn

Agriculture, Industry, and Trade

That agriculture and industry interact both in the domestic and international economy seems to be a triusm, but it is not easy to ascertain how they actually do so or whether there is an optimum balance between them. All one can say with certainty is that the precise state of the interaction is subject to the constraints of resource endowment and to the choice-making of political leadership that a country has at a given moment of time. Depending on the actual condition of resources and political processes, therefore, there can be different modes of agricultural-industrial interaction both in domestic and in international economic activities. Whatever modes Pacific Basin countries may choose, however, their economic lives are increasingly interdependent, not only by virtue of geographical proximity but also by virtue of changing differentiation in comparative advantage. Hence, there is need for these countries to coordinate and cooperate in their industrial and trade policies to enhance areas of reciprocal and common interests.

In this brief essay, an attempt will be made to shed light on the agricultural-industrial interaction that is being formed under different contexts. Concomitantly, two related issues will be addressed. The first concerns the issue of priority and sequence in developing agriculture and industry and the resulting interaction between the two. The second issue concerns the way in which a particular country goes about relating agriculture with industry and, more specifically, the degree to which a country opens its economy to other economies and depends on trade in securing its food needs. Related to this issue is the agricultural-industrial interaction among different countries.

In terms of priority, a country can take up the development of agriculture prior to the development of industry, or vice vesa, or it can attempt both simultaneously. If a country sets out to put the primary emphasis on industry at the expense of agriculture, its growth pattern is often called "unbalanced," as defined by Albert O. Hirschman. If it aims at developing both sectors simultaneously, its growth is called "balanced."

In carrying out industrialization, the initiative can be taken by individuals, the state, or both the state and individuals. In the latter two cases, policymakers of industrializing countries can adopt either inward-looking development strategies by protecting their domestic production, including agriculture, from the vagaries of international trade, or outward-looking strategies by promoting exports and subjecting their economy to the mechanism of international trade. Both of these strategies have their strengths and weaknesses.

The case of South Korea illustrates the strategy of facilitating a rapid industrialization by joint initiatives of the state and individuals and by taking an outward- and export-oriented economic policy. South Korean agriculture was initially given less attention as a result. Only after the economy underwent a structural transformation from a base of subsistence agriculture to that of a newly industrializing country—thereby causing stagnation in agriculture—did policymakers seek to redress the resulting imbalance by increasing investments in agriculture and undertaking a self-help campaign called the Saemaul (New Community) Movement, in the early 1970s. Yet in the attempt in recent years to balance growth with stability, Korea has not relented in its drive to increase exports and to liberalize imports, including food items.

Like any public choice, each course of action involves costs and benefits in terms of economic rationality and political feasibility. From the economic point of view, however, a new consensus seems to have emerged that unbalanced and outward-oriented development strategies are better able to generate growth and employment, other things being equal. There is evidence that countries that have followed such a strategy have been better able to overcome the external shocks wrought by the two oil crises in 1973 and 1979. It goes without saying that outward-oriented strategies are more conducive to facilitating free trade and economic cooperation in the Pacific Basin. But how a country molds its agriculture, industry, and trade policies still remains its own business and the domain of its domestic political process.

In theory, the linkage between agriculture and industry within a country is provided by food, labor, raw materials, and capital funds. But in practice, this linkage is predicated upon the specific domestic and international context of resource endowment and decision making, as pointed out above. In the following pages, I will delineate alternative patterns for this linkage and discuss their implications. I will first enumerate some different approaches to this problem in general. Then I will focus on the Korean case as an example. Lastly, I will comment on agricultural-industrial interactions in the Pacific Basin and offer some of my own biases toward free trade and the negotiations necessary for building an economic community in this region. An overall theme underlying this exercise is that agriculture, industry, and trade are inseparable but intertwined in this age of instant communication and interdependence.

Different Approaches in Agricultural-Industrial Interactions and Trade

Hypothetically, a country can remain agricultural without ever going through industrialization. But historically, it appears that industrialization has been a universal phenomenon. In broad terms, therefore, the sequence and the method by which modern countries have approached industrialization provide an insight into the actual interaction between agriculture and industry. From this interaction emerge the new political and social forces that preside over the process of modernization understood as industrialization.

From modern history we can extrapolate three roads to industrialization, and from the contemporary experiences of trade, two diverging development strategies. The earliest case of industrialization was characterized by agricultural commercialization and gradual industrial development. This manner of development was achieved mainly by the initiatives of individuals over a period of three centuries. A late case of industrialization was the Communist revolution, after which the totalitarian state began to carry out agricultural collectivization and forced industrialization. A later case of industrialization, now occurring in many countries, is characterized by the combined efforts of the state and individuals to try to achieve agricultural reform or land reform and then rapid industrialization.

In terms of trade policy, the developing countries can be divided into two categories: those that seek inward-oriented strategies with protective policies geared to import-substitution, and those that seek outward-oriented strategies with free-trade policies designed to increase export earnings and raise industrial efficiency. The contrast between these two is quite distinctive among the so-called newly industrializing countries (NICs) in the Pacific Basin.

Agricultural Commercialization and Gradual Industrialization

Human civilization was originally based on agriculture, and consequently all traditional societies were more or less self-sufficient in terms of agriculture. But by the eighteenth century in England, modern science and technology began to have an impact on agricultural production. By using the inventions made available, the peasants were able to increase the size of their farm units and to produce surplus products. They also had to reorganize their farming methods by ending open-field farming and by introducing enclosure to produce wheat and barley for overseas markets. In short, agriculture was becoming commercialized. The peasants turned into farmers who began to mechanize agriculture and to transform it into business enterprises.

The industrial revolution (actually evolution) made this transformation possible by making steam power and machinery available for the farmers. The growth of the cotton and textile industries created further market opportunities for farmers, but comparative advantage shifted gradually to manufacturing industries.

The evolutionary progress of industrialization in the nineteenth century compelled the British Parliament to repeal the Corn Laws and liberalize grain trade. Then, agriculture in that country declined as industries expanded by relying on foreign raw materials, and as liberalism replaced mercantilism. In this sequential industrialization, agriculture and industry interacted through the market mechanism until they formed an equilibrium of modus vivendi over a long period of time. As a result, individuals in general and town people in particular performed the leading roles. As society controlled politics, pluralist systems of liberal democracy emerged. Later on, this prototype of industrialization was transferred to the United States, Australia, and New Zealand, where extensive agriculture continued to prosper along with industry because of the land and resource endowments existing in these new nations or colonial states.

Agricultural Collectivization and Forced Industrialization

In countries like the Soviet Union and China where agricultural commercialization had not progressed and the traditional aristocracy had ruled for a long period, a group of the elite imbued with new Western ideas about industrialization carried out the Communist revolution by mobilizing the peasants and workers. After having established a totalitarian system, the Soviet state forcefully collectivized agriculture and embarked upon crash programs of industrialization. In the process, industry was developed at the expense of agriculture. Lacking in investments and incentives, agriculture became a weak link in the Soviet economy, and the peasants were treated like wage-earning workers.

In China, too, Mao attempted in the late 1950s to collectivize agriculture, even beyond the Soviet experience, by means of the Great Leap Forward. Having failed in this application of the original ideals of people's communes, however, the People's Republic later adopted a strategy of developing agriculture and industry in a balanced effort under the slogan of "Agriculture as the Foundation and Industry as the Leading Factor." In making adjustments in the current Four Modernizations program, the Chinese seem to be adhering to the priority of developing agriculture, light industry, and heavy industry in that order. Of interest here is the outward-oriented trade policy and the attempts to increase the size of private plots and to encourage the "responsibility farm system" whereby production quotas are entrusted to small groups and even to private households. Yet as long as the Communist parties in both China and the Soviet Union advocate socialism as their official ideology, collective agriculture will continue to serve the state plans. More recently, China has joined the International Monetary Fund and the World Bank, and it remains to be seen how that country will interact with the market economies in the Pacific Basin.

Agricultural Reform and Rapid Industrialization

In most developing countries, industrialization reached its greatest impetus after World War II. It was characteristic of these newly independent countries that the state usually initiated land reform programs not only to enhance social equality of land distribution but also to pave the way for labor-intensive private farming in place of sharecropping or landowner-tenant arrangements. As such land reform projects have been completed, the tillers own their land and try to make the best out of it. As productivity rises in the food sector beyond the subsistence level, the surplus is transferred to the industrial sector through various channels of interaction.

Again, in most developing countries, the population density is high and the arable land limited. Because most of the agricultural products are inelastic in terms of price, these countries usually attempt to achieve industrialization by implementing five-year development plans. In undertaking planned economic development, however, they usually rely on the combined efforts of the state and private sector. Depending on the given resource endowment, a country can determine the mix of agriculture and industry in its investment priority. More often than not, developing countries put more emphasis on industry in their efforts to overcome economic backwardness. No matter what they do, their economy invariably remains a "dual structure," showing both a relatively traditional sector and a highly modern industrial sector. Exposure to the workings of international trade and investment tends to accelerate the trend toward such a dual economy.

Faced with a task of simultaneously realizing both industrialization and social justice, the developing countries encounter crisis after crisis. In the midst of these crises, authoritarian single parties or the military often take over the state in the name of justice, reform, and development. Regardless of their professed pronouncements, the leaders who emerge from these crises have tended to establish corporatist political systems whereby the state controls, coopts, and often subsidizes the societal groups and organizations existing in it rather than allowing their autonomous competition for the sake of their own interests. It is a distinctive characteristic of these systems that the state deliberately designs a proper relation between agriculture and industry by planned programs of taxation and investment. As long as the groups do not challenge the legitimacy of the government in power, however, they are allowed and even encouraged to expand their economic activities. In varying degrees, therefore, the private sector in these countries is dependent upon the state authorities for protection and support.

Inward- Versus Outward-Oriented Strategies

A crucial choice that a country faces after having gone through the first stage of agricultural-industrial interaction is whether it should pursue inward- or outward-oriented development strategies. This choice becomes an acute dilemma especially for the NICs, for it touches upon the delicate issue of determining the degree to which they can protect their agriculture and industries against those of both advanced and other developing countries.

According to a widely known analysis by Bela Balassa, industrialization generally starts in response to an increased domestic demand generated in the primary sector; a surplus arising in this sector can be used as investment for manufacturing industries.[1] At this initial stage, all developing countries have a tendency to protect the incipient manufacturing industries producing for their domestic markets; these countries try to pursue import-substitution policies for developing such nondurable consumer goods as clothing and shoes. This stage is the first in import-substitution.

When the domestic production of these goods rises above the level of domestic consumption, the country enters a second stage of import-substitution. At this stage, the country has to make a choice as to whether it should continue and upgrade import-substitution, by developing such durable producer and consumer goods as steel, automobiles, and refrigerators for domestic markets. Raul Prebisch recommended this inward-oriented strategy for Latin America and so did Gunnar Myrdal for India, so that they could avoid a "dependency relationship" with the advanced industrialized countries.

By contrast, a country can choose outward-oriented strategies by trying to manufacture labor-intensive goods for foreign markets, and thereby pursue export-oriented industrial policies. Because the capital and the technology necessary for capital-intensive industries are generally limited, but their populations are overly dense, developing countries can decide to produce goods for both domestic and foreign markets by setting competitive interest rates and prices, and by subjecting their industrial production to the requirements of international trade. In fact, some of them have deliberately provided positive incentives for exports instead of protecting their domestic production. In this case, their priority is to accelerate industry first even if such a policy adversely affects agriculture.

The evidence so far is conclusive that outward-oriented strategies have shown a superior performance in terms of exports and in terms of growth in industry and employment. This initial outcome is so because the countries pursuing these strategies have developed and exported their industries according to their comparative advantage. As a result, they have been able to achieve a structural transformation in their economies. Yet in most of these countries, the initiators of industrialization are still peasants-turned-workers and peasants-turned-leaders. Hence, psychologically and politically, they can hardly ignore agriculture completely. Moreover, their outward-oriented strategies are not without costs.

In the Pacific Basin, all the categories of economies elaborated thus far are found. In the category of agriculture commercialization and gradual industrialization, such advanced countries as the United States, Australia, New Zealand, and even Japan fall, although Japan presents an early case of land reform and rapid industrialization. In the category of collectivization and imposed industrialization, China and Vietnam can be placed, even though these relatively young Communist countries are still pre-industrial states. The remainder of the countries can easily be put in the category of agricultural reform and rapid industrialization, even though there is a great deal of variety in how they are going about it.

Turning to the inward versus spectrum, South American countries such as Mexico, Chile, Brazil, and Argentina have at least initially belonged to the inward category, and the four East Asian countries and protectorates of South Korea, Hong Kong, Singapore, and Taiwan to the outward category. The performance of these eight selected countries except Taiwan in terms of economic development can be observed in Table 6.1.

The Case of South Korea

South Korea is a formerly agricultural country that has successfully carried out land reform and rapid industrialization by opting for outward-oriented strategies. On the whole, the Korean government has made industry its first priority. In the 1960s, therefore, the agricultural sector supported the industrial sector by providing cheap food and labor and by accepting overpriced imported goods. In the 1970s, however, the government began to redress the imbalance that resulted from the industry-first policy by instituting price supports and by launching the Saemaul Movement. In this period, the industrial sector supported the agricultural sector. As in other countries, food self-sufficiency has been a national goal but is yet to be realized. Despite the continuing deficits in the balance of trade, Korea has steadily liberalized its imports, including food. In many ways, therefore, Korea is a good example of agricultural-industrial interaction at both domestic and international levels.

Export-Led Industrialization and Structural Transformation

Korea used to be an agricultural country with a poor resource endowment with which to increase the agricultural surplus or other exportable primary products. After the Korean War of 1950-1953 devastated the economy, South Korea was dependent primarily on the United States for economic assistance. South Korea's economic growth in the 1950s was less than 4 percent per year and its exports were negligible, while population growth was reaching almost 3 percent per year. Under these circumstrances, perhaps the only viable choice for South Korea was to concentrate on labor-intensive manufactures and to export the products in order to gain momentum in economic development. Indeed, when the Park Chung Hee government revealed its first five-year plan (1962-1966) in 1962, it deliberately chose to encourage production for exports instead of continuing import-substitution. To promote exports, the government offered tax incentives and monetary subsidies for export industries, and set prices and interest rates more realistically to increase domestic saving and industrial efficiency.

The result, extended far past the initial five-year plan to a second, third, and fourth—today there is a fifth—was spectacular growth, especially in exports, which in turn brought about a rapid structural transformation from an agricultural to a manufacturing economy. From 1962 through 1981, South Korea's per capita income, measured at current prices, rose from US $87 to US $1,636; its exports increased from US $54 million to US $21 billion; its manufacturing exports grew from 9 percent of GDP in 1953 to 22 percent in 1973-1975, making up 83 percent of total exports. By the

TABLE 6.1
Average Annual Growth Rates of Economic Sectors of Selected Pacific Basin Countries, 1960-1979 (percentages)

	GNP		Agriculture		Industry		Manufacturing		Services	
	1960-1970	1970-1979	1960-1970	1970-1979	1960-1970	1970-1979	1960-1970	1970-1979	1960-1970	1970-1979
Mexico	7.2	5.1	3.8	2.2	9.1	6.4	9.4	6.4	6.9	4.7
Chile	4.5	1.9	2.6	3.5	5.0	0.3	5.5	-1.0	4.5	2.8
Brazil	5.4	8.7	--	5.0	--	9.6	--	10.9	--	8.7
Argentina	4.2	2.5	2.2	2.5	5.9	2.4	5.7	1.9	3.4	2.5
Korea, Rep.	8.6	10.3	4.4	4.8	17.2	16.5	17.6	17.8	8.9	8.8
Hong Kong	10.0	9.4	--	-11.0	--	4.3	--	6.1	--	10.1
Singapore	8.8	8.4	5.0	1.7	12.5	18.6	13.0	9.3	7.7	8.5

Source: *World Development Report* (Washington, D.C.: World Bank, 1981), p. 137.

TABLE 6.2
Percentage of GNP by Industrial Group in the Republic of Korea, Selected Years from 1956 to 1981

Year	Primary	Secondary	Tertiary	Total
1956	44.2	12.8	43.0	100
1961	43.8	14.9	41.3	100
1966	37.9	19.8	42.3	100
1971	24.2	29.9	45.9	100
1981	18.0	30.9	51.1	100

Source: Economic Statistics Yearbook (Seoul: Bank of Korea, various years).

TABLE 6.3
Projected Growth Rates of Economic Sectors in National Economic Plans of the Republic of Korea, 1962-1981 (percentages)

	First Plan (1962-1966)	Second (1967-1971)	Third (1972-1976)	Fourth (1977-1981)
Exports	42.9	39.5	43.1	21.2
Industrial exports	76.1	48.7	44.3	22.0
Manufacturing	16.0	21.8	18.7	10.6
Mines and industry	14.3	20.0	18.0	10.3
Growth rate	7.8	9.7	10.1	5.4

Source: Economic Planning Board, Republic of Korea.

beginning of the 1980s, South Korea had become a middle-income industrial power whose role has to be reckoned with in international life.

Because South Korea had a comparative advantage in labor-intensive manufactures, it made a swift switch from a traditional import-substituting economy to a manufacturing export-producing economy in the 1960s. This strategy has worked well in transforming its economic structure, as shown by Tables 6.2 and 6.3.

It should be clear from these tables that South Korea's rapid growth rate has been slowing down. In 1980 in particular, it plummeted to −6.1 percent for the first time in recent decades. It should also be understood that rapid industrial expansion has taken place in the urban areas and has been concentrated specifically in Seoul, Pusan, and Daegu. In the course of this growth, industry indirectly interacted with agriculture by absorbing disguised unemployment from the countryside; industrial employment rose by 7.9 percent per year in 1960-1974, showing more of a "pull" by industry than a "push" by agriculture. Interaction was increased by the production of fertilizers and agricultural implements, and by the building of such infrastructures as transportation and communication facilities.

The primary task of the Korean government was to generate pressures for industrial development. It did this by making export promotion a national commitment, by restructuring the tax system so as to maximize domestic saving, and by sustaining administrative coordination and evaluation, vividly illustrated in the monthly report meetings personally presided over by the president.

The method by which the South Korean government implemented the development plans was rather flexible and practical, using the market mechanism as a means of planning and management. In 1965, for example, it raised interest rates to 34.5 percent annually on eighteen-month time deposits, and raised trade to keep foreign exchange rates floating within manageable limits. Since 1975, it has also sponsored the formation of general trading companies, so that these large corporations can have a competitive advantage in the international market in terms of "economy of scale." Despite this pragmatism, the government often made important economic decisions on the basis of political considerations, too.

Within the constraints of a physical environment in which only 20 percent of the land is arable and the rest is rugged mountains, the manufacturing sector has a comparative advantage given the densely populated country and highly talented Korean people. In addition, the capital resources available for investment are limited. Against this background, South Korea has to export to earn foreign exchange, and import in order to export. But this policy initially left agriculture stagnating. In fact, the government kept the price of agricultural products low in order to maintain low wages among the industrial labor force.

The industrial sector itself had revealed a series of difficulties by the early 1970s. At least in its outward form, its performance was quite impressive at the aggregate level in terms of its growth rate, employment, and exports, but its inner workings contained a great many distortions. The ability of enterprises at the firm level, for example, to generate an economic surplus and efficiency in resource use was not as impressive as one would expect, for the very survival of these enterprises in terms of fiscal solvency depended either on government-backed bonds or on the unofficial money market, providing ample room for corruption. More than anything else, the government was compelled to do something about the deteriorating agricultural sector at the beginning of the 1970s.

Fiscal Supports for Grain Products and the Saemaul Movement

Traditionally, Korea regarded agriculture as "the great foundation under the heaven." Because of the deepening imbalance and the keen concerns of the people in the city as well as the countryside about each year's crop, which helped determine the health of the economy, the government could not permit the agricultural sector to decline further. With the third five-year plan (1972–1976), it took steps to reverse the trend by raising the prices of grain that it purchased and by incorporating the New Community Movement into the subsequent development plans, to stimulate self-help among the rural population. These measures were instrumental in arresting

TABLE 6.4
Food Production in the Republic of Korea, 1976-1980 (thousand metric tons)

	1976	1977	1978	1979	1980
Rice	5,215	6,006	5,797	5,565	3,551
Barley	1,847	862	1,388	1,556	906
Miscellaneous	103	117	123	165	170
Beans	352	390	355	326	279
Wheat	667	595	565	501	431
Total	8,184	7,970	8,228	8,113	5,337

Source: Economic Statistics Yearbook (Seoul: Bank of Korea, 1981), p. 95.

the existing trend but contributed to huge fiscal deficits, creating another set of dilemmas about distortion of prices and inflationary pressures.

Food production did not meet the increasing demands generated by industrialization and urbanization. As Table 6.4 shows, food output fluctuated around 8 million metric tons in recent years and the government had to import the shortfall from abroad.

From 1968 on, the Korean government began to raise the prices of agricultural products relative to the prices of other goods and services. In 1968, for example, it increased the purchase price of rice by 17 percent; in 1970 it raised the price again by 36 percent. As the government purchased grains at higher prices from the farmers, it also tried to sell them to urban dwellers at lower prices. The erosion of rural political support in the 1971 presidential election in particular prompted the government to continue this policy. To enforce this policy, the government devised two special accounts: the Fertilizer Fund and the Grain Management Fund. As these funds constituted about 15 percent of the government's expenditures, however, they became heavy financial burdens. To alleviate this situation, the government decided to increase the price of fertilizer by 69 percent in 1976 and subsequently decreased the purchase price of grains.

Faced with the need for improving the terms of trade for the agricultural sector and, at the same time, constrained by the scarce financial resources available for investments, the Korean government set out to cope with this difficult situation by launching the New Community Movement in 1971. The professed goal of this movement was twofold: to improve the physical environment of rural villages and to increase rural income with some government help but primarily by voluntary efforts. To a certain degree, it was also an ideological campaign. The often repeated slogans of this movement were "self-help, self-reliance and cooperation." Basically, it was a bold attempt by the government to mobilize farmers to help themselves so that they could build economic infrastructures (by improving roads, irrigation, and water conservation). They were also called upon to innovate in their farm methods by adopting new varieties of seeds.

In the course of this movement, farm households did respond to the government's calls by replacing their thatched roofs with tiles or metal roofs, renovating their houses, and reshuffling their wells and toilet systems. In addition, over 40 percent of their rice acreage was planted in the high-yield Tongil variety. But most of the peasants were still careful in weighing their expected returns from the new variety against the time-tested seeds and methods they had used for years. Besides, the "green revolution" was more dependent on irrigation, fertilizer use, and intensive care—and also was more susceptible to insect damage and climate changes. As a result, the average rice yield of about 4 metric tons per hectare in Korea, though relatively high, is below the Japanese yield of 6 metric tons per hectare.

In order to raise rural income, the government in 1973 started the New Village Factory program by calling upon villages to set up small factories. The Ministry of Commerce and Industry provided financial and technical assistance to those villages that developed such factory-building programs. But most of the factories so built produced goods either for export or for larger enterprises under contract arrangements. The government offered financial help only when the rural villages were prepared to run their factories with their own labor and resources. In addition to the organizational supports, the government has sponsored an elaborate system of training for leaders and activists. The government assumes about 20 percent of the total expenses of the New Community Movement and the remaining portions are shouldered by the villages in the form of labor and also partly by donations made by entrepreneurs. Of interest in this regard is the practice of recognizing substantial donations from businessmen, in return for which President Chun commends their contributions by writing personal letters. Thus, the current government under President Chun has committed itself to continuing this movement.

Besides the export drive and the New Community Movement, there is another policy of which South Korea is proud: family planning. Beginning in the first five-year plan, the government has integrated this program into the economic plans. In the current, fifth five-year plan (1982-1986), it is trying to upgrade family planning into a more positive population program by offering a system of incentives for (and disincentives for ignoring) population control. As a result of these programs, the rate of annual population growth had declined from 3 percent in 1960 to 1.5 percent in 1980. There is reason to believe that these programs have interacted with other social mobilizations such as industrialization, urbanization, and the New Community Movement in bringing about this decline in population growth rate. But at the same time, migration to urban areas has become a more difficult problem as the urban population increased from 24 percent in 1955 to 51 percent in 1980, aggravating housing shortages, traffic congestion, environmental pollution, and the strain on public services. Twenty percent of the population live in Seoul, which represents only 6 percent of the land. In 1982 there were about 8 million people in this city. Thus, the price support and the New Community Movement have not changed the basic trend of rural migration to the cities for better standards of living and education.

It is clear that the policy of supporting agriculture implemented in the 1970s has also revealed its limits in many ways. Nowhere is this more acute than in the dilemma between the attempt to achieve food self-sufficiency by domestic production and the attempt to realize food security by stable imports.

Food Self-Sufficiency or Security by Imports

Should South Korea endeavor to achieve food self-sufficiency, or food security by continuing imports? Politically, the goal of accomplishing food self-sufficiency is highly desirable, but economically it may be not only infeasible but also undesirable, given the poor resource endowment of Korea for agricultural production. Yet self-sufficiency at least in rice production is desirable and may be feasible. Import of other agricultural products is inevitable and rational for Korea's industrial development. By and large, Korea has opted for the import approach to food security; over 76 percent of its imports had been liberalized by 1982.

Even though agriculture has lagged behind industry, one should not belittle the role of agriculture in the Korean economy, for it has provided over 75 percent of the grains consumed. Unless the habit of eating rice as the main food item in the diet drastically changes, it remains necessary for Korea to produce adequate supplies of rice. In 1977, the rice crop almost reached a level of self-sufficiency. In fact, no country can be totally dependent on other countries for food, even if its industry remains trade-dependent. As long as the rice crop serves as a sort of barometer for measuring the people's mood about the economic condition of the year, good crops are politically necessary.

Food imports have been a controversial issue in South Korea. In general, imports adversely affect agricultural development and, naturally, the farmers are opposed to the imports. Yet without imports, it becomes extremely difficult for the government not only to meet the nation's food requirements, but also to stabilize the prices of grains and meat. Financially, however, food imports take up about 10 percent of total imports and place a substantial burden on the balance of trade, especially when export prospects are not bright. Hence, it makes economic sense to try to raise agricultural productivity. To do so will stimulate industry as well, by generating demand for industrial goods and improving the level of employment (34 percent of the work force is still engaged in agriculture). Raising agricultural productivity can also minimize the income distribution gap between the urban and rural areas. But in the short run, this attempt will be far short of achieving food self-sufficiency.

On the other hand, excessively high rice prices may discourage farmers from engaging in other cash crops and off-farm activities. Moreover, the continuation of the fiscal support will result in distortion of prices and deficits. Purely from the economic point of view, therefore, such price supports do not seem to be preferable to importing grains and meat; for example, the domestic prices of rice, barley, and wheat are two times, and that of beef five times, the price of imported products. Such price supports will also adversely affect Korea's export competitiveness. For these reasons, Korea began importing beef from Australia and New Zealand from 1978 on. But such imports obviously hurt domestic cattle industries; hence, they have become a hotly debated issue in Korea.

So long as Korea's comparative advantage lies in manufacturing industries, it is rational to upgrade this sector and thereby induce off-farm employment. In a similar vein, it is necessary for the Korean government to gradually reduce price supports for grains and to import the shortfall of grain and beef from the international market.

Korea is now in the midst of structural readjustments as the government is actively seeking to achieve a private-sector-led economy. From the current efforts to reduce inflation and foreign debts and to overcome disruptions in the money market may emerge an optimism relationship between agriculture and industry.

Agricultural-Industrial Interactions in the Pacific Basin

The Pacific Basin encompasses all types of countries, highly industrialized, middle income and developing, and both food surplus and deficient. Theoretically speaking, therefore, these countries can have a division of labor by specializing in both industrial products and agricultural crops according to the principle of comparative advantage and free trade. But the reality is not quite so because in actuality, all countries are busy protecting their own interests from one another. Yet if these countries are serious about building an economic community based on common and reciprocal interests they should try to conduct their domestic and trade policies according to that principle by negotiating their differences and working toward their common interests.

Even a cursory look at this region reveals that the economies of the countries are becoming more and more interdependent. But more important than this reality is the phenomenon that as these countries make their economic and trade policies mainly through their domestic political processes, they tend to define and seek solutions to the interdependent problems from their nationalistic points of view. Because of this central dilemma, the highly industrialized countries are imposing protectionist restrictions on manufactured imports from the NICs; and the cereal- and beef-producing countries are trying to protect the prices of and the markets for their products. On the other hand, the NICs and other developing countries are beginning to compete in the production and export of labor-intensive goods. In all probability, though, the NICs and even Southeast Asian countries will have to import food from the United States, Australia, New Zealand, and Argentina, and the latter nations will have to import manufactured goods from the former. In the short run, therefore, conflicts are inevitable among these Pacific Basin countries, although in the long run, the division of labor will benefit all by raising productivity and the levels of imports.

Ideally, the suppliers and consumers of industrial goods and agricultural crops can negotiate and reach satisfactory agreements on the reciprocal flow of and stable access to these commodities. But this is easier said than done. Toward this goal, some sort of institutionalized forum seems to be in order not only to study these matters but also to discuss them on an ongoing basis. What may be called "the Pacific Council" can be organized to provide a more systematic framework for such discussion and for creating public opinion.

Notes

1. What follows in this section is based on Bela Balassa, *The Newly Industrializing Countries in the World Economy* (New York: Pergamon Press, 1981), pp. 1–14.

7
Agricultural Development and Policy in the People's Republic of China

Wu Daxin

Achievements in Agriculture

In China before the mid-twentieth century, peasants were exploited by the feudal landlords and the ruling class was indifferent to agricultural development. As a result, the Chinese agricultural production level was very low. Prolonged war in the 1930s and 1940s (the war of resistance against Japan and the war of liberation) brought further deterioration to the rural economy and grain production dropped to a very low level.

After the founding of the People's Republic of China in 1949, peasants and cadres in the hundreds of millions, under the leadership of the Chinese Communist Party, began to carry out land reform; they realized the collectivization of agriculture and adopted a series of measures to transform the production conditions and to promote agricultural productivity. Since that time, the years of progress have greatly surpassed other periods, and China's agriculture has achieved a high degree of rehabilitation and development.

Rural Economic Organizations

Rural economic organizations with a collective economy as their main goal have been formed on different scales and with various management systems. At present, China has more than 50,000 people's communes, over 600,000 production brigades, and more than 5 million production teams. In addition, there are state farms and also household economies as a supplementary sector. This multiform structure of socialist agriculture contributes to the development of social production forces and brings advantages of the socialist system into full play.

The Growth of Agricultural Output

The total value of agricultural output for 1981 was 172 billion yuan, 4.3 times higher than that of 1949, with a yearly average increase of 5.3 percent. The output of grain increased from 113 million metric tons in 1949 to 325 million metric tons in 1981, 2.9 times that of 1949, with an average annual growth rate of 3.4 percent (see Table 7.1). The total output of ginned cotton was 2.9 million metric tons in 1981, 6.7 times that of 1949, with an average rate of increase of 6.2 percent a year. The total output of oil-bearing crops, and of sugarcane and sugar beet, was 3 times and 11.7 times that of 1949, respectively.

Compared with 1949, the number of hogs by the end of 1981 was 5.1 times as great, that of sheep and goats was 4.4 times as great, and that of large animals was 1.6 times as great. Their annual growth rates were 5.2 percent, 4.8 percent, and 1.5 percent, respectively.

The 1952 gross agricultural output value was 48.4 billion yuan, which was calculated according to 1952 constant prices; the corresponding output values for 1957 and 1965 were 53.7 billion yuan and 59 billion yuan respectively, according to 1957 constant prices; output values for 1978, 1980, and 1981 were 145.9, 162.7, and 172.0 billion yuan respectively, according to 1970 constant prices. The 172 billion yuan of 1981 was 5.7 percent more than that in 1980. If measured in constant prices of 1980, the total value of agricultural output in 1981 was 231.2 billion yuan, which was much higher than that in 1980.[1]

Table 7.2 shows that grain output in 1981 was only 1.4 percent greater than the previous year. Apart from grains, the output of other crops—except for silkworm cocoons, but including cotton, oil-bearing crops, sugar-bearing crops, jute and ambary hemp, and tea—all increased by a large margin. Although increases were also registered in the output of major animal products on the basis of the sharp increases in 1980, the number of hogs in the national herd at the end of 1981 had dropped.

In 1983, there was another bumper harvest following four consecutive years of increased agricultural output. The total 1983 output value of agriculture was 312.1 billion yuan, up 9.5 percent from 1982 and exceeding the planned target of 4 percent growth. After deducting the industrial output value of 36.8 billion yuan for other enterprises run by production brigades and teams, the total value of agricultural output was 275.3 billion yuan, up 7.9 percent from 1982. The output of nearly all major farm products hit all-time highs, reaching or exceeding the planned figure. Total grain output was 387.28 metric tons, topping the state plan by 13.1 percent, or 9.2 percent more than in 1982. Cotton output was 4,637,000 metric tons, topping the state plan by 37.6 percent, a 28.9 percent rise over 1982. (Details are shown in Table 7.3).

Improvement of Conditions in Agricultural Production

Since its founding, the People's Republic of China has been undertaking a large-scale agricultural capital construction program. In order to lessen

TABLE 7.1
Output Comparisons of Some Major Farm Products and Livestock, People's Republic of China, 1949 and 1981 (million metric tons; head)

	Output and Number of Animals		1981/1949
	1949	1981	(percent change)
Grain	113.18	325.02	287.17
Cotton	0.44	2.968	674.55
Oil-bearing crops	2.564	10.205	398.63
Sugarcane and sugar beets	2.833	36.028	1,271.73
Hogs (by the end of the year)	57,750,000	293,702,000	508.57
Sheep and goats (by the end of the year)	42,350,000	187,730,000	443.28
Large animals	60,020,000	97,641,000	162.68

TABLE 7.2
Output of Major Farm Products and Number of Livestock, People's Republic of China, 1981 (million metric tons; head)

	1981 output	Percent change over 1980
Grain[a]	325.02	1.4
Cotton	2.68	9.6
Oil-bearing crops	10.205	32.7
Sugarcane and beetroot	36.028	23.8
Jute and ambary hemp	1.26	14.8
Silkworm cocoons	0.311	-4.6
Tea	0.343	12.8
Hogs in stock at year end	293,702,000	-3.8
Sheep and goats at year end	187,730,000	0.2
Large animals at year end	97,641,000	2.5
Meats (pork, beef, and mutton)	12.609	4.6

a. The 1981 grain output was adjusted from 318.22 million tons (statistical figures for output of plots for peasants' personal needs were incomplete in some provinces) to 325.02 million tons.

TABLE 7.3
Output of Major Farm Products and Number of Livestock, People's Republic of China, 1982 and 1983 (million metric tons; head)

	1982	1983	Percent Change, 1982/1981	Percent Change, 1983/1982
Grain	353.430	387.280	8.7	9.2
Soybean	9.090	9.760	-3.2	8.1
Cotton	3.598	4.637	21.3	28.9
Oil-bearing seeds	11.817	10.550	15.8	-10.7
Sugarcane and beetroot	43.594	40.323	21.0	-7.5
Jute and ambary hemp	1.060	1.019	-15.9	-3.9
Silkworm cocoons	0.314	0.340	1.0	8.2
Tea	0.397	0.401	16.0	0.8
Meats (pork, beef, and mutton)	13.508	14.021	7.1	3.8
Milk	1.618	1.845	25.4	14.0
Hogs in stock at year end	300.780	298.540	2.4	-0.7
Sheep and goats at year end	171.790	166.950	-3.2	-8.2
Large animals at year end	101.130	103.500	3.6	2.3

the occurrence and the degree of scourge of flood, waterlogging, and drought, priority was given to harnessing the system of China's main rivers, such as the Yellow River, the Yantze River, the Huai River, and the Hai River. By the end of 1980, there were 86,000 reservoirs of all sizes and 2.09 million diesel and electric pump wells. The total irrigated areas increased from 13 million hectares to more than 47 million hectares, 48 percent of the total cultivated land. About 13 million hectares of arable land exposed to all kinds of waterlogging, 40,000 hectares of saline and alkaline land, and 20,000 hectares of barren land composed of lateritic and yellow soils were transformed to some extent. This improvement helped raise the resistance to natural disasters and the productivity of land. Up to 1979, 28 million hectares of land in China had been forested or reforested; the total area of forest increased to 122 million hectares, a coverage rate of 12.7 percent. The nationwide afforestation campaign has been developed vigorously in the last two years. In all, 4.5 and 6.32 million hectares were afforested in 1982 and 1983, respectively.

Enhancement of Technical Equipment and Investment in Agriculture

In 1980, a total of 12,694,000 metric tons of chemical fertilizers (counted on the basis of 100 percent effectiveness), or 150 times more than in 1949, was applied, averaging 127.8 kilograms per hectare. A total of 16,598,000 metric tons of chemical fertilizers was applied in 1983. By the end of 1983, China had 841,000 large- and medium-sized tractors; 2,750,000 small-capacity and walking tractors; power-driven drainage and irrigation equipment for rural use with a total of 78,492,000 horsepower; and 275,000 farm trucks. By the end of 1980, tractor-plowed farmland came to 40,991,000 hectares, accounting for 41.3 percent of all arable land. Total power capacity of farm machines in 1983 reached 245 million horsepower, and total electricity used in the rural areas was 43,520 million kilowatt-hours, averaging 423 kilowatt-hours per hectare of arable land. To solve the energy problem in the countryside, more than 100,000 small hydroelectric power stations have been built, marsh gas (methane) has been used in rural areas where the conditions allow, and experiments have been made in the exploitation of solar, wind, and geothermal energy resources.

Improved strains of seeds for the three major crops of rice, wheat, and cotton have been popularized, and the area under cultivation with hybrid corn and hybrid sorghum has been extended to more than 60 percent of the total area sown in corn and sorghum. Hybrid rice varieties, developed in 1973, were planted on large areas and their output increased significantly. The wide use of farm chemicals and implements has made a great contribution to the control of such serious insects and diseases as migratory locusts, wheat midges, and smut of cereals.

Development of Agricultural Scientific Research and Education

The Chinese Academy of Agricultural Sciences, established in 1956, is now the highest institution of agricultural sciences in China. There are about 652 agricultural scientific research institutions above the prefecture level, with 24,000 agricultural scientific research workers and technicians, and there are 25,000 agricultural extension services in which about 12,000 staff and workers are on the payroll of the public budget. There are more than 50,000 animal husbandry and veterinary stations in communes, with 280,000 staff and workers. In addition, there are about 250,000 part-time farmer technicians who have a little agricultural science training and good experience and practice in farming, who are playing an active part in the countryside. A widespread system of research and extension has been formed.

In 1979, the number of graduates from agricultural universities and colleges increased 3.7 times, and graduates of secondary technical schools 4.5 times, over the comparable numbers in 1949. A total of 860,000 graduates of the agricultural institutions of higher learning and the secondary agricultural technical schools have been registered in this thirty-year period. In 1983, China had fifty-nine agricultural colleges and universities and 358 secondary agricultural schools with a total enrollment of 200,000 students and with graduating classes totaling 40,000 to 50,000 students.

Since the founding of the People's Republic of China, agriculture has made significant progress as summarized earlier, beginning especially during the period of eight years from 1949 to 1957, when the socialist transformation of agriculture was first being accomplished. Grain production increased more than 10 million metric tons each year on average, and all other major cash crops and livestock increased significantly. However, the continued development of agriculture was not plain sailing but full of twists and turns. After 1957, overeagerness to achieve quick results in economic construction resulted in activities that were not responsive to the laws of nature and economics, and agricultural production suffered a setback for a time. In 1960, the output of some farm products was actually lower than what it had been in the initial period after 1949.

Thanks to the principles and measures of adjustment adopted from 1963 to 1965, the annual growth rate of agricultural production returned to 6.7 percent. But subsequently, during the ten years of the "Cultural Revolution," which occurred between 1966 and 1976, China's agricultural production did not improve as much as it should have. After the downfall of the "gang of four" in 1976, the Central Committee of the Communist Party of China formulated in 1978 "The Decision on Some Questions Concerning the Acceleration of Agricultural Development" and followed up by adopting a series of policies designed to fire the enthusiasm for production of our hundreds of millions of peasants and broad masses of cadres, thus setting right the normal course of the development of agriculture in a positive, gradual way.

The Present Situation of Grain Production and Consumption in China

Even with setbacks, China's grain production increased more than twofold from 1949 to 1983. Average annual grain production was well above 300 million metric tons during the 1978 to 1983 period despite serious natural calamities in two years out of the four. China's grain area is comparatively small, but its yield per hectare reached 4,275 kilograms.

Per capita grain production in China was around 380 kilograms in 1983, which was lower than the world average level. In recent years, China has imported a bit of grain every year with a view to regulating grain supplies. For example, the amount of grain imported in 1981 was less than 5 percent of total grain production in that year; thus, the degree of self-sufficiency in grain production reached 95 percent. Most Chinese people can afford to eat and there is only a small number whose grain ration is slightly inadequate. In 1983, the per capita net income of the peasants rose to 309.8 yuan, an increase of 14.7 percent over the preceding years.

The situation of food consumption for the Chinese people is changing for the better. Compared with 1952, each Chinese in 1980 ate 8.2 percent more grain (213.8 kilograms). The figures for pork consumption were up 88.6 percent, and for sugar consumption, 320 percent. In 1981, each Chinese consumed about 12 kilograms of meat, 2.4 kilograms of eggs, and 4.1 kilograms of sugar.

The daily caloric intake of the Chinese people averaged 2,666 calories per capita in 1981, compared to 2,311 calories in 1978—an increase of 15.4 percent (more than 350 calories). In 1981, daily caloric intake for urban people was 2,966 calories and for rural people, 2,598 calories. During several preceding years (1978-1981), the daily caloric intake of rural people had increased 16.8 percent, compared with a 9.2 percent increase for urban people. Therefore, although the daily caloric intake of rural people was less than that of urban people, the rate of growth in caloric intake was much faster for rural than for urban people. Moreover, according to the data of the State Statistical Bureau, the average daily caloric intake per capita reached 2,779 calories in 1982. Daily protein intake of the Chinese people increased from 70.8 grams in 1978 to 80.5 grams in 1982, and daily intake of fats from 29.9 grams to 44.4 grams. It is said that a daily intake of 2,600 calories and 70 grams of protein is needed for an average Chinese to ensure normal physiological functions of the body.

At present, although the daily caloric intake of the Chinese people compares favorably to that for most of the other developing countries, it is still lower than that of the developed countries, which take from food a daily average of 3,000 to 3,500 calories per capita. In addition, a large proportion of the Chinese diet is grain. Hence most of the caloric, protein, and fat intake for the Chinese people is from vegetable food. In view of this fact, the food problem China faces has two dimensions: to increase grain production and to improve the nutritional quality of food as well. In other words, the continued development of agricultural production includes the effort to change progressively the composition of the average diet.

The present condition of grain production and food consumption reflects two consequences of China's huge population: a very low ratio of person/ arable land, and the weak foundation of the economy. It is for these reasons that the course of fundamental change in China's food situation has a long way to go. The nutritional situation can be improved only gradually on the basis of first having enough food for the people to eat. The population growth rate must be controlled strictly—the rate of increase must be reduced as much as possible—to guarantee the realization of agricultural modernization and an improvement in the standard of living of the Chinese people. At one time the importance of crop planting, especially grain production, was overemphasized to the neglect of the development of animal husbandry. This situation must ultimately be altered, but without slackening efforts to increase grain production; to the contrary, every effort must be made to increase it. This is a strategic problem with regard to the development of China's agriculture.

In China, annual per capita grain production has long been in the neighborhood of the 300-kilogram level. Given this level, it is totally impractical for China to turn several kilograms of grain into one kilogram of meat. Grain cannot be turned to use as feed grain to develop animal products in a big way.

China has 220 million hectares of grassland, of which 80 million hectares are located in sandy areas. This grassland and the 46 million hectares of hillside pastures in the agricultural area amount to 260 million hectares, most of which have to be improved. Thus, the carrying capacity for animals is relatively low. If a good job is done, China's grasslands can provide 1-1.5 million tons of meat annually, averaging only 1-1.5 kilograms for each person.

If annual per capita grain production for each Chinese can reach 400 kilograms by the end of the century, the food situation will be much better. This goal is feasible and is certain to improve the diet to a more reasonable composition in which grain, animal products, fruits, and vegetables are arranged in proper proportions. The demand for food grains will be somewhat alleviated as the consumption of meat is increased.

China is a large country of 1 billion people. To import a small amount of grain each year to regulate temporary fluctuations in supply and demand is permissible, but to rely on the importation of grain is not—let alone to develop animal husbandry by means of imported grains. The only correct way to proceed is to develop agriculture, increase production, and improve progressively the people's livelihood. The system of planned supply of grain is still in force in order to ensure the necessities of life for the most people.

China has great potential for increasing grain production. In 1979, the area sown to grain crops was 119,263 million hectares, with an average yield of 2,782.5 kilograms per hectare. But the yield varied a great deal from place to place, being quite high in some places and very low in others. For example, the per-hectare yield of grain in the provinces of Jiangsu, Zhejiang, and Hunan was above 7,500 kilograms, but the yield in most provinces was below 3,750 kilograms. Moreover, there were a few provinces in which the yield was as low as 1,500 kilograms.

On the scale of counties devoted to grain production, about 170 base counties have a marketable surplus of grain in the east, middle, and northeast of China. Their population is only 10 percent of the total and their arable land makes up 7.3 percent of the arable land for the whole country. But they produce 15.3 percent of the total grain and 23.4 percent of the marketable grain from the gross national grain production. By contrast, there are 241 low-yield and grain-deficient counties in the northwest and southwest. Their population is 9 percent of the total and their arable land 11.9 percent of all of China. But their grain production is only 8.4 percent of the total. The per-unit yield of grain in the low- and medium-yield areas can be increased considerably by applying advanced agricultural techniques and improving the conditions of production.

The average annual growth rate of grain production in the thirty-two-year period from 1949 to 1981 was 3.4 percent. If one takes the total grain production of 325.02 million metric tons in 1981 as the base and assumes an average annual growth rate of 2 percent, total grain production would be 473.49 million metric tons by the end of the century. It is estimated that China's population would then have increased to about 1.2 billion. Hence, each citizen would then have an average amount of grain of 395 kilograms—about 20 percent higher than the current level.

Agricultural Policy

Since the Third Plenary Session of the Eleventh Central Committee of the Chinese Communist Party, held in 1978, a series of agricultural policies and rural economic measures has been formulated to correct the problems that then existed in the countryside. The implementation of these policies has increased the enthusiasm for production of our country's hundreds of millions of peasants, pushed forward the development of agricultural production, and enlivened the rural economy. The following are the major policies.

Reducing the Burden of the Peasants

Beginning in 1979, the state has raised the purchasing prices for farm and sideline products while reducing rural taxes in some areas. As a consequence, the peasants received 52,000 million yuan more in the period from 1979 to 1981. The prices for farm machinery, chemical fertilizers, pesticides, and plastic products for farm use were also reduced, by 10 to 15 percent.

The amount of grain to be delivered and sold to the state for the period 1976–1978 remained the same as it was for the years 1971–1975 and was not raised even where there had been a bumper harvest. Moreover, starting in 1979, the amount of grain to be delivered and sold to the state was reduced by 2,500 million kilograms.

Agricultural loans have more than doubled in the period from 1979 to 1985. The state has issued long-term, special-purpose loans at a minimal or very low rate of interest, to be paid back in ten to fifteen years or even at the end of the century.

Effecting a Policy of Respecting the Power of Self-Management of Production Teams

The ownership of the people's communes, production brigades, and production teams, and their power of self-management, are to be protected by state laws. The requisition or use of labor power, land, draught animals, machinery, funds, products, and other materials of a production team without compensation is no longer allowed. As long as they keep to the socialist orientation, carry out government policies, observe the laws and decrees of the state, and accept the guidance of state planning, all the basic accounting units under a people's commune have the right to cultivate whatever is suited to the season and to local conditions, to determine measures for increased production, to decide on the methods of management, and to distribute their own products and cash income.

Adopting the System of Responsibility in Production

The system of responsibility in agricultural production takes various forms, but all forms have one thing in common: the adoption of contracts for fixed quotas and remuneration according to output, with extra pay for above-quota output. Generally speaking, the forms of responsibility fall under several categories: (1) the system of individuals undertaking to fulfill certain quotas in farm work under the unified management of the production team; (2) the system of fixed output quotas on the basis of specialized groups, households, or individuals under the unified management of the production team; and (3) the system of peasant households assuming full responsibility for most of the farm work. The new system of responsibility has resulted in a clear-cut division of labor and effectively puts into practice the principles "from each according to his ability, to each according to his work." It has resulted in equal pay for equal work between men and women, and it has greatly enhanced the enthusiasm of the peasants and boosted agricultural production.

Relaxing Restrictions on Private Plots, Livestock, Sideline Occupations, and Rural Trade Fairs

Land plots allotted to commune members for personal use, livestock for personal needs, household sideline occupations, and rural trade fairs are supplementary and accessory to the socialist economy. The collective economy will continue to be consolidated and developed, and the household sideline occupations will be encouraged and supported at the same time.

In general, the area of private plots allotted to commune members can be 5 to 7 percent of the total farmland cultivated by each production team, the upper limit being 15 percent. Since 1979, rural trade fairs have been opened in cities and towns, and the farm and sideline products of peasants can be sold at the fairs.

New Circulars on Rural Work

The nation has reaped good harvests for a number of years in succession, thanks to the implementation of these policies and economic measures. More recently, China has been divulging in more detail the basis of its agricultural policies, with relaxed restrictions on some aspects. In the Circulars on Rural Work in 1983 and 1984, the Central Committee of the Chinese Communist Party affirmed the rural policies and principles of the last two years and formulated work plans and policies for the years to come. The circulars emphasized that China's countryside is now in a historical period in which the self-supporting and semi-self-sufficient, traditional agricultural economy is developing into a modern economy with large-scale commodity production. This major trend provides the background for peasants in the 1980s to take part in economic activities. The circulars also pointed out that the main tasks ahead are to raise productivity, open more channels of circulation, and develop community production, on the basis of stabilizing and improving the production responsibility system. The main elements of the accompanying new policies are as follows:

1. *Stabilizing and Improving the Responsibility System in Agricultural Production.* The year 1983 was one in which the contract responsibility system linking remuneration with output was widely adopted, and economic reform in the rural areas developed in depth. It was a year in which agricultural production advanced with giant strides. Finally, it was a year in which commodity production in the countryside developed vigorously and on an unprecedented scale.

Under the new system, state planners advise each production team (or collective) in general terms on how farming in its area should proceed and what results are expected. The production team then draws up a contract with each household, under which the household is allotted land, draft animals, and small- and medium-sized farm equipment. These contracts are binding on the state, the production team, and each household.

The household is responsible for working its allotment (which remains the property of the collective) and for caring for its livestock and machinery, which it can use exclusively. The collective is responsible for providing and maintaining large farm equipment and water conservation projects.

Farm produce is divided three ways: the state buys its quota at a set price, the collective takes a certain amount for the common reserve, and the household, which must pay a state agricultural tax, keeps the remainder for personal use or sale.

The contract responsibility system, which links remuneration with output, has taken root in China. It is not merely an expedient policy to solve the problem of feeding the people, but a fundamental reform of the economic system in the countryside. It is inestimable in its significance for building socialism with Chinese characteristics.

What is more inspiring is that throughout the country there have sprung up great numbers of specialized households that have prospered through hard labor. The number of such households (which specialize in operating an enterprise such as food grain or cotton and derive the main portion of their income from that enterprise) has reached 24.8 million, or about 13 percent of all households in the countryside in 1983. They can sell 70 to 90 percent of their products to the state.

2. *Insisting on the Collective Ownership of Land and Preventing the Irrational Use of Arable Land.* China has a vast population but not enough arable land, and this contradication will become more and more acute as the population increases. The nation had 111.33 million hectares under cultivation in 1977 (including 17.07 million hectares of arable land reclaimed during this period). Hence, 29.07 million hectares had actually been lost from production in twenty years. Per capita arable land has now declined to about 0.10 hectare. To control population and to treasure and use every inch of land rationally therefore has to be state policy, of necessity. All farmland, gardens, woodlands, grasslands, water-surface, coastal lands, wastelands, and barren mountains must be used under the direction of the collective, and no one is permitted to take possession of them. Farm plots, hillside land, and farmyards allocated to the peasants for their own use over a long period are still owned by the collective.

3. *Giving Priority to the Development of Commodity Production in the Rural Economy.* The proportion of commodity production in the rural economy rose from 40 percent in 1978 to more than 50 percent in 1983. About 100 million peasants have switched from farming to tapping and developing other natural resources.

With a view to promoting the further development of commodity production, the Chinese Communist Party has put forward some new flexible stipulations to invigorate the rural economy. One is that the quantity and variety of farm and sideline produce subject to unified or fixed purchase by the government should be reduced as production and market supplies increase. The government at present exercises complete or partial control over grain, cotton, and essential agricultural products, as well as sideline products like valuable medicinal herbs.

Peasants are permitted under current policies to sell in or outside their areas what is left after meeting quotas for government purchase and tax payment. The peasants are now allowed to transport goods long distances for sale, and to buy farm machinery and transport vehicles either individually or collectively.

Another new stipulation is that in order to help peasants enlarge their production scale and sell the produce, the period of land contracts should in general be extended to fifteen years from their present three to five years. The terms should be extended even further for long-term undertakings and development projects, including afforestation and the development of barren hillsides and wastelands. The peasants should be encouraged to invest more in the land to enrich the soil, and to run various rural enterprises with their own funds.

It is necessary to consolidate and improve the various forms of the contracted responsibility system that is based on the household, to promote specialized household and various forms of economic associations, to continue to improve the structure of the agricultural economy, and to support the peasants in actively expanding commodity production.

4. *Advocating an All-around Development of Agriculture and Rural Collective Enterprises.* The development of a diversified economy has been encouraged since the 1950s. The general principle is to completely and rationally capitalize on local natural conditions and resources in developing a diversified economy. It is expected that in this way the rural economy will flourish and peasants will earn more income.

The development of cooperative industry, commerce, and sideline occupations is not restricted by regions or trades. The policy of free circulation of workers, capital, and technology was reaffirmed in the Circular of 1984. Compared with the policy of the 1950s, the policy of free circulation is a marked change, positive both in its significance and its function.

Today the total output value of cooperative industries throughout China amounts to 80 billion yuan, with fixed assets of 40 billion yuan. A large number of peasants earn very high incomes from these small industries. In some places, peasants engaging in lines of work other than industry may also become well off, provided they plant crops and trees, grow fruit, vegetables, and local products, and engage in animal husbandry or horticulture. One path alone will not do. To put it in a nutshell, peasants may engage in whatever lines of production are best suited to local conditions.

As agriculture, forestry, animal husbandry, sideline occupations, and fishery are developed in an overall way, attention will be paid in the future to enterprises that integrate agriculture, industry, and commerce so as to gradually change the face of the rural areas.

5. *Releasing Surplus Labor from Farmland.* China's population is too large and consumes a large proportion of the grain output, leaving only a limited amount of marketable grain. The ratio of persons per hectare of arable land is high. Therefore those who depend on farming receive a higher income if they have large tracts of arable land. In the many areas where the tracts of cultivated land are small and the population large, income is low or relatively low.

Under the present policy, the peasants are allowed to leave their land and run small-scale industries with their partners, or run cooperative commercial or transportation enterprises and engage in large-scale animal husbandry. The different factors of production are allowed to circulate freely, which means a free flow of workers, capital, and technology.

A vision of the future holds that 30 to 40 percent of rural labor will engage in industries and sideline occupations, and that these people will get together to set up small towns, thereby cutting down the trend toward urban population by increasing the population in rural towns. In a situation of surplus rural labor, this view, as policy, may be a proper way to increase employment and people's incomes, to raise their cultural level, and to speed up rural development. In short, this vision becomes a policy for comprehensive development of the countryside, and the vision will probably come true in twenty years or so. The concomitant hope exists that as people make their choices, farmland will gradually be placed in the hands of more efficient farming families, to improve management and increase output.

As an increasing number of peasants is able to shift from farming to industry, commerce, sideline production, and services, they should be able— provided they decide to abandon farming—to return all or part of their contractual land to the collective or pass it to others with the approval of the collectives. Such approval should extend to decisions made during the contract period. Contracts cannot, however, be transferred without the approval of the collectives, which own the land. Peasants are not allowed to sell or let the plots they are farming under contracts. In addition, contractual plots must not be diverted for uses other than farming.

6. *Restructuring of the Economy by the State.* The people's commune system was founded in 1958. Later, adjustments were made to its scale and management powers, leading to the institution of "three-level ownership by commune, production brigade, and production team, with the production team as the basic accounting unit." At the same time, the communes functioned as a level of political power.

This system had remained intact until investigated anew in 1983. Based on the opinions of commune members, local cadres, and economists, the investigators unanimously agreed that the communes played a positive role in some aspects. However, some insurmountable contradictions existed because the economic organization and the organs of political power were identical. That the system of combining government administration with commune management was not adapting to the needs of the development of production became more obvious through many sample surveys and experiments conducted in different counties of different provinces over a period of two years.

The separation of government administration from commune management is a big issue that involves the political and economic life of the 800 million Chinese peasants. It will have a great impact on the development of China's countryside. The state will institute the reforms step by step in order to ensure the smooth progress of production and other work.

7. *Reforming the System of Supply and Marketing Cooperatives.* In keeping with the new situation marked by growing commodity exchange in the rural areas, the system of supply and marketing cooperatives must be reformed. The essential thing is to change them from being run by the government to being run by the people, that is, to change them into cooperative commercial enterprises that are collectively owned by the peasants. It is necessary to restore the characteristics of mass participation, democratic management, and flexible operation, and to boldly encourage peasants to buy shares by abolishing restrictions on their buying; thus, the cooperatives' undertakings will be much more closely linked than before with the economic interests of the peasants. It is also essential to reform the labor and personnel system of the supply and marketing cooperatives so that cadres can be elected and can work at higher or lower levels as

required, and so that workers and office staff can be recruited or dismissed according to a contract system.

8. *Making the Most Energetic Efforts to Run Various Services Well.* When a traditional subsistence or semi-subsistence type of agriculture begins to develop into commodity production, it requires infrastructural elements of various kinds to promote farm technological advance and to move information and supplies into the area undergoing development, as well as to store surplus products, handle them, and move them out of the area. The projected development of the agricultural sector without the services that flow from the required infrastructural elements is impossible. Commodity production in the countryside cannot make a single step forward if there are not the necessary circulation channels, guidnce in science and technology, transportation and communication facilities, means of production, and information services. Thus, the commercial, scientific and technological, transportation and communications, agriculture-serving industrial, and educational departments should fully understand the urgent demands of the peasants and further enhance efforts (and consciousness) to serve the countryside. The credit cooperatives—the financial organizations in rural areas—will shift the emphasis of their work to serving the peasants.

A new technological revolution is currently taking place in the world. It is a long-term strategy for China to intensify the development of intellectual resources and constantly improve the qualities of workers and staff members working in the field of agriculture.

Notes

2. All statistical data in the text and tables were provided by the Chinese State Statistical Bureau.

Part 4

The International Migration of Labor

8
The U.S.-Mexican Labor Market

Wallace E. Huffman

Among migrant labor markets in the Pacific Basin countries, the U.S.-Mexican labor market seems to be the largest. Great numbers of Mexicans have entered and continue to enter the United States to work, mostly illegally in recent years.[1] The United States is the only Pacific Basin country that has been the destination of such large numbers of international workers in recent years. Although Canada, Australia, and New Zealand have been open to citizens of the Commonwealth, relatively few others have entered these countries legally or illegally. Their relative geographic isolation from low-income countries has undoubtedly been a factor in keeping illegal immigration low. Japan, Taiwan, and the Philippines, on the other hand, have not been open to immigrants. Mexico, although one of the largest exporters of labor within the Pacific Basin, is also the destination of some Central Americans who have been migrating northward to that country. Other Latin American migration patterns include Colombians migrating to Venezuela and Ecuador, and Chileans migrating to Argentina.[2]

In the U.S.-Mexican case, most of the illegal aliens have come to the United States seeking temporary or permanent employment and real wage rates that are much higher than they can obtain in Mexico.[3] Employment of illegal aliens fills an otherwise excess demand for labor of a low-skilled type in the United States and removes part of an excess supply in Mexico. Thus, large-scale immigration can be expected to raise wage rates for workers from Mexico and to lower wage rates for low-skilled labor in the United States. Some of this excess demand and supply would be expected to disappear if commodity trade restrictions among countries were reduced and if population growth rates in developing countries, such as Mexico, were reduced.

The objective of this chapter is to present an economic perspective on the U.S.-Mexican labor market. Section one presents a historical perspective of Mexican emigration to the United States. Because output and factor markets are linked together, a general equilibrium model of immigration and trade is investigated in section two for possible predictions about the long-run economic effects of significant immigration of low-skilled labor to the United States.[4] Immigration and trade policies seem unlikely to be truly exogenous or independent. Section three presents a model of joint determination of endogenous immigration and trade policies. The final section contains policy recommendations.

Mexican Emigration

Temporary and permanent illegal labor flows from Mexico to the United States have become large especially during the 1970s and 1980s. Before 1921, permanent legal U.S. immigration was largely unrestricted (see chapter appendix). The United States had a large endowment of land, timber, and other natural resources that were undeveloped, and labor to develop these resources was relatively scarce.[5] Furthermore, a variety of policies had been established during the colonial era to attract and bring people to America— policies such as low-priced or free land, ownership of slaves, indenture as servants in return for the cost of the trip, and religious freedom.

The United States chose at an early date to invest in the schooling of its people, beginning with public schools in the East. Public lands then were set aside to help establish and support public elementary schools in the Midwest and West,[6] to provide a basic elementary education for rural people. A basic education was necessary for starting the transformation of unskilled to skilled labor and for developing the skills required to process information in a changing economic environment.

Concern for the wage-depressing effects of large numbers of low-skilled workers led Congress to end unrestricted permanent U.S. immigration in 1921. Small nation-specific immigration quotas were established for non-Western hemisphere countries.[7] These quotas were based on national origins of the then-current U.S. population. This policy changed the ethnic mix of immigrants during the post-1921 period from what it had been during 1901-1920, when relatively large numbers of southern and eastern Europeans were emigrating. The new policy tended to preserve the northwestern European ethnic mix of the pre-1900 U.S. population. Canada, Mexico, and the West Indies, which are Western hemisphere countries, also became major sources of emigrants during the later period (see Table 8.1).

Temporary or nonimmigrant worker programs first became important sources of labor in the 1940s for meeting seasonal or other temporary increases in the demand for U.S. labor.[8] World War II brought a dramatic increase in the total demand for labor in the United States, and the Bracero program was established to bring Mexican workers to the United States during the 1942-1965 period.[9] This program was the largest legal immigrant program for temporary workers ever set up by the United States; it permitted Mexicans to enter the United States temporarily to work in agriculture, and to be exempt from social security and income taxes. The expected earning prospects were so attractive that an excess supply of Mexicans wanted to participate in the program, and bribes to Mexican officials were frequently used by prospective migrants as a means of rising nearer the head of the list of eligible individuals.

TABLE 8.1
U.S. Immigration by Country of Origin, for Selected Periods from 1820 to 1977[a] (percentages in parentheses)

Countries	Years				
	1971-1977	1921-1970	1901-1920	1820-1900	1820-1977
Germany[b]	53,086 (1.8)	1,421,399 (12.4)	485,443 (3.3)	5,010,248 (26.2)	6,970,176 (14.5)
Italy	110,900 (3.8)	980,606 (8.5)	3,155,401 (21.7)	1,040,479 (5.4)	5,287,386 (11.0)
Great Britain	89,927 (3.1)	896,709 (7.8)	867,358 (6.0)	3,028,151 (15.8)	4,882,145 (10.2)
Ireland	8,753 (0.3)	355,518 (3.1)	485,246 (3.3)	3,873,104 (20.3)	4,722,621 (9.8)
Austria-Hungary[c]	12,643 (0.4)	233,066 (2.0)	3,041,608 (20.9)	1,027,195 (5.4)	4,314,512 (9.0)
Canada	112,654 (3.9)	1,996,022 (17.3)	921,411 (6.3)	1,051,275 (5.5)	4,081,362 (8.5)
USSR	21,822 (0.8)	66,566 (0.6)	2,518,507 (17.3)	761,728 (4.0)	3,368,637 (7.0)
Mexico	438,454 (15.1)	1,295,943 (11.3)	268,646 (1.8)	28,008 (0.1)	2,031,046 (4.2)
West Indies	509,084 (17.5)	733,430 (6.4)	230,972 (1.6)	125,598 (0.7)	1,599,084 (3.3)
Sweden[d]	4,355 (0.2)	150,687 (1.3)	344,608 (2.4)	807,760[b] (4.2)	1,271,281 (2.6)
Japan	36,554 (1.3)	123,203 (1.1)	213,634 (1.5)	28,547 (0.1)	401,938 (0.8)
Others	1,502,653 (51.8)	3,254,686 (28.3)	1,998,363 (13.8)	2,341,518 (12.2)	9,133,335 (19.0)
Total	2,900,885 (0.23)[e]	11,507,835 (0.15)	14,531,197 (0.78)	19,123,606 (0.66)	48,063,523

a. For the period 1820-1867, numbers are "passengers arrived"; 1886-1891 and 1895-1897, "immigrant aliens arrived"; 1892-1894 and 1898 to present, "immigrant aliens admitted." Data before 1906 relate to country from which alien came; thereafter, to last country of permanent residence.
b. Austria is included with Germany from 1838 through 1945.
c. Data for Austria-Hungary not reported until 1861. Austria is included with Germany from 1838 through 1945.
d. Includes a few immigrants from Norway for 1820-1860.
e. New immigrants annually as percentage of total population.

Source: U.S. Department of Justice, Annual Report of the Immigration and Naturalization Service (Washington, D.C.: Immigration and Naturalization Service, 1978).

When the Bracero program ended in 1964, Mexicans did not have legal means for obtaining temporary access to the U.S. labor market. Some of the demand for labor in the United States was successfully replaced by mechanization, so that significantly less low-skill or unskilled labor was required to produce goods and services. For example, the tomato harvester was perfected and quickly adopted by California processed tomato producers, largely in response to the anticipated rise in wage rates caused by the termination of the Bracero program.[10] Some other industries, such as fresh fruit and vegetable production, could not easily mechanize given current technology, and they continued to need low-cost, unskilled labor to produce competitively.

Illegal immigration can be viewed as an uncontrolled international worker program.[11] During the post-1965 period, only a few Mexican workers have qualified for entry into the U.S. labor market under legal (H-2) temporary worker programs.[12] At the prevailing U.S. wage rate for low-skill and unskilled workers, large numbers of Mexican workers have voluntarily entered the United States illegally to obtain work, and U.S. emloyers have voluntarily hired them. A relatively large share of these illegal workers seem to enter the United States temporarily, work part of a year at seasonal jobs, and then return to Mexico for the balance of the year to be employed or unemployed. Other individuals enter illegally and obtain more-or-less permanent jobs and try to stay in the United States. No hard data exists on the number of permanent or temporary illegal immigrants.

The main reason that Mexicans are willing to risk illegal entry into the United States seeking jobs is that real wage rates, even minimum wage rates, have been five or more times greater in the United States than in Mexico (see Tables 8.2 and 8.3). Thus, Mexicans can work in the United States at a wage rate that is below what domestic U.S. workers would voluntarily accept, but still receive a wage rate that greatly exceeds Mexican rates. Furthermore, the U.S. unemployment rate has generally been much lower than the Mexican rate.

To increase the probability of successfully crossing the U.S.-Mexican border and finding a job quickly, Mexicans frequently pay for border crossing and employment assistance.[13] U.S. employers are willing to hire Mexicans because (1) the Mexicans will work for a lower wage, (2) they place less emphasis on nonwage aspects of jobs, and (3) the employers bear no penalty for being identified as employers of illegal aliens.

A large proportion of Mexicans attempting to obtain temporary employment in the United States are successful in entering the United States and in finding work. About half are employed in U.S. agriculture, as Ranney and Kossoudji point out. Their recent study[14] reports results from a 1978 special national survey of return migrants. In this survey, 94.5 percent of the Mexican temporary migrants to the United States were noncommuters and 90.6 percent of them were males. Eighty-nine percent of the males and 65 percent of the females were illegal entrants to the United States. However, only 29 percent of the noncommuters were apprehended at least once by the U.S. Immigration and Naturalization Service. (A maximum of 2 percent were apprehended and returned to Mexico three to five times.) About 4 percent came to the United States seeking work but did not obtain it. Fifty percent of the noncommuters paid for assistance in crossing the U.S.-Mexican border. All in all, Mexicans seeking temporary employment in the United States seem to have adopted a fairly effective strategy.

Among male noncommuting temporary migrants, the level of schooling was relatively low (with a mean of 4.2 years) and 52 percent were employed in U.S. agriculture as farm workers. On the average they spent 144 days (40 percent of a year) in the United States during 1978, were employed 92 percent of these days, and earned about $25 per day. Thus, employment in U.S. agriculture continues to be a very important source of work for Mexican males seeking temporary employment in the United States. Only 3 percent of the noncommuting females were employed in U.S. agriculture during 1978 (69 percent of them were employed as private household workers).

Vegetable and horticulture farms are believed to be the largest employers of illegal workers in U.S. agriculture. Labor expenses are 50 percent or more of the production costs for vegetables, melons, fruits and nuts, and horticultural specialities, and production of these crops has a large seasonal demand component that is generally associated with harvesting the crop. States leading in the expenditures on hired and contract labor for vegetable and horticultural crops are California and Florida, with 58 percent of the total in 1978. States of lesser importance are Washington, Pennsylvania, New York, Michigan, Texas, Oregon, Arizona, and Ohio.[15] These ten states produced about 80 percent of U.S. vegetable and horticultural crops in 1978. Some other states also have small vegetable and horticulture producing areas that employ significant numbers of seasonal hired laborers. These employers include apple producers in western Maryland, northern Virginia, and eastern West Virginia; peach producers in the Spartanburg area of South Carolina; and vegetable and horticultural specialty crop producers in Colorado.[16] Thus, seasonal or temporary illegal immigrants (rather than permanent illegal immigrants) seem likely to be the main source of low-skilled labor for producing labor-intensive U.S. agricultural crops.

Illegal Mexican immigrants are also employed in nonagricultural jobs. The survey of return migrants illustrates that the important secondary occupations of employment for temporary Mexican migrants in 1978 were, for males, craft work, nonfarm labor, and public service work, and for females, operators of various processes and equipment, exclusive of transportation. Although hard data on employment of permanent illegal Mexican immigrants do not exist, their occupational employment pattern seems to be concentrated in the nonfarm low-skilled occupations.

Permitting Mexicans to continue to enter the United States temporarily to obtain jobs that have a seasonal nature or a finite term seems likely to create a minimum of social problems, especially during periods of economic growth. Such has been the experience of western European and South

TABLE 8.2
A Summary of Macroeconomic Indicators—Real Output, Investment, Population,
Labor Force, Wage Rates, and Price Levels—for the United States, 1950–1980

Indicator	1950	1955	1960	1965	1970	1975	1980
GNP:							
Current ($ billions)	286.5	400.0	506.5	691.1	992.7	1,549.2	2,626.1
Real (1972 = 100)	534.8	657.5	737.2	929.3	1,085.6	1,233.9	1,480.7
Decade growth rate of real GNP (%)	41.3	22.9	46.3	31.1	25.6	36.5	
Population:							
Total	152.3	166.0	180.7	194.6	204.9	216.0	227.7
Decade growth rate (%)	17.2	17.0	14.8	10.3	10.5	10.6	
Labor Force:							
Decade growth rate (%)	8.9	13.7	13.4	21.2	25.0	26.3	
Participation rate (%)	40.9	39.1	38.5	38.3	40.4	43.9	48.0
Engaged in agric. (%)	11.2	9.9	7.6	5.7	4.0	3.8	3.1
Engaged in mfg. (%)	23.9		23.3	23.4	22.5	19.4	
Unemployment rate (%)	5.3	4.4	5.5	4.5	4.9	8.5	7.1
GNP per capita:							
$/person	1,881	2,310	2,803	3,551	4,845	7,172	11,533
Real (1972 = 100)	3,511	3,961	4,080	4,775	5,298	5,713	6,503
Decade growth rate of real GNP (%)	24.1	5.9	31.5	20.8	15.1	25.9	
Consumer Price Index:							
1967 = 100	72.1	80.2	88.7	94.5	116.3	161.2	246.8
Decade rate of change (%)	21.3	20.1	12.7	41.5	65.3	85.2	
Wage Rates:							
Mfg. (prod., $/hr)	1.44	1.86	2.61	3.35	3.35	4.83	7.27
Real (1967 = 100)	1.99	2.32	2.76	2.88	2.88	3.00	2.95
Agr. ($/hr)	0.58	0.72	1.01	1.51	1.51	2.25	3.37
Real (1967 = 100)	0.81	0.89	1.30	1.30	1.30	1.40	1.36

Investment:						
Domestic:						
Gross fixed capital formation ($ billions)	47.3	61.4	71.3	106.6	137.0	213.0	401.2
Ratio to GNP (%)	16.5	15.4	14.1	15.4	13.8	13.7	15.3
Direct foreign in U.S. ($ billions)[a]	0.320	0.282	0.315	0.415	1.464	2.54	10.64
Other private long-term (approx.) ($ billions)	0.180	−0.193	0.289	−0.328	3.302	0.44	1.98[b]
Foreign:						
Direct foreign outside U.S. ($ billions)	1.145	1.677	2.653	5.010	7.358	13.73	18.21
Other private long-term ($ billions)[a]	0.571	−0.062	0.910	0.759	1.102	6.02	3.66[b]

a. Private sector securities—corporate bonds and equities, net new issue and outstanding.
b. For 1979.

Sources: Economic Report to the President (Washington, D.C.: Executive Office of the President, 1982); Handbook of Labor Statistics (Washington, D.C.: U.S. Department of Labor, 1980); International Financial Statistics and Balance of Payment Statistics (Washington, D.C.: International Monetary Fund, various issues).

TABLE 8.3
A Summary of Macroeconomic Indicators—Real Output, Investment, Population,
Labor Force, Wage Rates, and Price Levels—Mexico, 1950-1980

Indicator	1950	1955	1960	1965	1970	1975	1980
GNP:							
Current (billions of pesos)	53.0[a]	88.2	155.9	252.0	418.7	988.3	4,159.3[b]
Real (1975 = 100)	129.6[a]	215.0	381.1	537.6	751.0	988.3	1,207.6[b]
Decade growth rate of real GNP (%)		126.5	114.5	68.8	66.9	54.9	40.1
Population:							
Total	25.8	30.01	36.05	42.69	50.69	60.15	71.91[b]
Decade growth rate (%)		30.2	36.7	33.8	34.4	34.2	35.7
Labor Force:							
Decade growth rate (%)		30.6	30.6	13.4	13.4	24.8	24.8
Participation rate (%)	32.3		31.4		25.6	27.6	28.3[b]
Engaged in agric. (%)	57.8		54.2		39.5	40.9	40.1[b]
Engaged in mfg. (%)	11.6		13.7		16.7	17.8	18.2[b]
GNP per capita:							
Pesos/person	1,574	2,940	4,325	5,903	8,260	16,431	57,840
US $/person	325	235	346	472	661	1,314	2,520
Real (1975 = 100)	5,023	7,164	10,571	12,593	14,618	16,431	16,793
Decade growth rate of real GNP (%)		71.0	77.8	35.0	29.8	23.4	4.4
Consumer Price Index:							
1967 = 100[c]	40.9	63.7	84.9	93.1	111.0	169.2	514.2
Decade rate of change (%)		88.6	57.5	18.4	35.2	113.9	192.7
Wage Rates:							
Mfg. (pesos/mo.)[d]	194[a]	268	402	656	807	1,617	3,654
(US $/mo.)	16	21	32	52	65	129	159
Real (pesos/mo. at 1967 = 100)	474	421	473	705	727	824	711
Agric. (pesos/day)	—	—	—	16.5	26.2	50.1	135.0
(US $/day)	—	—	—	1.32	2.09	4.08	5.88
Real (1967 = 100)	—	—	—	17.72	23.6	25.53	26.25

Investment:
Domestic:
Gross fixed capital formation (billions of pesos)	4.8	12.6	23.2	44.2	82.3	211.7	1,032.9
Ratio of GDP (%)	11.8	14.3	14.9	17.5	19.7	22.4	24.8[b]
Direct foreign in Mexico (billions of pesos)	0.422	1.34	1.725	2.038	4.038	7.619	15.44
Other private long-term[e] (billions of pesos)	–	0.050	0.138	0.25	1.815	4.523–	.4.39[b]
Exchange rate (pesos/US $)	4.854	12.50	12.50	12.50	12.5	12.5	12.5

a. Data for 1951 used for 1950.
b. Data for 1979 used for 1980.
c. Covers only food, clothing, utilities, and household goods in Mexico City before 1969.
d. Monthly earnings.
e. Net long-term loans received.

Sources: International Financial Statistics and Balance of Payments Statistics (Washington, D.C.: International Monetary Fund, 1981 and other issues); Handbook of Labor Statistics (Washington, D.C.: U.S. Department of Labor, 1980).

American countries. Europe had a guest-worker program during 1960-1974 that permitted large numbers of individuals from southern European countries and northern Africa to work in northern European countries, especially in Germany, Switzerland, and France.[17] Both workers from the European Economic Community (EEC) and other countries were eligible; however, under an EEC treaty, EEC workers had a privileged status. In West Germany, France, and Switzerland, the work-permit system restricted the type and location of work that aliens could take, but they could work for up to ten years and change employers. In addition, these individuals received greater political and economic privileges as they accumulated years of continuous residency.[18] Guest workers became a significant share of the labor force in these countries by the mid-1960s, and in the case of Switzerland, guest workers comprised 30 percent of the work force by 1964.

In 1973, when the first significant economic recession occurred since initiation of the guest-worker programs, serious problems developed in Germany and France because of conflicts between guest workers and native residents. Guest workers demonstrated in France and struck in Germany. Guest-worker programs were ended in 1974, but guest-worker permits could not be withdrawn from workers with five years of residency in a country. Host countries could not send many of the alien workers home, and voluntary repatriation has been slow. It is estimated that Germany and France had a 6-8 percent permanent increase in population due to the guest-worker program, and Switzerland had a 25 percent increase.[19] Workers from EEC member countries continue to have relatively unrestricted access to labor markets in other EEC countries.

Although some seasonal worker programs have been established in Europe since 1974, they have not functioned very well. The workers have been given contracts for less than one year, they can take only "temporary jobs," and they cannot bring families. Frequently, temporary workers have been rotated through permanent jobs, but it is very difficult to terminate a worker when a job does not end with his termination.[20]

Since the termination of the guest-worker program, illegal immigration has become a serious problem in some European countries. A significant quantity of illegal alien labor is being employed in Germany and France.[21] Although employer sanctions—fines or prison terms—have been imposed in all EEC countries except Great Britain, employment of illegal aliens has not stopped. Switzerland and Germany have rejected adjustments of legal status for illegal aliens, but the Netherlands, Great Britain, Belgium, and France have sometimes given amnesty.

In summary, the United States and several western European countries that have tried to restrict immigration have similar illegal immigration experiences, whereas more geographically isolated but equally advanced countries such as Japan, Canada, and Australia have minimal problems with illegal immigration. The higher-income South American countries of Venezuela and Argentina have chosen to have a relatively open policy toward temporary immigration, and illegal immigration seems to be a minor problem for them.

A General Equilibrium Approach to Immigration

Although migration or immigration is frequently analyzed in a partial-equilibrium framework, this approach ignores important interrelationships between input and output markets. Because labor and other inputs are employed to produce commodities demanded ultimately by domestic and foreign consumers, domestic and international commodity and factor markets are linked together in a general-equilibrium framework.[22] These linkages are important when migration or immigration represents a significant change in the size of the population and labor force of a country and adjustments are made to these changes. Also, immigration policy and costs affect patterns of commodity trade and income distribution; and tariff, quota, and transport cost policies affect the incentives for immigration and migration.

Jones' three-factor, two-commodity, two-country trade model[23] seems to fit the description of the economic situation between the United States and Mexico better than the standard 2 × 2 × 2 Hechscher-Ohlin-Samuelson (HOS) model. Three strands of thought are central to the choice: (1) Mexico, a developing economy, has a large primary sector, and trade in primary commodities cannot easily be explained by the endowment of labor and capital;[24] (2) Mexican immigrants to the United States are largely unskilled, while the U.S. nonimmigrant labor force consists mainly of skilled labor; and (3) given the large intercountry factor-endowment differences, a model permitting complete specialization rather than complete factor-price equalization seems reasonable.

Jones[25] developed a three-factor, two-commodity model of trade that can be adapted to these aspects of reality. The distinctive features of Jones' model is that each commodity requires only two factors of production as inputs; one factor is specific to each sector, and one factor is mobile between the two sectors. The assumptions for the U.S.-Mexican analysis are as follows: the three inputs are designated as unskilled labor (U), skilled labor (S), and capital (K); and the two sectors are a primary sector, like agriculture, producing a commodity designated by (A), and a nonprimary sector, like high-technology manufacturing, producing manufactured goods designated by (M). Skilled and unskilled labor are commodity- and sector-specific inputs. Unskilled labor and capital are the variable inputs for producing A, and skilled labor and capital are the variable inputs for producing M.[26] Strong assumptions are that capital has intersectoral national mobility, but it is internationally immobile,[27] and labor, both skilled and unskilled, is internationally mobile but it is not intersectorally mobile.[28] Additional assumptions include constant returns to scale in production, competition in commodity and input markets, common intercountry production technologies, and full employment.

For given (international) prices of commodities A and M, an equilibrium is described by the following conditions: (1) equality of the rental rate on capital between the two sectors; (2) full employment of all three factors of production, with the services of skilled and unskilled labor valued at their

FIGURE 8.1
An Isocost, Isoquant Relationship in a Three-Factor (U, S, K), Two-Commodity (A, M) Trade Model

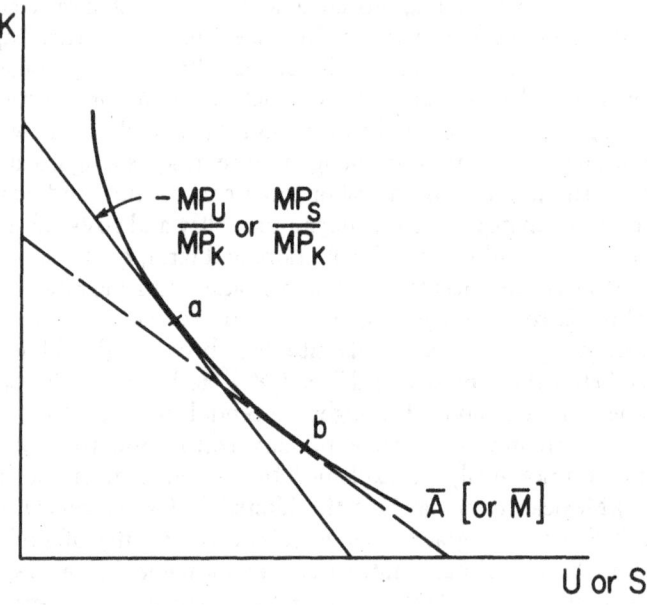

marginal product, and (3) competition among cost-minimizing firms within each sector. Unlike the 2 × 2 HOS model, factor rewards are neither independent of factor endowments nor determined solely by output prices.

For a given quantity of capital services, the rental rate on capital will be higher in this model when the endowment of either unskilled or skilled labor is larger, holding the other sectorally specific factor constant (see Figure 8.1). For a given quantity of unskilled [skilled] labor, the fraction of capital employed in the primary sector (agriculture) will be large [small], when the quantity of available skilled [unskilled] labor is small. These results follow from the assumptions of sectoral capital mobility and competitive factor rewards. If the quantity of unskilled or skilled labor increases, the marginal product of capital in the sector experiencing the increase must rise. Maintenance of capital rental-rate equality between sectors thereby implies that some capital must move from the other sector. With a given amount of the sectorally specific factor, this observation implies a lower wage for labor as well as reduced output in the sector that is losing capital.

If a country has no skilled labor, none of M is produced, all capital is employed in the primary (agricultural) sector, and the rental on capital will be determined by the capital-unskilled labor ratio formed by the national endowments of these two inputs (Figure 8.1). A transformation curve of OT_1 is implied in Figure 8.2. Presumably some primary (agricultural) products would be exported for other (manufactured) products. If skilled labor is obtained, capital must move from the primary (agricultural) sector to the

FIGURE 8.2
A Three-Factor (U, S, K), Two-Commodity (A, M) General Equilibrium Model

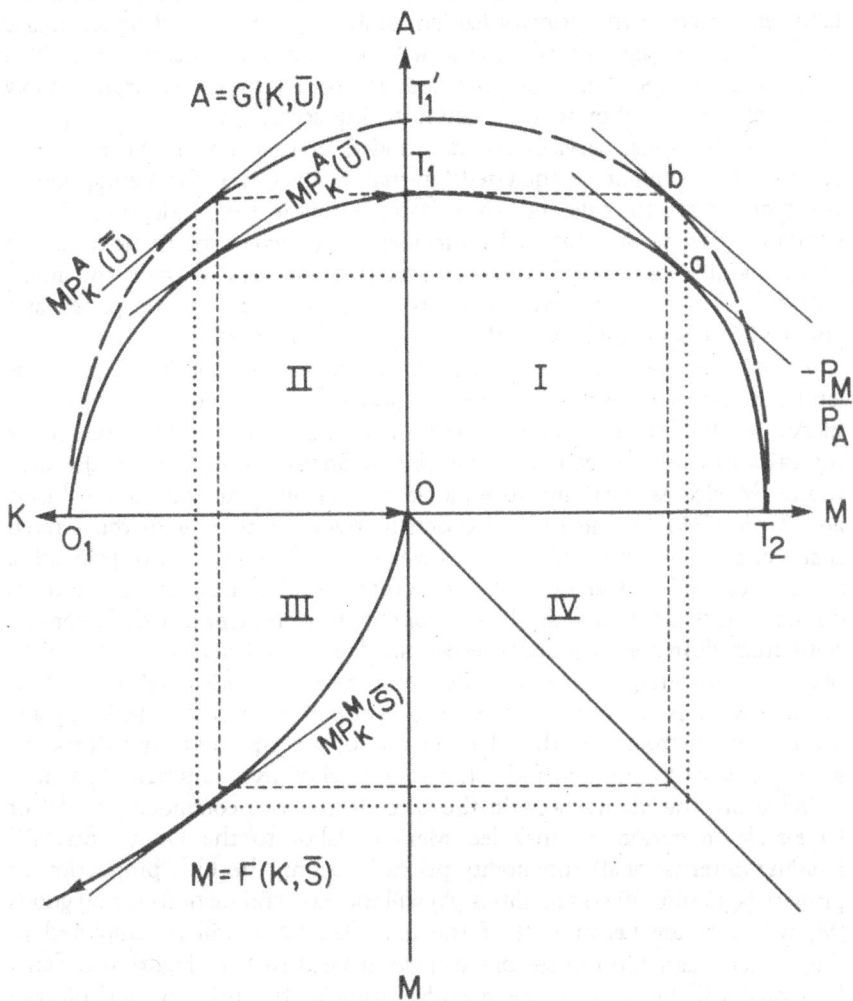

manufacturing sector in order to keep the rental rate on capital equal in the two sectors. The product transformation curve shifts from OT_1 to T_1T_2 when skilled labor becomes available. When capital is transferred to the manufacturing sector from the primary (agricultural) sector, the return to capital must rise because the capital-to-unskilled labor ratio declines in the primary sector.

Once a manufacturing sector is established, further increases in available skilled labor imply a rise in the ratio of capital rental to the skilled wage, a fall in the wage for unskilled labor in the primary (agricultural) sector, and a reduction in the production of primary (agricultural) goods, given that the same quantity of unskilled labor is combined with less capital. Thus, the size of the primary (agricultural) sector must shrink as the quantity of skilled labor increases. If skilled labor is obtained by investing in unskilled labor employed in the primary (agricultural) sector, the resulting shrinkage of the primary (agricultural) sector will be even faster because unskilled labor is being removed from the primary (agricultural) sector to supply additional skilled labor to the manufacturing sector.

Although capital services are not traded in this model, the return to capital services might be equalized internationally. Given the assumption of constant returns to scale and two variable inputs in the production of each commodity, these international returns are equal when international prices of commodities and wage rates are equalized. Barriers to trade and international labor mobility make equality of international factor prices and commodity prices unlikely in this three-factor model.[29]

A large increase in Mexican exports of unskilled-labor–intensive goods (and imports of skilled-labor–intensive goods) would reduce the economic incentives for Mexican immigration of unskilled labor. However, large increases in trade, at least with the United States, are unlikely in the near future. Mexico is unwilling to endorse the General Agreement on Tariffs and Trade (GATT). Mexico's approach to trade relations with the United States and other developed countries seems to be based upon two principles: (1) unquestioned sovereignty of its natural development policies and (2) claimed entitlement as a developing country to nonreciprocal trade concessions from developed countries, especially the United States.[30] The United States is unwilling to remove its countervailing duties against certain inexpensive Mexican commodities because of perceived unfair Mexican trade practices.[31] Furthermore, the Mexican economy seems unlikely to produce large increases in the demand for domestic labor from internal growth.

What are the implications in the three-factor, two-commodity model of large-scale migration of unskilled Mexican labor to the United States?[32] Holding (international) commodity prices constant, the U.S. production of primary (agricultural) commodities (A) will increase and manufacturing goods (M) will decrease because all of the unskilled labor will be employed in the primary (agricultural) sector—a move from a to b in Figure 8.2, Panel I. Capital will move from the manufacturing to the primary (agricultural) sector, the U.S. wage rates for unskilled *and* skilled labor will decline, and the marginal product of capital will increase. The reasoning is as follows. The increase in the available (and assumed to be employed) unskilled labor lowers the U.S. capital-to-unskilled labor ratio in the primary (agricultural) sector, thereby lowering the marginal product and wage for unskilled labor and raising the marginal product of capital. To equalize the marginal returns to capital in the two sectors, capital, the sectorally mobile input, must be transferred to the primary (agricultural) sector from the manufacturing sector. This transfer lowers the ratio of capital to skilled labor in the manufacturing sector, which reduces the U.S. wage for skilled labor, given the full employment assumption. The net result is that the U.S. wage rate for unskilled labor falls by a larger percentage than the wage for skilled labor, so the relative wage of skilled labor versus unskilled labor rises.[33]

The story does not end here, however, because the increased production of primary (agricultural) goods and the decrease in manufacturing goods may not match changes in the quantities demanded of these commodities. The relative output prices may need to change. For the quantitites of A and M represented by point b in Figure 8.1 to be a new equilibrium, an income elasticity of demand for primary (agricultural) goods larger than 1 is required. Empirical studies suggest that this is not the case.[34] Thus, the relative price of primary (agricultural) goods must decline. In turn, the production of primary (agricultural) goods must decrease and of manufacturing goods must increase. This change can be accommodated by transferring some of the units of capital from the primary (agricultural) sector back to the manufacturing sector. The capital-to-unskilled labor ratio declines, causing a further decline in the wage rate of unskilled labor. The capital-to-skilled labor ratio rises, raising the wage of skilled labor. The net effect of the return to capital is ambiguous.

If individuals specialize in factor ownership (skilled labor, unskilled labor, or capital), and domestic and foreign laborers of a given skill type have the same preferences for consumption goods, these second-round adjustments make unskilled U.S. domestic labor worse off. The percentage decline in the unskilled wage exceeds the percentage decline in the price of primary (agricultural) goods, and the price of manufacturing goods has risen. U.S. skilled workers may be better off because their wage has risen and the price of primary (agricultural) goods has fallen; however, the rise in the price of manufactured goods must be weighed against these gains. If skilled workers have a high income elasticity of demand for primary (agricultural) goods, the likelihood of them being made better off in terms of purchasing power over final goods increases. The U.S. owners of capital may lose some of their initial gains, but they show a net gain in purchasing power over final goods, caused by the immigration of unskilled laborers. Thus, U.S. owners of capital are the big winners, U.S. skilled laborers may be small winners, and unskilled U.S. domestic laborers are the major losers from immigration of unskilled labor. These conclusions would be modified, however, if the immigration of unskilled labor increases the rate at which investments are made to convert unskilled into skilled labor, or if immigrant labor also brings capital.

When Mexico temporarily exports part of its labor force to the United States, its trade policy may affect both its citizens who remain at home and those who emigrate to the United States. If the United States adds protection against Mexican producers for U.S. producers of primary (agricultural) products such as fresh winter vegetables and fruits, the tendency will be for the welfare of the nonemigrating Mexican population to decline. However, the Mexicans who emigrate temporarily to the United States to work for U.S. fresh fruit and vegetables farmers are made better off by U.S. protection of its own producers. Thus, the U.S. protection against fresh winter fruits and vegetables from Mexico might improve—overall—the welfare of Mexican workers, both immigrants and nonimmigrants.[35]

Even when U.S. producers of fresh winter fruit and vegetables fail to obtain direct protection from Mexican imports,[36] they are aided indirectly by a lax policy of illegal immigration that reduces their costs of production from what these costs otherwise would be. Moreover, the nationality of immigrants and the nation of origin for imports of goods frequently differ. For example, U.S. textile firms may be employing low-skilled immigrant labor from Mexico and facing strong competition in the U.S. textile market from Taiwan, Sri Lanka, or China. Tightening immigration restrictions will make U.S. producers of these products less competitive.

Endogenous Immigration and Trade Policies

There is a growing belief among economists that government policy is not exogenously determined. In the past, formation and enforcement of governmental policies were viewed as a costless process with socially benevolent outcomes.[37] More recently, government officials have been treated as being captured by the interest groups that they attempt to regulate. Thus, government policies are frequently diverted to promoting the private interests of one group rather than the public interest. Furthermore, theories of competitive interest or pressure groups now treat policy outcomes as the result of continuous struggles between affected groups; policy is a compromise among the competing interest groups[38] and does not in general reflect perfectly the interests of any one of the competing groups.

The new view of public policy is important for two reasons, when attention is focused upon U.S.-Mexican immigration and trade. First, public policy outcomes dealing with immigration and trade are behavioral relationships, which need further research. Second, a large proportion of immigration from Mexico to the United States is illegal. The only hard data on illegal immigration are the U.S. Immigration and Naturalization Service's (INS) data on illegal aliens apprehended. But apprehended aliens are not a random sample of illegal aliens present in the United States. The apprehended aliens are, on the average, younger, less experienced, and working in occupations where detection is relatively easy. Furthermore, the relationship between the number of illegal aliens apprehended and the number of illegals present is unlikely to be a fixed proportion over time. The resources and technology of INS enforcement change, and illegal aliens become more experienced and efficient in evading INS officials. Thus, to improve policy analysis of U.S.-Mexican immigration and trade, the number of illegal aliens apprehended must be linked in a behavioral relationship to the number of illegal aliens present in the United States.[39]

Because U.S.-Mexican trade and immigration policies have factor and output market effects, public determination of these policies should be considered jointly. Consider a political-economic model of endogenous immigration and trade policies. Immigration policy includes the passage and enforcement of immigration legislation. More restrictive legislation and stronger enforcement of given legislation will provide welfare gains to U.S. domestic low-skilled workers and welfare losses to U.S. capital owners. Nontariff, rather than tariff, trade barriers are considered because countries that have endorsed GATT cannot raise tariffs. Nontariff trade barriers, such as minimum quality, size, and special packaging requirements reduce trade and can be converted into tariff equivalents. Higher trade barriers against Mexican primary (agricultural) goods bestow gains on some U.S. groups at the expense of losses by other groups.[40]

U.S. policy on trade barriers and immigration is determined by one or more U.S. government agencies. Let us assume for simplicity that U.S. policies are determined by the president, and competing interest groups are formed to achieve benefits or to mitigate losses from the political process. The president can be expected to weigh the gains and losses of these interest groups when he considers changing policies, because he needs political support to remain in office, to get re-elected, and to obtain funds for policy enforcement efforts.

The president is assumed to choose trade and immigration policies that maximize his expected political support from affected groups.[41] Thus, politically optimal trade and immigration policies must meet the joint criteria that (1) the marginal expected gain in political support from beneficiaries of higher nontariff trade barriers equals or exceeds the marginal expected loss of political support from losers, and (2) the marginal expected gain in political support from beneficiaries of a more restrictive immigration policy equals or exceeds the marginal expected loss of political support from those adversely affected by the policy. Thus, politically optimal policies depend on the characteristics of beneficiaries and losers under both policies.

Some Policy Recommendations

The Pacific Basin countries, as well as others, would benefit from a coordinated migrant or immigrant labor policy. The national boundaries of countries are not insurmountable walls, and it is very expensive for countries to police their borders effectively when large economic incentives exist for people to leave or to enter the countries. Furthermore, trade, foreign capital, exchange rate, and macroeconomic policies may not be adjusted to improve the problem. A pragmatic view is that people will find ways of crossing borders, especially when large wage differences exist between countries that share a common border. In such cases, the affected countries need to cooperate so that economically important issues do not become a politically sensitive problem.

Two main issues must be addressed. First, will aliens be admitted (or permitted to leave) for work on a temporary or a permanent basis, and second, will preferential treatment be granted to workers with particular skills, or citizens of adjoining countries, and so on? If a country does not want to have its emigrant or immigrant-worker policy change the permanent size of its population, then the program must be structured so that there are built-in incentives for workers to return home on a regular basis. Workers might be permitted to leave, or admitted, for periods of one year or less and be required to return home at the end of that period. This policy is facilitated when aliens have access to (or are permitted to take) seasonal or temporary jobs only, and when political-social rights do not change with length of tenure in a foreign country.

If a country wants to expand or to restrict the permanent size of its population and work force, then the program should be structured so that there are built-in economic incentives for immigrants to come or emigrants to leave and obtain permanent residence. This policy is facilitated when workers may take jobs in a foreign country for longer periods of time than a year and when their political-social rights increase, or decrease, with tenure in the foreign country.

Furthermore, it seems acceptable for countries to have either a temporary or permanent immigrant or emigrant program, provided that basic human rights are guaranteed and individuals are informed about their eligibility for gain or liability for loss of political-social benefits. Then prospective immigrants can weigh the net advantage (income plus non-income benefits) of working and living in different international locations. However, one can reasonably expect that the economic cost of obtaining this information and moving from one country to another will be lower on the average for individuals moving between countries with common borders. Thus, it seems pragmatic to grant preferential treatment to alien workers who are citizens or permanent residents of adjacent countries. Finally, preferences might also be granted to individuals in general who have skills.

Acknowledgments

Ed Schuh, Steve Torok, Chiho Kim, and Robert Coltrane provided comments on an earlier draft of this paper. Financial assistance is acknowledged from the U.S. Department of Agriculture, Economic Development Division, and the Iowa Agricultural and Home Economics Experiment Station. (Journal Paper No. J-11961 of the Iowa Agricultural and Home Economics Experiment Station, Ames, Iowa. Project No. 2590.)

Notes

1. U.S. Congress, Committees on the Judiciary, House of Representatives and Senate, *U.S. Immigration Policy and the National Interest*. Joint Committee Print No. 8, 97th Congress, August 1981.

2. Mary M. Kritz, "International Migration Patterns in the Caribbean Basin: An Overview"; Adriana Marshall, "Structural Trends in International Labor Migration: The Southern Cone of Latin America"; and Jerry Zubrzycki, "International Migration in Australasia and the South Pacific," all in *Global Trends in Migration*, ed. Mary M. Kritz et al. (New York: N.Y. Center for Migration Studies, 1981).

3. Mexicans also come to the United States seeking nonwage benefits (e.g., U.S. citizenship for children born in the United States, and access to social programs).

4. Other perspectives on trade are presented by Jagdish M. Bhagwati and T. N. Srinivasan, "On the Choice Between Capital and Labor Mobility," *Journal of International Economics* 14(3 and 4), 1983:209-221; Robert E. B. Lucas, "International Migration: Economic Causes, Consequences and Evaluation," in *Global Trends in Migration*, ed. Mary M. Kritz et al. (New York: N.Y. Center for Migration Studies, 1981); Robert D. Emerson, "Trade in Products and International Migration in Seasonal Labor Markets," *American Journal of Agricultural Economics* 64 (May 1982):339-346; Wallace E. Huffman, "International Trade in Labor versus Commodities: U.S.-Mexican Agriculture," *American Journal of Agricultural Economics* 64 (December 1982):989-998; and Steven J. Torok and Wallace E. Huffman, "U.S.-Mexican Trade in Winter Vegetables and Illegal Immigration," Department of Economics, Iowa State University, October 1984.

5. Willard W. Cochrane, *The Development of American Agriculture: A Historical Analysis* (Minneapolis: University of Minnesota Press, 1979), and Simon Kuznets, "Two Centuries of Economic Growth: Reflections on U.S. Experiences," *American Economic Review* 67 (February 1977):1-14.

6. Cochrane, *The Development of American Agriculture: A Historical Analysis*.

7. Nation-specific quotas were first imposed on Western hemisphere countries in 1976.

8. Vernon M. Briggs, Jr., "Nonimmigrant Labor Policy: Future Trend or Aberration?" in *The Unavoidable Issue: U.S. Immigration Policy in the 1980s*, ed. Demetrious G. Papademetriou and Mark J. Miller (Philadelphia: Institute for the Study of Human Issues, 1983; and Larry C. Morgan and Bruce L. Gardner, "Potential for a U.S. Guest-Worker Program in Agriculture: Lessons from Braceros," in *The Gateway: U.S. Immigration Issues and Policy*, ed. Barry R. Chiswick (Washington, D.C.: American Enterprise Institute for Public Policy Research, 1982).

9. Harry E. Cross and James A. Sandos, *Across the Border* (Berkeley: University of California, Institute of Governmental Studies, 1981).

10. Andrew Schmitz and David Seckler, "Mechanized Agriculture and Social Welfare: The Case of the Tomato Harvester," *American Journal of Agricultural Economics* 52 (November 1970):569-577.

11. Briggs, "Nonimmigrant Labor Policy: Future Trend or Aberration?"

12. Virginia tobacco growers and Arizona citrus producers have used Mexican workers under the H-2 program for the past 4 or 5 years. Also, some Mexicans have been hired under H-2 to herd sheep in several western states for several years. U.S. Congress, *U.S. Immigration Policy and the National Interest*, August 1981.

13. Susan Ranney and Sherrie Kossoudji, "Profiles of Temporary Mexican Labor Migrants to the United States," *Population and Development Review* 9 (September 1983):475-493.

14. Ranney and Kossoudji, "Profiles of Temporary Mexican Labor Migrants to the United States."

15. Robert Coltrane, *Immigration Reform and Agricultural Labor* (Washington, D.C.: U.S. Department of Agriculture, ERS, Agricultural Economic Report No. 510, April 1984).

16. Coltrane, *Immigration Reform and Agricultural Labor*.

17. Mark J. Miller and Demetrios G. Papademetriou, "Immigration Reform: The United States and Western Europe Compared," in *The Unavoidable Issue: U.S. Immigration Policy in the 1980s*, ed. D. G. Papademetriou and M. J. Miller (Philadelphia: Institute for the Study of Human Issues, 1983); and Mark J. Miller and Philip L.

Martin, *Administering Foreign-Worker Programs* (Lexington, Mass.: Lexington Books, 1982).

18. Miller and Martin, *Administering Foreign-Worker Programs*.

19. Miller and Papademetriou, "Immigration Reform: The United States and Western Europe Compared."

20. Miller and Martin, *Administering Foreign-Worker Programs*.

21. Miller and Papademetriou, "Immigration Reform: The United States and Western Europe Compared," and U.S. Congress, *U.S. Immigration Policy and the National Interest*.

22. Jagdish N. Bhagwati, "Shifting Comparative Advantage, Protectionist Demands, and Policy Response Options," paper presented at National Bureau of Economic Research (NBER) Conference on Import Competition and Adjustments: Theory and Policy, Cambridge, Mass., 1980; Jagdish N. Bhagwati and Richard A. Brecker, "National Welfare in an Open Economy in the Presence of Foreign-Owned Factors of Production," *Journal of Interntional Economics* 10 (1980):103–115; and Ronald Findlay and Stanislaw Wellisz, "Endogenous Tariffs, the Political Economy of Trade Restrictions, and Welfare," in *Import Competition and Response*, ed. Jagdish N. Bhagwati (Chicago: Univ. of Chicago Press for National Bureau of Economic Research [NBER], 1982), pp. 223–243.

23. Ronald Jones, "A Three-Factor Model in Theory, Trade and History," in *Trade, Balance of Payments and Growth*, ed. Jagdish N. Bhagwati et al. (Amsterdam: North Holland Publishing Co., 1971), pp. 3–21.

24. Anne Krueger, *Trade and Employment in Developing Countries*, vol. 3 (Chicago: University of Chicago Press for NBER, 1983).

25. Jones, "A Three-Factor Model in Theory, Trade and History."

26. Clearly this model is a major simplification of the real world. Some skilled laborers are employed in the production of primary goods like agricultural goods and some unskilled laborers are employed in the production of other goods. The key issue is relative importance, and applying this criterion, the assumed factor specializations seem reasonable.

27. Mexico has extensive controls on investments by foreigners. Foreigners cannot own farmland, and Mexico has a 51 percent rule on ownership of companies by Mexican nationals. This restriction insures control by Mexican nationals, which increases the risk to foreign ownership. U.S. capital investments in Mexico are encouraged mainly within a twenty-kilometer band adjacent to the U.S.-Mexican border. The Mexican government allows U.S. firms operating in Mexico under the 51 percent Mexican ownership provision to import recognizable parts and equipment duty-free on the condition that the resulting products leave Mexico.

28. Mexico takes no significant measure to deter emigration. The activities of the U.S. Immigration and Naturalization Service do impose barriers to free immigration. However, a large share of the Mexicans who attempt to enter the United States illegally are successful within two attempts. Thus, it is only an approximation to describe the real situation as one where capital is immobile between the United States and Mexico and labor is mobile.

29. Jones, "A Three-Factor Model in Theory, Trade and History."

30. Guy F. Erb, "An American View of Mexican Trade Policy," Overseas Development Council, U.S.-Mexico Project working paper, Series 2, Washington, D.C., April 1982.

31. Andrew J. Samet and Gary C. Hufbauer, "'Unfair' Trade Practices: A Mexican-American Drama," Overseas Development Council, U.S.-Mexico Project working paper, Series 1, Washington, D.C., April 1982.

32. See Bhagwati and Srinivasan, "On the Choice Between Capital and Labor Mobility," for an alternative discussion of welfare effects of international labor (and capital) mobility. Their analysis is applied to the U.S.-Mexican situation.

33. Clearly, a model with different assumptions might yield different results.

34. Food and Agriculture Organization, *Agricultural Commodity Projections for 1970: FAO Commodity Review, Special Supplement* (Rome: Food and Agriculture Organization, 1962).

35. See Jagdish N. Bhagwati and R. Rivera-Batiz, "Protection in the Presence of Immigrant Workers and the Sending Country's Welfare: Some Paradoxes," Massachusetts Institute of Technology, Cambridge, Mass., 1980 (mimeographed); see also Bhagwati, "Shifting Comparative Advantage, Protectionist Demands, and Policy Response Options."

36. Maury E. Bredahl, Jimmeye S. Hillman, Robert A. Rothenberg, and Nicolas Gutienez, *Technical Change, Protectionism, and Market Structure: The Case of the International Trade in the Fresh Winter Vegetables* (Tucson: University of Arizona, College of Agriculture, Agricultural Experiment Station Technical Bulletin 249, 1983).

37. Richard A. Posner, "Theories of Economic Regulation," *Bell Journal of Economics and Management Science* 5 (1974):335-358.

38. Sam Peltzman, "Toward a More General Theory of Regulation," *Journal of Law and Economics* 19 (1976):211-240; Gary S. Becker, "A Theory of Competition Among Pressure Groups for Political Influence," *Quarterly Journal of Economics* 98 (August 1983):371-400; George J. Stigler, "The Theory of Economic Regulation," *Bell Journal of Economics and Management Science* 2 (1971):3-21; and William A. Brock and S. P. Magee, "The Economics of Special Interest Politics: The Case of the Tariff," *American Economic Review* 68 (May 1978):246-250.

39. Torok and Huffman, "U.S.-Mexican Trade in Winter Vegetables and Illegal Immigration"; and Gustavo E. Sain, Philip Martin, and Quirino Paris, "A Regional Analysis of Illegal Aliens," *Growth and Change* 14 (January 1983):27-31.

40. Bredahl et al., *Technical Change, Protectionism, and Market Structure*, and G. A. Zepy and R. L. Simmons, *Producing Fresh Winter Vegetables in Florida and Mexico: Costs and Competition* (Washington, D.C.: U.S. Dept. of Agriculture ESCS-72, November 1979).

41. Two policies are clearly a simplification of alternatives facing a U.S. president.

APPENDIX
Outline of U.S. Immigration Policy, 1783-1980

1783 George Washington proclaims that the "bosom of America is open to receive not only the opulent and respectable stranger, but the oppressed and persecuted of all nations and religions whom we shall welcome to a participation of all our rights and privileges."

1819 For the first time, the U.S. government begins to count immigrants.

1864 Congress passes law legalizing importing of contract laborers.

1875 The first federal restriction on immigration excludes admission of prostitutes and convicts.

1882 Congress curbs Chinese immigration; it also excludes convicts, lunatics, idiots, and persons likely to become public charges, and it places a head tax on each immigrant.

1885 Legislation prohibits the admission of contract laborers.

1891 Ellis Island opens as an immigrant processing center.

1903 The list of excluded immigrants is expanded to include polygamists and political radicals such as anarchists.
1906 The Naturalization Act makes knowledge of English a requirement.
1907 Congress establishes the Dillingham Immigration Commission. The head tax on immigrants is increased, and the list of excluded immigrants is expanded to include persons with physical or mental defects that may affect their ability to earn a living, persons with tuberculosis, and children unaccompanied by their parents. A gentlemen's agreement between United States and Japan restricts Japanese immigration.
1917 Congress requires literacy in some language for those immigrants over 16 years of age, except in cases of religious persecution, and bans virtually all immigration from Asia.
1921 Quotas are established limiting the number of immigrants of each nationality to 3 percent of the number of foreign-born persons of that nationality living in the United States in 1910. The limit on European immigration is set at about 350,000.
1924 The National Origins Law (Johnson-Reed Act) sets temporary annual quotas at 2 percent of a nationality's representation in the U.S. population as determined in the 1890 census, and sets an upper limit of 150,000 upon immigration in any one year from non-Western hemisphere countries.
1929 The quotas of 1924 are permanently set to be apportioned according to each nationality's proportion of the total U.S. population as determined in the 1920 census.
1939 Congress defeats a refugee bill to rescue 20,000 children from Nazi Germany—despite willingness of U.S. families to sponsor them—on the grounds that the children would exceed the German quota.
1942 Bilateral agreements are reached with Mexico, British Honduras, Barbados, and Jamaica for the entry of temporary foreign laborers to work in the United States (the Bracero program).
1943 Laws excluding Chinese immigrants are repealed.
1946 Congress passes the War Brides Act, facilitating immigration of foreign-born wives, husbands, and children of U.S. armed forces personnel.
1948 Congress passes the Displaced Persons Act (amended in 1950), enabling 400,000 refugees to enter the United States.
1950 The Internal Security Act increases the grounds for exclusion and deportation of subversives; aliens are required to report their addresses annually.
1952 The Immigration and Nationality Act of 1952 (McCarran-Walter Act) reaffirms the national origins system that gives each nation a quota equal to its proportion of the U.S. population in 1920; limits immigration from the Eastern hemisphere to about 150,000, leaving immigration from the Western hemisphere unrestricted in total; establishes immigration preferences for skilled workers and for relatives of U.S. citizens; and tightens security and screening standards and procedures.
1953 The Refugee Relief Act admits more than 200,000 refugees beyond existing quotas.
1957 The Refugee-Escape Act defines "refugee-escapee" as any alien who has fled from any Communist country or from the Middle East because of persecution or fear of persecution on account of race, religion, or political opinion.
1960 A Cuban refugee program is established.
1964 The Bracero program is ended.

1965	The Immigration and Nationality Act Amendments of 1965 abolish the national origins system; establish an annual ceiling of 170,000 immigrants from the Eastern hemisphere, with a 20,000 limit per country; establish on immigrant visa distribution system according to seven categories of preference, favoring close relatives of U.S. citizens and permanent resident aliens, those with needed occupational skills, and refugees; and establish an annual ceiling of 120,000 immigrants from the Western hemisphere with no preference system or limit per country.
1975	The Indochinese Refuge Resettlement Program begins.
1976	The Immigration and Nationality Act amendments of 1976 extend the 20,000 limit per country and the seven-category preference system to the Western hemisphere, and maintain the separate annual ceilings of 170,000 for the Eastern hemisphere and 120,000 for the Western hemisphere.
1978	The Immigration and Nationality Act Amendments of 1978 combine the ceilings for both hemispheres into a worldwide total of 290,000, with the seven-category preference system and the 20,000 limit per country uniformly applied.
1978	Congress establishes the Select Commission on Immigration and Refugee Policy. It also passes a law excluding, and providing for deportation of, former Nazis guilty of persecution.
1980	The Refugee Act establishes clear criteria and procedures for admission of refugees.

9
International Migration Within the Pacific Basin: Characteristics, Causes, and Consequences

Michael J. Greenwood
P. Lynn Stuart

In the decades leading up to and following World War II, a new awareness by older nations of a large part of the world has evolved. Imperial empires and the concomitant system of control once characterized many nations. But as an increasing number of former colonies gained independence in those years, they could no longer be accurately perceived as appendages to the more established European countries that had ruled them for so long. Many of the Pacific Basin nations share this scenario of conception. By the late 1950s, it became evident that these new political entities had lives of their own and problems with which to contend. Their peoples, freed from colonial constraints, were making their presence felt in the world as they began to grasp the enormity of the change that had befallen them. Disparities in economic development between the ex-colonies and the long-time independent nations put the problems of these less-developed countries into stark relief. Change and dynamism moved through the region. Population migration has been and continues to be an important part of this dynamism.

A study of migration within the Pacific Basin is bound to be complex. People migrate to many different places and for a variety of reasons. In order to comprehend even a small bit of what is going on, we will organize our efforts toward answering a few basic questions, all of which pertain to relatively large-scale phenomena. The chapter focuses on migration of labor-force members within the region, but not to the exclusion of all else.

This paper draws heavily from Michael J. Greenwood, "The Economics of Mass Migration from Poor to Rich Countries: Leading Issues of Fact and Theory," *American Economic Review, Papers and Proceedings* 73 (May 1983):173-177.

We begin by discussing the shortcomings of the data that record international migration flows and their implications for our study. As it turns out, we are restricted to looking at U.S. immigration for the answers to most of our questions. Next, an outline of the institutional setting for migration to the United States is given. We then examine questions relevant to three important issues: (1) the identification of dominant migratory flow patterns, and how these patterns depend importantly on the motivation for migration; (2) a descriptive profile of the demographic and labor-force characteristics of migrants; and (3) a consideration of the probable effects of migration on both the receiving and the sending countries. We conclude by reflecting on other issues that may be of special interest to migration within the Pacific Basin.

Constraints and Issues of Fact

Several underlying problems make valid intercountry comparisons of international migration data difficult, if not presently impossible. The source of international migration data differs from country to country. Whereas certain countries employ censuses or sample surveys to collect their data, others use administrative records, which include population registers, employment registers, alien registration, border control, exit or entry visas, and other means.

Not only do data sources differ widely, but also the manner in which emigrants and immigrants are defined differs greatly between countries. Many countries define emigrants in terms of intended duration of stay in the country of destination, but this duration varies widely. Certain countries base their information on the number of persons intending to relinquish residence in the country of emigration. Others base theirs on the expressed intention to establish residence in the country of immigration. Some countries require that the emigrant intend to take a job in the destination country. And whereas certain countries count all departing persons who meet their definition, others count only residents, or only nationals, or only aliens, or only persons with exit visas. For some countries the mode of transportation of those departing is crucial. Finally, certain countries do not even attempt to gather data on emigration. The above list is not exhaustive. Problems associated with comparing immigration data are equally troublesome.

Such differences in the definition and measurement of international migration make the formation of even a 2 × 2 matrix of international migration flows for virtually any two nations in the world extremely doubtful as to accuracy and comparability. The number of emigrants recorded by country A as moving from A to B would almost never equal the number of immigrants recorded by country B as moving to B from A. Within the Pacific Basin group, for example, Japan and Korea report both emigration and immigration for selected years. Japanese data stated that 1,726 emigrants went to Korea in 1969, whereas Korean data for the same year show that 30,916 immigrants arrived from Japan.[1] No footnotes to explain the discrepancy are provided. This example is by no means atypical.

In order to get a consistent, albeit incomplete, idea of migration patterns in the Pacific Basin, we have limited our study to use of only U.S. official historical data on immigration to the United States.[2] (The United States does not report emigration statistics.) A shortcoming of these data is that they do not include estimates of the numbers of illegal immigrations, which have probably risen dramatically over the past twenty years. On the positive side, however, these data are categorized by age, sex, and occupation to provide rich detail on the characteristics of immigrants. This information is extremely useful in sorting out the dynamics of international labor movements.

Studying Pacific Basin immigration only to the United States can be justified on grounds other than the purely practical matter of data availability. Despite the fact that strict comparability of the immigration data from different nations is precluded by the problems noted above, the accounts of emigration compiled by each source country reveal a significant fact: the United States is named as the dominant destination for seven of the nine Pacific Basin countries reporting such data.[3] The exceptions are New Zealand and Australia, for which the United States is listed as the third major recipient of emigrants after the United Kingdom and each other. Japan is the only close contender for this distinction within the Pacific Basin group, and it is significant only for other Asian countries. Thus, looking at immigration solely to the United States is warranted on the grounds that it appears to be of particular importance to the region.

The fact that the United States and, to a lesser extent, Japan have become main destination countries is not surprising. Nearly all theories of migration postulate that relative economic prosperity and political stability act as magnets to prospective migrants. What may seem curious is that Australia, New Zealand, and Canada—other Pacific Basin countries that possess these same attractions—have not emerged in the same role. The explanation for this lack of drawing power lies in the fact that these countries have restrictive immigration policies that keep them from accepting large numbers of Asian or unskilled immigrants. Domestic labor-force considerations are dominant in the admission policies of these countries and have acted to suppress migration flows within the region.

Prior to being revamped in 1965, U.S. laws governing immigration were similar to the stringent policies of Oceania and Canada. At that time the national origins quota system of the 1920s was abandoned in favor of a more liberal system with a primary emphasis on family reunification. The previous regime, formulated to maintain the turn-of-the-century ethnic balance among migrants, was one of de facto discrimination on the basis of nationality, or, as in the case of the Asian-Pacific Triangle provisions, on the basis of race. For the majority of U.S. immigrants during the national origins era, quota numbers were allocated by country of birth, but those of 50 percent or more Oriental ancestry were required to obtain visa numbers through one of the Asian-Pacific countries, regardless of country of birth. Because nearly all of the Asian countries were limited to an allotment of 100 quota immigrants annually, this condition imposed a harsh constraint on immigration from that area of the world. (Oriental spouses and children of U.S. citizens were exempt from the provisions.) The new laws in 1965 were enacted not so much to change the total amount of migration to the United States as to alter its composition. No other area in the world has been affected by these changes to the extent that the Asian countries have been.

The new system imposed a worldwide ceiling on immigration of 290,000: 170,000 for the Eastern hemisphere countries and 120,000 for those of the Western hemisphere. (Subsequently the distinction between hemispheres was dropped in favor of a worldwide quota of 290,000.)[4] Immediate relatives of U.S. citizens—spouses, children, and, for the first time, parents—continued to be exempt from numerical limitations. (The sum of the quotas for Eastern countries prior to 1965 was roughly 158,000; immigration from Western hemisphere countries had not been numerically restricted.) Although concern was expressed about the reaction of our American neighbors to the new policy, the greater worry was that mounting population pressures in many of the Western hemisphere nations would soon prompt a deluge of new immigration if left unchecked. During the early 1960s, immigration to the United States from other American countries had increased from 98,000 to 144,000.

In addition to the overall hemispheric caps, the 1965 revisions also restricted each Eastern country to a maximum of 20,000 quota immigrants per year. Within the prescribed limits, a seven-category system of preference was established to facilitate the distribution of immigration visas. Four of the categories allocated up to 74 percent of available visas for certain family members of U.S. citizens and permanent resident aliens. Brothers and sisters were covered within these classifications, for example, but aunts and cousins were not. The third and the sixth categories were the occupational preferences, and each absorbed 10 percent of the overall limitation. Spouses and children accompanying immigrants entering within either of these categories also were counted against the quota limitations for occupational preferences. The remaining 6 percent of preference visas were reserved for the now-defunct seventh category, refugees. Any visa numbers not applied for on a preference basis were made available on a nonpreference basis.

Neither the limitation per country nor the preference system was implemented for the Western hemisphere until additional amendments to do so were passed in 1976. Except for some changes pertaining to the treatment of refugees made within the Refugee Act of 1980, essentially the same preference system is still in effect today. Because the data we look at in this chapter are for the years 1960–1979, the 1980 changes are not relevant to the following discussion of Pacific Basin immigration.

The revisions to U.S. immigration laws legislated in 1965 were not made fully effective until 1 July 1968, but provisions for pooling unused national origins quotas among all Eastern hemisphere countries during the intervening transition period allowed the profile of U.S. migration to change almost immediately. A major impetus for removing the national origins system was that a few western European countries had a monopoly on nearly 70 percent of the total quota slots. Although these slots were underutilized by the proprietary nations, no channels were set up for transferring unused visa numbers to areas with excess demand. The result was that a substantial backlog of visa applicants appeared, while the overall quota remained undersubscribed. The national origins visa assignment scheme remained in place during the three transition years, but pooling provided for unused visa numbers from the previous year to be made available to other Eastern hemisphere countries. Only those prospective immigrants qualifying for preference status had access to the pool, however.

A basic understanding of the legal constraints outlined above is extremely important for interpreting the data on immigration to the United States from other Pacific Basin countries. Although our primary purpose in this chapter is to provide a framework for making sense of migration within the region, and not to show the effects of the 1965 law changes, the latter intent must also be adopted because it is those changes that have brought us closer to the theoretical paradigm of laissez faire. In addition, a comparison of immigration to the United States before and after the changes allows speculation about the possible consequences of restructuring other, currently strict, immigration policies.

Migration Within the Pacific Basin

An account of the statistics describing Pacific Basin immigration to the United States is most meaningful within some theoretical context. This task is best accomplished by first suggesting a theory based on (unobservable) motivations, and then deriving hypotheses that are testable using the facts. Unfortunately, the availability of "facts" will usually circumscribe the ability to follow through with the testing procedure. The descriptive approach we follow below does not constitute a rigorous check of economic theory, but may indicate a fruitful path for the design and implementation of statistical tests.

Economic theory suggests that the pursuit of an increase in material well-being will be paramount in the decision to migrate. For most people, the ability to achieve a higher standard of living depends primarily on labor market involvement. Thus, people would be motivated to migrate so that they may become affiliated with a more attractive labor market—one that offers relatively high rates of remuneration along with opportunities for career advancement. If international migration is motivated by the desire for economic advancement through the labor market, then we can expect to see several patterns take shape as we examine the data on immigration. Limitations imposed by the level of detail given in the data will be noted as they become apparent.

One pattern that should manifest itself if our economic theory is accurate is that countries boasting relatively high wages and a healthy rate of economic growth will be net receivers of migrants, and low-wage, slow-growth countries will be net suppliers. We have already mentioned that problems of data availability and reliability make it difficult to gauge this issue for all Pacific Basin migration with precision. Furthermore, the constraints imposed by immigration laws prevent economic incentives from freely working themselves out. However, the fact that the countries listed as primary destinations of emigrants within the Pacific Basin, namely Japan and the United States, are relatively rich and developed does not negate the view that the search for economic betterment in the labor market is a probable motivation for migration. Moreover, with the exception of Indonesia, the relatively poor Eastern hemisphere countries have been sending increasing numbers of immigrants since the 1965 changes in U.S. law, whereas flows from Japan and Oceania have remained nearly constant since 1960.[5] The picture for American countries is less clear. Mexico is now by far the largest Western hemisphere supplier of immigrants to the United States, but the level of Canadian immigration has plummeted from its peak levels of the unrestricted mid-1960s. A deeper exploration of the issues is necessary to see what is going on in this area.

A second pattern to look for has to do with labor-force participation rates. If labor-force attachment is important, we would expect the percentage of the migrating population that is economically active to be greater than the same measure for the source population. A breakdown of labor-force participation rates by age groups would be best for evaluating this difference. Unfortunately, U.S. immigration data do not provide us with that much information. The best we can do is compare the percentage of the total home country population that is economically active with the percentage of all immigrants declaring an occupation. These two statistics obviously measure slightly different concepts, and this makes the comparison troublesome.

One problem is that the majority of migrants to the United States are not required to declare an occupation. Aside from those entering within one of the two occupational preference categories, only those nonpreference immigrants intending to work in the United States face the labor certification process that obliges them to state an occupation. Labor certification involves getting a statement over the secretary of labor's signature declaring that the prospective immigrant relating to occupation is requested on all visa applications, relatives of resident aliens and citizens may opt to leave the answer blank. Possible reasons for this omission include difficulty in filling out the forms, or with finding an equivalent for one's native occupation. The result is that the percentage of immigrants declaring an occupation may be an understatement of the true labor-force participation rate for that group.

No doubt biases exist in the reporting of participation in the source country as well. The International Labor Office compiles these data using survey techniques where possible and relying upon government figures otherwise. For 1975 an effort was made to achieve comparability among all countries, but cultural differences in defining labor-market work still posed difficulties. For instance, persons who work for family enterprises, such as small farms, are not considered to be economically active in some lesser-developed countries; this is especially true for women. Perhaps these figures also underestimate the true population value. No definitive statement about the net direction of these biases can be made without better documentation than is currently available for these statistics.

Statistics on the economically active population are available for nine of the Pacific Basin countries, but in most cases only the 1975 figures are comparable.[6] Because factors that affect these percentages are bound to change slowly over time, we will assume they are roughly constant for the years in our sample, 1960–1979. For the sake of convenience in making comparisons between the percentage of immigrants declaring an occupation and the percentage of the source population that is economically active, the term "labor-force participation rates," or simply "participation rates," will be used even though neither of the two measures we have is strictly equivalent to the term as it is normally used. Eastern hemisphere countries will be discussed separately from the Western countries due to the fact that U.S. immigration laws treat the two differently.

With the exception of Canada, all of the Pacific Basin countries in the Western hemisphere report a participation rate close to 30 percent for the sending population. For migrants, the rate is erratic (35 percent to 64 percent), but 40 percent is roughly the predominant rate. During the 1966–1968 transition period, the participation rates for all Western hemisphere immigrants, including Canadians, dipped markedly. Accompanying the dip was an upward surge in the share of female immigration.

Canada, which is by far the richest Western hemisphere country being considered for emigrants to the United States, has a labor-force participation rate just above 40 percent. Prior to the 1965 changes, the percentage of Canadian immigrants declaring an occupation hovered around 46 percent—in line with what we would expect—but in the subsequent years, the rate dropped into the mid-thirties. For several reasons, the character of U.S. immigration from Canada is unique among the Pacific Basin group. The Canadian labor market is not very different from that of the United States, and the two countries share a common language, a similar culture, and a long border. Therefore, U.S. drawing power should not be as great for working Canadians, and workers' decisions to migrate may be more heavily influenced by conditions in the home labor market. Cyclically unemployed workers in Canada would find it relatively easy to move to the United States if the U.S. economy is not experiencing the same downturn in the business cycle.

Trends in the relevant statistics bear out this idea. In the early 1960s, when the Canadian unemployment rate oscillated between 6 and 7 percent, total immigration to the United States soared to historical highs. The return of unemployment rates to the 3.5 to 4 percent range, as occurred in 1965–1966, was greeted by a 25 percent fall in the amount of emigration from

Canada. The percentage of migrants declaring an occupation simultaneously dropped 11 percentage points. Further decreases in total migration occurred in 1969, the first year of numerical limitations for the Western hemisphere, and increasing competition for scarce visa numbers within the Americas has prevented the reemergence of former high levels of total Canadian immigration. Nevertheless, labor-force participation rates for Canadian immigrants have followed the steady upward climb of unemployment rates in that country throughout the 1970s. What this suggests, not surprisingly, is that the factors determining migration between rich countries are not the same as those in play for flows from poor to rich countries.

Within the Eastern hemisphere, the labor-force profiles of U.S. immigrants from Korea and Japan are more difficult to interpret because of the extremely high number of wives of U.S. citizens who emigrate from those countries. Between one-third and one-half of the total number of immigrants fell into this category during the 1960s for Korea. When total immigration skyrocketed with the increased availability of visa numbers for Asian countries, the share of wives fell, although the actual number remained about the same. For Japan, which, as noted previously has sent a nearly constant number of immigrants since 1960, the share of the total accounted for by wives of U.S. citizens has remained above 30 percent. For both countries, the participation rate of immigrants lies considerably below that of the home population, because the majority of U.S. citizens' wives do not declare an occupation upon entry.

For the Philippines, Indonesia, and China, immigrants display labor-force participation rates ranging from 40 to 50 percent after the changes made in 1965. The rate for the source population is reported only for the Philippines, where it is 35 percent—a good deal lower than the migrant rate. Total immigration from both China and the Philippines rose dramatically when the provisions for pooling were made in 1966, and have continued to soar ever since. Most remarkably, Filipino immigration to the United States increased by a factor of 13 within this period.[7]

A third pattern that will corroborate our economic theory can be seen in relation to the age profile of migrants coming to the United States. Specifically, young workers should be most prone to seek labor-force advantage by migrating. In making the decision to migrate, they will weigh costs against benefits. The bulk of the costs will be borne at the outset, whereas benefits, which tend to be known with less certainty, may not appear until some distant future. The stream of returns on a move to a more favorable labor market will accrue slowly; net positive benefits may not be realized for quite some time. In this context, it makes sense to expect that a disproportionate share of migrants will be of relatively young labor-force age. If we assume entry into the labor force at age 19 and retirement at 65, the majority of labor-market migrants can be expected to be in the younger half. Because of the classifications used for data reporting, we will use ages 20 and 39 as the cutoff ages for this younger group. It is this group of workers who will have the most time to collect returns and recoup the costs of a move. Moreover, younger people tend to be more willing to break ties with their families and native cultures. Finally, the labor-force positions of younger workers are not as established as those of older workers. In short, younger workers typically have the most to gain and the least to lose by migrating.

To assess the accuracy of this claim, we will again use data on the source country population as a benchmark. The percentage of the sending population aged 20 to 39 is virtually identical for males and females, and ranges between 25 and 31 percent for all of the Western hemisphere countries. Immigrants in the same age category account for an average of roughly 45 percent of the population moving to the United States. Generally speaking, the female and the male immigrants move together in their rates, although the percentage of male migrants 20 to 39 follows the immigrant labor-force participation rate more closely. This phenomenon is particularly true for downturns of the participation rate. Most of the troughs in the participation rate coincide either with peaks in the percentage of total immigrants who are female, or with drop-offs in total immigration. Thus, migration motivated by family reunification continues although labor-force migration appears to be slowing.

The observed large spread that predominates between the percentages of home and migrant populations aged 20 to 39 is just what theory would predict. This spread is greatest for the South American countries, where the percentage of immigrants aged 20 to 39 is a full 30 points higher than the same measure for the home population. We should note that the greatest difference between the two rates occurred prior to 1969.

Eastern hemisphere countries report similar proportions of persons 20 to 39 years of age in the source populations as do the Western countries, except that Japan's population share in that age group is somewhat higher, at 32 percent. For the immigrants, 1965 marked an upturn in the ratio of young immigrants of labor-force age to the total migrant population, for both sexes. (We are ignoring the female measures for Japan and Korea because of the special case of wives already noted.) The percentage of males who were 20 to 39 continued to rise steadily throughout the sample period for immigrants from Japan (to a high of 68 percent) and Australia (to a high of 55 percent). Other Eastern hemisphere countries in the sample showed a gradual falling off of immigrants of ages 29 to 39, after five years of increase to roughly 50 percent in the late 1960s.

A possible explanation for this roller-coaster profile is that a wave of labor-force immigration was unleashed by the augmentation of visas available for Asian countries in 1965, followed by reunification of families through the 1970s, as total immigration from these countries continued to grow. Again, the disproportionately high share of persons aged 20 to 39 among the immigrant populations lends credence to the notion that labor-force opportunities prompt migration.

The final aspect of the immigrants' characteristics we will inquire into is the skill level of those immigrants declaring an occupation. An important question by itself, it may take on additional weight if skill level is thought of as a proxy for income level, or for wealth.[8] We have treated this variable as a dichotomous one: immigrant workers are either skilled or they are not. In the former category are those who claim to be professional, technical, and kindred workers, or managers and administrators, except farm.

The question concerning the predicted skill level of migrants can be addressed by either of two hypotheses. On the one hand, if a considerable amount of time or money has been invested to enhance earning capabilities, the worker may be particularly keen to seek out the highest possible return by migrating. Moreover, skilled workers are apt to have the resources necessary to support the transition to a new country. These workers may also find their skills more easily transferable from their home countries to the U.S. labor market. On the other hand, the highly skilled workers are likely to be among the relatively well-off in their home countries, and thus they may have little incentive to leave. The latter scenario depends upon how well the home labor market functions to reward investment in human capital. A look at the percentage of workers who declared an occupation in the skilled group may shed some light on the question of which of these two claims seems most applicable to the Pacific Basin countries. Unfortunately, we have no reliable statistic on the home labor markets for comparison.

If we first look at the Western hemisphere countries, Canada shows a most interesting pattern in the skill levels of its workers emigrating to the United States. During the unrestricted era of Western hemisphere immigration, approximately 30 percent of Canadian immigrant workers were skilled. The 1966 decline in total immigration, previously discussed, was matched by an upward leap in the share of workers declaring a skilled occupation, and this upward trend continued, to reach a high of 60 percent in the late 1970s. This high figure, along with the accompanying decrease in total immigration, clearly reflects the new competition for obtaining visa numbers in the Western hemisphere. And yet the skill level profile for other American immigrants is wholly disparate from that of Canadians. Only 4 to 8 percent of Mexican workers immigrating to the United States during the sample period have been in the skilled category. Even when Mexican immigration was at its lowest—around 33,000 per year, compared with current levels above 70,000—the percentage of skilled workers did not climb above 9 percent.

A higher percentage of immigrant workers from the South American nations fall into the skilled classification, but the figure declines in periods of increased total immigration. Chile is the source of a relatively greater share of skilled workers (30-50 percent) than are Peru, Colombia, and Ecuador (all 20-40 percent). The fact that Mexico, with a higher per capita income than any of the South America countries, sends the greatest share of unskilled workers may be accounted for by its proximity to the United States, which makes migration both more immediately enticing and less costly. Income distribution in the sending countries is no doubt highly influential as well.

Eastern hemisphere Pacific Basin countries are among the most plentiful sources in the world of skilled immigrants to the United States. Between 45 and 80 percent of the workers from these countries declare skilled occupations, and the large absolute numbers of labor-force migrants from the Philippines and, to a lesser extent, Korea, make the issue of skill transfer via migration an important one for this region. Total immigration from Australia and Japan, the rich nations of the eastern Pacific Basin countries, is relatively small; each supplies between 1,000 and 5,000 immigrants annually, but roughly 50 percent of those who come to work in the United States declare a skilled occupation. Factors such as distance, which is a proxy for the costs of moving, and, in some instances political stability of the source country or its ties to the United States, may play important roles in determining who migrates from these countries. More explicitly, the higher costs of emigrating from the far-away Asian countries may be affordable for only the higher-income workers, and in the Philippines, U.S. investment in the industrial infrastructure has created a pool of workers who not only are skilled, but also have become accustomed to a mode of work similar to that in the United States (but for a fraction of the wages). Per capita incomes alone do not tell us enough to explain why the patterns of skill level for these relatively poor Eastern hemisphere countries differ so markedly from those of the poor Western hemisphere countries. Particularly for the Asian countries, the 1965 law changes have facilitated greater labor-force migration, as indicated by both the increased percentages of immigrants declaring an occupation and the increased percentages of immigrants of the appropriate age group.

Some Economic Consequences of International Migration

Among the most visible and controversial issues regarding the impacts of immigrants on the economy of the receiving country are those concerning employment opportunities, wages, and working conditions for domestic workers. Do immigrant workers displace domestic workers from jobs, cause a reduction of domestic wage rates, and encourage undesirable working conditions? These questions are particularly difficult to resolve because immigration may have negative effects on certain workers but positive effects on others.

The idea underlying the debate is that the level of employment (E) at the end of a given period t is dependent upon the amount of net employment migration (M) that occurs during t. Thus, $E_t = f(M_t, X_t)$, where X_t is a vector of variables other than migration. The partial derivative $\delta E_t / \delta M_t$ shows the employment effect of one additional employed migrant. The value (hereafter = β) can be greater than, equal to, or less than one, depending upon whether one more employed migrant causes employment to increase by more than one job, by one job, or by less than one job. The segmentation hypothesis ($\beta = 1$) suggests that employment rises by precisely the migrant's contribution to it, whereas the replacement hypothesis ($\beta < 1$) indicates that employment rises by less than the migrant's contribution, which implies substitution of migrant for indigenous labor. Finally, $\beta > 1$ suggests that an employment increase occurs over and above that of the migrant's employment contribution.

Under free-market conditions, migration appears frequently to be a self-reinforcing and cumulative phenomenon because it increases labor demand as well as labor supply in receiving areas. (Fragmentary evidence on internal U.S. migration suggests that $\beta \geq 1$.) Many factors may underlie such a relationship. Among these are, first, the skills, inventiveness, and innovativeness of the migrants themselves, who may possess differential endowments of human capital (in the form of education, accumulated skills, or entrepreneurial talent, as examples) relative to the population of the sending or receiving area. This alternative seems less applicable when immigrants are mainly poor, unskilled individuals from poor countries. Second, apart from their human capital, migrants may own physical and financial capital that they bring with them. Third, migrants may possess sources of income other than their labor services. Each of these possibilities, of course, is less likely if the migrants themselves are poor. Fourth, migrants may cause investment (as in social infrastructure and housing) in receiving localities. Fifth, migrants may influence the price of locally produced goods and services due to the changed demand they may cause for such goods and services. Finally, migrants may contribute to the growth of markets and to the achievement of scale and agglomeration economies. Many economic historians believe, for example, that this last factor was operable in the United States up to about 1900 or 1920, but that it has not been important since then. Each of the above factors thus appears to cause a dampened employment effect from a poor immigrant relative to a rich immigrant.

Regardless of the value of β, the distributional consequences of immigration have been a serious issue. Even if $\beta \geq 1$, low-income, poorly educated, unskilled immigrants may be competing primarily with comparably educated, comparably unskilled U.S. residents. Certain participants in the debate argue that the jobs filled by immigrants from poor countries are of no interest to U.S. citizens, but little concrete evidence is presented to support this view. The other view is that low-income U.S. residents, primarily Blacks, Hispanics, and Puerto Ricans, are hurt by job competition from immigrants. Historical precedent exists for this latter position, in that after the Civil War, the flow of immigrants to northern U.S. cities appears to have fluctuated inversely with the flow of Blacks out of the South and into these cities, as well as with the flow out of rural areas in general. The effects of immigration also appear to be dependent upon the timing of the migration over the business cycle, with negative effects on poor domestic workers being most pronounced during periods of high unemployment. Finally, much attention has been directed at specific U.S. regions that have been particularly affected by immigrants.

In general, then, issues dealing with economic growth and employment have probably received the most emphasis in North America. Immigration's effects on inflation and the balance of payments have not been at the center of the debate. These latter two topics are much more widely discussed with reference to European migration, as are various issues focused on the externalities of migration. Moreover, except for research on the earnings behavior of immigrants and their offspring, little emphasis has been placed on the short-run versus long-run benefits and costs of North American immigration.

Whether international migration has helped or hindered the economic development of poor source countries is a noteworthy issue. The brain-drain debate focused on the negative consequences of emigration of the most highly educated from their native countries. These consequences were typically identified in terms of the opportunity cost of investment in education and training or of the lost talent made possible from such investments. Recently, however, the emphasis appears to have shifted, probably in response to the fact that migration from poor countries now seems to be much more heavily oriented toward migration of poor people.

One important issue on which little agreement exists deals with the effects of remitted earnings on countries of emigration. Though their precise magnitude is difficult to measure, remittances appear frequently to be substantial, and they also appear to be closely related to the permanency of the move, falling in magnitude and regularity with increased duration of the migration. In this sense remittances are closely related to the conditions that give rise to the migration. Whether the remittances are channeled into investment or are used primarily for current consumption seems to depend upon economic and social conditions in the countries of emigration. The effects are difficult to generalize.

A second important issue deals with the effects of skills learned abroad by migrants who later return to a poor country. Little is known about the applicability of skills learned in a rich country to a poor country of origin of migrants, but a body of literature is emerging on this issue. A hypothesis central to this literature is that a labor force oriented toward agricultural skills can be transformed into one oriented toward urban industrial skills through a period of employment in an industrialized economy. If Western hemisphere migration to the United States is more likely to entail later return to the source countries, the issues of remitted earnings and remitted skills will assume an importance in the Western hemisphere similar to that accorded them in international migration elsewhere in the world.

Conclusion

We began by describing the institutional framework within which Pacific Basin migration to the United States takes place. Changes legislated in 1965 dramatically altered the profile of immigration to the United States and clearly show that the institutional setting is of key importance in determining global migratory flows.

The skeletal theory presented here suggests that migration is motivated by the desire to achieve economic gains through the labor market. The validity of such a theory was assessed by describing characteristics both of migrant populations and of sending and receiving countries. Available data on age, labor-force involvement, and skill level of U.S. immigrants generally supports the labor-force hypothesis, as does the prevailing flow of migrants from poor to rich countries.

Additional issues mentioned as being of possible importance, but not explored in any depth in this chapter, are income distribution in the sending country and historical ties with countries that have more developed economies (e.g., ties to the United States in the Philippines). These two issues may in fact be closely related if links to developed economies allow the emergence of a relatively small well-to-do class in the midst of widespread poverty. Moreover, exposure to the higher standard of living brought by foreign investment may initiate emigration to the developed nations, particularly if the benefits of that investment are bestowed upon a privileged few.

Finally, issues we did not discuss, but that are no doubt important, include sociological ones such as the role of ritual and the value placed on cultural and other noneconomic aspects of life. The absence of any notable increase in immigration from Indonesia since the 1965 changes may well be better understood in the context of these kinds of considerations.

Several issues are likely to be at the forefront in the debate regarding the impacts of international migration. For the destination country, the way in which immigrant labor impinges on economic growth and employment opportunities for citizens is of prime importance. Impacts on the source country vary greatly, depending on whether or not the emigrants are taking needed skills with them and on whether or not the emigration is long term or short term. If money is sent back to the home country, immigration may provide for small-scale international income redistribution, but perhaps the exchange of workers will negate such an effect. These issues are particularly difficult to evaluate because quantitative evidence is lacking in most instances.

Notes

1. UN *Demographic Yearbook* (New York: United Nations, 1977), Special Topic: International Migration Statistics, p. 672 (Japan) and p. 679 (South Korea). Both data from Table 29: "Long-term Emigrants and Immigrants by Country or Area of Last or Intended Long-term Residence: 1958-1976," pp. 535-824.

2. U.S. Department of Justice, *Annual Reports of the Immigration and Naturalization Service*, 1960-1979 (Washington, D.C.: U.S. Department of Justice), Table 6: "Immigrants Admitted by Classes under the Immigration Laws and Country or Region of Birth;" Table 8: "Immigrants Admitted by Country or Region of Birth and Major Occupation Group;" and Table 9: "Immigrants Admitted by Country or Region of Birth, Sex, and Age."

3. The statistics for the following countries are derived from the sources in note 1: Canada, Mexico, Colombia, Peru, Japan, South Korea, Philippines, New Zealand, and Australia.

4. Eastern hemisphere: Europe, Asia, Oceania; Western hemisphere: North, Central, and South America.

5. We are using the terms "rich" and "poor" based on the per capita incomes reported for 1975. For all countries listed in the national accounts section of the UN *Statistical Yearbook*, median income was approximately US $1,500 in 1975, which was the figure chosen to separate rich from poor. Of the Pacific Basin countries, the United States, Canada, Australia, New Zealand, and Japan are rich by this criterion.

6. International Labor Organization: "Percent of Population which is Economically Active," in *Yearbook of Labor Statistics* (Geneva: ILO, 1983). The nine Pacific Basin countries for which this statistic is available are Mexico, Chile, Colombia, Ecuador, Canada, Japan, South Korea, the Philippines, and Australia. We also have this data for Peru, China, and Indonesia.

7. See note 6.

8. See note 2.

Part 5

Technological and Research Capacity, Exchange, and Diffusion

10
Resources for the Production of Agricultural Growth in the Pacific Basin Region

M. Ann Judd
Robert E. Evenson

The capacity to produce *low cost* growth in the agricultural sector has been and continues to be a central feature of economic development. For the past decade or so many writers dealing with development problems have emphasized distributional issues rather than growth, and much of the literature produced betrays an anti-growth, anti-technology quality. Even this literature has in many ways demonstrated that growth in the supply of food and other agricultural products is important. It has generally been easier to achieve improvements in distribution when food supply is ample than when severe shortages prevail.

Agricultural growth can be produced in a number of alternative ways and these alternatives have different costs. For purposes of this chapter we will classify these alternatives in five groups:

1. The elimination of market interventions that produce inefficient resource allocations.
2. The lowering of transactions and related costs through public-sector investments in market information, communication, etc., and through improvements in legal systems regarding contracts.
3. The use of improved technology, beginning with technology produced elsewhere, adapting the technology through applied adaptive research, undertaking broad programs of basic and adaptive research, and investing in extension of technology to farmers.
4. The investment in land improvements through drainage, irrigation, clearing, leveling, fertilizing, etc.
5. The addition of labor, animal power, and chemicals per unit of land and fixed assets.

History has shown that all five alternatives produce growth. Alternatives 4 and 5 provide the basis for the classical analysis of growth, and for most of the countries of the world prior to the twentieth century growth could be understood as mainly determined by investment in land and increases in conventional inputs per unit of land. Japan prior to the Meiji restoration, Java, and much of the Indian subcontinent have long histories of agricultural growth understandable in these terms. The classical economists, notably Malthus and Ricardo, pointed out that when growth is based solely on these sources the prognosis for development is dim. The history of these situations also demonstrates that the cost of such growth is high. Alternative 4, however, has been a low-cost source of growth in countries with a large land frontier.

The modernizing and developing countries of today have achieved general economic growth in both the agricultural and nonagricultural sectors by utilizing varying combinations of alternatives 1, 2, and 3. These alternatives can produce low-cost—indeed very low-cost—growth. Further, because all five alternative sources are interdependent, achieving growth through alternatives 1, 2, and 3 results in a lowering of the cost of achieving it through the classical alternatives 4 and 5.

Alternatives 1 and 2 require substantial institutional reforms in many cases, and although they offer much potential growth, many countries are unable to implement them quickly. Market interventions in most poor countries of the world are instigated for the benefit of an urban middle class and are generally characterized by policies designated to hold agricultural commodity prices to urban consumers below world price levels and below prices that would guide efficient resource allocation. Negative effective protection is provided to the agricultural sector while most industrial sectors are provided strong positive protection. These policies tend to be altered only after low-cost growth is achieved using alternatives 2 and 3. Once a period of such growth is achieved, there is a tendency for a reversal of market interventions in favor of agriculture. The Pacific Basin includes countries on both ends of the spectrum regarding market intervention policy. Virtually all developing economies and most semi-industrialized economies intervene against agriculture. Most industrialized countries intervene to assist agriculture. All could achieve growth in their economies through alternative 1.

Alternative 2 provides the basis for most "rural development" projects, which in the developing economies are generally well-funded. Indeed the promise of low-cost growth through lowering the cost of credit, community development programs, and related "integrated-intensive" and institution-building programs has induced investments in these activities by both national and international aid agencies that are substantially greater than those observed in the histories of contemporary developed economies. In fact, rather little evidence exists that these programs, which promise the "quick-fix" or rapid payoff, have been low-cost sources of growth. One critical element of this alternative is the legal institutional structure of the economy and its effect on transaction costs. Transaction costs are high, sometimes very high, in many developing countries partly because of inefficiencies in court systems. Credit programs, for example, are almost impossible to run efficiently if farmers face no penalties or sanctions for default. The costs of enforcing all but the simplest contracts can add greatly to production costs and can be a severe hindrance to growth. The failure of many rural development projects to achieve their stated objectives is often attributable to an inefficient legal system.

Alternative 3, which involves delivering improved technology to farmers, has clearly proven to be the major low-cost source of growth for most countries of the world (except for a few countries favored with abundant land during certain periods of their history). A large number of studies have documented high returns to investment in agricultural research that translate into low-cost growth.[1] Further, because of international transmission of technology there is some scope for "free riding" by some poor countries, enabling them to realize even lower-cost growth. A system of international agricultural research centers has been established in the past twenty-five years designed to facilitate this international free riding. Even with technology transfer, however, growth through technology is not free. Virtually no country in the world has realized much growth through technology without investing something (e.g., Burma). But those countries that make even modest investments have purchased considerable low-cost growth.

Our concern in this paper is primarily with this capacity to achieve growth through technology. In the following section we discuss the public sector programs of support for agricultural research and extension programs in the region and compare the Pacific Basin countries with other similar countries. The second section discusses the private sector, with emphasis on the role of legal systems in encouraging invention. A concluding section offers a brief policy discussion.

Public-Sector Investment in Research and Extension

A region's potential for increasing agricultural productivity can be measured in part by the resources it commits to agricultural research and extension. It is important to know not only the levels of expenditures and manpower available for agricultural research and extension, but also the relationship between spending levels and the value of agricultural production, expenditures per research scientist or extension worker, and the degree to which the focus of research and the makeup of production are the same.

We will present a variety of data that should give a fairly complete picture of the state of agricultural research and extension in the countries of the Pacific Basin. The data we have will also allow us to compare agricultural research in the Pacific Basin to research in other countries. In presenting this data, our primary emphasis will be on research as opposed to extension. This emphasis is the result of (1) our judgment that research plays a more important role in increasing agricultural productivity, and (2) the fact that our data on research are more complete and tend to be more reliable.[2]

TABLE 10.1
Agricultural Research Expenditures and Manpower for Pacific Basin Countries by Industrial Class, 1959-1980

	Expenditures (Thousands in Constant 1980 US $)			
Countries	1959	1962	1965	1968
Middle-income developing				
Thailand	1,552	4,231	7,476	9,652
Philippines	2,781	3,663	4,255	4,877
Indonesia	564	2,256	4,750	6,783
Peru	1,073	2,104	4,154	8,479
Colombia	14,104	13,428	17,746	25,464
Ecuador	704	1,411	2,768	4,226
Guatemala	862	1,025	1,218	1,474
Nicaragua	451	803	1,385	1,827
Total	22,091	28,891	43,752	62,782
Semi-industrialized				
Malaysia	3,386	5,924	9,136	9,653
Korea, Rep.	2,538	2,820	3,332	4,567
Taiwan	1,975	3,245	3,877	4,539
Mexico	5,079	5,924	6,922	8,871
Panama	345	410	487	589
Chile	1,693	2,963	6,229	6,915
Costa Rica	775	930	1,108	1,043
Total	15,791	22,216	31,081	36,177
Industrialized				
Japan	135,414	197,479	334,992	420,064
Australia	76,169	95,918	156,421	169,591
New Zealand	14,952	16,927	27,131	29,484
Canada	104,664	108,614	129,013	211,336
United States	562,224	648,858	808,409	939,275
Total	893,423	1,067,796	1,455,966	1,769,750
People's Republic of China	54,166	169,265	332,223	469,638
Total Pacific Basin	985,417	1,288,168	1,863,022	2,338,347

TABLE 10.1 (cont.)

Expenditures (Thousands in Constant 1980 US$)			
1971	1974	1977	1980
11,740	11,463	23,547	21,600
5,499	6,844	8,637	9,533
8,688	8,023	42,229	33,231
11,740	12,895	6,871	8,163
30,806	31,329	29,668	32,231
5,260	8,901	8,132	6,100
2,247	2,963	4,083	5,332
1,878	1,719	1,711	2,211
77,858	84,137	124,878	118,370
11,740	11,463	19,564	30,391
23,381	24,400	26,607	20,012
5,400	5,539	12,520	14,000
14,558	22,924	20,393	70,929
899	1,185	1,515	2,482
16,436	10,315	11,960	11,319
2,747	2,374	1,935	2,168
75,161	78,200	94,491	151,301
575,260	611,306	645,543	684,276
281,760	267,447	286,823	306,199
44,612	68,773	73,713	78,683
234,800	229,240	277,925	241,246
1,056,600	1,050,683	1,072,880	1,094,338
2,193,032	2,227,449	2,356,884	2,404,742
535,344	623,434	663,420	643,555
2,881,395	3,013,220	3,209,673	3,317,968

TABLE 10.1 (cont.)

Countries	Manpower (SMYs)							
	1959	1962	1965	1968	1971	1974	1977	1980
Middle-income developing								
Thailand	150	250	350	475	600	725	1,134	1,264
Philippines	200	300	400	500	600	620	630	640
Indonesia	15	70	140	240	340	592	914	1,473
Peru	32	65	131	155	180	220	295	290
Colombia	200	338	300	550	809	870	824	881
Ecuador	12	20	34	64	94	200	183	208
Guatemala	19	22	27	43	47	58	71	123
Nicaragua	8	10	17	22	29	34	44	57
Total	636	1,075	1,399	2,049	2,699	3,319	4,095	4,936
Semi-industrialized								
Malaysia	40	90	150	156	195	149	284	386
Korea, Rep.	300	320	340	450	744	807	880	960
Taiwan	250	275	310	350	375	400	404	452
Mexico	190	220	280	520	540	711	1,074	1,079
Panama	11	13	16	25	44	49	29	51
Chile	32	58	113	162	171	192	171	177
Costa Rica	40	48	59	55	61	71	60	75
Total	863	1,024	1,268	1,718	2,130	2,379	2,902	3,180
Industrialized								
Japan	7,200	8,500	10,000	11,500	13,700	14,000	14,784	15,671
Australia	1,500	1,700	1,900	2,130	3,000	3,200	2,425	2,589
New Zealand	250	250	450	475	590	700	707	713
Canada	950	1,050	1,150	1,300	1,450	1,520	1,820	1,836
United States	5,740	6,150	6,570	7,000	7,400	7,500	8,303	8,469
Total	15,640	17,650	20,070	22,405	26,140	26,920	28,039	29,278
People's Republic of China	1,250	4,000	8,000	11,000	13,500	16,000	17,000	17,272
Total Pacific Basin	18,389	23,749	30,737	37,172	44,469	48,618	52,039	54,666

Sources: Data for 1959-1974 were taken from J.K. Boyce and Robert E. Evenson, National and International Agricultural Research and Extension Programs (New York: Agricultural Development Council, 1975); the 1977 and 1980 figures are from J.K. Boyce, M. Ann Judd, and Robert E. Evenson, "Inter-country and Inter-regional Comparisons of the Allocation of Resources to Agricultural Research and Extension" (unpublished manuscript, 1982).

Table 10.1 provides agricultural research expenditure and manpower data for twenty-one Pacific Basin countries for eight time periods between 1959 and 1980. The data show that most countries have steadily increased their spending levels during this period. Overall, the middle-income developing countries increased research expenditures 184 percent between 1959 and 1968, and 89 percent between 1968 and 1980. The growth in manpower was somewhat different—SMYs (scientist man-years) increased over 300 percent between 1959 and 1968, and approximately 140 percent between 1968 and 1980.

Expenditures in the semi-industrialized countries increased even more dramatically, 130 percent between 1959 and 1968 and over 300 percent between 1968 and 1980. It is interesting to note, however, that SMYs increased more slowly than they did in the middle-income developing countries, doubling between 1959 and 1968 and increasing 85 percent between 1968 and 1980.

The differences in the growth rates of expenditures and SMYs are caused, in part, by increases in capital as opposed to operating expenditures. Most of the data we collected did not allow us to distinguish between capital and operating expenditures, but we would judge that sudden and substantial increases in spending tend to be the result of program-building, capital expenditures. It is also likely that there is a considerable lag between capital expenditures and resulting increases in manpower. Indonesia provides a good example. Expenditures on research in Indonesia increased by over 400 percent between 1974 and 1977, probably as the result of a major program-building effort. During the same period, manpower increased by only slightly more than 50 percent. Expenditures in 1980 were about 20 percent lower than in 1977, while SMYs continued to increase by approximately 60 percent. A similar pattern can be seen in the data for other countries like Thailand, South Korea, and Mexico, which have experienced periods of rapid growth in research expenditures as they spend the capital necessary to develop their research systems.

The industrialized countries of the Pacific Basin have increased their spending and manpower but at rates slower than for the middle-income developing and semi-industrialized countries. Expenditures increased by 98 percent between 1959 and 1968 and 31 percent between 1968 and 1980. The increases in manpower were 43 and 31 percent for the two periods, more nearly matching changes in spending than for the middle-income developing and semi-industrialized countries. These data provide further evidence that much of the increase in spending in the latter countries is due to substantial capital expenditures rather than increases in operating expenses.

Our data for the People's Republic of China are based primarily on estimates, but we believe that the data give a fairly accurate picture of spending on agricultural research, especially for the 1970s. The earlier data are not as reliable, so it is difficult to make comparisons between the growth rates of the 1960s and 1970s. China's expenditures have increased steadily since 1959 and its spending level is now almost equal to that of Japan.

TABLE 10.2
Agricultural Research Expenditures and Manpower by World Region (Pacific Basin or Other) and by Industrial Class, 1959-1980

Industrial Class and Region of Countries	Expenditures (Thousands in Constant 1980 US $)			
	1959	1962	1965	1968
Middle-income developing				
Pacific Basin (8)[a]	22,091	28,891	43,752	62,782
Other (16)	44,838	66,169	88,902	99,748
Total (24)	66,929	95,060	132,652	162,530
Share of Pacific Basin in total (%)	(33.0)	(30.4)	(33.0)	(38.6)
Semi-industrialized				
Pacific Basin (7)	15,791	22,216	31,081	36,177
Other (14)	134,119	183,478	255,762	296,354
Total (21)	149,910	205,694	286,843	332,531
Share of Pacific Basin in total (%)	(10.5)	(10.8)	(10.8)	(11.2)
Industrialized				
Pacific Basin (5)	893,423	1,067,796	1,455,966	1,769,750
Other (13)	257,833	423,865	588,099	812,893
Total (18)	1,151,256	1,491,661	2,044,065	2,582,643
Share of Pacific Basin in total (%)	(77.6)	(71.6)	(71.2)	(68.5)
People's Republic of China	54,166	169,265	332,223	469,638
Low-income developing (26)	67,810	71,214	91,514	112,146
Eastern Europe (6)	554,180	924,983	1,058,567	1,183,617
All countries				
Pacific Basin (23)	985,471	1,288,168	1,863,022	2,338,347
Other (75)	1,058,780	1,669,709	2,082,844	2,240,758
Total (98)	2,044,251	2,957,877	3,945,866	4,579,105
Share of Pacific Basin in total (%)	(48.2)	(43.6)	(47.2)	(51.1)

TABLE 10.2 (cont.)

	Expenditures (Thousands in Constant 1980 US $)			
	1971	1974	1977	1980
	77,858	84,137	124,878	118,370
	113,688	113,459	242,677	230,424
	191,526	197,596	367,555	348,794
	(40.7)	(42.6)	(34.0)	(34.0)
	75,161	78,200	94,491	151,301
	325,345	415,975	465,542	532,292
	400,506	494,175	560,033	683,593
	(18.8)	(15.8)	(16.9)	(22.1)
	2,193,032	2,227,449	2,356,884	2,404,742
	895,504	979,048	1,101,282	1,386,326
	3,088,536	3,206,497	3,458,166	3,791,068
	(71.0)	(69.5)	(68.2)	(63.4)
	535,344	623,434	633,420	643,555
	145,883	155,500	205,498	221,696
	1,332,020	1,471,546	1,457,766	1,457,766
	2,881,395	3,013,220	3,209,673	3,317,968
	2,812,420	3,135,528	3,472,765	3,828,504
	5,693,815	6,148,748	6,682,438	7,146,472
	(50.6)	(49.0)	(48.0)	(46.4)

TABLE 10.2 (cont.)

Industrial Class and Region of Countries	Manpower (SMYs)			
	1959	1962	1965	1968
Middle-income developing				
Pacific Basin (8)[a]	636	1,075	1,399	2,049
Other (16)	968	1,187	1,434	1,697
Total (24)	1,604	2,262	2,833	3,746
Share of Pacific Basin in total (%)	(39.7)	(47.5)	(49.4)	(54.7)
Semi-industrialized				
Pacific Basin (7)	863	1,024	1,268	1,718
Other (14)	3,556	4,369	5,648	6,959
Total (21)	4,419	5,393	6,916	8,677
Share of Pacific Basin in total (%)	(19.5)	(19.0)	(18.3)	(18.8)
Industrialized				
Pacific Basin (5)	15,640	17,650	20,070	22,405
Other (13)	5,284	7,192	8,956	10,672
Total (18)	20,924	24,842	29,026	33,077
Share of Pacific Basin in total (%)	(74.7)	(71.0)	(69.1)	(67.7)
People's Republic of China	1,250	4,000	8,000	11,000
Low-income developing (26)	1,731	1,938	2,470	3,078
Eastern Europe (6)	16,621	26,793	34,012	39,488
All countries				
Pacific Basin (23)	18,389	23,749	30,737	37,172
Other (75)	28,160	41,479	52,520	61,894
Total (98)	46,549	65,228	83,257	99,066
Share of Pacific Basin in total (%)	(39.5)	(36.4)	(36.9)	(37.5)

a. Number of countries in parentheses.
Sources: Data for 1959-1974 were taken from J.K. Boyce and Robert E. Evenson, National and International Agricultural Research and Extension

TABLE 10.2 (cont.)

	Manpower (SMYs)			
	1971	1974	1977	1980
	2,699	3,319	4,095	4,936
	2,056	2,447	4,952	6,203
	4,755	5,766	9,047	11,139
	(56.8)	(57.6)	(45.3)	(44.3)
	2,130	2,379	2,902	3,180
	8,029	8,989	11,000	11,330
	10,159	11,368	13,902	14,510
	(21.0)	(20.9)	(20.9)	(21.9)
	26,140	26,920	28,039	29,278
	11,665	13,157	17,083	17,443
	37,805	40,077	45,122	46,721
	(69.1)	(67.2)	(62.1)	(62.7)
	13,500	16,000	17,000	17,272
	3,708	4,401	7,265	7,543
	44,310	50,286	49,608	49,608
	44,469	48,618	52,039	54,666
	69,768	79,280	89,908	92,127
	114,237	127,898	141,947	146,793
	(38.9)	(38.0)	(36.7)	(37.2)

<u>Programs</u> (New York: Agricultural Development Council, 1975); the 1977 and 1980 figures are from J.K. Boyce, M. Ann Judd, and Robert E. Evenson, "Inter-country and Inter-regional Comparisons of the Allocation of Resources to Agricultural Research and Extension" (unpublished manuscript, 1982).

In Table 10.2 we compare the expenditures and SMYs of the Pacific Basin countries to those of other countries in the same industrial classes. Several interesting patterns emerge from these data. Among twenty-four middle-income developing countries, the share of eight Pacific Basin countries in both expenditures and SMYs has remained relatively constant over time, increasing in the late 1960s and early 1970s, but then returning to previous levels. On the other hand, the seven semi-industrialized Pacific Basin countries have steadily increased their share of the total expenditures for this industrial class. The expansion of agricultural research programs in Malaysia, Mexico, Taiwan, and South Korea is responsible for most of the increase in the Pacific Basin's share. In terms of manpower, the share of semi-industrialized Pacific Basin countries has remained fairly constant.

Among industrialized countries, those of the Pacific Basin clearly dominate both agricultural research expenditures and SMYs, although the magnitude of this domination has been decreasing. The share of expenditures of these countries has dropped from 77.6 percent in 1959 to 63.4 percent in 1980, and the share of SMYs from 74.7 to 62.7 percent.[3]

Research and extension expenditures per SMY are presented in Tables 10.3 and 10.4. It is readily apparent that expenditures on research scientists are much higher than expenditures on extension workers for all regions and industrial classes. The reasons for this difference are obvious—salaries for scientists are higher than for extension workers and the amount of capital (laboratory equipment and the like) needed to maintain a productive research program is substantial.

In general, expenditures per SMY have increased for all the industrialized countries. For the middle-income developing and semi-industrialized countries, expenditures per SMY have been somewhat erratic. As mentioned previously, large capital investments can inflate expenditures in one year while SMYs remain relatively unchanged, and then expenditures in the next period will drop while SMYs increase in response to the previous capital investment.

Among the industrialized countries, those in the Pacific Basin spent more per SMY in all years. There is no clear trend in expenditures per SMY for middle-income developing and semi-industrialized countries. Expenditures per SMY were generally higher in middle-income developing countries throughout the 1960s, and this has continued to be the case among the non-Pacific Basin middle-income developing countries during the 1970s. If one could correct for the distortions caused by large capital investments, it would probably be the case that the relative cost per scientist has been approximately the same in both middle-income developing and semi-industrialized countries.

Finally, Tables 10.5 and 10.6 present publications data by commodity or type of crop for middle-income developing and semi-industrialized countries. To the degree that publications can be used as a rough measure of the output generated by agricultural research programs, the commodity mix of subjects of the publications can be seen as a reflection of the commodity

TABLE 10.3
Agricultural Research Expenditures per Scientist Man-Year by World Region (Pacific Basin or Other) and by Industrial Class, 1959-1980 (constant 1980 US $)

Industrial Class and Region of Countries	1959	1962	1965	1968	1971	1974	1977	1980
Middle-income developing								
Pacific Basin	40,789	41,350	45,558	42,837	40,764	35,147	35,100	28,840
Other	56,366	57,997	59,974	55,628	52,135	48,280	49,884	45,657
Semi-industrialized								
Pacific Basin	33,055	30,766	30,321	26,752	41,908	37,800	43,362	49,598
Other	43,919	39,674	39,844	43,616	40,746	41,942	40,779	41,407
Industrialized								
Pacific Basin	67,573	71,262	82,270	94,994	103,248	103,279	109,625	106,581
Other	45,477	54,714	63,409	75,727	78,194	78,096	73,647	92,968
People's Republic of China	43,333	42,316	41,528	42,694	39,655	38,896	37,260	37,260

Sources: Data for 1959-1974 were taken from J.K. Boyce and Robert E. Evenson, National and International Agricultural Research and Extension Programs (New York: Agricultural Development Council, 1975); the 1977 and 1980 figures are from J.K. Boyce, M. Ann Judd, and Robert E. Evenson, "Inter-country and inter-regional Comparisons of the Allocation of Resources to Agricultural Research and Extension " (unpublished manuscript, 1982).

TABLE 10.4
Agricultural Extension Service Expenditures per Scientist Man-Year by World Region (Pacific Basin or Other) and by Industrial Class, 1959-1980 (constant 1980 US $)

Industrial Class and Region of Countries	1959	1962	1965	1968	1971	1974	1977	1980
Middle-income developing								
Pacific Basin	21,342	21,407	22,457	16,815	17,115	13,680	16,678	28,840
Other	12,659	12,345	10,549	11,687	9,739	8,763	10,455	45,657
Semi-industrialized								
Pacific Basin	13,255	13,807	19,481	16,253	14,046	13,279	14,595	49,598
Other	18,148	20,279	25,583	26,135	24,640	17,269	24,073	41,407
Industrialized								
Pacific Basin	25,350	30,057	31,811	33,868	33,180	36,480	81,435	106,581
Other	15,722	16,894	20,174	21,348	21,549	20,524	23,308	92,968

Note: Data not available for the People's Republic of China.

Sources: Data for 1959-1974 were taken from J.K. Boyce and Robert E. Evenson, National and International Agricultural Research and Extension Programs (New York: Agricultural Development Council, 1975); the 1977 and 1980 figures are from J.K. Boyce, M. Ann Judd, and Robert E. Evenson, "Inter-country and inter-regional Comparisons of the Allocation of Resources to Agricultural Research and Extension." (unpublished manuscript, 1982).

TABLE 10.5
Average Number of Publications on Selected Agricultural Commodities for Pacific Basin and Other Countries by Industrial Class, 1972 and 1976

Industrial Class and Region of Countries	Wheat 1972	Wheat 1976	Rice 1972	Rice 1976	Corn 1972	Corn 1976	Cotton 1972	Cotton 1976	Sugar 1972	Sugar 1976	Other[a] 1972	Other[a] 1976
Middle-income developing												
Pacific Basin	5.0	2.8	107.0	152.6	32.8	37.4	8.4	7.8	12.8	21.0	377.2	688.0
Other	52.3	43.3	36.0	33.0	93.3	98.5	66.8	53.3	22.0	17.8	1105.3	1491.0
Semi-industrialized												
Pacific Basin	27.6	30.4	81.8	94.4	29.6	37.2	1.2	2.0	25.0	35.2	536.0	809.8
Other	35.8	45.5	29.3	40.3	80.5	127.5	22.5	28.0	46.5	60.3	1294.3	1943.3

a. Includes other crops and livestock.

Sources: Data for 1972 were taken from J. K. Boyce and Robert E. Evenson, National and International Agricultural Research and Extension Programs (New York: Agricultural Development Council, 1975); the 1976 figures are from J. K. Boyce, M. Ann Judd, and Robert E. Evenson, "Inter-country and Inter-regional Comparisons of the Allocation of Resources to Agricultural Research and Extension" (unpublished manuscript, 1982).

TABLE 10.6
Ratio of Number of Publications to Value of Agricultural Output (Thousands in Constant 1980 US $) for Pacific Basin and Other Countries by Industrial Class, 1972 and 1976

Industrial Class and Region of Countries	Wheat 1972	Wheat 1976	Rice 1972	Rice 1976	Corn 1972	Corn 1976	Cotton 1972	Cotton 1976	Sugar 1972	Sugar 1976	Other 1972	Other 1976
Middle-income developing												
Pacific Basin	.32	.21	.15	.12	.18	.13	.39	.29	.07	.08	.29	.43
Other	.33	.21	1.35	.28	.53	.51	1.85	.26	1.46	1.59	.50	.56
Semi-industrialized												
Pacific Basin	4.85	12.33	.13	.18	.61	.86	.004	.10	.41	.39	.30	.44
Other	.16	.06	.07	.05	.16	.22	.09	.13	.14	.15	.28	.33

Sources: Data for 1972 were taken from J. K. Boyce and Robert E. Evenson, National and International Agricultural Research and Extension Programs (New York: Agricultural Development Council, 1975); the 1976 figures are from J. K. Boyce, M. Ann Judd, and Robert E. Evenson, "Inter-country and Inter-regional Comparisons of the Allocation of Resources to Agricultural Research and Extension" (unpublished manuscript, 1982).

mix of the subjects of the research itself. Further, if one looks at the relationship between publications and agricultural production, one can also judge whether a particular commodity is being given too much or too little weight in research.

Table 10.5 reveals that the commodity mix of subjects of publications in Pacific Basin countries is quite different from that in other countries. The presence of two international centers, the International Rice Research Institute (IRRI) in the Philippines and the International Wheat and Maize Improvement Center (CIMMYT) in Mexico, has undoubtedly increased the number of rice publications in Pacific Basin countries (Table 10.5) and the number of corn and wheat publications in the semi-industrialized Pacific Basin countries. However, numbers of publications alone do not reveal anything about the relative importance of a particular commodity in a region's research programs. When one looks at the ratios of rice publications to the value of rice production for the Pacific Basin countries (Table 10.6), they indicate that rice is not being overemphasized in research (despite the single focus of IRRI). On the other hand, the high ratios for corn and very high ratios for wheat (Table 10.6) in the semi-industrialized Pacific Basin countries suggest that the presence of CIMMYT in Mexico may be distorting the commodity mix of research for these countries.

Table 10.6 indicates that research investment for the three staple food crops (wheat, rice, and maize) tends to be moderate to low with the exception of that for wheat and corn for the semi-industrialized Pacific Basin countries. The semi-industrialized countries outside the Pacific Basin have low ratios for all commodities, especially rice. One somewhat surprising fact revealed by the data in Table 10.6 is that there does not appear to be any consistent overinvestment in sugar research. Sugar is an important export crop for many developing countries, so that it might have been expected that sugar research would receive more emphasis than research on several of the basic food crops.

This section has shown that public-sector agricultural research programs have been expanding throughout the 1960s and 1970s in all industrial classes and regions of the world. This expansion will, of course, have an impact on agricultural productivity, but the actions of the public sector are only one of many things that influence the potential for growth. As the following section will show, the private sector also plays an important role in changing a country's capacity for growth.

The Private Sector and Technology Production in Agriculture

We noted in the introduction that the reform of legal systems to achieve lower costs of transactions has proven to be very difficult for many countries. Legal systems are also critical to the size and efficiency of private-sector research and development directed toward improvement of agricultural technology. In this section we first review the very limited data available regarding private-sector research spending. These data show that most developing and semi-industrialized countries of the Pacific Basin and the rest of the world expend very little in the private sector to produce new agricultural technology. By contrast, the private sector is very significant in the developed countries, being of approximately equal magnitude with the public sector in the United States.

We then turn to an examination of the factors behind these data. Part of the explanation, of course, lies in the size of the purchased input markets. In low-wage economies there is little demand for farm machinery, hence little demand for mechanical technology. A similar observation is much less true for chemical technology. However, we conclude that the type of legal systems in place is also an important factor. Most developing and semi-industrialized economies of the region have legal systems that serve them poorly regarding technology production. The Philippines and South Korea, and possibly Taiwan, are exceptions to some extent. Many other legal systems are designed to provide protection to types of inventions for which foreign firms and individuals enjoy a comparative advantage; these legal systems provide little incentive or encouragement for the types of inventions for which developing countries enjoy a comparative advantage.

Consider first the available data for private research expenditures and scientist man-years devoted to agriculturally related research. These data are summarized in Table 10.7 (data are available for relatively few Pacific Basin countries). These data indicate that the United States has a major private-sector research enterprise, accounting for 40 percent or more of total private plus public effort. Australia and New Zealand have modest private efforts accounting for 10 percent or so of the total. The private sector in South Korea, Malaysia, Taiwan, and, surprisingly, Japan, is of minor importance. Some of these data are for the 1960s and if updated might show somewhat more private research. We should also acknowledge that the scope of agriculturally related research in the private sector is not well defined in most countries, hence these data should be regarded with more than usual caution. Even granting the limitations of the data, however, the fact that the private sector is investing little in the production of agricultural technology in most countries listed in the table emerges clearly enough. The same is true in most of the Pacific Basin countries, and we want to ask why this is so and to turn to data on patenting activities for further insight.

Invention in the private sector can be encouraged and stimulated by several policy instruments. The general industrial policy toward new entrants and toward monopoly, tariff protection, and price controls can encourage or discourage inventive activity in important ways. It can also provide different incentives for domestic and multinational firms. It particularly affects process and product inventions by firms large enough to capture significant added profits from inventions. Contracts can also be used to encourage invention, and many defense department sources use contracts as such an instrument. Trade secrecy laws by which penalties are imposed

TABLE 10.7
Private-Sector Agricultural Research Activity in Selected Countries for Selected Years

Country	Year	Expenditure	SMYs	Percentage of Total Public-Sector and Private-Sector Exp.	SMY's
Austria	1970	ASh. 7.75m	10	6	5
Belgium	1963	BFr. 24.3m	27	15	10
	1960	BFr. 23m	--	7	--
France	1960	-	71	--	13
Greece	1963	-	2	--	1
Italy	1973	Lire 2033m	--	8	--
	1970	Lire 1536m	--	9	--
	1969	Lire 1903m	--	12	--
	1964	-	117	--	11
Netherlands	1960	G. 5.5	62	17	10
Norway	1963	NKr. 13.1m	189	44	48
Portugal	1960	E. 3.5m	9	8	3
Spain	1960	P. 6.2m	--	6	0
Sweden	1963	SKr. 3m	142	9	35
	1960	SKr. 16m	101	34	12
Australia	1973	-	260	--	8
New Zealand	1973	-	91	--	10
United States	1960s	-	--	40	--
	1950s	-	--	25	--
Chile	1974	E. 255m	8	5	4
Kenya	1970	-	5	--	2
Nigeria	1966	N.580,000	--	12	--
South Africa	1970	R. 860,000	--	4	--
Japan	1972	Yen 3870m	544	4	3
	1963	-	580	--	3
Korea, Rep.	1973	-	5	--	1
Malaysia	1973	-	3	--	2
Taiwan	1973	-	15	--	5

Source: James K. Boyce and Robert E. Evenson, National and International Agricultural Research and Extension Programs (New York: Agricultural Development Council, 1975).

on parties convicted of stealing or pirating trade and invention secrets tend to reinforce the industrial-structure policies.

It has long been recognized that monopolistic industrial-structure policies reinforced by trade secrecy laws have inhibitory features regarding invention and technology development. Such policies limit the incentives to invent to a relatively small number of firms. Further, by encouraging secrecy, the "disclosure" effects of invention are discouraged.

The conventional *invention patent* was designed as a means to (1) encourage exchange of inventions, (2) bring inventions out of secrecy by forcing disclosure, thus enabling other inventions to be made, and (3) provide an additional incentive to invent. In return for these benefits the inventor receives a limited monopoly on his or her invention. Encouraging invention by this means has the added advantage that it broadens the base for inventions. Inventors need not be associated with large firms to be able to profit from inventions. This feature has turned out to be quite important in mechanical agricultural invention. In the United States thousands of patents were obtained on a broad array of agricultural inventions before the public research system was established. Inventions were produced by farmers, farmhands, blacksmiths, and numerous other noncorporate inventors.

Table 10.8 summarizes agriculturally related invention in the United States. Data for thirteen technology fields are reported. Prior to 1860 or so, all reported inventions were individual inventions. Many of these inventions formed the basis for the development of agricultural implement firms. By 1910 or so, perhaps 25 percent of these inventions were assigned to an organized corporation. The agricultural machinery industry was the largest industry in the United States in terms of value added in 1906, and much of the growth of the industry was due to the continuous series of inventions from both individual and corporate inventors.

The proportion of corporate inventors rose from 25 percent around 1910 to roughly 70 percent by 1950 and has remained roughly constant since then. The proportion of patents granted to foreigners (the table reports only on patents granted to U.S. citizens) was less than 5 percent prior to 1930, but it had risen to 15 percent by 1950 and roughly 30 percent by 1980. Individual inventors have been of critical importance to the general processes of machinery improvement (and to a lesser extent, chemical and biogenetic improvement). They have served a role similar to "wildcat" oil-exploration firms by investing their efforts in highly uncertain, highly innovative inventions, while corporate inventors have concentrated on the safer inventions associated with product and process improvements. Virtually all new agricultural implements developed throughout U.S. history, and even its recent history, were the product of wildcat inventions made outside the corporate sector.

In many other countries, however, the invention patent has not encouraged broad-scale invention by those countries' nationals, as can be seen in Table 10.9, which reports data on all invention patents (including agricultural patents) for numerous countries. Here we note that most semi-industrialized and developing countries grant high proportions of their invention patents to foreigners. We also note that the ratio of patents granted to nationals in foreign countries to patents granted in all nations is low for these countries. This observation indicates two important characteristics of technology markets. First, there is considerable international trade or exchange in technology. Second, invention varies between countries in its degree of adaptiveness. Most of the low-income, low-wage economies, including countries in the Pacific Basin, engage in heavily adaptive invention as measured by the ratio of patents granted abroad to patents granted at home.

The table suggests the basis for understanding the widespread dissatisfaction with the international invention patent system, particularly as regulated by the major patent conventions (notably the Paris Convention). Developing countries and, to a lesser extent, semi-industrialized countries enter into a rather poor bargain. They commit themselves to recognition of patents by foreigners (mostly multinational firms) and hence are forced to enter into a royalty or similar arrangement when they have the option of "pirating" inventions (i.e., provided they have the capacity to pirate). Although in return their inventions are given similar protected treatment in developing countries, the data show that they have few national inventions. Even these highly adaptive or derivative from developed countries' inventions. Hence they have limited "upstream" markets, and "downstream" markets in poorer economies are not large.

Perhaps the most important aspect of membership in the international invention system is that it tends to inhibit the development of legal systems truly suited to Third World countries. Such systems would be designed to provide incentives for national invention where the country has a comparative advantage. They would also be designed to facilitate the purchase or imitation of technology from abroad on the best terms possible.

Most countries of the Third World, including those in the Pacific Basin, have not moved toward more effective legal systems and have chosen instead to vent frustration in international forums and to simply weaken their patent systems, with the result that they reduce patenting by foreigners but do little to encourage local inventions. An important exception to this tendency exists. Table 10.10 reports data on *utility models*, usually described as "petty" patents, for countries utilizing this legal device. Here we may note that for all of the semi-industrialized countries, utility model patents outnumber invention patents granted to nationals, and they are predominantly granted to nationals.

The standard invention patent must meet three standards:

1. The invention must be "novel," i.e., new.
2. The invention must be "useful."
3. The invention must exhibit an "inventive step"; i.e., it must be unobvious to practitioners skilled in the technology field.

With international conventions, courts generally accept evidence from anywhere in the world that would contravene the patent.

Utility models, on the other hand, generally have a narrower search field, in that only evidence from the country or region is accepted for overturning a utility model patent. Further, the inventive step requirement is typically weaker. Thus, with appropriate court interpretations, utility models can be quite successful in encouraging local adaptive invention.

TABLE 10.8
Patent Activity as Reflected by Number of Patents for Agricultural Technology Fields, United States, 1800s and 1900s

Period	Harvesting Equipment				Animal-Related Fields			
	Hay Handling	Grain Reaping and Threshing	Corn Husking	Cotton and Other Husking	Dairy Equipment	Livestock Housing	Poultry Equipment	Animal Harness
Pre-1830	2	13	0	0	0	0	0	1
1830-1839	17	89	38	0	0	1	0	1
1840-1849	22	74	32	0	0	5	3	10
1850-1859	216	178	121	8	2	35	1	59
1860-1869	903	401	143	30	10	292	11	226
1870-1879	742	455	186	37	17	514	21	393
1880-1889	668	544	142	94	16	923	97	727
1890-1899	411	246	102	97	30	849	112	529
1900-1909	484	355	171	183	77	717	343	456
1910-1919	441	241	124	331	196	1100	385	302
1920-1929	213	182	128	387	139	808	367	91
1930-1939	147	162	97	622	62	425	282	28
1940-1949	181	137	23	340	91	212	79	10
1950-1959	379	118	45	901	244	399	96	9
1960-1969	315	103	61	753	260	530	70	9
1970-1979	257	185	79	638	218	582	34	11

TABLE 10.8 (cont.)

Period	Tillage Equipment			
	Husbandry	Planters, Drills	Cultivation	Plows
Pre-1830	0	0	0	91
1830-1839	0	12	7	108
1840-1849	2	52	18	97
1850-1859	17	332	55	225
1860-1869	84	997	691	934
1870-1879	104	1172	640	660
1880-1889	80	1661	656	438
1890-1899	83	1263	489	341
1900-1909	83	1131	470	392
1910-1919	225	875	381	339
1920-1929	156	274	242	228
1930-1939	239	421	112	125
1940-1949	86	202	65	122
1950-1959	209	179	69	135
1960-1969	455	236	47	98
1970-1979	457	227	56	75

Sources: Data from J.K. Boyce and Robert E. Evenson, National and International Agricultural Research and Extension Programs (New York: Agricultural Development Council, 1975); J.K. Boyce, M. Ann Judd, and Robert E. Evenson, "Inter-country and Inter-regional Comparisons of the Allocation of Resources to Agricultural Research and Extension" (unpublished manuscript, 1982).

TABLE 10.9
Industrial Design Patents and Trademarks Granted in Selected Countries
(grouped by Level of Economy), 1975 and 1980

	Industrial Designs Granted				Trademarks Granted			
	Nationals		Foreigners		Nationals		Foreigners	
Countries	1975	1980	1975	1980	1975	1980	1975	1980
1. Industrial market economies								
A. Moderate- to rapid-growth								
Japan	34,129	30,696	700	593	104,156	41,577	5,010	5,290
Austria	3,987	4,260	1,517	1,744	1,458	3,333	1,247	2,143
France	11,320	13,209	857	1,560	12,645	37,332	4,312	9,784
Denmark	390	314	486	630	1,520	1,324	3,704	3,339
Germany, Fed. Rep.	54,231	70,701	2,609	4,844	9,396	13,006	3,432	3,533
Benelux	1,671	1,691	1,376	1,262	5,529	4,418	3,571	3,082
Norway	243	252	364	434	522	464	2,531	2,675
B. Slow-growth								
Canada	337	337	1,168	978	3,507	8,779	3,391	6,755
Ireland	34	46	176	284	107	162	893	2,093
Switzerland	465	351	213	325	2,552	2,462	1,508	1,507
Sweden	1,283	1,558	364	588	1,397	1,577	2,591	2,603
United States	3,428	3,056	854	892	28,353	17,319	2,578	1,566
Australia	1,165	1,377	568	580	2,835	1,860	4,252	2,715
United Kingdom	1,665	2,166	1,354	2,799	5,878	3,356	5,562	3,352
Finland	165	371	222	350	276	703	1,126	3,542
New Zealand	157	170	167	173	845	524	2,015	1,318
2. Semi-industrialized economies								
A. Rapid-growth								
Spain	3,234	2,239	224	407	--	11,119	--	12,822
Israel	115	266	42	56	224	255	1,064	868
Greece	--	--	--	--	1,546	1,260	1,469	1,800
Singapore	--	--	--	--	--	784	--	2,499
Portugal	266	335	216	228	770	1,035	481	581
Brazil	--	136	--	81	--	136,808	--	42,821
Korea, Rep.	1,583	3,917	6	154	--	--	--	--
Hong Kong	--	--	--	--	348	603	1,182	1,647

TABLE 10.9 (cont.)

Countries	Industrial Designs Granted				Trademarks Granted			
	Nationals		Foreigners		Nationals		Foreigners	
	1975	1980	1975	1980	1975	1980	1975	1980
B. Moderate- to slow-growth								
Chile	--	--	--	--	2,883	1,986	2,810	1,735
Venezuela	59	77	34	16	635	2,360	1,452	1,961
Argentina	2,426	n.a.	159	n.a.	12,428	--	2,032	--
Costa Rica	--	--	--	--	521	--	974^a	--
Mexico	--	--	--	--	3,352$_a$	8,637$_b$	3,117	8,292^a
Turkey	--	--	--	--	557^a	1,129^b	1,171^a	1,181^b
Uruguay	--	--	--	--	1,293	6,414	1,152	541
3. Developing economies								
Ecuador	--	--	--	--	210	513	612	1,007
Iraq	19	9	--	--	68	184	236	885
Morocco	82	116	15	40	428	541	309	443
U.A.R. (Egypt)	127	166	8	27	234	145	396	408
Colombia	11	n.a.	5	n.a.	702	584^a	1,542	672
Philippines	151	n.a.	19	n.a.	539	1,225	341	1,013
Kenya	--	--	--	--	153	443	585	747
Ghana	--	--	--	--	27	8	263	167
India	723	n.a.	29	n.a.	3,019	n.a.	640	n.a.
Sri Lanka	8	n.a.	--	n.a.	43	160	130	376
Indonesia	--	--	--	--	1,160	6,479$_b$	697	2,741
Pakistan	74	93	14	36	283	494^b	640	780
Zambia	--	--	3	--	22	4	441	215
OAPI	26	--	57	--	62	n.a.	954	n.a.
4. Centrally planned economies								
Germany, East	-	-	--	--	299	150	325	265
Czechoslovakia	577	1,304	8	20	182	134	302	258
USSR	-	-	--	--	48	1,627	5	559
Hungary	165	120	11	28	107	149	290	194
Poland	139	124	16	28	288	116	640	544
Bulgaria	27	38	5	6	15	73	434	492
Yugoslavia	102	n.a.	30	n.a.	156	n.a.	154	n.a.
Romania	-	-	--	--	205	418	334	53

a. 1976.
b. 1979.
n.a. - not available.

Source: WIPO, *Industrial Property* (Geneva: World Intellectual Property Organization, annual issues).

TABLE 10.10
Utility Models (Petty Patents) Granted in Selected Countries, 1967, 1975, and 1980

Country	Applications						Utility Models Granted					
	Nationals			Foreigners			Nationals			Foreigners		
	1967	1975	1980	1967	1975	1980	1967	1975	1980	1967	1975	1980
Germany, Fed. Rep.	42,214	30,114	26,094	11,344	11,938	8,153	20,948	12,099	10,252	2,400	2,181	1,879
Italy	4,418	—	n.a.	778	n.a.	n.a.	3,935	n.a.	n.a.	702	n.a.	n.a.
Japan	109,154	178,992	190,388	1,906	1,668	1,397	20,601	47,449	49,468	721	957	533
Philippines	141	565	762	2	7	24	94	331	465	—	9	3
Poland	1,647	1,896	2,523	22	31	36	411	1,775	1,680	4	25	20
Portugal	139	78	118	25	13	15	77	153	159	9	25	6
Spain	7,601	7,650	5,830	710	1,353	1,162	6,177	4,128	3,845	600	2,041	1,131
Brazil	—	—	1,657	—	—	89	—	—	131	—	—	13
Korea, Rep.	—	7,052	7,936	—	238	622	—	1,032	1,315	—	14	438

Sources: Data for 1967 were taken from J. K. Boyce and Robert E. Evenson, National and International Agricultural Research and Extension Programs (New York: Agricultural Development Council, 1975); the 1975 and 1980 figures are from J. K. Boyce, M. Ann Judd, and Robert E. Evenson, "Inter-country and Inter-regional Comparisons of the Allocation of Resources to Agricultural Research and Extension" (unpublished manuscript, 1982).

Table 10.11 reports the distribution, by industry, of patents granted from 1970–1974 in selected countries to both nationals and foreigners. The data show that the importance of the agricultural and food sectors is considerably higher in the lower-income countries generally. A high proportion of these patents were granted to nationals, whereas most of the chemical patents in these countries were granted to foreigners.

Legal systems vary considerably in their coverage of agricultural invention, particularly regarding biogenetic inventions. A review of Latin American legal systems illustrates this diversity. Although Latin American countries have various forms of copyright and seed- and breed-certifying systems, we will concentrate only on the patent and plant variety protection systems, because these are the primary modes for protecting the results of agricultural research. Although all patent systems encompass at least some agricultural research results, all Latin American legal systems that we considered exclude patent or like protection to much of the agricultural research activity. To depict the differing approaches to what is appropriately patentable or protectable under a plant variety protection statute, we will assume a hypothetical "Latin American Agricultural Research Corporation" (LAARC). LAARC is presumed to be involved in an extensive agricultural research program covering the entire spectrum of invention and development research activities directed toward improving agricultural productivity. Following is a listing of probably tangible results of the LAARC research activities. For the purpose of this discussion, it is assumed that all of these research results have been developed exclusively by LAARC using LAARC funds, were never before existent or described anywhere in the world, and were in fact better than the state of the art.

Mechanical/Electrical Inventions

1. LAARC Plow I: A basic innovation in plows that is adaptable to a wide range of soil and climatic conditions.
2. LAARC Plow II: A minor modification for adapting a plow to be utilized in a specific localized soil condition.

Chemical Inventions

3. LAARC Chemical Fertilizer: A new fertilizer, a mix of chemical compounds that optimize tolerance to extremes in soil moisture conditions.
4. LAARC Insecticide: A new chemical compound that is a useful insecticide.
5. LAARC Herbicide: A new chemical compound that is a useful herbicide.
6. LAARC Pharmaceutical for Animals: A chemical compound that is a new pharmaceutical for controlling disease in farm animals.

TABLE 10.11
Average Annual Distribution of Patents Granted in Selected Countries (by Industrial Sector), According to the International Patent Classification, 1970-1974 (percentages)

Country	Agri-culture	Food-stuffs and Tobacco	Personal and Domestic Articles	Print-ing	Trans-portation	Metal-lurgy	Textiles	Paper	Build-ing	Mining	Instru-ments
Canada	1.5	1.5	2.3	2.2	8.8	3.3	4.2	1.3	2.6	0.9	10.3
France	2.1	1.3	3.5	2.3	10.8	1.8	2.7	0.3	4.9	0.4	13.5
Germany, Fed. Rep.	1.5	1.0	2.6	2.4	8.9	2.8	3.6	0.6	4.5	1.0	13.3
Switzerland	2.3	1.6	3.7	2.0	8.4	1.7	5.1	0.2	5.1	0.1	12.1
United States[d]		1.3			6.3	1.0	1.0		2.3		10.4
United Kingdom	0.8	0.9	2.4	1.3	7.2	2.2	3.1	0.03	3.6	e	11.1
Chile	8.2	3.9	2.4	1.0	7.4	4.7	3.2	1.5	3.6	0.5	5.1
India	0.8	1.6	2.1	1.0	6.0	4.0	4.0	0.4	2.7	0.5	4.8
Kenya	6.4	8.0	1.4	1.3	4.0	2.2	1.0	0.2	2.2	0.8	1.3
Philippines	5.2	5.7	3.0	0.9	2.8	3.5	3.7	1.0	2.2	0.5	0.7
Venezuela[f]	4.0	0.7	10.7	0.04	1.7	4.2	2.1	0.2	0.9	0.3	3.1
Korea, Rep.[g]	5.6	12.8	6.6	3.6	1.4	7.2	3.8	4.4	5.9	2.5	3.8

Country	Electricity–Related[a]	Chemical–Related[b]	Machinery–Related[c]	Total
Canada	14.0	25.2	21.6	100
France	14.5	18.9	22.9	100
Germany, Fed. Rep.	19.8	15.6	22.2	100
Switzerland	13.9	26.4	17.2	100
United States[d]	19.6	19.5	38.5	100
United Kingdom	15.4	19.2	20.0	100
Chile	6.9	37.5	13.9	100
India	16.4	32.9	22.6	100
Kenya	3.7	58.0	9.4	100
Philippines	2.8	58.2	9.7	100
Venezuela[f]	0.05	70.7	1.3	100
Korea, Rep.[g]	8.0	20.8	13.5	100

a. Includes the following subsections of the International Patent Classification: electricity, lighting and heating, and nucleonics.
b. Includes medicine and hygiene, and chemistry.
c. Includes separating, shaping, and engines and pumps.
d. The source used for the United States grouped patents according to the industrial classification.
e. Included under machinery-related.
f. Up to 1972.
g. Some patents are unclassified.

Sources: For all countries except the United States, WIPO, *Industrial Property* (Geneva: World Intellectual Property Organization, various issues); for the United States, *Science Indicators 1976* (Washington, D.C.: National Science Board, 1977).

Biogenetic Inventions

7. LAARC Soybean: A new, improved soybean variety developed in a plant breeding program.
8. LAARC Corn: A new hybrid corn seed variety developed in a plant breeding program, with LAARC retaining control over the hybrid parents.
9. LAARC Rose: A new variety of ornamental rose that can be asexually reproduced.
10. LAARC Beef Cattle: A new pure breed of beef cattle developed in a selective breeding program.
11. LAARC Bacteria: A new, improved nitrogen-fixing bacterial strain developed using recombinant-DNA techniques.
12. LAARC Vaccine: A live-virus vaccine.

Other Inventions

13. LAARC Computer Program: A new computer program utilized in the determination of the optimal mix of chemicals used in the LAARC Chemical Fertilizer (Invention 3).
14. LAARC Accounting System: A new accounting system used for optimally allocating research personnel and facilities in various research projects, adaptable to any large agricultural research organization.

Table 10.12 despicts the availability of patent and plant variety protection for the various LAARC inventions in various Latin American countries, as well as in the United States. The United States has been treated in this table for comparison purposes because it has a quite comprehensive scheme of protection.

For mechanical/electrical inventions such as the LAARC Plow I, all of the countries provide some type of utility patent protection. For the minor adaptation of the LAARC Plow II, only Brazil has a utility model or petty patent system that would provide protection. Otherwise, unless the LAARC Plow II was sufficiently innovative to satisfy utility patent statute requirements for "level of invention," no protection would be available for it.

As to the chemical inventions, only Argentina and the United States provide patent protection for the fertilizer, insecticide, and herbicide. Most countries' patent statutes specifically preclude patents on certain types of inventions related to food production and health. In Argentina, pharmaceutical drugs are expressly precluded from protection.[4]

For the biogenetic inventions, none of the countries provides patent or variety patent protection for the beef cattle breed. Only Argentina and the United States provide much in the way of protection for the new plant varieties. The United States does not provide plant variety protection for the hybrid corn; presumably, such protection is not needed because corn breeders can effectively maintain control over the hybrid parents and thus already have "genetic" protection. Although there are legal systems in some countries (e.g., Hungary, Romania) that provide breeder's rights to new animal breeds, none of the countries of Table 10.12 has such a provision.

The possibility of patent protection for the nitrogen-fixing bacteria and the live-virus vaccine was only recently ruled upon by the U.S. Supreme Court, the matter having been an open question of whether a "utility" patent on living organisms could actually be obtained.

The exemplary "other" inventions, namely, the computer program and the accounting system, are not provided with patent or variety protection under any of the legal systems; except for a copyright system that may provide some limited protection for the computer program.

Historically, inventions and discoveries involving living organisms have contributed greatly to increases in agricultural productivity. Until recently, most advances stemmed from domestication and selective breeding of plants and animals, a technology that could be termed the application of "classical genetics." In the recent past, much has been learned about the genetic makeup of living things and new techniques have been developed for manipulating the genetic structure to speed development of new strains of microorganisms, new plant varieties, and new animal breeds—a technology that could be termed the application of molecular genetics. In addition, there have been technological innovations that speed up the process of selective breeding, including sperm storage, artificial insemination, estrus synchronization, super-ovulation, embryo recovery, embryo transfer, embryo storage, sex selection, twinning, in vitro fertilization, and the like.[5]

Based on the new biogenetic technologies, it is reasonable to expect that biogenetic inventions will play an increasing role in agricultural research. However, in the past, patent or variety protection for living organisms has been much more restrictive than patent systems for devices and chemical compositions, even in the United States. Indeed, most countries, and especially developing countries, have not gone nearly as far as the United States in providing private protection for recent inventions in living organisms. Neither have developing countries, in general, participated in the industrial biogenetic research boom currently underway. The largest part of the current new private biogenetic research is directed toward health and pharmaceutical products, but significant research directed toward agriculture is already underway (at least US$100 million in effort in 1982). If only a small part of the market projected by a recent assessment in the agricultural sector is realized within a 10- or 20-year time span—a market estimated at US$50- to-100 billion—it will have important implications for developing countries, and indeed worldwide. The new biogenetic technology emerging from this work may be less location-specific than current technology, although this outcome is highly unlikely. It is clear that developing countries will have to be concerned about their capacity to undertake this research in both the public and private sectors. At present, they have virtually no capacity to do so.

There are a number of reasons for differences in patenting activity between developed and developing countries. Perhaps the most important

TABLE 10.12
Comparison of "LAARC" Research Developments and Inventions with Availability of Patent or Variety Protection in Various Latin American Countries and the United States

	Mechanical/ Electrical Inventions		Chemical Developments or Inventions			
	Plow I Major	Plow II Minor	Fertilizer	Insecticide	Herbicide	Disease-Controlling Chemical
Argentina	yes Art. 1 Law 111	no	yes Rule 27/74	yes Rule 27/74	yes Rule 27/74	no Art. 4 Law 111
Brazil	yes	yes Art. 10	no Art. 9b (Process)	no Art. 9b (Process)	no Art. 9b (Process)	no Art. 9C (Process)
Chile	yes Art. 4a	no	no Art. 9a (Process)	no Art. 5a (Process)	no Art. 5a (Process)	no Art. 5a (Process)
Mexico	yes Art. 4	no	no Art. 10 §V	no Art. 10 §IV	no Art. 10 §IV	no Art. 10 §IV
Peru	yes Art. 1	no	no Art. 5C	maybe	maybe	no Art. 5C
Venezuela	yes Art. 5 & Art. 14.2	no	no Art. 15.1	no Art. 15.1	no Art. 15.1	no Art. 15.1
United States	yes	no	yes	yes	yes	yes

TABLE 10.12 (cont.)

	Biogenetic Developments or Inventions					
	Soybean	Hybrid Corn	Rose	Beef	Nitrogen-Fixing Bacteria	Live Virus Vaccine
	yes Plant Protection Act	yes Plant Protection Act	yes Art. 2B, Law of Seed	?	yes Rule 27/74	no
	no Art. 9C	no Art. 9C	no Art. 9J	no Art. 9J Product of Nature	no Art. 9J	no
	no Art. 5a	no Art. 5a	no Art. 5c	no Art. 5a	no	no
	no Art. 10 §I	no Art. 10 §I	no Art. 10 §I	no Art. 10 §I	no Art. 10 §I	no
	no Art. 5b	no Art. 5b	no Art. 5b	no Art. 5b	no Art. 5b	no
	no Art. 15	no Art. 15	no Art. 15.3	no Art. 15.1	no	no
	yes	no	yes	no	no	no

TABLE 10.12 (cont.)

| | Other Inventions ||
	Computer Program	Accounting System
Argentina	maybe Rule 15/75	no Art. 4
Brazil	yes Art. 9h	no Art. 9h
Chile	old law (1935)	no Art. 5b
Mexico	no Art. 10 §V Art. 9 §III	no Art. 9 §III
Peru	maybe Art. 3 Art. 4C	no Art. 4C
Venezuela	no Art. 14.5	no Art. 15.2
United States	no	no

is the fact that the technological opportunity for types of inventions is heavily biased toward biogenetic inventions and against mechanical/electrical inventions in developing countries; yet biogenetic inventions have not been afforded patent protection in developing countries.

The bias against mechanical/electrical invention in low-wage economies is created by the basic dilemma of hand-versus-machine performance of tasks. In the lowest-wage economies, there simply is no potential for the invention of machines to replace hand labor. In most low-wage economies, crops are harvested by hand. Harvesting machines, even after a century or more of continuous improvement in high-wage economies, continue to be uneconomical in these economies. In general, as we move from low-wage to high-wage economies, we first observe that plows and cultivators replace hoes and hand-tillage tools, and that animal power replaces human labor. At later stages, planters and seeders replace hand seeding. Later still, cultivators are used for weed control. Mechanical threshers replace hand threshing at moderately high-wage levels, and mechanical harvesting machines tend to become economical only at relatively high-wage levels in developing countries.

The data on patents for selected countries in Table 10.13 reflect these considerations to some extent. These data show total patents in the International Class A01 (agriculture, forestry, animal husbandry, hunting, trapping, and fishing) and thus include patenting activities in areas that we have not included in our public-sector research data. However, the series is dominated by agricultural patents, as the table title indicates. We would judge that approximately 80 to 90 percent of the patents were related to agricultural production.[6]

Table 10.14 provides a summary of the data in Table 10.13 according to the level of per capita income in the countries involved. Middle-income and semi-industrialized countries have the highest patent intensities. The data include patents to both nationals and foreigners and reflect to some extent the scope for invention in countries where the basic economies of hand-versus-machine methods have recently favored machine methods.

On the whole, the data on patenting show the following:

1. The poorest developing countries grant few patents in agriculture. They generally have not devised legal systems to encourage indigenous invention of any kind.

2. The medium-income developing countries grant a significant number of patents but, with few exceptions, these patents are granted to foreigners protecting their products in growing national markets. Many of these patents are in chemical fields. Countries in this group (notably the Philippines) have attempted to devise petty patent systems to encourage local adaptive invention and appear to be doing so.

3. The advanced developing countries do still more patenting. However, except where some imagination is employed in designing legal systems, many of these countries grant most patents to foreigners. Where utility models or other devices are used to stimulate domestic invention, as in Brazil, they

TABLE 10.13
Patents Granted in Relation to Agricultural Production, Selected Countries, 1965-1972

Region and Country	Annual Number of Patents	
	1965-1968	1969-1972
Northern Europe		
Denmark	186.3	179.5
Finland	44.2	49.7
Ireland	48.7	45.5
Norway	n.a.	70.8
Sweden	206.2	185.2
United Kingdom	476.7	427.0
Central Europe		
Austria	304.0	327.0
Belgium	415.3	362.7
France	1,178.5	835.0
Germany, Fed. Rep.	473.7	299.2
Netherlands	76.5	65.0
Switzerland	497.0	417.5
Southern Europe		
Italy	n.a.	792.5
Portugal	35.0	n.a.
Spain	448.0	395.7
Eastern Europe		
Bulgaria	48.0	61.7
Czechoslovakia	95.7	162.5
Hungary	34.5	115.5
Poland	n.a.	49.5
USSR	828.0	1,231.3
North America		
Canada	576.7	444.7
United States	785.0	830.0
Oceania		
Australia	116.5	133.5
Latin America		
Chile	53.0	79.7
Colombia	26.0	30.5
Costa Rica	22.0	10.0
Cuba	11.0	4.0
Trinidad and Tobago	7.2	5.3
Uruguay	32.0	24.0
Venezuela	25.5	111.7

TABLE 10.13

Region and Country	Annual Number of Patents	
	1965-1968	1969-1972
Africa		
Kenya	8.0	10.2
Malawi	22.0	15.0
Mauritius	n.a.	6.5
Morocco	29.3	19.0
Rwanda	0	0
Sierra Leone	0	0.5
South Africa, Rep.	326.5	n.a.
Zimbabwe	55.0	86.5
Tunisia	5.7	5.7
Uganda	7.0	6.7
Zaire	n.a.	6.0
Zambia	26.7	8.0
Asia		
India	32.5	33.7
Israel	87.2	118.7
Malaysia	8.7	14.0
Philippines	19.2	43.7
Korea, Rep.	7.4	11.0
Sri Lanka	8.0	n.a.
Syria	7.7	n.a.

n.a. = not available.

Source: WIPO, Statistical Reports, 1965-1972 (Geneva: World Intellectual Property Organization).

TABLE 10.14
Patents Granted in Relation to Agricultural Production, by Level of per Capita Income in the Countries Involved, 1965-1972

Per Capita Income Level in US $	Annual Number of Patents		Patents per US $ billion Agricultural Product	
	1965-1968	1969-1972	1965-1968	1969-1972
More than $1,750	5,574	4,745	65	51
$1,001-$1,750	1,998	2,792	50	64
$401-$1,000	1,089	1,171	80	80
$150-$400	111	113	21	20
Less than $150	116	97	10	8

Source: James K. Boyce and Robert E. Evenson, National and International Agricultural Research and Extension Programs (New York: Agricultural Development Council, 1975.).

appear to have a significant impact. Only the more advanced countries in this semi-industrialized category appear to be generating inventions that, in turn, are patented in other countries.

4. Among developed countries the patenting pattern has changed quite rapidly in recent years, as Japan and the European countries (notably France) have expanded their foreign patenting. The United States, which once dominated many of these technology fields, is now relegated to a lesser role.

Conclusions and Policy Recommendations

Our data generally show that in the more developed countries of the region, the level of public-sector investment in both research and extension is relatively high. Legal systems provide incentives for mechanical and chemical invention in the private sector. Private-sector investment, however, is quite modest except in the United States, partly due to the fact that countries other than the United States do not encourage biogenetic invention.

For the semi-industrialized and developing countries of the region, public-sector investment in extension and rural development projects is relatively high. Investment in research programs is low to modest, with all countries of the region showing high rates of growth in investment and probably in quality as well. Only the Philippines and South Korea are really encouraging much private-sector invention (Malaysia may also belong to this category), due to their use of the utility model patent rather than the invention patent.

Our data show that, with few exceptions, developing and semi-industrialized countries have joined international patent conventions, although at the same time expressing great concern over technology transfer form developed countries and technology dependence. For the most part the strong statements regarding technology in North-South and Third World international forums have not been translated into serious efforts to design legal systems suited to the conditions of the countries in question. The only modification to the standard-invention utility model system undertaken by developing countries has been some form of preclusion of technology fields from patentability. The preclusion usually affects foods and drugs.

Few developing countries have designed petty patent systems. None to date have attempted to use plant patents, including plant variety protection systems. The developing countries are thus not encouraging biogenetic inventions.

We could understand the reluctance to provide stimulus to indigenous private-sector inventions somewhat better if public-sector investment was high and its institutions strong. However, this is not the case in most countries. Public investment in agricultural research is considerably less intensive than it has been in developed countries for the past half-century. Public investment in mechanical/electrical and most chemical fields is of minor importance in most developing countries.[7]

Why is it that the developing and semi-industrialized countries of the region show such great reluctance to use legal systems to stimulate indigenous inventions? Why, at the same time, do most join international patent conventions, which result in automatic and mandatory recognition of intellectual property rights of foreign inventors, thus cutting off their option to imitate at low cost? These same countries intervene in commodity markets regularly through tariffs and quotas to limit the payment of rents to foreigners.

We believe that several factors are involved. These factors include a belief on the part of policymakers that there is little scope for adaptive invention in developing countries and that most technology must be imported. General industrial policy toward transnationals and toward local firms affects attitudes toward legal systems. In a number of countries, existing industrial firms see legal systems that would broaden the invention base as a threat because they would encourage more competition. We believe, however, that there is a fundamental misconception regarding monopoly rights in patents, which has led to a great reluctance to use them.

In this final section we first address the issue of monopoly rights in patent systems. We then discuss the compatibility of public and private invention in agriculture and the problems attendant on building effective public-sector institutions.

Monopoly Rights, Rents, and Patent Systems

Perhaps the first point to be made regarding monopoly rights and the ability of an inventor to collect monopoly rents is that patent systems are not the only means by which such rents accrue. In the absence of formal patent systems a few inventions that can be freely and easily imitated will be made, but most inventions will tend to be held in trade secrecy, enabling the inventor to collect monopoly rents through the sale of products embodying the invention.

The second point of importance here is that monopoly rights are limited in two ways. The first is relatively unimportant. It is the legal time limit over which monopoly rights are granted (usually eighteen years or so). The most important limit on monopoly rights is the erosion of monopoly due to subsequent invention. The major point here is that an effective legal system not only grants monopoly incentives but provides a disclosure mechanism that helps make possible subsequent invention and, in turn, erodes the original monopoly rents.

Inventions, whether biogenetic, chemical, or mechanical, have a "public good" character. They are also fundamentally conceptual even if embodied in plants, animals, machines, or chemicals, so that they are not scarce in any economic sense once they are discovered. They may be employed in an added use without sacrifice to other employment effectiveness. Thus, the marginal cost of employing an invention in another use, say to produce an added bushel of wheat, is simply the cost of imitation.

From the perspective of standard welfare economics at the current moment, a known invention will be of maximum advantage to society if employed in all uses where its value exceeds the costs of imitation. There are several types of policy instruments utilized to stimulate invention: monopoly, prizes, contracting, legal systems, private associations, and public systems. Of these, three tend to meet the foregoing standard. When the public-sector research systems produce inventions they usually make them available at little or no cost to all parties interested in using the inventions. Similarly, if a public-sector agency induces inventions by a prize system or by contracting with a research organization and then makes the inventions freely available to the public, the efficiency requirement is met. In the case off the private growers' association, the requirement is often met as well, in that inventions are usually made available to all members.

In the other two cases, monopoly and legal systems, the requirement is usually not met. Monopolistic firms do not produce where marginal costs equal the social value of the goods produced and do not employ inventions efficiently. Trade secret protection and patent protection allow the inventor to charge a price for use of an invention. This price will be higher than the cost of imitation. As a consequence, inventions are not optimally used. A social or welfare loss is thus incurred with monopoly, trade secrets, and patents. Yet most Western countries justify some monopoly on the grounds that it increases invention and usually gives patent protection, trade secrecy protection, or both to private firms.

The argument for these policies is that for a certain range of potential inventions, private self-interested firms and individuals are superior to public-sector research systems in producing inventions for the following reasons: (1) many more individuals can be stimulated to work on a problem in the private sector than could be stimulated in a public-sector system, thus improving the probability of discovery; (2) the private sector knows what is required in the way of making inventions more highly tailored to the market clientele, whereas many public systems do not have an effective clientele; (3) private systems can be of many sizes and types, utilizing informal and formal institutional arrangements; and (4) private, self-interested individuals have more "animal spirit" than public employees who are too security-oriented and lack boldness.

We do not have extensive evidence to support the judgment that all of these arguments have credence. We observe that most major inventions have, in fact, been generated under the protection of legal systems. We also observe that when public-sector agricultural research program compete directly with the private sector (as in hybrid corn, for example), they come out second best. We do believe that the arguments of this section will show, however, that if an effective patent system is in place, there is reason *not* to provide trade secrecy protection and little reason to encourage industrial monopoly. (We also wish to argue in the final section that combinations of public-sector research systems, public-sector contracts with private firms, and imaginative patent systems are optimal.)

The cost of the limited monopoly associated with patents is qualitatively quite different from the standard cost argument regarding industrial monopoly.

The monopoly in question is granted only for the new or improved technology component. The holder of a patent can collect rents only to the degree that his or her invention is superior to the next-best alternative. Further, as the next-best alternative is improved, the original inventor's ability to collect rents is eroded. The disclosure requirement in the patent is designed to provide information to encourage other, competing inventions and thus lead to an erosion of rents from the first invention. As these rents are eroded the benefits pass into the public domain as lower prices on consumer products in a competitive economy.

Patent disclosure is not the only form by which invention potential is increased. In fact, public research systems often concentrate on providing genetic materials, technical concepts, instrumentation, etc., freely to inventors so as to stimulate invention by making discovery more probable. Much technology is transferred in this form. In biogenetic technology new varieties or lines produced in one station or location add to the gene pools available to public and private breeders in other locations.

Many public-sector scientists and administrators fear that the provision of publicly produced genetic material and the like to private firms will produce monopoly rents to these private firms. This fear is simply without basis where the private firms in question are competitive. In that situation, the full benefits of research findings in the public sector will be passed on to the consumer, and thus into the public domain. Private firms will capture rents only on the "value added" component that they provide, if this component is patentable. As long as competition prevails, public-sector genetic materials will enable a competitor to produce another variety that limits the rents on the first.

The situation is different if the public material is made available to a monopolistic firm. In that case it will result in private monopoly gains whether or not the monopolist is able to patent it. In any situation where full monopoly power is allowed to exist, the monopolist will benefit from any publicly produced technology that lowers the monopolist's costs. The availability of a patent system actually should help the public research system limit the transfer of rents to monopolists; the system could, for example, force a monopolist to pay royalties or licensing fees. We will argue in the final section, however, that in situations where monopolists have control over final technology, the public system has a responsibility to provide competition.

The experience of the Philippines, Brazil, Japan, and other countries with petty patent systems seems to have been generally good in terms of stimulating indigenous inventors. By providing a weaker and narrower standard of patentability and by administering the system efficiently, these countries have stimulated local adaptive inventive activity. This stimulation is important in agriculture where a great deal of minor modification to farm machines for different types of soil, crops, etc., is desirable.

On the matter of the extension of patent protection over new varieties of plants and animals, we would suggest that a system that adequately safeguards public programs and stimulates private activity makes good sense. This type of invention is generally so location-specific that it has to be done in situ; thus, the issue of international patent recognition may not be too important. It would be unwise to allow a legal system to hamper the work of public research systems. These systems should play two roles in the private-public mix of research systems: they should provide raw materials to private breeders and they should provide competition. Thus, laws have to be carefully drafted to insure that public systems can serve both roles. There is always a question of adequacy of incentives from private activity. One has to be careful to provide sensible incentives to invention. It is critical for both public and private research institutions that competition be monitored. It would be a serious mistake to franchise the right to produce technology to any private or public institution.

There is probably some scope for more research contracts to private firms from public agencies. This step may become much more feasible in the future. The international research centers could lead the way by more experimentation with contracts to produce materials meeting certain standards. Fundamentally, however, the fact that indigenous inventive effort is at very low levels should be borne in mind. Almost any program that stimulates more indigenous inventive activity is likely to have a beneficial effect.

Public-Private Research Compatibility

As private research activities expand, they have several effects on existing public research systems. These effects can sometimes be unproductive as the public and the private systems work toward a compatible relationship. By private systems here we mean research programs conducted by private profits making firms, not research by semi-public commodity associations such as sugarcane growers' associations. The latter present rather different problems to be discussed below.

Experience in the United States has generally shown that the public system finds two roles compatible with its responsibilities. The first is to undertake a range of immediate or basic research and to make findings available to all private firms. The second is to serve as an alternative source of technology and to undertake various testing and verification activities designed to curb abuses of the private sector. In some areas of technology the two roles work quite effectively. In hybrid corn production, for example, public experiment stations have produced inbred lines and other types of basic or general research on corn production, particularly on agronomic practices. The inbred lines have been made freely available to private breeders. At the same time, public stations have produced hybrids in direct competition with private breeders. They have been unsuccessful in terms of achieving large sales, but they have provided important competition. It appears to be the case that in situations where private firms have adequate incentives to product technology, they are more effective in doing so than are public bureaucracies.

The public stations have been successful at producing inbred lines in competition with private breeders. Thirty years ago most inbred lines were produced by private breeders. Today almost all important inbred lines in use have been produced by public experiment stations. (It might be noted that the economic value of hybrid corn varietal improvement since 1957, the data at which Zvi Griliches calculated benefits in his classical study, has been several times as great as the early improvements. Much of this result is attributable to improvements in inbred lines.)

In terms of engineering research, public-sector agricultural experiment stations have not been highly effective in producing much of value to the private sector except in new machines where the potential market is small. In fact, if one looks at the history of invention of farm machinery in the United States, several interesting patterns emerge. The first pattern is that all distinct "new" items of farm machinery were brought to a commercial stage by small independent firms engaging in what might be called "wildcat" invention. This observation holds true for machines and implements developed after 1890 or so, when large manufacturing firms with sophisticated engineering staffs has been established (most of them originating as small wildcat invention firms). The large firms have tended eventually to dominate the production of new farm implements because of superior capacity to produce, market, and repair these implements.

Public systems thus have reason for concern at the prospect of more private activity and more competition. All public institutions have reason to fear competition because of the basic nature of bureaucracies. The tendency of bureaucracies without competitive alternatives to become inefficient and to serve their own rather than clients' interests is great. Bureaucracies want monopoly power to protect their inefficiency in many cases.

Yet competition has been vital to the success of public-sector agricultural research systems. In the United States this competition takes place between states. Plant breeders in Indiana are pressured by clientele farmers with political clout to match results in Iowa. International centers are providing some competition for national programs in the developing world.

If more effective legal systems are devised for some developing countries and encourage more invention, the major impact on public systems will be in biogenetic inventions. The major impact on the economies in question may well be in mechanical and chemical invention, but the public role is not large in these inventive efforts. It is possible that more hybrid corn situations will develop. If private soybean breeders in the United States, for example, are successful in developing new varieties protected by PVPCs (plant variety patent conventions), the situation will raise some issues for developing countries.

Public research centers such as the international centers for rice and other crops will have a responsibility to see that they provide their own material with broad protection and then make it available to other breeders. They also have a responsibility to encourage competition among users of the material and to provide some competition themselves. We have noted that providing technology to monopolists is not optimal, but private-sector breeding activities can be quite competitive if actively encouraged (there are large numbers of hybrid corn producers, for example).

The use of private activity will create problems of another sort. Private firms are likely to be able to hire scientists away from public-sector experiment stations—already a serious problem in many countries. Agricultural scientists are trained at very high cost (usually supported by aid funds). However, the public institutions employing them may provide low salaries and poor working conditions, and thereby lose them to the private sector and to international agencies.

The building of effective research institutions is not easy under the best of circumstances. Effective research institutions are characterized by (1) a dedicated, skilled, and imaginative scientific staff, (2) an effective clientele, and (3) a means by which the "pool" of potential inventions or research discoveries can be recharged or kept current. If the first requirement is not met, the research institutions produce little. If the second is not met, they produce the "wrong" products. If the third is not met, they are subject to exhaustion.

Successful agricultural experiment stations have met these requirements in various ways. First, they have provided stable and attractive working environments to scientists and have obtained the full attention and devotion of scientists to the institutions. Many of the semi-industrialized and developing countries of the region cannot achieve this end because of restrictions on salaries. They often pay salaries much lower than scientists can earn in alternative jobs. They either lose the scientists to other jobs or retain them on a part-time basis. Research and teaching institutions cannot be effective with part-time staff. This situation is aggravated when international institutions recruit scientists from these countries, usually without considering the damage done to local institutions.

The second requirement, that of an effective clientele group (in this case farmers), is very difficult to meet in countries lacking political institutions that give farmers and farm interest groups power. In the absence of these interest groups, the direction and guidance of the research institutes tend to be from above and reflects the interests of the bureaucrcy. Effective research programs do not serve their own interests. In many parts of the Pacific Basin, research programs have been built with international aid even though the local political support base for them has been weak. The presumption is that by demonstrating effectiveness and productivity, the research programs will generate a local support base. They have not done so in many countries; many programs or systems are stalled between declining aid support and slow-growing local support.

The final requirement, that of a recharge mechanism for invention potential, is usually met by bringing various basic research programs into the agricultural research institutions themselves. History has shown that basic research in the universities devoted to arts and sciences has little recharge value, but that research guided by agricultural research interests has been highly productive. Most of the newer research systems in the lower-income countries are highly committed to applied research, with little attention given to recharge. The international centers and stronger national programs provide some recharge, but they too are far more applied in their approach than, say, the U.S. Agricultural Experiment Stations.

The lack of recharge and the loss of scientists are problems that tend to be remedied only after they have already become serious. They tend to be regarded as serious sooner by effective clientele groups demanding output from the system, than possibly by many system administrators. The Pacific Basin has a rich variety of research and other institutions producing technology today. Although their progress is far from optimal in many, perhaps most, countries in the region, undeniable progress is being made.

Notes

1. See Robert E. Evenson, Paul Waggoner, and V. W. Ruttan, "Economic Benefits from Research: An Example from Agriculture," *Science* 205 (September 1979).

2. In most cases, data for 1959-1974 were taken from J. K. Boyce and Robert E. Evenson, *National and International Agricultural Research and Extension Programs* (New York: Agricultural Development Council, 1975); the 1977 and 1980 figures are from J. K. Boyce, M. Ann Judd, and Robert E. Evenson, "Inter-country and Inter-regional Comparisons of the Allocation of Resources to Agricultural Research and Extension," unpublished ms., 1982. All of the data (as well as sources) which were compiled for the later work are available from the authors.

The extension data we have is too sketchy to allow us to produce a table comparable to Table 10.2. Subsequent tables do contain measures based on our limited extension data, and the authors have data on extension expenditures and workers for a number of countries.

3. It should be noted here that the other tables in this section (i.e., Table 10.1 and Tables 10.3-10.8) do not include any low-income developing countries or Eastern European countries. Data for these countries were not included because none of the Pacific Basin countries for which we have data falls into either group. We have added them to Table 10.2 in order to show the role that Pacific Basin countries play worldwide in the area of agricultural research. As the data show, this role has been and continues to be an extremely important one. The share of expenditures on agricultural research by Pacific Basin countries in the world total has ranged between 43.6 and 51.1 percent since 1959. One final point regarding the data should be made here. We have, as consistently as possible, not included data on expenditures/manpower for either forestry or fisheries in any of the data we report, although forestry and fisheries are often included in agricultural research budget figures.

4. The rationale for precluding certain types of inventions from protection appears to be related to a basic "needs" concept and to an interest in preventing transnational firms from capturing monopoly rents. However, the resulting elimination of national protection is a serious hindrance to local invention.

5. A comprehensive discussion of the development of biogenetic technology is contained in a report titled "Impact of Applied Genetics," published by the Office of Technology Assessment of the Congress of the United States, April 1981.

6. The series does not include food-processing patents.

7. India is an exception. The Council for Scientific and Industrial Research engages in a broad range of inventive activity.

11
Development of Agricultural Research Capacity: Some Perspectives from Asian Experience

Vernon W. Ruttan

Throughout most of human history, increases in agricultural output have been achieved chiefly by expansion in the area cultivated. By the end of the twentieth century almost all increases in agricultural output will have to come from improved and more extensive use of existing crop area. As a result of this transition, the capacity to develop and manage agricultural technology in a manner consistent with a nation's resource and cultural endowments has become the single most important variable accounting for differences in agricultural productivity among nations.

This chapter addresses four interrelated topics in the development of agricultural research capacity. First, it reviews some recent changes in the environment for international assistance for the development of national agricultural research systems. Second, it characterizes the recent developments in some of the national agricultural research systems on the Asian side of the Pacific Basin. Third, it identifies some of my concerns about the development of agricultural research systems, and finally, it suggests some change in the structure of international support for national agricultural systems.[1]

International Assistance for the Development of National Agricultural Research

The architects of the post–World War II set of global institutions included the problems of meeting world food needs and reducing poverty in rural areas as essential elements of their vision of a world community that could assure all people freedom from want and insecurity. They sought to achieve this vision by the creation of a set of global bureaucracies—the UN specialized agencies.

The establishment of a UN Food and Agriculture Organization (FAO), headquartered in Rome, was the major institutional response to the concern for freedom from hunger and the reduction in rural poverty. The explosion in the number of new nation-states associated with the decolonization of the 1950s and 1960s placed new demands for assistance on the FAO system— demands that the FAO intellectuals failed to recognize, that the FAO bureaucracy was unprepared to accept, and that the FAO governing council was unwilling to support. The result has been the emergence of a welter of bilateral and multilateral agricultural programs designed to support or coordinate agricultural development efforts in poor countries. The effect by the late 1970s was to create a "tower of babel" in which competition and aggression among and between assistance agencies and assistance recipients were often as characteristic as cooperation and accomplishment.

The National Aid Agencies

Bilateral technical assistance to agricultural development during the postwar period has been dominated by three major national programs— those of the United States, the United Kingdom, and France. More recently the Federal Republic of Germany has become an actor of major significance. A number of other nations—Canada, Australia, Sweden, Holland, Belgium, Switzerland, and Japan—occupy smaller and more specialized roles.

In recent years a number of bilateral agencies have experienced serious difficulties stemming from weakened domestic support, declining professional capacity, and difficulty in adapting their style of operations to the changing political and professional environments in the countries in which they work. The bilateral programs have also been weakened by their tendency to let political objectives subvert program content. Let me illustrate by referring to the U.S. bilateral assistance programs of the U.S. Agency for International Development (US/AID or merely AID).

In 1973 the U.S. Congress mandated, under its "new directions" legislation, that U.S. development assistance be targeted at meeting the basic needs of the poorest people in the developing countries. Yet during the 1970s there has instead been a decline in US/AID real resources allocated, under development assistance, to countries where technical and institutional development needs are most severe, and an increase in resources allocated, under the Economic Support Fund, to countries considered politically sensitive (Table 11.1).[2] In many countries the once powerful U.S. programs of assistance for agricultural and rural development have been reduced to filling in the technical assistance, research, and training gaps resulting from overambitious World Bank projects. On the positive side, a larger share of U.S. development assistance has been allocated to the agricultural sector and, within the agricultural sector a larger share has apparently been devoted to research on food crops.

The Development Banks

The World Bank has become an increasingly important source of funding for agricultural development. During its early years support for agricultural

TABLE 11.1
U.S. Multilateral and Bilateral Assistance to Developing Countries for Selected Fiscal Years from 1970 to 1979 (millions of constant 1972 US $)

	1970	1972	1974	1976	1978	1979
Bilateral assistance (Budget Authority)						
Development assistance	1,206	1,036	752	765	858	947
Economic Support Fund[a]	437	559	559	1,332	1,488	1,322
Other[b]	165	107	190	131	142	231
Receipts						
Principal	-54	-45	-23	-153	-203	-194
Interest	-21	-16	-29	-116	-146	-167
Net Total	1,553	1,641	1,449	1,959	2,139	2,250
Multilateral assistance (Budget Authority)						
Multilateral development banks	769	1,422[c]	2,028[c]	533	1,292	1,522
Callable capital	(231)	(954)	(1,072)	(74)	(551)	(545)
Paid-in capital	(538)	(468)	(956)	(459)	(740)	(1,007)
International organizations[d]	147	152	132	155	161	160
Total Multinational Aid	916	1,574	2,160	688	1,453	1,712
Public Law 480 Food Aid (Outlays)						
Program costs	1,397	1,320	873	744	799	848
Receipts	-437	-307	-294	-215	-258	-246
Total P.L. 480 Outlays	960	1,013	579	529	541	602

Note: A U.S. GNP deflator was used throughout this chapter to convert current dollars to constant 1972 US $ (1972 US $ = 1).

a. Includes Mideast Special Requirements Fund, Indochina Postwar Reconstruction Fund, and peacekeeping operations.
b. Includes International Narcotics Control, Inter-American Foundation, refugee assistance, and the Peace Corps.
c. In 1972, includes $1.08 billion to maintain gold value of U.S. dollar contributions; in 1974, includes $1.31 billion to maintain U.S. dollar value of contributions.
d. Voluntary contributions to the international organizations. Assessed contributions are part of budget subfunction 153.

Source: Congressional Budget Office, Assisting the Developing Countries: Foreign Aid and Trade Policies of the United States (Washington, D.C.: U.S. Government Printing Office, September 1980).

development was largely a byproduct of major multipurpose infrastructure investments in hydroelectric, transportation, and related development areas. Over time, project funding for agricultural resource development achieved increased emphasis. Beginning in the mid-1960s, the World Bank began making loans for the development of agricultural research and training institutions. The first of these loans was for the development of the University of the Philippines College of Agriculture.

As lending for agricultural development has increased, the World Bank has rapidly expanded its project lending and management staff capacity. The smaller regional banks—the Inter-American, Asian, and African Development Banks—have not been able to match World Bank professional capacity in these areas and have tended to focus on smaller-scale projects and to piggyback on larger World Bank projects.

As the World Bank's emphasis on agricultural research, extension, and education projects has expanded, there are indications that its effectiveness has declined. During much of the last decade a concern with the transfer of resources has increasingly dominated the capacity of the recipient country to implement and manage bank-funded projects. In the area of agricultural research, World Bank support for facilities development has often outrun the development of capacity to manage and staff the new research facilities. The result has often been resource dissipation rather than resource transfer.

The International Agricultural Research System

Since the mid-1960s, a new system of international agricultural research institutes has emerged as perhaps the most dynamic component of the global agricultural support system. The initial units in the system, the International Rice Research Institute (IRRI), the International Wheat and Maize Improvement Center (CIMMYT), the International Center for Tropical Agriculture (Centro Internacional de Agricultura Tropical, or CIAT), and the International Institute for Tropical Agriculture (IITA) were at first funded by the privately endowed Rockefeller and Ford Foundations. The further expansion of the institute system was made possible by the major national aid agencies and by the World Bank and regional banks organized as the Consultative Group on International Agricultural Research (CGIAR). The governance of the system is characterized by a highly innovative system of funding and management. Although system funding and planning are centrally coordinated, research management is decentralized to the individual institute level.

The new technologies developed by the institutes have contributed to significant expansion in commodity production, particularly in wheat and rice in a number of poor countries. The effectiveness of the CGIAR system is, however, constrained by the lack of capacity of many national research systems to make effective use of the new knowledge and prototype technology that the CGIAR system of institutes is capable of producing. It is also increasingly recognized that some of the dramatic contributions of the institutes have been the result of the ability to exploit lags in the application of scientific and technical knowledge. There is currently a perception that the easy gains have been realized and that the institutes themselves have begun to lag in their capacity to take advantage of recent advances in biological science and technology in their crop and livestock development programs.

Foundations and Private Voluntary Agencies

From the mid-1950s to the late 1970s the two major U.S. foundations, Ford and Rockefeller, were major innovators and supporters of agricultural development. The Rockefeller Foundation provided much of the entrepreneurial professional leadership for the new agricultural research institutes. The Ford Foundation field offices attracted some of the best intellectual talent of American universities to their very substantial agricultural and rural development programs. By 1980, as a result of the effect of inflation on the value of endowment portfolios and conscious decisions to reorient program activities, neither the Rockefeller nor the Ford Foundation was playing more than a marginal role.

A number of private voluntary agencies that have been active in the food aid and agricultural development field have expanded their programs in the 1970s. In the United States this expansion has occurred primarily with government support. Some of the private voluntary agencies have been a source of imaginative program initiatives. As their public support has risen, however, their relationship to US/AID has increasingly tended to evolve into a patron-client mode (more than 75 percent of the CARE and Catholic Relief budgets come from public sources). In turn, they have often taken on a major role in mobilizing political support for the AID programs.[3]

Six Asian Agricultural Research Systems

I would now like to turn to a characterization of several of the major national agricultural research systems, with a focus on some of the contrasts and similarities among three pairs of Asian countries—Japan and India, Korea and the Philippines, and Indonesia and Malaysia.

The Japanese agricultural research system, like that of the United States, drew heavily on Germany's experience for its inspiration. In the United States, the German model had its primary impact on the organization of the state agricultural experiment stations. In Japan the central government played a stronger role relative to the prefectural governments in establishing the agricultural research infrastructure. Initially the prefectural system developed somewhat more slowly than the national system. This relation began to change in the late 1890s, and since 1910 between two-thirds and three-fourths of the expenditures for agricultural research have been at the prefectural level.

The development of the Japanese system has been characterized by a series of four stages: The first stage, at the beginning of the Meiji period (1868), involved an attempt to transfer Western mechanical technology from Great Britain and the United States to Japan. This stage was quickly followed by the transfer of more appropriate biological and chemical science and technology from Germany. The second stage, which began in the 1880s, involved the rationalization and extension of indigenous technology. The third stage, from the 1920s to the 1940s, emphasized scientific research capacity and nationally coordinated crop development programs. After World

War II the research system was reorganized to give the branch stations of the national system and the prefectural stations greater autonomy.

The commitment of resources to agricultural research has been substantial by any standard. In 1977 there were about 3,400 researchers (plus about 3,000 technical and clerical workers) located at the thirty research and experiment stations operated by the Ministry of Agriculture and Forestry. There were in addition approximately 7,000 researchers and over 11,000 technical and clerical employees located at the 379 stations managed by Japan's forty-seven prefectures. This commitment of resources approximately equaled that in the United States. One measure of the effectiveness of the Japanese system is that agricultural productivity in Japan has grown at approximately the same rate as in the United States over the last century in spite of the much more serious resource constraints that confront Japanese farmers.

The Indian agricultural research system was initially modeled more along an institutional pattern transferred from the United Kingdom. Since independence, India has developed one of the world's larger and more sophisticated agricultural research systems. At the time of independence, India inherited the elements of a research system that had already made important contributions to agricultural production. This system was strengthened during the 1950s and 1960s with support from US/AID and the Rockefeller and Ford Foundations. In terms of both the number and quality of professional resources, the Indian agricultural research system ranks among the leading half-dozen research systems in the world.

There is no question that the investments in agricultural research by the government of India and by US/AID and other donors have paid off handsomely. Studies by Robert Evenson and Dayanath Jha and by A. S. Kahlon, H. K. Bal, P. N. Saxena, and Dayanath Jha indicate rates of return in the 40-60 percent range for the system as a whole.

The foregoing summarization is not to suggest that there are no serious weaknesses in the system. The mixed federal-state system has not yet reached the level of maturity that characterizes the U.S. federal-state or the Japanese national-prefectural systems. It performs better in some Indian states and for some commodities than in others. A great deal of concern has been expressed as to the effect of excessive bureaucratization on research entrepreneurship and productivity. But the impressive performance of Indian agriculture over the last decade is testimony to a level of effectiveness that many skeptics were unwilling to credit until very recently.

Both the Philippines and Korea have emerged with substantial capacity to contribute to agricultural production over the past two decades. Yet there are important contrasts in their organization and capacity. In the Philippines, approximately 840 scientists trained at the MS and PhD levels were, in the late 1970s, employed by research and training institutions. Even after discounting for teaching, consulting, and administrative commitments, there are probably over 300 scientist-years available for agricultural research at the MS and PhD levels. The Korean system is considerably smaller than the Philippine system. About 190 scientists trained at the MS and PhD levels are employed by the Office of Rural Development, and a somewhat smaller number are employed by the universities. A larger share of available scientist-years is probably devoted to research in Korea than in the Philippines.

The two systems present a striking contrast in terms of research organization and management. In Korea, a "concentrated" management style is employed.[4] Both agricultural research and extension are organized under the semi-autonomous Office of Rural Development. Administration of research is highly centralized. The universities, except for Seoul National University, play a relatively modest role in agricultural research. Strong links are maintained with the relevant international agricultural research institutes in order to facilitate technology transfer (borrowing, screening, adaptation) as well as technology development. Major attention has been focused on rice. Rice yields have risen rapidly and are now the highest in Asia, with the possible exception of those in Japan.

In contrast, the Philippines has employed a more diffuse pattern of administration. Research is conducted by a diverse group of ministry research bureaus, colleges and universities, research centers and institutes, and commodity authorities and regional commissions. In 1972, the Philippine Council of Agricultural Research was established to attempt to achieve some coordination of these diverse elements. The system is characterized by a number of centers of very substantial strength and productivity and by a large number of exceptionally weak institutions and locations. In contrast to Korea, research on rice by national institutions in the Philippines is probably weaker than a decade ago—due apparently to a decision that with the IRRI located in the Philippines there is a higher pay-off to Philippine research resources in other commodity or research areas.

The agricultural research systems in both the Philippines and Korea have developed substantial capacity for technology generation as well as for technology transfer, screening, and adaptation. In both countries this capacity is limited to a few commodity and resource categories. There are other commodity and resource categories where capacity is still rudimentary.

The Indonesian system seems to be evolving more along the lines of the Korean system, with primary support for research being channeled through the Agency for Agricultural Research and Development (AARD). It should be noted, however, that this concentrated style of management, which is replacing the extremely diffuse pattern that existed a decade ago, continues to be under continuous challenge from the universities, the National Science Development Board (LIPI), and the Science Ministry.

The Indonesian agricultural research system is approaching a level of manpower development (100–150 scientists at the MS and PhD levels) that should enable it to begin to become an effective source of new technology. This capacity is less effective than it might be because substantial numbers of the scientists with the best training are located at universities that receive limited research support. The university scientists are not effectively linked with the national research institutions and lack incentives for technology-oriented research.

In spite of these limitations the Indonesian system has evolved significant capacity to transfer, screen, and adapt technology and to serve the information needs of the extension agencies. In addition, the Indonesian system has achieved limited capacity as a source of new rice technology.

The Malaysian agricultural research effort was, until the late 1960s, heavily concentrated on a single commodity (rubber) at a single research institute, the Rubber Research Institute of Malaysia (RRIM). The RRIM, organized in 1925, was one of the great colonial research institutes. It was responsible for much of the genetic improvement and development of cultural practices that resulted in a several-fold increase in rubber yields.

Although the transition to national leadership in the early 1960s was not easy, the RRIM quickly compensated for the departure of expatriate staff with an aggressive program of training and retraining. By 1980 half of its 220-member research staff had received training at the PhD level and the rest at the MS level. Additionally, although while under colonial leadership the research program had focused primarily on problems of estate rubber production, in recent years greater attention has been given to the problems of small-holder rubber production. During both the colonial and post-colonial periods the program was funded by a cess (tax) on rubber exports.

After independence there was increasing concern about the relative neglect of research on other crops. In 1967 an autonomous Malaysian Agricultural Research and Development Institute (MARDI) was established to absorb the limited research on other crops. In spite of substantial support by the World Bank and from bilateral donors, MARDI has not yet become a major source of new technology for Malaysian agriculture.

Concerns About the Development of National Research Systems

Let me now turn to some of the challenges and concerns that have emerged as I have participated in a series of reviews of several Asian agricultural research systems over the last several years. I will also, for comparative purposes, occasionally refer to Latin American experience. The examples refer to observations made in the early 1980s.

1. *Excessive investment in development of research facilities relative to development of scientific staff.* There are too many facilities without programs. Premature investment in facilities represents a burden on the research system rather than a source of productivity.

Example: It will be at least well into the 1990s before there will be staff capacity in place at the Sukamandi rice station (Indonesia) to make effective use of the very substantial investment in station development. Lack of effective consultation with scientific and administrative staff during the initial design stage has resulted in the necessity for substantial redesign and reconstruction of facilities even before their completion.

Example: At Bicol University College of Agriculture (Guinobatan, Albay, Philippines), two new laboratory buildings and screen houses were constructed for abaca research. But they have not been equipped, staffed, or provided with research leadership. Meanwhile, the BPI research station in the same province (Buong, Albay) has discontinued abaca research. At the University of Southern Mindanao (Kabacan), the animal science unit has new buildings that are unoccupied. The crop research units have begun to occupy new buildings but the laboratories are not being used. The laboratory equipment that has been delivered remains in shipping crates.

2. *Excessive administrative burden that stifles both routine investigations and research entrepreneurship.* It appears that a concern for fiscal responsibility has often been carried to the point where it becomes an excessive burden on research productivity.

Example: In the Philippines the complicated project review process, involving both the Philippine Council on Agricultural Research and Resources (PCARR) and the Budget Commission, requires a *minimum* of 18 months and a huge amount of staff time between the time a project is proposed and the time funds become available to initiate the project.

Example: At the Indonesian National Vegetable Research Center at Lembang, it has sometimes taken as long as eighteen months to obtain the repairs and servicing of simple equipment (for preparing distilled water, for example) needed for routine analysis.

3. *Location decisions for major research facilities, often made with the advice of consultants from an assistance agency, have frequently failed to give adequate weight to the factors that contribute to a productive research location.* These factors include: (1) location in a community that includes related education and professional infrastructure; (2) location in an agro-climatic environment that is representative of an important part of the area in which the particular commodity is grown, or that is representative of a major resource (soil, water) problem area; and (3) selection of a site with appropriate resources (soil, water) and characteristics of infrastructure (electricity, transport, amenities).

Example: In the early 1970s, the Indonesian Ministry of Agriculture decided to move its Central Rice Research Station from Bogor to a major rice-growing area on the north coast of Java. The decision was correct but was followed by two costly errors. The first error was in locating the station in an isolated area completely lacking in either physical or institutional infrastructure. The station has had to build its own power plant, housing for scientific and technical staff, and the facilities for health, education, and cultural amenities. The second major error was the choice of the specific site. The station was located on a former cassava plantation at the insistence of the Ministry of Agriculture and over the strong (verbal) objection of the members of at least one World Bank review team. The site is not representative of major rice soils on the north coast, and its soil is too arid to permit high rice yields. At a very minimum, consideration should have been given to alternative sites near a north coast urban center such as Tjirebon or Semarang. The Sukamandi mistake is, in the judgement of many observers, being repeated at the Rubber Research Station near Medan.

Example: The Philippines have made an opposite error. There were, in the early 1900s in the PCARR system, some 130 cooperating research stations. Some of them were federal ministry research stations that were poorly staffed and inadequately equipped. Others were small agricultural colleges (more appropriately junior colleges) with poorly trained faculty and with no research management experience. On the other hand, the PCARR has made some very good facility investments. One example is the establishment of the La Granja Agricultural Research Center, which integrates (1) the Carlata Stock Farm of BAI, (2) the La Granja Experiment Station of BPI, (3) the La Granja Sugarcane Experiment Station of PHILSUGEN, and (4) the La Granja Research and Training Center of UPLB.

If the objective of investment in agricultural research is to generate growth, it is clear that many of the research facility investments being made by donor agencies will not measure up. The costs of these errors are measured in terms of the maintenance burdens imposed on national research systems, the delayed flow of technology to producers, and the delayed growth of production.

4. *Lack of congruence between research budgets and the economic importance of major commodities or commodity groupings.* If new knowledge and new technology were equally easy (or difficult) to come by in each commodity area, a good rule of thumb would be to allocate research resources roughly in proportion to the value (or value added) of commodity output or resource input. Good reasons for departure from such a rule often exist, however. In a small research system, critical mass (i.e., scale economies) implies the desirability of focusing resources on areas that account for a large share of output (i.e., rice) or on a commodity where very large gains can be made in a short time (i.e., lowland irrigated rice in the 1960s). But extreme lack of congruence may suggest that little careful thought has been given to research resource allocation, or that particular interest groups have biased research allocation to their own benefit.

Example: In Bangladesh the rice crop accounts for more than half of the value of agricultural output. Yet less than one-fourth of the agricultural research budget was allocated to rice. Is this the correct proportion? Sugarcane research represents an even more extreme example. The Bangladesh Sugarcane Research Institute spent almost all of its efforts on improving sugarcane for use in sugarmills, despite the fact that 80 percent of the sugarcane is used to make gur (unrefined brown sugar).

Example: In the Philippines, the principle was adopted that equal funding should be available for commodities within each of three priority categories. The formula adopted to implement this principle, which implies that coconut research and carabeef research should receive the same level of funding, has even less to recommend it than the congruence approach referred to above.

5. *Lack of information and analysis that goes into establishment of research priorities and thrusts.*

Example: Farming systems (or cropping systems) research has been embraced as a major thrust by a number of aid agencies, national research systems, and some international institutes. But the enthusiasm for farming systems research has at times obscured both its limitations and its value. Among the limitations of farming systems research is that it is not a source of new technology. Its contribution to production derives from learning how to exploit more effectively the technological components available to it.

Farming systems research also has an important role in feeding back information on the value of improved components into the technology research and development activities of the central experiment station or international institute. The design of a farming system activity for this purpose will, however, be quite different from that of a farming systems program designed to feed information into outreach and extension activity.

Example: The Bangladesh Rice Research Institute established as an objective the development of improved varieties of deep water rice with the capacity to yield one ton per hectare. The objective prevailed for several years before it was discovered that farmers already were achieving yields of double that amount.

Example: There has been a great deal of rhetoric about the desirability of allocating research resources to meeting the needs of the poor. But there has been much less clarity about the operational implications of this concern. The most important implication is that research resource allocation should be biased toward the production of basic foods, such as beans instead of beef in Latin America, or more emphasis on palawija crops in Indonesia. The second implication is that research needs to be directed toward improving the productivity or improving the quality of the resources that can expand the economic size of small farms (e.g., water supply and use) and the factors that can increase intensity of labor and land use.

6. *The apparent presumption in some national systems that it is possible to conduct agricultural science without scientists.*

Example: Prior to the reforms of the late 1970s, the People's Republic of China failed to replace the agricultural science capacity represented by the human resources of scientists trained in the pre-1949 period. The mass campaigns of the Cultural Revolution resulted in the substitution of political for scientific qualifications in the training, recruitment, and promotions of agricultural scientists. China is now confronted with almost a complete generation gap in the staffing of its agricultural research institutions.

Example: The personnel in the Mexican agricultural research system rose from approximately 500 to 1,000 in number between 1970 and 1980. Yet the Mexican agricultural research system, after forty years of intensive development, still had fewer than 250 scientists in the early 1980s trained at the MS and PhD levels. The salary structure in the Mexican agricultural research system was so discriminatory, relative to other agencies, that there was not a single economist trained at the PhD level employed by the National Agricultural Research Institute (Institute Nacional de Investigaciones Agrarias, or INIA).

7. *Cycles of development and erosion of capacity that have characterized a number of national agricultural research systems.*

Example: In recent years most of the countries of Latin America have made major efforts to substantially strengthen their agricultural research systems. These efforts have been supported by bilateral and multilateral assistance agencies. There has been a tendency for capacity, measured in terms of both financial support and the scientific capacity of research staff, to erode following the reduction or withdrawal of external support. The losses in Argentina, Peru, and Colombia, documented by Ardila, Trigo, and Piñeiro,[5] have been particularly dramatic.

Example: During the past two decades a major effort has been made at the University of the Philippines College of Agriculture to develop graduate training capacity in the field of agricultural economics. The department has experienced three cycles of development and erosion of capacity during this period.

Concerning all the foregoing problems and examples, I do not want to be misinterpreted to suggest that the perspectives and concerns that I have expressed about agricultural research in Asia are the exclusive problems of new and growing research systems. Don Hadwiger[6] points out, for example, that in the United States the "pork barrel" approach to the location of agricultural research facilities resulted in 44 percent of all USDA research facility construction between 1958 and 1977 taking place in states represented by members of the Subcommittee on Agriculture of the Senate Appropriations Committee. He noted that this practice has forced "the federal Agricultural Research Service to operate a 'traveling circus' opening up new locations in current Senate constituencies, while closing some locations in states whose Senators are no longer members of the subcommittee."

It seems apparent that the institution-building efforts of the international assistance community and of many national governments have been, at best, less than fully effective in strengthening national research systems. The policies pursued by the donor community or agency have at times amplified the weaknesses rather than reinforced the strengths of a number of national systems.

Toward a Reform of Agricultural Research Support

What can be done to reform the system of international support for agricultural research? In my judgment the basic thrust of the reform should be largely to replace the project system by a "formula funding" or "revenue sharing" approach in the support of national agricultural research programs.

There have been many criticisms of the project approach followed by the major bilateral and multilateral development assistance agencies. The criticism most frequently heard is that the assistance agencies exert undue influence on the content of national agricultural development programs. This criticism is partly correct. It is not too difficult to identify cases where close patron-client bonds have been established between particular officers in the aid agencies and the leaders of favored national program agencies. Such relationships have often appeared to give particular national programs a degree of stability and continuity that would be difficult to achieve in the unstable political environments that characterize many developing countries.

The criticisms that focus on selectivity in program support and bias in the direction of program activity are not, however, my major concern. Rather, my concern is that the project support approach to agricultural development assistance has rarely been effective in contributing to the development of viable national agricultural development institutions. It might be argued, in contrast to this assertion, that the project system has, in a number of countries, contributed to the rapid development of professional capacity and facilities. But the period of rapid development has too often, as noted in the previous section, been followed by the erosion or collapse of program capacity when external project support has declined.[7]

In my judgment, cycles of development and erosion are inherent in the project approach. The reason for this inherent contradication is that external project assistance provides an alternative to the development of internal political support for program development. National program directors have frequently found that the generation of external support requires less intensive entrepreneurial effort than the cultivation of domestic political support. Domestic budget support required by donors is typically achieved by creative manipulation of budget categories rather than by increments in real program support, particularly when donor representatives are under pressure from assistance agency management to "move resources." Most existing project systems thus have built-in incentives for the national program leadership to direct entrepreneurial effort toward the donor community rather than toward the domestic political system.

Any effective alternative should attempt to reverse the perverse incentives that characterize existing programs. The system should be reformed to provide incentives for national program directors to redirect their entrepreneurial efforts toward building domestic political and economic support for agricultural development.

I am increasingly convinced that the long term viability of agricultural research systems depends on the emergence of organized producer groups who are able to bring their interest to bear on legislative and executive budgetary processes. The support of finance and planning ministries for agricultural research is undependable. Their support tends to fluctuate with perceived severity of food crises, foreign exchange demand, and changes in governments. Where, for example, will the political support necessary to assure fiscal support for Empresa Brasilera de Pesquizas Agropecuarias, or EMBRAPA (Brazil); PCARR (Philippines), and PARC (Pakistan Agricultural Research Council) come from when donor resources are phased out? Such support requires a long-term political development effort on the part of national research program leaders and program beneficiaries.

TABLE 11.2
Illustration of a Funding Model for Agricultural Research Support

	Program Support and Assistance Level (in millions of US $)					
	Low		Medium		High	
National Fiscal Capacity	National Support	Donor Assistance	National Support	Donor Assistance	National Support	Donor Assistance
Low (40% assistance)	20	8	50	20	100	40
Medium (20% assistance)	20	4	50	10	100	20
High (10% assistance)	20	2	50	5	100	10

What alternatives to the existing system do I suggest? I suggest that the donor community move toward a program support approach in which the amount of external program support is linked to growth in domestic program support. This linkage implies the development of a "formula" approach in which the size of donor contributions would be tied to the growth of domestic program support. The formula should include an adjustment that adjusts the ratio of external to domestic support to take into account differences in domestic fiscal capacity.

An example of how such a system might work is presented in Table 11.2. In the model presented in the table, external donors agree to support a specific share of the national agricultural research budget. In the example, the share declines from 40 percent for a country with low fiscal capacity to 10 percent for a country with high fiscal capacity. The amount of external assistance within each capacity group varies with the level of national resources that a particular country is willing to devote to agricultural research. The advantages and disadvantages of alternative models should be explained. One alternative would be a formula in which external donor support would be related to increments in national program support rather than to the absolute level of national support.

A dialogue on donor assistance to national agricultural research programs was initiated at a meeting called by the World Bank in 1981. It is imperative that these dialogues be continued. The issue of reform of agricultural assistance should be recognized as one of the most urgent items on the agenda.

Other options should also be examined. A partial approach toward the principles suggested in this section is implicit in the World Bank practice of making project loans within the framework of a program development plan. Program performance then becomes an important consideration in the negotiations for support beyond the initial loan period. At US/AID, internal discussion is focusing on the development of "common theme" regional approaches to the transfer of technology and the development of institutional capacity. One objective of the proposed approach is to achieve sufficient agreement on regional priorities to overcome the tendency for each new mission director or program officer to impose his/her personality on program priorities and objectives.

Opposition to the proposed reforms in the method of supporting national agricultural development support can be expected from a number of sources. The major *policy* level opposition can be expected from the foreign affairs ministries of the developed countries. In the case of the United States, the State Department could be expected to be unhappy about the loss of discretion to direct agricultural development support to or from strategically important countries, toward Egypt or Pakistan and away from Nicaragua and India, for example. This objective might be muted in the case of a formula funding experiment that included only a relatively low ticket item such as agricultural research rather than the total agricultural development support budget.

Major *bureaucratic* objection could be expected from the staff of the assistance agencies. Transfer of funds on a more objective program basis would be less intensive in its demands on administrative and professional resources of the aid agencies than under the present system. The use of technical assistance personnel from developed country universities and consulting firms would decline as the agricultural development agencies of less-developed countries substituted lower-cost domestic personnel for "tied" technical assistance staff. (Even in countries where technical assistance personnel outnumber local counterparts, the technical assistance personnel rarely regard their presence as counterproductive.)

Donor *legislative* bodies might object that the proposed program looks like an "open checkbook" activity with little donor control over program level or content. Opposition might also be expected from the aid *constituencies* in the developed countries. The aid constituencies typically have their own reform agendas which they would like to see national aid agencies impose on recipient countries. A partial answer to the legislative and constituency concerns is that the program would encourage internal program review capacity as the level of national resources devoted to the program rises. A second answer is that donor representatives should focus their attention on national research strategy and policy rather than on the details of program management. A regular schedule of reviews of policy, strategy, and impact (at five-year intervals, for example) should be part of the program extension process.

With this kind of opposition, where does one look for support for reform of international support for the development of national agricultural research capacity? My response is that the crises that I have identified in assistance in the development of agricultural research capacity are most imperative. The problems described here also characterize other areas of development assistance such as agricultural extension and rural health. The aid constituencies in both the developed and the developing countries are confronted with a growing lack of confidence in the impact of development assistance efforts.

Notes

1. In this chapter I draw primarily on my book *Agricultural Research Policy* (Minneapolis: University of Minnesota Press, 1982); on the initial findings of the US/AID Asian agricultural review as described in Vernon Cardwell, James C. Moomaw, and Vernon W. Ruttan, *Agricultural Research in Indonesia* (Minneapolis: University of Minnesota, Economic Development Center Bulletin 81-0, March 1981), as well as in Robert E. Evenson, Paul Waggoner, and Paul Bloom, *The Agricultural Research System of the Philippines: A Reconnaissance Report* (Minneapolis: University of Minnesota, Economic Development Center Bulletin 81-3), and, again, in my book *Agricultural Research Policy*; and on the InterAmerican Institute for Agricultural Research Policy; and on the InterAmerican Institute for Agricultural Cooperation's project on national agricultural research systems in Latin America, as reported in Jorge Ardila, Edward Trigo, and Martin Piñeiro, *Human Resources in Agricultural Research: Three Cases in Latin America* (San José, Costa Rica: Instituto Interamericano de Cooperación Para La Agricultura, March 1981). For data on the development of national agricultural research, the reader is referred to the reports in James K. Boyce and Robert E. Evenson, *National and International Agricultural Research and Extension Programs* (New York: Agricultural Development Council, 1975) and in Peter A. Oram and Vishua Bindlish, *Resource Allocations to National Agricultural Research: Trends in the 1970s* (Washington, D.C.: International Food Policy Research Institute, and the Hague: International Service for National Agricultural Research, November 1981).

2. In recent years over 80 percent of the Economic Support Fund has been allocated to three countries—Israel, Egypt, and Jordan (Development Coordination Committee).

3. The Peace Corps should also be mentioned. The Peace Corps has played a major role in educating young Americans to the realities of village and urban life in developing countries. The education has come at a stage in the life of most Peace Corps volunteers when they are highly receptive to such learning experiences. Many returned Peace Corps volunteers who have gone on to acquire the graduate education necessary to help them understand and interpret the significance of their experience are now highly skilled AID staff members, productive scholars, and citizens who have an acute sensitivity to international affairs. But investment in the Peace Corps (and in the youth volunteer agencies in other countries) should be charged against the nation's education budget rather than its foreign aid budget.

4. This term has been used to describe the Brazilian system by Jose Pastore and Eliseu R. A. Alves, "Reforming the Brazilian Agricultural Research System" in *Resource Allocation and Productivity in National and International Agricultural Research*, ed. Thomas M. Arndt, Dana G. Dalrymple, and Vernon W. Ruttan (Minneapolis: University of Minnesota Press, 1981), pp. 394-403. Alves and Pastore were contrasting the Brazilian system to the more "diffuse" federal-state system in the United States.

5. Ardila, Trigo, and Piñeiro, *Human Resources in Agricultural Research: Three Cases in Latin America*.

6. Don Hadwiger, *Politics of Agricultural Research* (Lincoln: University of Nebraska Press, 1982).

7. See, for example, the cases documented by Ardila, Trigo, and Piñeiro in *Human Resources in Agricultural Research: Three Cases in Latin America*. At a subnational level one can point to cycles in the strength of particular institutions such as the Bangladesh Agricultural University (at Mymensingh).

12
The Changing Institutional Nature of Technology Diffusion in Latin America: Policy Implications

Martin E. Piñeiro
E. J. Trigo

Over the years the countries of the Pacific Basin have gradually developed closer economic and political ties. These ties, together with considerable differences in factor endowment and economic structure, provide excellent opportunities for economic and institutional cooperation. Some of these countries, like the United States, Canada, and Australia, are important agricultural producers and exporters and serve as major centers for the generation and diffusion of agricultural technology to the other countries in the Pacific Basin and to the rest of the world.

Although food supply no longer seems to be the main problem in the Pacific Basin, agricultural technology continues to be a major policy issue. It has a broad effect on production, international trade, and the very nature of society. During past decades, technology has been visualized mainly as a policy issue related to the development and effective operation of national research institutions. The problem, however, has much wider implications, especially in view of the increasing importance of international technology transfer and the vital role of the private sector in this process.

This picture is of fundamental importance in the analysis of possible avenues of collaboration among the countries of the region. It has profound policy implications in regard to the nature of the technology process and the role of the public sector. This chapter discusses some of these issues from a Latin American perspective and attempts to draw some general policy implications.

The chapter focuses on two main topics. First, it draws attention to the importance of international and national efforts that have been made in the last few decades for the creation and development of National Research Institutes. In retrospect, we find that relatively little effort has been made to understand the implications of the international nature of the innovative process, or the role of what Edquist and Edqvist have called the social carriers of technology.[1] Although publicly supported extension programs have received attention as the chief mechanisms of technology dissemination inside national borders, the role of the private sector and of other informal mechanisms of technological diffusion have been the most ignored.

With the advantage of hindsight, we would like to hypothesize the presence and nature of social carriers of technology as an extremely important element in the process of agricultural modernization in the developing world. We believe that this element will be even more important in the future.

The second main topic of the chapter is the recent history of technological change in Latin American agriculture. We have defined three main historical phases, each with a different institutional mechanism by means of which the productive structure had access to technical innovations and which, for the most part, originated in the developed world.

The first phase extended through World War II. During this period, technology was disseminated through three main mechanisms: immigrant laborers, the initiative and efforts of large productive units, and the immigration of university scientists.

The second phase lasted until the mid-1970s and was a period of strong participation by the public sector through the National Research Institutes. Diffusion mechanisms were formalized and autonomous research became the main policy objective.

Finally, in the third phase the private sector has become increasingly predominant. This predominance is particularly true of the transnational firms that manufacture the inputs and capital goods implied by technological innovations.

The chapter will describe and analyze these three phases, identifying in each of them the principal social carriers of technology, the social and economic forces that brought these carriers into existence, and the consequences of their efforts. However, the analysis will stress the second phase and the National Research Institutes that were so important during that period.

Two different perspectives will be employed in the analysis. First, we will try to place the National Research Institutes in an appropriate historical perspective, highlighting their relationships witth the institutional setting that preceded them and with the institutional developments that were eventually set in motion, in part by the National Research Institutes' very existence. Second, we will briefly trace their research contributions and their real impact on agricultural development. In doing so, we will suggest that their real contribution was primarily their role in diffusing international technology and in developing human capital, rather than any direct contribution to building new knowledge.

On the basis of these findings, we will state our conclusion that the whole process of technical change in the developing world is increasingly determined by developments that take place in the industrialized world and by the existence of institutional mechanisms that facilitate the emergence and operation of appropriate social carriers of international technology. Then we will suggest that in economies whose activities are organized with markets, it is the social forces underlying development that make the emergence of such carriers possible and, indirectly, will bring about drastic changes in the nature of public-sector institutions.

Finally, on the basis of the preceding arguments, we will highlight some of the policy issues that in our judgment should have the highest priority in the years ahead. Although these issues are analyzed from a Latin American perspective, we feel they have a wider relevance.

We would like to state from the beginning that most of the chapter is highly tentative in nature. It is intended to call attention to the broad social and institutional phenomena related to the process of agricultural modernization as observed in Latin America during the post-World War II period.

The chapter is organized in six sections, including this introduction. The second section briefly describes the early phases of technological history in Latin America. The third section provides a description and analysis of the second historical phase. It describes the development of National Research Institutes and interprets the social forces that conditioned their impact on agricultural production. The fourth section describes the main elements of the third phase, which witnessed the emergence of private-sector institutions as social carriers of technology and discusses the implications of the process. The fifth section provides a tentative interpretation of the social and economic forces that led to the creation of the research institutes and those that have eroded their original position and mandate. Finally, the sixth and last section analyzes some of the policy implications of the study.

Phase One: The Pioneers

The first phase of the technological history of Latin America was characterized by unstructured institutional mechanisms for technological diffusion. Most of the countries had little or no publicly supported research until about 1930. Even then, only minor efforts were made by the ministries of agriculture of the larger and richer countries.

Three main sources of technological innovation were important during the early part of the century. The first source was the European immigrants who settled in the fertile and abundant farmland of Latin America. Important examples of these immigration processes and their technological impact are reflected in grain production in Argentina and Uruguay. Immigrants introduced technical know-how and specific varieties of wheat and other grains being produced at that time in Europe, especially Italy. This immigrant activity defined the initial type of agriculture in the countries receiving such immigrants.

A second important form of technological diffusion took place through the special efforts and dedication of farmers and ranchers who traveled to

Europe and brought back certain technological innovations they considered useful for the special production conditions in Latin America. This process was particularly important for cattle and sheep breeding in the Southern Cone countries, which became international centers of purebred stock of British origin.

The third mechanism by which technology was spread to the countries of the region was more structured and very similar to the mechanisms by which industrial technology is diffused at the present time: the activities of large and usually transnational firms that had developed large plantations for the production of mostly tropical crops. These firms had foreign managers who brought specific technological experience and developed mechanisms by which technological innovations, developed elsewhere and particularly in other subsidiaries of the firm, were diffused.

Concurrent with these developments were two types of efforts that took place in the public sector. The first was the development of agricultural universities, which included certain research activities mainly in botany, agronomy, and soils. To a great extent, these universities were developed through the special talents of a few outstanding academicians who were hired mainly from Europe.[2]

In the second public-sector effort, a number of experimental stations were established. The most important were today's Estanzuela in Uruguay; the Pergamino Experimental Station established in Argentina in 1914; the National Agricultural Society established in Chile in 1925; the Palmira, Medellin, and Bogota Experimental Farms founded in Colombia in 1915; the Cañete (1924) and La Molina (1927) Experimental Stations in Peru; and the Central Agricultural Experimental Station established in Ecuador in 1941.

During this first phase of activity, and particularly in the case of the experimental stations, efforts were geared primarily to overcoming crises in certain crops. Examples include the Cañete Experimental Station in Peru, founded to study the breakdown of genetic potential in Tanguis cotton, and the Palmira Experimental Farm in Colombia, consolidated in the face of outbreaks of mildew on sugarcane plantations of the Cauca Valley.

The process of technological diffusion in these relatively weak and unstructured mechanisms was slow and very fragmentary. It concentrated on crops and production conditions most closely resembling those in other parts of the world. Furthermore, little or no adaptive research was done and, therefore, only those technologies closely fitted to productive needs could be profitably adopted.

Phase Two: Public-Sector Institutional Development

The National Research Institutes

In the mid-1950s, the postwar reorganization of the international economy had important effects on economies and polities in Latin America. One fundamental outcome was a new awareness of the needs for agricultural development and the importance of technological institutions in this process.

A direct result of this new awareness was the creation of autonomous and relatively well-funded research institutes in a number of countries. Thus, with some variations from one organization to another, but always within the same general framework, the Instituto Nacional de Tecnología Agropecuaria (National Institute for Agricultural Research, or INTA) was created in Argentina in 1957, the Instituto Nacional de Investigaciones Agrícola y Pecuarias (National Institute for Agricultural and Livestock Research, or INIAP) was created in Ecuador in 1959, the Instituto Nacional de Investigaciones Agrarias (National Institute for Research in Agriculture, or INIA) was created in Mexico in 1961, the Instituto Colombiano Agropecuario (Colombian Institute for Agriculture, or ICA) was created in 1962, and the Instituto Nacional de Investigaciones Agrícolas (National Institute for Agricultural Research, or INIA again) was created in Chile in 1964. (Note that from country to country, the acronyms were sometimes the same.) The trend toward decentralization was not limited to the technological institutions; it also affected other service areas such as marketing, credit, etc., all under the aegis of sectoral planning offices responsible for coordinating overall sectoral policy.

In the 1970s, Empresa Brasilera de Pesquizas Agropecuarias (the Brazilian Enterprise for Agricultural Research, or EMBRAPA) was created, along with Fondo Nacional de Investigaciones Agrícolas y Pecuarias (National Fund for Agricultural and Livestock Research, or FONAIAP) in Venezuela, the Instituto Boliviano de Tecnología Agropecuaria (Bolivian Institute of Agricultural Technology, or IBTA), the Instituto Centroamericano de Tecnología Agropecuaria (Central American Institute of Agricultural Technology, or ICTA) in Guatemala, INTA (again) in Nicaragua, and INIA (again) in Peru. During this period, Venezuela and Peru departed significantly from the general model. In the case of Venezuela, the private sector participated intensely through foundations like Fundación Shell para la Agricultura (Shell Foundation for Agriculture, Venezuela, or FUSAGRI). In Peru, innovation emerged from the active participation of the University (the La Molina Agrarian University).

From an organizational standpoint, these National Research Institutes, which became the keystones of the systems in 1960, were decentralized, autonomous, and covered a broad range of products, regions, and farmers. Functionally, they integrated research, especially applied research, with technology-transfer activities, in some cases including postgraduate education (INTA and ICA). Slight differences in the integration of functions occurred in Ecuador and in Mexico. In Ecuador's INIAP, technology transfer is not a formal function of the institution, and Mexico's INIA conducts no livestock research.

In most cases the institutes were administratively organized to include National Research Centers that were specialized by subject area or product and that were responsible for developing basic research. The experimental stations and extension agencies performed applied and adaptive research and transferred new technology. The purpose of this particular kind of organizational structure was to achieve institutional integration of the different stages of the technology generation and transfer process, and to tie the process directly to the production problems of the different regions and types of farmers.

Operationally, programs by discipline and by product were superimposed on this decentralized structure. They provided a basis for developing activity programming, selecting priority actions, allocating resources, and coordinating national programs.

During the first decade or so these institutes received substantial and increasing funds, which enabled them to develop an infrastructure and initiate ambitious human resource programs. Table 12.1 shows the funding received by these institutions and the regional totals. As can be seen, in most cases funding grew until the middle of the 1970s and then stabilized.

The development of training programs was based primarily on technical assistance programs with developed countries, although in a few countries autonomous programs were initiated with close participation by the National Research Institutes. Table 12.2 shows the number of matriculating graduate students in three countries: Argentina, Colombia, and Peru. Table 12.3 shows the total number of personnel with graduate training in the main agricultural research institutions of these three countries. Both tables suggest the considerable effort made in this field.

Almost simultaneous with the development of national research systems, international interest began to focus on the "international centers."[3] The rationale for this idea grew from the urgent need to develop technological know-how in basic food crops. Given their wide applicability, it was expected that the findings could then be used by National Research Institutes to help develop site-specific technical innovations.

The research system thus created was logical, at least in principle, in the sense that the full process of discovery could be performed adequately. Scientific knowledge would be expended by academic institutions in the developed world, and technological know-how for basic food crops would be generated by the system of international centers. The national institutes would be responsible for generating technnical information on the remaining products and for developing technological innovations, adapting them to each ecological niche, and, in most cases, diffusing them into the production system through the use of extension services that in this case were relevant to all agricultural products.

The comprehensiveness of the system and the successful experiences of most countries in the developed world in previous decades encouraged an optimistic outlook regarding food production and rural development in Latin America. Now, after three decades, it is quite clear that the institutional system as developed has had a considerable impact on food production in the continent. However, it is also quite evident that the degree of success has been uneven for different crops in the various countries, and that few of the success stories have touched small-scale producers. The reasons for these characteristics of the process are analyzed in the following section.

Social Articulation and Technical Change

The establishment of the National Research Institutes ushered in a strong process of technological innovation in Latin America. The institutes represented a new or renewed effort by the public sector to generate and transfer technology, and they mobilized public opinion concerning the need to make national efforts in this area. In addition, they played an important role by articulating national efforts with developments in the international arena.

The efforts in the area of technology had a heavy impact on a number of products whose economic conditions lent themselves to the process of technology adoption or adaptation. Thus, a number of products have shown sharp increases in yield and production in several countries of the continent (see Table 12.4), reflecting both the growing international transfer of technology and the national efforts in the area. However, a detailed study based on seven case studies suggests that technical change was present only under some very specific economic and sociopolitical conditions that made possible the articulation of research and technological diffusion activities with an economic policy that made technical change profitable to specific and politically powerful social groups.[4] The results of these studies indicate that the existence of available technology was a necessary but not sufficient condition for the development of successful processes of agricultural modernization.

Table 12.5 provides data on the annual rates of increase in production and the per hectare yields of the products studied. Comparisons are made at the world level on different continents, and for the Latin American country showing the highest overall growth rate. The figures indicate that for the eight products studied, yields at the world level, and more particularly in given Latin American countries, made significant progress. These findings suggest that technology for increasing land productivity was internationally available. In the cases under study in Latin America, however, only rice production in Colombia and corn production in Argentina showed increases that approached those of countries with the highest yields.

In general, the empirical findings indicate that two principal types of social phenomena are connected with the processes of technical change. These two types are framed by the nature of the process of social articulation that caused them and by the quality of technical change that took place.[5]

In one type, represented by rice production in Colombia and corn production in Argentina since the mid-1960s, the state mediated between the interests of the industrial urban centers and the more specific interests of the farmers. In both cases, state mediation was motivated by a crisis in the production of the commodities under study. The state helped to reach negotiated solutions that, at least in an ex-ante evaluation, respected the overall interests of the social sectors involved.

TABLE 12.1
Funding for Agricultural Research in Latin America and the Caribbean for Selected Years from 1960 to 1980 (values in thousands of constant 1975 US $ at the national exchange rate)*

Subregion[a]	1960	1965	1970	1974	1980
Southern zone (except Brazil)	31,446[b]	31,298	32,594[c]	44,702[d]	42,599[e]
Brazil	8,280[f]	15,553[g]	24,178[h]	32,879[i]	116,797
Andean zone	15,631[j]	20,003[k]	43,056[l]	57,393[m]	60,541[n]
Panama and Central America (except Mexico)	4,412[o]	4,967[p]	4,904[q]	5,961[r]	10,215
Mexico	4,666[s]	5,218	9,723	14,637[t]	48,357[u]
Caribbean (except Dominican Republic)	1,530[v]	1,530[w]	3,280[x]	2,940[y]	2,128[z]
Dominican Republic	441[aa]	496[aa]	490[aa]	2,278	1,642
Total, Latin America and the Caribbean	66,406	79,045	118,225	160,790	282,239

*Preliminary figures, still subject to adjustment.
a. The Southern zone includes Argentina, Uruguay, Paraguay, and Chile; the Andean zone includes Bolivia, Peru, Ecuador, Colombia, and Venezuela; Central America includes Costa Rica, Nicaragua, Honduras, El Salvador and Guatemala; the Caribbean includes Guyana, Suriname, Jamaica, Haita, Barbados, Grenada, and Trinidad and Tobago.
b. The information for Chile is for 1961.
c. The information for Paraguay is for 1971.
d. The information for Chile and Uruguay is for 1973; the information for Paraguay is for 1972.
e. The information for Argentina is for 1979.
f. The information is for 1962.
g. Estimated from figures by J.K. Boyce and Robert E. Evenson, National and International Agricultural Research and Extension Programs (New York: Agricultural Development Council, 1975).
h. The information is for 1972.
i. The information is for 1973.
j. The information for Bolivia, Venezuela, and Peru is for 1962; for Ecuador, 1965.
k. The information for Bolivia is for 1962.
l. The information for Bolivia is for 1972 and for Venezuela, 1969.
m. The information for Bolivia and Ecuador is for 1973; for Venezuela and Peru, 1976.
n. The information for Colombia is for 1979.
o. The information for Nicaragua and Guatemala is for 1962; for Honduras, 1963.
p. The information for El Salvador is for 1966; for Guatemala, 1962, and for Panama, 1961.
q. The information for Honduras and Nicaragua is for 1965; for Guatemala, 1973; the information for Panama is estimated at US $ 600,000.
r. The information for El Salvador is for 1973; for Honduras and Panama, 1976, the information for Nicaragua is estimated at US $ 1,000,000.
s. The information is for 1962.
t. The information is for 1972.
u. The information is for 1979.
v. The information for Barbados, Jamaica, Suriname, Grenada, and Trinidad and Tobago is for 1965; the information for Guyana is estimated at US $ 250,000.

TABLE 12.1 (cont.)

w.The information for 1960 was used again.
x.The information for Barbados, Jamaica, Suriname, Grenada, and Trinidad and Tobago is for 1972; for Guyana, 1973; and for Haiti, 1976.
y.The information for Barbados and Haiti is for 1976; for Jamaica and for Trinidad and Tobago, 1972.
z.The information for Haiti is for 1978; for Suriname and Grenada, 1974; and for Guyana, 1978.
aa.Estimated from figures at about 10 percent of the total for Panama and Central America.

Sources: E. J. Trigo and M. E. Piñeiro, La investigación agropecuaria a nivel nacional en América Latina: problemas y perspectivas en la década de 1980 (San José, Costa Rica: Inter-American Institute for Cooperation on Agriculture [IICA], 1981). Document of Cooperative Research Project on Agricultural Technology in Latin America (PROTAAL) No. 77 (52pp.).

TABLE 12.2
Personnel Entering Agriculturally Related Postgraduate Studies at INTA (Argentina), ICA (Colombia), and La Molina Agrarian University (Peru), 1965-1978 (totals and in national programs)

Year	INTA (Argentina)		ICA (Colombia)		La Molina (Peru)	
	Began Studies	National Program	Began Studies	National Program	Began Studies	National Program
1965	15	2	11	-	15	2
1966	22	3	22	-	13	2
1967	34	-	24	8	27	1
1968	28	10	35	7	24	6
1969	23	2	40	8	16	2
1970	21	5	51	15	20	4
1971	39	21	37	8	10	3
1972	24	8	110	59	10	1
1973	24	16	96	52	11	5
1974	4	-	57	40	13	5
1975	1	-	53	51	7	1
1976	2	-	28	23	6	2
1977	1	-	7	-	1	-
1978	-	-	4	3	-	-

Source: E.J. Trigo, M.E. Piñeiro, and J. Ardila, "Aspectos institucionales de la investigación agropecuaria en América Latina: problemas y perspectivas," Desarrollo Rural en las Américas (Costa Rica) 12(1), 1980: 3-25.

These processes of social articulation are remarkably similar to those that occurred in the developed countries after the 1950s, and more recently in some Asian countries. The overwhelming need to increase production, and the presence of dominant social sectors capable of implementing public policies consistent with technical change, are the cornerstones of the process.

TABLE 12.3
Total Staff with Postgraduate Training (MS or PhD) at INTA (Argentina), ICA (Colombia), and La Molina Agrarian University (Peru), 1965-1978

Year	INTA	ICA	La Molina
1965	56	47	49
1966	70	60	68
1967	87	90	70
1968	105	100	77
1969	120	107	90
1970	133	123	104
1971	141	142	123
1972	169	163	124
1973	193	192	126
1974	209	256	128
1975	221	311	127
1976	197	336	120
1977	195	371	117
1978	189	382	102

Source: E.J. Trigo, M.E. Piñeiro, and J. Ardila, "Aspectos institucionales de la investigación agropecuaria en América Latina: problemas y perspectivas," Desarrollo Rural en las Américas (Costa Rica) 12(1), 1980: 3-25.

In these two cases, technological articulation depended upon (1) the introduction of a technological package based on improved or hybrid varieties developed through research carried out primarily at the international level, by organizations funded and controlled independently of the productive sectors, but for which national public agencies played an important role in diffusion; and (2) the implementation of an economic policy that stabilized prices and that paid large subsidies for direct investment in technology adoption or capital-embodied technology. These characteristics of the process, in addition to the qualitative nature of technological change and the low concentration of supply, resulted in a relatively equitable distribution of the surplus among the different social sectors.

The impact of these processes of technical change on both production and yields was notable, even in comparison with international results (see Table 12.5). Moreover, the use of labor and land was capital intensive and exerted only a minor effect on the organization of the productive process, the relations of production, and other aspects of the productive structure, including the degree of concentration and vertical integration.[6]

In the second type of modernization process, illustrated by sugar production in Colombia and milk production in the Ecuadorian highlands, social articulation was generated from inside the agricultural sector. In both cases, corporate actions enabled these sectors to negotiate with the state a series of policies that served their specific sectoral interests and enabled them to begin processes of technological innovation. However, the productive sector firmly controlled the quality of these processes by defining their form and appropriating a good part of the benefits of technical change. In every

TABLE 12.4
Latin America: Average Annual Percentage Yield Increases of Thirteen Products in Eighteen Countries, 1958-1978

	Wheat	Rice	Corn	Sorghum	Soybean	Cassa.	Potato	Bean	Cotton[a]	Sugar[a]	Coffee[a]	Banana	Milk
Latin America	1.1	0.5	1.7	4.1	2.9	-0.3	2.8	-0.1	—	0.5	0.9	—	—
Chile	0.8	1.2	2.4	—	—	—	0.9	0.8	—	—	—	—	0.4
Colombia	2.4	5.5	0.5	0.6	2.5	3.8	1.5	2.2	2.3	1.7	1.7	0.9[b]	-1.2
Ecuador	1.6	2.8	1.7	-78.8[c]	3.2	0.1	2.7	-0.6	10.0	-2.0	1.4	-0.1[b]	7.0
Paraguay	1.1	-1.2	0.3	1.1	-0.2	0.0	3.0	-0.9	5.0	-0.1	-4.9	2.2[b]	-6.2
Peru	-0.6	0.4	1.8	3.9	-1.6	-1.2	1.5	01.4	2.6	1.1	0.1	—	5.3
Uruguay	1.3	1.5	4.3	15.3	6.2	—	1.3	-1.6	-5.0	1.8	—	—	9.2
Venezuela	-3.8	5.1	0.4	-0.1	—	0.2	2.6	-1.0	5.0	0.4	-1.7	-1.8[b]	5.1
Guatemala	4.1	2.6	3.2	5.0	—	0.6	1.1	-0.2	-0.1	3.1	0.8	-3.5[d]	-1.8
Honduras	3.2	-1.4	2.6	0.6	—	-3.0	11.2	1.0	2.0	2.1	0.0	1.2[d]	1.9
Mexico	5.5	2.1	2.4	3.1	0.6	—	5.1	2.5	4.7	1.2	3.7	1.6[d]	-6.0
Argentina	1.1	0.3	2.8	4.9	3.8	-1.1	3.4	-0.7	2.9	-0.6	—	4.2[d]	10.8
Bolivia	1.1	0.6	0.6	—	-3.9	-1.1	4.3	7.6	7.3	1.3	0.0	5.6[d]	2.0
Brazil	2.6	-0.4	0.9	3.4	2.0	-0.5	3.0	-1.6	7.2	1.2	-3.2	-1.3[d]	4.6
Costa Rica	—	4.6	3.0	1.5	—	3.3	1.5	3.0	-7.6	3.5	3.1	6.0[b]	1.2
Dom. Republic	—	2.5	3.0	-1.4	—	0.3	9.9	-1.4	28.7	1.7	-1.4	-3.9[b]	5.7
El Salvador	—	3.5	4.0	1.7	—	2.5	9.4	2.0	-1.7	2.0	-1.4	1.9[b]	3.2
Nicaragua	—	4.6	0.3	1.1	—	6.6	0.2	1.7	1.5	2.2	9.7	-8.2[b]	-9.9
Panama	—	2.7	0.3	—	—	-1.2	5.1	-0.5	—	3.3	0.8	—	1.4

a. 1971-1978.
b. From 1961-1963 to 1973.
c. Only two years.
d. Until 1973.

Source: Prepared by authors on the basis of the Food and Agricultural Organization's (FAO's) figures from various issues of FAO Yearbooks.

TABLE 12.5
Average Annual Percentage Rates of Increase in Production and Yields of Eight Products in Different World Regions, 1958-1978

Region	Rice Prod.	Rice Yield	Sugar Prod.	Sugar Yield	Beef Prod.	Milk Prod.	Corn Prod.	Corn Yield
World	2.37	1.27	---	---	4.59	1.56	3.17	2.38
Western Europe	0.73	0.21	-0.54	-0.58	4.81	1.47	5.00	6.06
North America	4.38	1.74	3.09	-1.17	2.87	-0.31	2.57	3.09
Latin America	3.91	0.50	2.96	0.46	6.81	2.53	3.28	1.72
Far East	1.93	1.59	3.32	0.56	8.38	-0.85	3.18	1.33
Africa	3.17	0.90	1.60	-1.30	12.24	-3.35	2.53	0.62
Country studied[b]	7.39	5.02	6.64[c]	1.67[c]	0.90	3.60	3.70	2.80
Zone studied[e]	7.39	5.02	6.64[c]	1.67[c]	0.90	---	17.60[f]	---
Latin American country with highest growth rate[g]	14.60	5.10	10.70	3.50[h]	11.70	7.30	6.20	4.30

Region	Beans		Potato		Tomato[a]	
	Prod.	Yield	Prod.	Yield	Prod.	Yield
World	--	--	-0.03	1.37	4.84	1.09
Western Europe	-0.61	2.22	-2.25	1.00	2.87	1.91
North America	0.29	0.12	1.75	2.03	2.93	2.95
Latin America	2.14	-0.15	2.73	2.77	5.03	1.02
Far East	2.37	0.72	5.92	0.25	3.28	0.98
Africa	3.24	-0.57	5.82	-0.11	5.05	0.68
Country studied[b]	1.70	-1.60	2.30	1.50	2.85[d]	4.16[d]
Zone studied[e]	1.55[c]	-4.21	--	--	4.91[d]	2.14[d]
Latin American country with highest growth rate[g]	10.30	7.50	14.80	11.20	--	--

a. 1964-1978.
b. Country studied: Colombia (rice and sugar); Uruguay (beef); Ecuador (milk); Argentina (corn); Peru (potato); United States (tomato); Brazil (beans).
c. 1960-1977.
d. 1950-1972.
e. Zone studied: Valle Del Magdalena (rice); Valle Del Cauca (sugar); Uruguay (beef); Ecuadoran highlands (milk); "Corazon Maicero" (corn); Valle Del Manitaro (potato); California (tomato); State of Pernambuco (beans).
f. 1950-1970, calculated on the basis of indices.
g. Rice production and yield, Venezuela; sugar production, Guatemala; sugar yield, Costa Rice; beef production, Nicaragua; milk production, El Salvador; corn production, Paraguay; corn yield, Uruguay; potato production, Dominican Republic; potato yield, Honduras; bean production, Argentina; bean yield, Bolivia.
h. 1964-1978.

Source: Prepared by authors using data obtained from Food and Agricultural Organization (FAO) Yearbooks, various issues.

case, the public policies implemented were specifically designed to overcome particular obstacles to development in the dominant productive sectors. In addition, these sectors created organizational mechanisms that gave them a certain amount of control over the supply of technology. Qualitatively, the technical change had moderate effects on yields, while production expanded through the vigorous incorporation of new areas. In addition, important changes took place in the organization of work activities. Moreover, the concentration and vertical integration of production increased.

It is important to emphasize that independently of the type of social process that originated technical change, its impact was to increase capital use and to homogenize the structure of production.

The Role of the Public Sector in the Process of Modernization

There is no doubt that the public sector as a whole played a fundamental role in the process of modernization described above. Agricultural policy and planning was strengthened considerably, and the design and application of specific policies, such as subsidized credit, were more aggressively pursued.

The research institutions in particular played an important role in this process. They generated public awareness of the importance of technology, they developed highly trained specialists, and they worked toward the domestic diffusion of technology. Their role as social carriers in transferring technology available at the international level is illustrated in the seven previously mentioned studies.

In the cases of milk production in Ecuador and beef production in Uruguay, public-sector institutions were primarily responsible for transferring technological packages from other parts of the world. The private sector participated through the sale of the inputs and capital equipment included in the technology package. But it was the public sector that mobilized the interest of producers and made major efforts to disseminate the required information around the country.

In the cases of rice in Colombia and corn in Argentina, the role of the public sector was shared with other institutions. In Colombia, major roles were played by the private sector, by Centro Internacional de Agricultura Tropical (the International Center for Tropical Agriculture, or CIAT), and by the Rice Producers' Federation. CIAT was the fundamental vehicle for transferring available technology internationally and for developing new technology particularly suited to Colombian conditions. The Rice Producers' Federation was mainly responsible for extension activities among rice producers.

Technological diffusion for corn production in Argentina was the result of two forces: (1) the international spread of technology and (2) the emerging work of the public sector (INTA) in developing new, more site-specific techniques. However, with time, the role of the private sector grew in importance, particularly in relation to new varieties. Private enterprise is now the major source of improved varieties.

Finally, the case of sugarcane in Colombia is an example of a very low level of participation by public institutions. For the most part, innovations were imported directly by the sugar mills, and very little indigenous research was developed.

Thus, with the exception of the case of sugarcane, public research institutions played a major role as social carriers of technology. Their role was important both at the international level and in the domestic diffusion of technology, including the mobilization of general interest in the innovation process itself. However, the role of National Research Institutes in the development of new technology applied to the productive process seems to have been less effective.[7]

Phase Three: Agricultural Modernization and Institutional Change

The modernization process of the past twenty years has introduced a number of institutional changes that have substantially modified the framework in which the national agricultural research systems must operate, both at home and abroad. In this context, two types of events have been particularly important in recent years: (1) the emergence of an industry that produces technological inputs; and (2) farmer organizations.

The Agricultural Inputs Industry

The qualitative nature of the innovative process experienced during the last two decades has motivated an increased private interest in participating in the research and development process for agricultural inputs. The evolution of Latin America's agricultural research organizations follows this general tendency. Over the past twenty years, Latin American research systems have evolved from an initial stage of state monopolies to a system of shared responsibilities among the public and private sectors. The seed, agrochemicals and fertilizers, and even the veterinary product industries represent major examples of private enterprises's increased participation in the supply of technology (see Table 12.6). This experience is neither new in general nor unique to Latin America. The evolution of the United States' agricultural experience indicates a similar trend in its change from an initial primarily public system, implemented through the creation of the Land Grant Colleges and the USDA Experimental Station System, to the present position where about half of all agricultural research expenditures are defrayed by private firms.

In Latin America, and probably in other less-developed regions, this process has developed beyond what regional and national modernization and development conditions would warrant, largely due to the increased importance of multinational firms operating in these fields. The multinational character of the firms has relaxed some of the market constraints because technological knowledge and innovations developed in one country can be used in another. The integration of national firms into multinational concerns

TABLE 12.6
Nitrogen and Phosphorus Consumption per Hectare of Arable Land or Land Under Permanent Crops in Latin America, 1961-1965 and 1977-1978

Country	Nitrogen Fertilizers (kg per ha)		Phosphorus Fertilizers (kg per ha)	
	1961-1965	1977-1978	1961-1965	1977-1978
Fertilizer producers				
Brazil	1.9	16.9	2.8	37.7
Mexico	8.0	34.2	2.1	9.4
Chile	6.0	6.9	13.4	9.5
Trinidad and Tobago	22.1	22.1	3.9	1.9
Colombia	7.8	28.2	9.5	13.6
Venezuela	2.5	27.7	1.2	10.0
Argentina	0.6	1.2	0.2	0.9
Costa Rica	49.5	59.2	9.3	24.5
Peru	27.6	31.2	10.3	5.3
El Salvador	32.5	105.5	10.5	34.6
Cuba	28.4	70.8	28.0	17.5
Guatemala	6.4	34.1	3.5	14.9
Jamaica	32.5	17.0	8.3	16.2
Ecuador	2.2	11.4	1.8	4.5
Uruguay	4.4	9.3	10.9	22.1
Countries exclusively importing fertilizers				
Honduras	8.1	16.6	0.6	6.0
Nicaragua	9.5	23.9	2.5	10.1
Haiti	0.1	1.8	-	0.8
Dominican Republic	9.9	31.3	1.2	12.8
Panama	15.7	15.9	-	11.0
Bolivia	0.3	0.6	0.3	0.5
Paraguay	0.2	0.3	0.9	0.6
Latin America	5.1	18.0	3.4	15.6
United States	8.9	48.2	6.8	24.6
Japan	122.3	138.2	82.2	149.8
Germany, Fed. Rep.	53.7	165.3	52.3	109.0

Source: E.J. Trigo and M.E. Piñeiro, "Dynamics of Agricultural Research Organization in Latin America," Food Policy (England) 6(1), 1981: 5.

also implies a differential access to technology potential through their larger scale of operation, which has also permitted their direct participation in the generation of new basic knowledge.

Technology Generation and Transfer by Farmer Organizations

In the late 1960s, and more intensely in the early 1970s, farmer organizations began to participate directly in activities related to the adaptation and diffusion of technology. Development was also made possible by the advances made in basic agricultural know-how and staff training by the National Research Institutes.

The first institutional development was the establishment of farmer organizations for technology transfer, using the same format as the Consortia of French Agricultural Technology Experimentation (CETA). These organizations acted to replace the extension systems of the research institutes and created farmer groups for the purposes of contracting private technical assistance. The first such organization appeared in Argentina in the late 1950s under the name of Regional Consortia of Agricultural Experimentation (CREA). Such organizations became more popular during the following decade, particularly in the 1970s. They have now extended to other countries, especially Chile and Uruguay.

A second institutional development is more complex and potentially far-reaching. Research and technology diffusion activities were directly undertaken by the pooled efforts of farmers producing specific crops.[8] The cases of rice and sugarcane in Colombia are interesting illustrations of this phenomenon. Although research and transfer activities on rice began at ICA, they were gradually taken over by the technical services of the National Federation of Rice Growers (FEDEARROZ), especially in the area of technical assistance. The presence of CIAT apparently played an important role in the development and consolidation of this process.

The case of sugarcane differs somewhat from that of rice. Most important among the differences was the creation of a research center, Centro de Investigaciones de la Caña (Sugarcane Research Center, Colombia, or CENICAÑA), with ties to the public system through participation of state representatives on CENICAÑA's board, but with a funding and decision-making process totally independent of the state and of the trade organization that created the research center—Asociación de Productores de Caña (Association of Sugarcane Producers, Colombia, or ASOCAÑA).

The Life Cycle of Public Sector Institutions: Elements for an Interpretation

Social Forces in the Creation of the National Research Institutes

The rationale for the creation of the National Research Institutes was that, in the absence of private research efforts, they were the most efficient institutional arrangement for conducting research. On the basis of scientific and technological findings available from developed countries, their work could result in the creation and adaptation of new technological innovations.

It is interesting to note that the founding of these decentralized institutes, with the possible exceptions of those in Brazil and Ecuador, followed a sequence consistent with the degree of industrial development achieved. Therefore, it is reasonable to hypothesize that the social forces necessary for this initiative to take place were present only after industrial development had occurred. Only then had the social structure progressed to the point where urban sectors interested in stimulating increases in food production had significant influence over government decisions to invest in agricultural research. Initially, these investments were (1) relatively high in cost due to the lack of trained personnel and the absence of an adequate research infrastructure; (2) high in risk due to the lack of experience, absence of markets of adequate size, etc.; and (3) difficult to recover because it was not certain that the private sector could appropriate research benefits when much of the new know-how in these cases concerned agronomic practices and simple technology that did not require capital inputs.

Under these conditions, technology had the characteristics of a simple public good. Consequently, the rational concern of the dominant socioeconomic groups was that society should assume the research costs.

In spite of these close associations between national social processes and the creation of the research institutes, it must be noted that they appeared simultaneously in many different countries under highly divergent socioeconomic and political conditions. This observation suggests that the process under way was only partially determined by the specific social processes in each country, and that other continent-wide determinants were also important.[9]

In general, these processes appear to be related to the heavy influence of ECLA and its work to make the economies more dynamic by transforming them through public-sector action. Another important influence was the international environment that emerged after the Punta del Este meeting, which gave rise to numerous international assistance programs for implementing new institutional models.

The following questions about this process came to mind: Why did technology become an important social issue only as recently as the 1960s? What was the origin of the institutional models adopted? How can the similarity of all the new agencies be explained? Why did the particular conditions of each country appear to have so little real influence over the organizational format of the institutions?

In answer to the first question, an analysis of the public policies and institutions for technology suggests that until the 1960s, conflicts over the organization of research were overshadowed by concern about public policies of more immediate significance, such as those that threatened the very existence of certain economic sectors (agrarian reform) or that had a clear, unequivocal economic impact (prices). Moreover, it was only recently that agricultural production stagnated, becoming a clear-cut constraint on development. Only then did it become essential to modernize agricultural production.[10]

The questions about the origin and similarity of institutional models bring into focus the special characteristics of the relationships between technological policies and the social context. In the case of economic policy instruments such as prices and credit, the effects are relatively specific for each agricultural commodity. As a result, the negotiation process was limited to those social sectors directly related to the product in question and concentrating on a small number of concrete decisions. By contrast, decisions concerning the founding, organization, and budgets of technological organizations include by their very nature the need to define comprehensive strategies for agricultural development. Thus the discussion and negotiation of state decisions assumes a more general nature, becoming more abstract and involving a much broader range of social sectors. All these factors not only delay and inhibit policies from reflecting the interests of the different sectors involved, but also complicate the mediation process between state and sector and the emergence of negotiated solutions.

The state bureaucratic apparatus was able to make technological decisions with considerably greater relative autonomy than it enjoyed in other fields. This greater relative autonomy, and the classic international dissemination of ideas in the areas of science and technology, made possible the adoption of institutional models developed in other countries. It also determined the selection of research priorities themselves.

In some cases this process resulted in institutional models and research priorities that had not been filtered through those social sectors that best understand the concrete conditions under which production takes place. Inconsistencies thus came to exist between the models and priorities and the actual economic and political situation in each context.[11]

Institutional Obsolescence as a Consequence of Changing Economic Conditions

Public-sector research institutes evolved from the perception that technology was essentially a public good. Recent evidence, however, suggests that in developing market economies, this concept needs to be substantially reformulated. As indicated above, private research and extension activities have gained considerable importance during the past decade. This fact, together with the growing importance of transnational corporations and international organizations, has modified the types of technology being produced, the nature of research in the public domain, and the role of public institutions as social carriers of technology.

In market economies, private organizations and activities move in the area of technology development whenever possibilities exist for private appropriation of technology-generated surpluses. These possibilities, and the consequent development of different types of private organizations, stem from a number of interrelated and mutually reinforcing processes.

The determining factor for the development of private research and extension activities, such as those performed by the fertilizer and pesticides industries, is the existence and size of markets for technological inputs. It is also essential that existing institutional instruments enable the private sector to protect its investments in technology generation, and for the private sector to internalize the possible benefits to be derived from technological change. Both these factors come about through agricultural modernization, making it increasingly attractive for the private sector to participate in technology generation and transfer activities.

As forward and backward linkages increase, agricultural production becomes more and more dependent on purchased inputs, thus increasing the market for technological goods. This process is generally accompanied by the public development of basic infrastructure that fosters the market integration of agricultural production. The infrastructure also activates the potential demand for modern inputs as farms become increasingly accessible to industrial sales efforts of new items. At the same time, the development of patent laws (royalties, regulations, etc.) leads to the private appropriation of the benefits of technical change by the producers of inputs.[12]

These market developments, especially those affecting market conditions for embodied technologies, have been accompanied by institutional developments that also affect more general farming technologies. Farming practices are frequently mentioned as an example of technologies in the public domain, inasmuch as they cannot be protected by patent law and can be easily shared among farmers. This situation discourages private interest in their development. However, the process of agricultural modernization often implies developments that tend to alter this situation.

In the first place, agricultural modernization introduces the specialization of agricultural production and homogenizes technological interests, particularly for the commercial agricultural sector. This process, especially when it goes hand in hand with regional localization, facilitates the development of producer organizations and fosters their involvement in a wide spectrum of service activities. These events, in turn, increase the possibility of private appropriation of the potential benefits of the development and incorporation of new farming practices and agronomic research in general. Whatever was not profitable at the farm level becomes attractive if the cost can be shared on a more aggregate sectoral basis.

The possibility of private participation in research activities is also altered by modernization and institutional development. First, investment levels fall as more basic scientific knowledge is accumulated and human resources are developed. Second, the level of risk for obtaining appropriate results also falls as better methodologies and human resources become more generally available. Under these conditions, profit levels are higher and more certain, making investment in technology generation increasingly attractive for the private sector.

It is important to note the unevenness of increases among crops or different types of technology. Because the supply of basic information and technological know-how, including research methodologies, comes from the developed world, economic incentives are concentrated in areas of activity and specific products that, because they are of interest in the more developed countries, have been more fully advanced.

Although the demand for technology by productive units is basically determined by their economic conditions, the qualitative nature of the process is at least partly determined by the international availability of basic know-how.[13] This availability not only makes some technologies possible and others impossible, but also differentially increases the private profitability of developing those that are possible.[14]

A final point has to do with the nature of public research institutions and their relationship with the state in market economies. National Research Institutes developed in earlier decades were one factor in the development of an overall state apparatus that was supposed to mobilize and coordinate the national productive system. This concept, which reflected the international atmosphere of the times, implied not only strong and centralized government activities, but also the capacity to plan and impose a general strategy for development.

An analysis of what has happened with public research organizations in a number of countries suggests that these assumptions are now, with the passage of time and the impact of the modernization process, less valid. As has already been argued, the growth of commercial agriculture and the gradual development of sectoral institutions whose specific purpose is to organize collective action imply a growing need for negotiation and consensus with each economic group with regard to the implementation of specific public policies.

However, in the case of research institutions, this process has had very special results. Its main characteristic has been the inability or unwillingness of state bureaucracies to protect the monopoly status they historically enjoyed, as they have done in other areas more crucial to the preservation of the system, at least in the short run. In this way, they have also lost their capacity to define and implement technological policy.

The basic argument presented above is intended to show that in market economies there is a dialectical and mutually reinforcing relationship between two trends: the nature of agricultural modernization as observed, which is characterized by the development of the commercial sector through capital-intensive inputs and the crops widely produced in the developed world; and the development of a multiorganizational institutional model for research, which removes the previous preeminence of public research institutions.

These complex and profound processes of institutional change raise a number of issues related to the implementation of technological policy. Some of them are discussed in the following section.

Reflections on Science and Technology Policy

Introduction

Scientific and technological policy for agriculture in Latin America has been dominated by two fundamental, closely interrelated concepts. The first is the role and nature of technology in the process of agrarian modernization. In accordance with the theory put forth by Schultz,[15] the lesser-developed countries can overcome their technological deficiencies by adopting the technology available in more-developed countries. This view does not take into consideration the possible undesirable effects that certain types of technologies might have on income distribution or development style. The second concept is the role assigned to the state in the technological process.

It is assumed that, given prevailing economic conditions, the private sector has no interest in the process of generating, adapting, and diffusing new technology. Consequently, the government must take the initiative and responsibility for agricultural research.

These concepts provided a useful basis for the policies on agricultural technology that were implemented in most of the countries of the region. The policies all tended to separate agriculture from the rest of the scientific and technological system and to provide for extensive participation in research by the public sector. Because the private sector was not participating in research, resource allocations within public-sector organizations dictated research priorities and, indirectly, the supply of technology.

The interpretive analysis of the process of modernization and technical change in the agricultural sector, as presented here, stands in contrast to the concepts that have guided technological policies in recent years. The contrast raises a number of questions.

The first and fundamental issue is that the technological process should be interpreted as a phenomenon endogenous to broader social processes that affect both the supply and demand for technology. Consequently, an effective technological policy cannot be restricted to actions directed to manipulating the supply of technology. The analysis clearly shows that the presence of technology has been only one of many ingredients in the process of technical change, which also requires economic conditions that make the adoption of new techniques attractive. Thus, an effective technological policy must include policy tools to affect the supply and demand of new techniques.

The second point to consider is the legitimacy of the role assigned to the public sector in generating technological knowledge. The growth and development of market economies requires the private sector to increase its capabilities and interest in participating in activities related to the creation and diffusion of new technologies.[16]

In actual fact, this means that the role of the state in research must be redefined. Institutional mechanisms should be developed to ensure that the functions of the public sector will be carried out, and to guide and coordinate the functions of the other sectors involved. In this general context, the following operational issues of technological policy are of considerable importance: (1) Is it possible or desirable to plan technological policy for market economies? (2) What is the best way to organize public-sector research institutions? (3) What functions should these organizations perform? (4) What is the role of the international organizations, and what should the countries expect and demand from these organizations for improving the efficiency of the overall system? (5) In view of the undesirable consequences of the qualitative nature of technical change in the past, and the limitations that science imposes on planning efforts, is it possible to define an autonomous technological pattern that has different requirements for the use of factors and with different effects on productive structures?

Although it is impossible at this time to discuss these questions in depth, we will briefly explore certain factors that emerge from the analysis.

Planning Technological Policy

The traditional model that became common in Latin America after the 1950s was based on public-sector manipulation of the technology supply as a means of influencing the modernization process. Experience in recent years has shown that market forces lead to major transformations in the operation of the technological process and, in particular, in the role that the state may play in guiding this process. Thus, the focal point of the discussion is the close relationship between the degree of planning of technical and scientific policies and the degree of planning of the economy for each particular society. If the planning capabilities are present, technical and scientific policy may become a tool for direct action on sectoral decisions. When the state's mechanisms for planning and controlling the economy are weak, the state is reduced to playing a subordinate role in the area of technology, and its sphere of action in scientific and technical policies is restricted.

The traditional approach has been to manipulate the technology supply. The unit adopting the innovations has been viewed as a simple receiver of a technological pattern defined by the public sector. However, experience seems to indicate that the important concern is not the type of technology that can be offered, but, quite the contrary, the ability to influence and guide the demand for new technological know-how. In this sense, policy tools of price, credit, inputs, etc., condition the economic context in which the production unit makes its technological decisions and, consequently, they serve as the pivotal points in defining the technological paths to be followed by specific productions.

Organizing Agricultural Research

The basic orientation of the institutional model adopted in Latin America for technology generation has been to improve the diffusion of technology by adapting innovations already available in the developed countries. The technological system in the region has thus taken shape within the boundaries of knowledge that are circumscribed by the priorities of the countries donating the technology; this knowledge is therefore adapted to the relative resource availability in the developed countries. In general, the resulting available technology has been capital intensive and has centered on products and forms of production appropriate to the ecological niches of the developed countries. Hence, the processes of economic concentration, noted above, have been set into action, and the production in developing countries of products from the temperate climates has prevailed over native products.

This trend has been further accentuated because the research organizations lack adequate mechanisms of integration into the productive sectors, often due to the public-sector nature of the organizations. The basic philosophy under which they were created is to develop institutional mechanisms that will transfer technological know-how already existing in other parts of the world. As a result, research priorities and resource allocations have not always reflected a clear understanding of the productive problems of the region, placing excessive emphasis on possible alternatives only from the body of knowledge already available.

This picture suggests the need to review whether today's institutional models are still appropriate for the generation and transfer of agricultural technology. The issues discussed previously also underscore the fact that such a review should include both the structural features and the operational components of the models.

The question of whether or not a given institutional model is truly functional calls a number of considerations into play. These include the overall and relative importance of the agricultural sector, the composition of the product and its concentration and regional homogeneity, target markets for the production, the prevailing type of social organization (types of enterprises, presence and types of trade unions or other organizations, etc.), the type of political organization, and the historical background of each institution. However, most models implemented to date have tended to imitate successful experiences instead of producing original institutional designs based on the needs, requirements, and limitations of each new case. Thus, a more in-depth understanding is needed of the basic principles in the dynamics of research organization in Latin America so that institutional readjustments can be better adapted to the socioeconomic, political, and ecological characteristics of the region. In operational terms, a key area of concern is to improve coordination with the productive sectors and to develop the capability for making fuller use of native productive potential.

The Role of the Public Sector in Generating Agricultural Technology

Special importance in the new multiorganizational context is attached to the gradual breakdown of the government's ability to guide the technological process, and the role that the government should play under present circumstances. As was noted above, when National Research Institutes were the only or most important sources of the technology supply, the process of resource allocation among organizations was an indirect means for the public sector to define technological policies.

As various sectors guided by market interest have increased their participation in the process of technology generation and transfer, the play of market forces has become the major force that governs how technological patterns determine commodities, priorities of clients, and types of technology. There are no policy tools to guide these private activities, and as a result, the technological variable has lost its influence as an active tool of agrarian policy. This phenomenon is particularly relevant in view of the importance that agricultural sectors have for national development in the region. These sectors help allay the balance-of-payments problems, and technology plays a crucial role in solving world problems of food production.

The situation today, as described, suggests the need to redefine how and to what degree scientific and technical policies for agriculture will be implemented. If this redefinition is made, the public sector will be better able to guide the multiplicity of public and private organizations that are taking part in the process of technology generation and transfer, for the purpose of tapping the full potential of the new organizations. Two basic elements underlie specific actions. The first involves introducing a level at which coordination can be accomplished between public agencies and the new institutions emerging in the private sector. This coordination could take place within the general framework of technological policy coordination (National Science and Technology Councils), or at the sectoral level through councils or coordinating committees for agricultural science and technology. The second element involves establishing or adopting specific tools that will permit the government to exercise its full capability to coordinate and direct technological change. These tools include patent laws, technology imports, monitoring and auditing the financial mechanisms for research investments, and so on.

In this general context, the government maintains its importance as a direct participant in agricultural research, but its functions and objectives emerge in a different pattern. The new organizations focus their attention on those types of technology that by their very nature lead to private appropriation of profits. Consequently, these activities cannot be expected to cover:

1. The development of functions for generating a "technological potential." Without these functions, the ability of the rest of the system to develop new technologies would quickly be exhausted.
2. Specific activities that are of generic nature (methodological research, etc.) and thus have a low probability of bringing about immediate results.
3. The development of certain types of technology that do not require inputs (such as cropping practices, pasture management, etc.) and that therefore offer no easy means for private appropriation of their benefits.

Private-sector institutions have a very specific coverage, associated with the products and conditions typical of commercial agriculture and particular forms of corporate organization. Consequently, a broad range of users neglected by the new institutional formats can be served only by public organizations. In this new context, the participation of the public sector should be selective, giving special attention to the groups bypassed by the private sector, and emphasizing missing elements of a comprehensive technology policy.

For a comprehensive policy, sector-wide mechanisms will be needed to guide the activities of the other components of the new institutional model. The institutional formats, as well as the type of mechanisms that will be used, depend on the nature and background of each particular situation.

The International Nature of the Technological Process

Worldwide developments also have a heavy influence on scientific and technological policy tools and on the role of the public sector in the technological process. The importance of new technological inputs has grown steadily, with international trade responsible for providing these inputs. Therefore, the mechanisms that control the flow of international trade must allow for adequate consideration to the implicit technological components.

The most important issue for the international centers is the development of effective liaison between the national and international levels. Liaison that goes far beyond lip service will make it possible to improve the use of available resources and to define international priorities consistent with the needs of the national programs. This topic cannot be discussed without taking into consideration the comparative advantages and functional limitations that each of the institutional components presents for the various types of research activities that must be developed.

Several authors have suggested that the research process can be oriented toward the following four types of activities:[17] (1) *basic research* for the discovery of new knowledge; (2) *strategic research* for solving specific and predetermined scientific problems; (3) *applied research* for the creation of new technology; and (4) *adaptive research* for matching technology to the specific conditions of a given locale or production system.

The international centers have a comparative advantage in applied research and, to a lesser extent, in strategic research for specific areas such as genetics. These advantages have been demonstrated by the actual outcome of research efforts, and the logical consequence is that national agencies should concentrate their efforts on adaptive research for those crops included in the mandates of the international centers, and on all types of research related to products not included in the mandates of the centers. These shifts in international priorities and changes in emphasis mean that national priorities must be reoriented and organizational structures altered.

The Limits of Autonomous Technology

Many studies have analyzed the effects of technical change on factor use, income distribution, and other economic variables directly related to development style. In response to the concerns generated by these studies, one school of thought suggests that the technological pattern can be guided by certain parameters determined by qualitative measurements. In its most extreme form this school of thought finds theoretical backing in the concept of appropriate technology as proposed by Schumacher.[18]

This viewpoint suffers from two important theoretical problems related to the implied assumptions on which the hypothesis is constructed. The first problem has to do with the limitations of planning efforts for science and with the growing role of the private sector in the technological process. These issues have already been discussed. The second problem is related to the concept of appropriate technology. The thrust of this concept is the search for a technological pattern adapted to the relative availability of factors in the lesser-developed countries, which are characterized by abundant labor, scarce capital, and small production units. However, there are two important points to keep in mind. In the first place, the new technologies must also be efficient for market economies. That is, they must be capable of generating an average factor productivity equal to that of capital-intensive technologies so that the production units can remain competitive in the domestic market. In the second place, the technologies must also be efficient for open economies so that the production will be competitive in international markets.

This problem must be analyzed in terms of the fact that the fundamental purpose of technical change is to develop more efficient productive processes for energy transformation.[19] Therefore, any restrictions on how much capital can be used or on how to use it serve to impose restrictions, in turn, on the range of possible scientific discoveries. This argument suggests that capital-intensive technologies are easier to invent than labor-intensive technologies, as has already been clearly demonstrated throughout the long history of technological innovation.

A related problem is the fact that the technology available to developing countries does not constitute the entire universe of theoretically possible technologies, but rather a subset of them, and they have been developed in the industrialized countries in accordance with the conditions of relative factor prices. As a result, the imposition of restrictions on the type of technology can also reduce the utilization of scientific discovery.

It is worthwhile to note that, historically, the processes of technology adoption in Latin America have been associated with price and credit policies that use capital subsidies to distort relative factor prices and place them on a par with the prices available in the developed countries where the technology was created. This situation leads Sábato[20] to suggest the idea of perverse but inevitable technology. If production is to increase, technology must be adopted, but the types of technology available imply shifts in relative factor prices. These shifts, in turn, lead to overuse of capital and the perpetuation of structural unemployment.

Concluding Remarks

The chapter has attempted to provide a broad overview of the development of institutions directly related to the creation and diffusion of agricultural technology in Latin America. We identified three phases, each one characterized by a different major institutional development. Of these, the most important and original to Latin America was the massive development of National Research Institutes during the 1960s and 1970s. It was a continental wave of institutional development that in most cases proved to be a very effective and profitable investment in terms of agricultural development.

In recent years, and in part as a consequence of the modernization process that these institutes helped to set in motion, the growth and expansion of the private sector, mainly concerned with the production and distribution of technological inputs, has started a new and different phase of technological development. For example, in some of the most advanced countries, research areas related to crop improvement and seed production (especially in temperate region crops) is dominated by private firms, most of which are of transnational origin. These new institutional developments pose a number of difficult policy issues related to the role of public-sector institutions and the nature of technical change in conditions where the private sector has an increasingly important role in the generation of knowledge.

The chapter has touched briefly on some of these issues. Without attempting to repeat the arguments here, we stress the importance of two fundamental elements. First, technology is a part of broader social processes. Institutional development—that is, the institutions that are created and the way they perform, and the qualitative characteristics of the technology produced and adapted, as well as its impact on productivity and income distribution—will be mainly determined by the characteristics of the economic and social organization that each country adopts. Second, the rapid and fundamental change in the organization of agricultural research suggests that it is necessary to take a hard look at the present organization and the functional roles of public research institutions—both their role as producers of technology and their role as formulators of technological policy. These adjustments should take into consideration the specificities of each country, as well as the growing importance both of the private sector in the development and diffusion of technology and of science as a basis for the development of agricultural technology in general. These elements result in an increasing interdependence of research at a global level. This new situation also defines new possibilities and new needs in relation to cooperation among countries with similar technological problems and development goals.

Notes

1. C. H. Edquist and O. Edqvist, *Social Carriers of Techniques for Development*, unpublished SAREC Report R3, Stockholm, Sweden, 1979.

2. For a discussion of this subject, see A. Marzocca, "Los pioneros," in *Las Ciencias Agrícolas en América Latina*, ed. Instituto Interamericano de Ciencias Agrícolas y Asociación Latinoamericana de Feitotechnia (San José, Costa Rica: Trejos, 1967), pp. 27-66.

3. Three of the thirteen international centers funded through the Consultative Group on International Agricultural Research (CGIAR) are located in Latin America: the International Center for Tropical Agriculture (CIAT), 1967; the International Wheat and Maize Improvement Center (CIMMYT), 1963; and the International Potato Center (CIP), 1971.

4. The studies were of sugar and rice production in Colombia, potatoes in Peru, milk in Ecuador, corn in Argentina, livestock in Uruguay, and a multiple-cropping consortium in Northeast Brazil. In addition, a study of tomato production in California was developed for social comparative purposes. See M. E. Piñeiro et al., *Relaciones sociales de producción, conflicto y cambio técnico: el caso de la producción azucarera de Colombia*, in *Comercio Exterior* (Mexico) 31(3), 1981:303-318 (Document PROTAAL [Cooperative Research Project on Agricultural Technology in Latin

America] No. 51, available in English); O. Barsky and G. Cosse, *Iniciativa terrateniente, cambio técnico y modelo institucional: el caso de la producción lechera en la Sierra Ecuatoriana*. Resumen de un estudio de caso (San José, Costa Rica: Inter-American Institute for Cooperation on Agriculture [IICA], 1980), Document PROTAAL No. 61 (71 pp.), Miscellaneous Publication No. 225; J. F. Sábato, *El agro pampeano argentino y la adopción de technología entre 1950-1978: un análisis a través del cultivo del maíz*. Resumen de un estudio de caso (San José, Costa Rica: IICA, 1980), Document PROTAAL No. 58 (94 pp.), Miscellaneous Publication No. 262; C. Barbato, *El proceso de generación, difusión y adopción de technología en la ganadería vacuna. Uruguay (1950-1977)*. Resumen de un estudio de caso (San José, Costa Rica: IICA, 1980), Document PROTAAL No. 59 (65 pp.), Miscellaneous Publication No. 263; M. Alves and R. Fiorentino, *La modernización agropecuaria en el Sertao de Pernambuco*. Resumen de un estudio de caso (San José, Costa Rica: IICA, 1981), Document PROTAAL No. 64 (82 pp.), Miscellaneous Publication No. 282; and A. de Janvry, P. LeVeen, and D. Runsten, *The Political Economy of Technological Change: Mechanization of Tomato Harvesting in California. Summary of a Case Study* (San José, Costa Rica: IICA, 1981), Document PROTAAL No. 63 (33 pp.). All the case studies referred to above are presented as Chapters 4, 5, 6, 7, 8, and 9 in M. E. Piñeiro and E. Trigo, eds., *Procesos sociales e innovación technológica en la agricultura de América Latina* (San José, Costa Rica: IICA, 1983).

5. For a detailed treatment of the subject, see Piñeiro and Trigo, eds., *Procesos sociales e innovación technológica en la agricultura de América Latino*.

6. In the case of irrigated rice, however, the number of farming units exceeding 30 hectares increased from 39 percent to 50 percent between 1959 and 1970.

7. Recent unpublished estimates for Colombia by Jorge Ardila suggest that the contribution of the National Research Institutes in the development of new varieties and hybrids was at one time quite important in commercial crops, but later decreased. In these crops (rice, cotton, sorghum, soybean, barley, oats, peanuts, palm oil, and forages) during the early 1970s, more than half of new releases were developed by ICA. After 1974 this proportion fell to about one-fourth.

8. This type of institutional organization is not new. The Colombian National Federation of Coffee Growers, for example, has run the Chinchiná Coffee Research Station for generating and transferring technology since the 1930s. It began operations in 1932 and has been operating until the present as the only center conducting coffee research in that country.

9. For a detailed description of the establishment and special characteristics of the national institutes, see Piñeiro and Trigo, eds., *Procesos sociales e innovación technológica en la agricultura de América Latino*, Chap. 10.

10. Ibid.

11. The increasingly international nature of an organizational ideology, and the social permeability of public policy, are reflected in the similarity among institutions founded after the 1950s.

12. For a discussion of this topic, see Piñeiro and Trigo, eds., *Procesos sociales e innovación technológica en la agricultura de América Latino*, Chapter 6, or de Janvry, LeVeen, and Runsten, *The Political Economy of Technological Change: Mechanization of Tomato Harvesting in California*.

13. J. Schmookler, *Invention and Economic Growth* (Cambridge, Mass.: Harvard University Press, 1966).

14. N. Rosenberg, *Perspectives on Technology* (Cambridge, Mass.: Harvard University Press, 1976).

15. T. Schultz, *Transforming Traditional Agriculture* (New Haven: Yale University Press, 1964).

16. This concept involves the role of private groups as carriers of technology. For a discussion of the subject, see note 1.

17. A detailed description can be found in Consultative Group on International Agricultural Research, *Second Review of the CGIAR* (Washington, D.C.: CGIAR, November 1981).

18. E. F. Schumacher, *Small Is Beautiful: Economics as if People Mattered* (New York: Perennial, 1975).

19. For a discussion of this subject, see K. E. Boulding, *Ecodynamics: A New Theory of Societal Evolution* (London: Sage View, 1978).

20. In discussions with the authors.

Part 6

Conclusions

13
Future Issues and Prospects for International Collaboration in the Pacific Basin

G. Edward Schuh

This chapter is divided into two main parts. The first provides an overview of the issues in food and agricultural development in the Pacific Basin countries in the decade ahead. The second part outlines opportunities for international collaboration in dealing with these issues. This chapter draws in part on the discussion at the conference at which the papers in this volume were originally presented. At the end of the chapter there are some concluding comments.

Issues for the Decade Ahead

It was noted in Chapter 1 of this volume that the world does not face a Malthusian crisis in the decade ahead, nor even a less serious food production problem, so long as past trends continue into the future. And there is no obvious reason why those trends cannot continue. In fact, one can be mildly optimistic that the world will be able to deal with its food production problems and promote a widely shared growth in per capita incomes and well-being.

This perspective changes significantly the way we need to think about the food and agriculture sector in the future. Hunger and malnutrition emerge as a problem of distribution and of poverty and low incomes—both within countries and among countries. The general issue then is to understand agriculture in the context of maximizing its contribution to general economic development. To do the latter requires that we make most efficient use of the world's agricultural resources, realizing the comparative advantage of individual countries and regions. It requires that we deal with the problem of poverty and low incomes. And it requires that we find ways of dealing with the short-term instability or food-security issue.

These problems can be discussed in more detail by addressing seven specific issues that almost every one of the Pacific Basin countries will face in dealing with its food and agricultural sector. Each following topic is one of the issues.

Growth in Productivity as a Policy Imperative

The importance of initiating and maintaining a process of growth in resource productivity within agriculture is now generally recognized. Moreover, the means by which this process can be initiated and maintained are also reasonably well understood.

There are at least four reasons why a broad-based growth in productivity in the agricultural sector is important. First, given that the easily utilized stocks of physical resources such as land have now for the most part been put into production, future increases in agricultural output will have to come from increases in productivity. Second, much of the generalized poverty in low-income countries is due to generalized low productivity in the agricultural sector. The key to raising per capita incomes is to raise resource productivity in that sector. Third, agriculture will make its maximum contribution to the general development of the economy only by experiencing a significant and sustained increase in resource productivity. Most countries start the development process with the bulk of their resources in the agricultural sector. Increases in productivity in this sector will result in the release of resources—both capital and labor—for the development and expansion of the nonfarm sector. Moreover, such an increase in productivity can accomplish this release of resources while supplying abundant food to the urban or nonfarm sector.

Finally, the key to maintaining a competitive position in international markets is a sustained growth in productivity. For many countries, agriculture is and can be an important source of foreign exchange. In the increasingly interdependent world economy of the late twentieth century, remaining competitive at the international level is the key to sustained economic development.

A consensus has emerged in recent years on how to obtain increases in productivity growth in agriculture. That consensus centers on investments in human capital, the introduction of modern inputs such as fertilizers and pesticides into the production process, the focusing of the process of technical change on the constraints to output expansion, and the provision of adequate incentives for producers.

Human capital has a number of important dimensions, including health and nutrition. For present purposes, however, interest focuses primarily on those aspects that have to do with the production and distribution of new knowledge and the application of that knowledge in conventional or new inputs. Hence, concern centers on agricultural research and development, agricultural extension, the schooling of the rural population (together with the provision of vocational skills), and the production or acquisition by other means of modern inputs that have new knowledge imbedded in them.

Operationally, the key factor for most countries is to either have access to or have the capacity to develop new production technology that is adapted to the local resource endowment. Given the location specificity of most agricultural technology, individual countries must in general have their own capability to produce the new production technology. Together with that capability there must be institutional arrangements that induce the process of technical change to focus on alleviating the existing constraints to output expansion. Other papers in this volume have addressed these issues, so that more detail is not required here. It is worth noting, however, that investments in human capital are important for at least two reasons. First, they are important sources of expanded output. Second, together with that contribution, they are important sources of expanded income streams. It is in this latter sense that they are the key to economic development and to the increase in per capita incomes.

Countries in the Pacific Basin differ widely in the capacity they have for the production and distribution of new production technology and in the investments they are now making to that end. Cooperation in expanding the base for the production of new technology is an important area in which the joint interests of countries in the region come together, and an important basis for continued collaboration in the future.

Mobilizing the Agricultural Surplus for Development of the Nonfarm Sector

Success in raising resource productivity on a sustained basis will generate an agricultural "surplus" (in Nicholls' sense) in most countries. Contrary to the labor "surplus" that was for so long the focal point of two-sector growth models, Nicholls' agricultural surplus refers to production above the level required to feed the agricultural population.

The mobilization and capture of this surplus for use by the nonfarm sector has been the objective of economic policies in most less-developed countries during the post-World War II period. Unfortunately, little attention was given in most countries to making the surplus larger, or to devising proper ways to manage the mobilization and transfer. The transfer has been accomplished in most cases by implicit means, in particular by shifting the domestic terms of trade severely against the agricultural sector. Particular policy instruments have included explicit export taxes on agricultural products, implicit export taxes in the form of overvalued currencies, and exorbitantly high protective tariffs or tariff equivalents for the industrial sector.

These policies have been responsible in large part for what is generally viewed as premature rural-to-urban migration in most less-developed countries.[1] The policies have also significantly reduced production incentives for agricultural producers; they have reduced the incentive for producers to adopt new production technology; and they have lowered the perceived rate of return for investing in the production and distribution of new production technology. The policies help explain why the bulk of poverty in most developing countries is in the agricultural sector.

The use of proper policies to mobilize and transfer the agricultural surplus is the key to broad-based and sustained economic development. Historically, various approaches have been used. In the United States, the bulk of the transfer took place through product and factor markets, with the incentive to save and invest provided through market forces. In Japan, an important share of the transfer during the critical period was accomplished through land taxes. The ability to implement and administer a land tax becomes an important prerequisite for using this approach.

One need not get bogged down in ideological arguments over whether it is better to use market forces or to depend on the government for the mobilization, transfer, and application of the surplus. The key issue is to accomplish the transfer in such a way as to not kill the goose that lays the golden egg. Put differently, the key issue is to make the transfer without stifling incentives to produce. There is quite an array of policies that can be used consistent with this criterion. The goal should be to mobilize and transfer the surplus so as to bring about as large a transfer of resources as possible and to invest it wisely for the general development of the economy. This goal will be second only to generating the surplus in the first place, as the key to capitalizing on the agricultural sector and obtaining broad-based economic development.

Facilitating the Transfer of Labor Out of Agriculture

It is inherent in the conditions of demand and supply for agricultural products that labor has to be transferred from agriculture to the nonfarm sector as development proceeds. Bruce Johnston of Stanford has noted that this requirement is as close to an "iron law" as one will find in economics. It is an issue about which there has been a great deal of naiveté over the last decade and a half, a naiveté promoted at least in part by premature rural-to-urban migration induced by dramatic shifts in the domestic terms of trade against agriculture. The premature migration, together with the difficulty of absorbing the flood of migrants in the nonagricultural sector, has caused many to argue that agriculture should be the employer of last resort for the economy. Many observers have taken this perspective without recognizing that to do so condemns those who remain in agriculture to chronic poverty.

Clearly, policies that induce premature migration from agriculture should be curtailed. Even with changes in these policies, however, there will still be a sizable rural-to-urban flow in most countries, especially if investments in agricultural research and development are being made at a socially optimal rate. Accommodating and facilitating the transfer of labor will therefore still be a critical policy issue. Moreover, dealing with this adjustment problem is likely to be the major policy issue in many of the Pacific Basin countries in the decade ahead.

Facilitating the transfer of labor at the proper rate will be the key to capitalizing on investments made in agricultural research and development. It will also be the key to providing for equitable growth, since it will be the means for reducing or eliminating the major income disparity in most countries that are undergoing economic development.

Two critical policy issues arise in dealing with this labor adjustment problem, neither of which has received the attention it deserves. The first is the need to invest in the schooling and skills of the rural population. Most countries substantially underinvest in the education and training of their rural population. It is little wonder, therefore, that large numbers of migrants arrive in urban centers with few skills and little potential to be absorbed in the nonfarm sector.

Conventional wisdom has it that farmers and farm people do not need schooling or vocational skills. This argument is specious even on the surface. When a flow of new production technology is being introduced into agriculture, Welch,[2] Schultz,[3] and others have shown that cognitive skills are needed to decode this new technology and that the rate of return to schooling will be quite high if the flow of new technology is large. Equally as important, schooling and the provision of skills will not only accelerate in due course the rural-to-urban transfer of labor but will increase the chances that a migrant will be absorbed when he or she reaches the urban center.

The second critical issue in facilitating the labor transfer is to decentralize the industrialization process. Unfortunately, the influence of neoclassical migration theory has caused many countries (including the United States) to experience development processes that are very wasteful of human resources. This theory failed to recognize the selective nature of the migration process, as well as the institutional arrangements that cause much of lower-level education to be financed by local means. These aspects of labor markets cause geographical migration to impose rather sizable negative externalities on both the supplying and the receiving region.[4] The result is a migratory process that eventually will reach an equilibrium, but only after the passage of two, three, or four generations. In the interim, a great deal of inefficient resource use and sacrificed output will be the result, together with the persistence of a serious equity problem.

The solution to this problem is to decentralize the industrialization process. To do so will reduce the need for geographic mobility while accelerating sectoral mobility. The result will be a more efficient use of a country's resources and a more equitable development process. Most countries provide incentives, either direct or indirect, to cause industry to locate in one place or another. They might just as well direct those incentives to activities and locations that encourage a more efficient development process.

To conclude, there is one final labor market issue—one having to do with the international migration of labor. This migration has two important dimensions—the migration of highly trained, skilled manpower, and the migration of unskilled labor in response to either economic incentives or political considerations. Much has been written on the former and little will be said about it until a later section. The international migration of unskilled labor, however, has become increasingly significant in recent years.

It is to this aspect that some remarks are in order, especially in light of its importance to some of the Pacific Basin countries.

In the absence of nation-states and geopolitical boundaries, there would undoubtedly be a great deal more geographic migration of labor than there is. Incentives for the international migration of labor arise from barriers to trade, barriers to the international migration of capital, and political considerations. Leaving the latter aside for present purposes, freer trade and open capital markets would practically eliminate the need for international migration of labor. Together or separately they would in most cases be an alternative to the migration of labor.

In dealing with this problem, these alternatives should be kept in mind. It should also be noted that acceptance of foreign workers is one means of preserving a particular industrial structure if that should be desired for national security or other reasons. The United States, for example, does not have a comparative advantage in labor-intensive manufactured products at the present time. If it should decide that it desires such industries, for whatever reason, it can sustain them by accepting the international migration of labor in lieu of high protective tariffs. Such policies obviously have political, efficiency, and income distribution consequences.

Deforestation and Conservation of Resources

Conservation is currently an important political issue in the United States. Much of this discussion reflects improved measurement ability that permits the use of quantitative statements for dramatic effect. Much of the discussion is also quite wide of the mark in that it assumes that farmers and resource owners are irrational in the management of one of their most important income-earning assets.

Countries in the Pacific Basin face at least two serious resource management or resource conservation issues in the future. The first is the deforestation that results from the pressures of the growing person-land ratios in selected countries. These pressures lead to the deforestation of lands that have no longer-term viable alternative. The loss of the forests eventually leads to denuding and loss of the topsoil, especially when the forests are on highly sloped hills. Hence, a climax vegetation that at one time had limited production potential is converted to one with no potential. Moreover, the runoff often goes to fill up lakes and reservoirs in the area below and to clog up streams and rivers.

The longer-term solution to this problem is a reduction in the person-land ratio, accomplished with the expansion of the nonagricultural sector and the absorption of the excess labor therein. The problem and its solution point up the importance of making effective use of the agricultural sector for the development of the nonfarm sector.

In the short run, zoning and other legal means must be used to prevent the destruction of such areas. Such forest lands require careful management so that the prevailing production potential can be sustained. Often, with proper management, agriculture and forestry can be developed on an integrated basis so that the benefits of both can be retained.

The second serious resource management problem is with water. The production and diffusion of land-saving production technology gives rise to increasing demands for water. In the future, water will probably be a more serious constraint to the expansion of agricultural output than will land. Hence, it is important that steps be taken to insure existing supplies of water and to assure that these supplies are used most effectively.

Two kinds of policies are needed. The first is a tax or tax equivalent on the extraction of water from underground aquifers that are being exhausted by too rapid a rate of exploitation. Mutual pumping by too many people results in the imposition of rising costs on each other. The tax should be devised so as to establish the optimal rate of draw-down of the underground water supply.

The second kind of policy needed is one that deals with present irrigation systems in which there is no charge for water. The lack of a "price" leads to wastage and nonoptimal use of water. It results in sacrificed output and, in turn, sacrificed income. The solution in this case is some system of pricing or rationing to make optimal use of the water.

Finally, the importance of efficient capital markets as a means of rationalizing the rate at which resources are exploited should be recognized. Viable capital markets provide a means by which present values can be compared with future values. They also provide a means by which private decision makers can borrow for investments, and a means to determine the rate at which resources can be utilized. The failure to have viable capital market alternatives is an important cause of the failure to use proper conservation practices—especially those that require the sacrifice of present income but whose benefits carry into the future.

The Promotion of Freer Trade

Policy perspectives toward trade are changing significantly on the international scene. During the 1950s and 1960s the advanced industrialized countries in general favored freer trade, while the less-developed countries and those with centrally planned economies for the most part pursued autarchic policies. Over the last decade these postures have tended to reverse themselves. For a variety of reasons, the less-developed countries and those with centrally planned economies are increasingly moving toward freer trade, while the advanced industrialized countries are becoming increasingly protectionist.

It is important to note that distortions and interventions in agricultural trade are about as strong as those in any other sector of the Pacific Basin economies. Agricultural interests are very strong politically in some countries, especially in the United States, Canada, Western Europe, and Japan. In other countries, self-sufficiency is a strong driving force of policy. In still others, especially those of the Third World, the political power of large urban population concentrations leads to trade distortions against agriculture that favor the urban consumer and labor force.

Two prominent books of the early 1970s dealing with world agriculture illustrate well the size of the distortions in international agricultural trade. Hayami and Ruttan[5] referred to "a massive disequilibrium" in describing world agriculture. D. Gale Johnson,[6] on the other hand, titled his important book on international agriculture *World Agriculture in Disarray.*

Trade in agricultural products is characterized by a number of important paradoxes. For example, much of the ideology of the Third World has argued that the less-developed countries were inadvertently exploited by trade because they were exporters of primary products and importers of manufactured products. In the Third World view the structure of trade was such that the international terms of trade inherently shifted against the former (primary products) and in favor of the latter.[7] Paradoxically, the United States—the world's preeminent industrial power—has emerged as the world's largest exporter of primary products, followed closely by Western Europe, also not unimportant in industrial power.

Similarly, the less-developed countries have long railed against trade barriers imposed by the advanced countries as turning the terms of trade against them and using the international system to exploit them. Yet it is fair to say that many, and perhaps most, of the barriers to trade in agricultural products are self-imposed.[8] Import-substituting industrialization policies have been the basis of development policy in most of the Third World until this past decade. These policies include high protection for the industrial sector, highly overvalued currencies (an import subsidy or an export tax, depending on the direction of trade), a wide array of explicit export taxes, and actual prohibitions against agricultural exports. The sum of these policies results in a significant shift in the domestic terms of trade against agriculture and serious discrimination against the producers in that sector.

There are at least five sets of issues in the trade area. The first is the loss in production potential and sacrificed incomes associated with distortions in agricultural trade. Agriculture, perhaps more than any other sector of the economy, is characterized by the resource specificity that causes existence of advantages to trade. Consequently, when one says that most of the world's agricultural output is being produced in the wrong place, it means that a great deal of both output and income are being sacrificed as a consequence of the sizable barriers to trade. The corollary is that freeing up agricultural trade can contribute importantly to dealing with the food and agriculture problems of the Pacific Basin countries, and that it can contribute importantly to the welfare of the people in the region.

The second issue its the growing importance of human capital as the basis of comparative advantage in trade. The United States became the world's major exporter of agricultural products not because of the outstanding quality of its "natural" agricultural resources. To the contrary, important parts of India, Brazil, and many other countries obviously are more well endowed, especially if one takes climate into account. The United States became the dominant exporter of agricultural products because it has invested heavily in agricultural research and development over the years, because it has invested heavily in the education of its agricultural labor force, and because it has maintained a strong physical infrastructure and efficient marketing arrangements.

By the same token there is nothing inherent in having low-priced labor that gives a country a comparative advantage in labor-intensive manufactured products. The issue is the cost of labor services, determined as much or more by the productivity of the labor as by its price.

The international economy is going through a major restructuring at the present time in response to changes in comparative advantage, changes in the international marketing system, changes in perspectives on trade, and the emergence of middle-income, newly industrialized countries that are becoming economic powers in their own right. Because of these significant changes, trade relations are likely to be an important source of international conflict in the decade ahead.

The third issue is the failure of either individual countries or the international community to devise an effective means of dealing with trade adjustment problems. Success in dealing with these problems is really the key to trade liberalization and the realization of the considerable benefits from trade. Unfortunately, trade conflicts are all too often perceived as a conflict between the domestic and the foreign producers. In general, of course, they really amount to conflicts between domestic consumers and domestic producers. When the argument is articulated in its traditional form, it is almost inevitable that the foreign producers (and the domestic consumer!) will be the losers.

Although trade adjustment problems are inherently a domestic problem, there will probably be little progress in dealing with them until international institutions are devised for dealing with them in a way consistent with the traditional rhetoric. This issue will be discussed further in the next section.

The fourth issue in the trade area is the growing significance of the international capital market. It is conventional to think of international economic intercourse in terms of the trade accounts only. Yet in principle the capital accounts are every bit as important. Moreover, the capital accounts have become empirically important for a number of different reasons. First, the volume of resources flowing through the international capital markets has become huge. In the aftermath of World War II most transfers of capital among countries were in the form of intergovernmental transfers, and often on concessional terms. Now, concessional capital transfers have declined significantly and countries—and groups within countries—use the international capital markets as a source of capital. These markets increasingly integrate the countries of the international economy, and do their task in a relatively efficient manner.

The international capital markets take on added significance now that the world has shifted to what is essentially a system of bloc-flexible exchange rates. In the presence of flexible exchange rates, changes in monetary and fiscal policy are reflected in changes in the trade sectors of the economy. International capital markets, together with floating exchange rates, have become an important source of instability in international commodity markets.[9] The instability of U.S. monetary policy has been an important source of this commodity market instability. But even in the absence of such factors as U.S. monetary policy instability, international capital markets would still remain a source of disturbances for international commodity markets.

The final issue is the use of trade policy to conduct economic warfare as an alternative to military warfare. It is obviously a great step in progress that military warfare has become increasingly intolerable to world public opinion, but with the unfortunate result that nation-states increasingly resort to economic means as the basis for punishing and rewarding other countries. The consequences to trade, and to the food and agriculture sector in particular, are very important. The use of economic measures in international diplomacy is not new, but the United States has put it on center stage once again, apparently with little appreciation of the limitations and strengths of such measures. This problem is likely to be a continuing issue in the decade ahead.[10]

Food Security

Food security involves the certainty with which a country can feed its population on a regular basis. Food security can be obtained by domestic means, such as by stockpiling grains or other food products, by carrying sufficient foreign exchange reserves to assure that supplies can be acquired on the international market when they are needed, or by pursuing self-sufficiency policies. It can also be attained by international means, such as by participating in the collective holding of international grain stocks, by simply depending on trade to fill any domestic shortfalls, or by depending on some other food-security scheme.

In addressing this issue it is important to recognize that the world has been remarkably free of major famines in the post–World War II period. The only famines that did occur occurred because governments did not want the international community to know about them or because the world did not learn about them in sufficient time to overcome transportation and bureaucratic barriers.

It is also important to note that the use of food embargoes by the United States to protect its domestic economy during the 1970s, and its recent use of food embargoes as part of its international diplomacy, has made other countries more sensitive to food-security issues, and has also provided strong incentives for individual countries to pursue self-sufficiency policies. The issue therefore looms high on policy agendas in the international arena.

Other papers in this volume deal with this issue. Consequently, only a few points will be emphasized here. First, it should be noted that carrying grain stocks is costly. Moreover, the incentive to carry such stocks lies primarily with the exporter, not the importing countries. Second, most estimates of the stocks required to provide food security are on the high side. Offsetting 100 percent of supply variability 100 percent of the time is obviously very costly. Moreover, it fails to recognize that higher prices on the occasion of shortfalls can reduce effective demand significantly. Third, self-sufficiency can also be a very costly means of providing food security. Countries that pursue such policies should carefully determine what it is they are giving up as a consequence of such policies. And finally, the pursuit of freer trade is probably the surest route to true food security. However, in the transition period to freer trade, some system of international collaboration on stock-holding or formal or informal insurance schemes will probably be needed.

Malnutrition and Hunger

Problems of malnutrition and hunger are to be contrasted with problems of food security and famine. The latter refer to acute problems that arise due to production shortfalls or the elimination of income opportunities of affected groups. The former refer to inadequate food supplies to particular groups in society on a chronic scale.

Although in many respects this problem is a domestic issue requiring domestic means to deal with it, it has a number of international dimensions. First, the bulk of malnutrition in most countries is a problem of poverty and low incomes. Consequently, international measures and collaboration that lead to higher rates of broad-based economic growth can play an important role in dealing with this problem.

Second, an increase in food supplies in the aggregate is another means of dealing with the problem. Other things being equal, an increase in food supplies leads to lower prices. Given that low-income groups spend a larger share of their budget on food, they will benefit in a relative sense. Moreover, a decline in food prices can result in significant income gains for such groups. It is for this reason that investments in new production technology, with the tendency of this technology to lower food prices, can be an important means of distributing the benefits of economic progress in a more equitable way.

Finally, targeted feeding programs can be an important means of dealing with malnutrition if the appropriate administrative and organizational skills are available. A variety of such programs has been established around the world, and considerable experience has been acquired in implementing them. The United States has long used a food stamp program that attempts to limit access to free or lower-priced food to low-income groups. India, as well as other countries, have used fair-price shops. And a number of countries use two-price systems to assure that low-income groups have access to food at reasonable prices.

Such targeted feeding programs can have important international implications. The availability of such programs will enable individual countries to pursue more rational domestic policies for their agricultural sector and reduce the use of policies that discriminate against the agricultural sector.

It is clear that the food stamp program has enabled the United States to avoid cheaper food policies. More generally, because trade and exchange rate policies are such an important means of keeping the domestic price of food down, the availability of targeted feeding programs can be an important means of bringing about a more open international trading system, and with it the more general realization of comparative advantage.

Opportunities for International Collaboration

The close of World War II witnessed a tremendous burst of creativity in the design and implementation of international institutions. These institutions stood the test of experience reasonably well for a considerable period of time, and in some cases for a longer period of time than their founders had a right to expect. However, at least three considerations suggest that new mechanisms are needed for international collaboration. First, most of the international institutions were designed by the advanced countries to serve the advanced countries. Although they served that purpose quite well, they are less and less relevant to the world economy that is emerging. In particular, the frustration of the South (the Southern hemisphere) in the North-South debate is due in large part to the fact that the international institutions are of so little value to most countries there.

Second, some of the international institutions designed at the end of World War II have broken down, but little has been put in their place. For example, that part of the Bretton-Woods convention dealing with exchange rates broke down when the world shifted to a system of floating exchange rates in 1973. Nothing has been put in its place, with the result that crises are dealt with on an ad hoc basis as they arise.

Third, trade patterns have evolved in such a way as to make the international institutions increasingly less relevant even for the countries they were designed to serve. The emergence of the centrally planned economies and the less-developed countries as major factors in international trade illustrates important cases in point. Many of these countries are not signatories to the General Agreement on Tariffs and Trade (GATT), yet GATT provides what regulations there are for international trade. This situation is particularly significant in agricultural trade, for it is the centrally planned economies and less-developed countries that have energed as major importers of food.

Similarly, nontariff barriers to trade have emerged as important means of interfering with trade, yet until the latest round of multilateral trade negotiations there was little in the rules of GATT that dealt with these interventions. State and quasi-state trade institutions are also largely outside the purview of GATT. Yet such entities are increasingly either a vehicle for trade or a source of trade intervention.

The time is ripe for a major reform of our international institutions, and in some cases the creation of new ones. In the discussion that follows, the perspective is toward the international institutions needed at the present time. None of these is specific to the Pacific Basin countries. However, they point to the direction in which international cooperation may be possible and suggest goals toward which the countries might wish to be working.

Support for International Research and Advanced Training

Agricultural research is one of the few areas in which new international institutional arrangements have emerged in the post-World War II period. The creation of the Consultative Group on International Agricultural Research (CGIAR) and its associated international agricultural research institutes was a major institutional innovation on the world scene. This system is designed to help develop a technological capability for the less-developed countries and to diffuse the results of this research on the international scene. More recently this system, through ISNAR, the International Service for National Agricultural Research, has begun the difficult task of helping to strengthen the research systems in individual countries.

Financial support for this system has come primarily from the advanced countries.[11] In some sense that is a limitation, for it tends to perpetuate the patron-client relationships that have dominated international relations in the post-World War II period. Bilateral collaboration in the area of agricultural research and institutional development has been structured for the most part in the same way. Consequently, the less-developed countries have had only limited opportunities to influence activities that are so important to them. Among the Pacific Basin countries there are a number of true bilateral collaborative efforts. But they serve more as exceptions to the general rule.

Funding for this system has been on a somewhat precarious basis. It depends on voluntary contributions by the developed countries, and often carries with it important influences on the character and shape of the research program. Over the longer term the basis of this funding needs to be changed, and the basis of the cooperation needs to be broadened. In addition, some means needs to be found by which international funds can be allocated to the strengthening of national research systems and programs.

Vern Ruttan has addressed this last question in Chapter 11 of this volume, so the remaining remarks deal with the other two. The first issue has to do with broadening the basis for international collaboration in building up the stock of human capital in individual countries. Some years ago international assistance for institution-building and for advanced graduate training was an important component of international foreign assistance. Despite the success of these efforts in at least some cases (Brazil and India are important examples), support for such activities has declined. National governments have offset part of this decline as the importance of advanced graduate training has become increasingly recognized. However, the need for institutional development still exists, and in some countries offers major opportunities.

This task should be broadly conceived. It isn't just agricultural research institutions that need to be strengthened. Graduate training programs are needed in many countries to train the future supply of researchers and teachers. After the capacity for research has been strengthened, extension services will be needed to diffuse the new knowledge. Institutions to train middle-level professionals will also be needed, so secondary schools and undergraduate institutions should be strengthened. And in many countries the capacity to provide formal elementary schooling in rural areas needs to be strengthened.

The opportunities for international cooperation in these various endeavors is legion. Bilateral collaboration can do a great deal. So can regional groupings with similar agricultures and similar cultural backgrounds. And there may be opportunities for fully international institutions. In all three of these dimensions, more attention should be given to devising means by which the existing stock of trained people can be shared more effectively.

A major challenge the international community faces is to develop the means to finance such programs. International organizations to date depend on what are essentially voluntary contributions by nation-states. If the respective organizations are to evolve and fulfill the important responsibilities and challenges they face, a more systematic means of financing them will be needed. It is time that more intellectual and political effort is directed to this problem.

Discussion at the conference focused on three issues. First, participants noted that producing and sharing in new technology should be beneficial to both developed and developing countries of the region because of the wide variety of technologies available in Pacific Basin countries. Second, participants stressed the importance of South-South cooperation, with emphasis on biological improvements, protection of soils in tropical areas, and post-harvest technology. Finally, the problem of domestic discrimination against locally trained researchers was discussed.

An International Central Bank

The increased instability that has characterized international commodity markets during the 1970s has been an important motivation for intervention in agricultural trade, the basis for a renewed interest in self-sufficiency, and the source of increased concern for food security. More generally, instability leads to inefficient resource use and with it sacrificed output.

An important part of the increased instability of the 1970s is due to monetary phenomena. In particular, as noted above, the combination of the shift to floating exchange rages, the emergence of a well-integrated international capital market, and the instability of U.S. monetary policy has contributed importantly to this commodity market instability. Under present institutional arrangements this instability is not likely to disappear. In the early 1980s the United States has forced a major realignment of exchange rates on the international economy as it once again has taken on the task of being banker for the world. Success in such a policy requires that the United States overvalue its currency, and that at least some others undervalue theirs. These moves are potential sources of distortions in world agriculture.

The solution to this problem is to establish an International Central Bank with responsibility for managing the growth of international monetary reserves. The creation of such an institution, which could be nothing more than an extension of the International Monetary Fund, would leave individual countries with the relatively more technical problem of managing the growth in their own money stock. The motivation for distortions in exchange rates would be reduced, and a system of discipline for the management of exchange rates would undoubtedly be required. Such a system would not only reduce the use of exchange rate policy as the basis for taxing or subsidizing agriculture, but it would also reduce the instability in international commodity markets. The time for such an institutional innovation is long past due. Participants in the conference agreed that some form of monetary reform was needed.

Reform of GATT

Simply put, GATT consists of a set of rules and regulations for managing trade and a mechanisms or mechanisms for settling trade disputes among countries. As noted above, these rules and mechanisms have become less and less relevant to trade as it has evolved over the last decade. Countries of the South have been saying this as they have attempted to put their requests for a New International Economic Order on the agenda of the international community. They have also complained about the injustices of the present system.

If GATT is not to become increasingly irrelevant, it badly needs a major reform. And if reform is beyond reach, a new set of rules and regulations and settlement mechanisms should be established. To date, the North-South debate has been a dialogue of the deaf. Neither side appears to listen to what the other side is saying. Perhaps if voices were lowered and attention focused on some of the pragmatic programs necessary to making a more effective GATT, piece-meal progress could lead to more general reform as confidence is built.

When the Tokyo round of multilateral trade negotiations came to a close, many observers felt that it would be the last attempt at such a comprehensive effort to lower trade barriers. However, just a few short years later pressure is already building for a new round. In this viewer's judgment, such an attempt is not worth the economic and political cost it would entail, in large part because conducting such negotiations under the auspices of GATT would no longer represent the true economic and political interests of the international community. Whether the advanced countries like it or not, economic and political power on the world scene has shifted toward the less-developed countries. Moreover, the centrally planned economies have become suffficiently important in international trade so that they also should be included in any international agreements.

The challenge is to break out of the somewhat artificial GATT-UNCTAD (United Nations Conference on Trade and Development) venues for trade negotiations and to develop a more constructive context in which to carry new negotiations forward. It will be difficult for the advanced countries to recognize that the political and economic realities of the world have changed. It will be equally difficult for the less-developed countries to give up some of their favorite shibboleths. But both sides must try if international institutions relevant to the changed political and economic realities of the world are to be developed.

Participants at the conference gave considerable attention to the potential of commodity agreements as a means of dealing with trade problems, especially if such agreements had funds for dealing with trade adjustment problems. The problem with this suggestion is that it is very difficult to specify operational rules for an agreement when exchange rates are fluctuating so greatly.

Trade Adjustment Problems

The failure to deal with trade adjustment problems ultimately imposes negative externalities on the world economy in the form of sacrificed output. Because of this, it makes sense to devise an international means of dealing with the problem, even though the adjustments required are within individual countries. One possibility would be an International Adjustment Fund that would provide external support for dealing with adjustment problems. Such a fund could be financed by a levy based on GNP. The advantage of such an approach is that it would attempt to provide a solution to the problem that is consistent with the way the problem is typically perceived and articulated. What is perceived as a problem whose source is in the international economy would be dealt with by an international means.

Participants at the conference agreed that adjustment in domestic markets must be a prerequisite for further cooperation in international trade. They also called attention to the role of price in facilitating the needed adjustment, and noted that domestic prices should be floated to world price equivalents in order to forestall the possibility of dumping.

Participants agreed on this point—that domestic prices must be allowed to adjust to world price levels to forestall dumping. They also agreed that solving domestic income distribution and equity problems is the key to dealing with trade issues, and that domestic structural constraints make it less likely that greater international cooperation will benefit the masses.

The Food-Security Problem

If the world were free of barriers to trade and had appropriate international monetary arrangements, there would probably be no need for international cooperation in order to deal with the food-security problem. Shortfalls in one part of the world would be offset by above-average levels of production in others, and international commodity markets would be reasonably stable. Moreover, international capital markets would provide the means for financing shortfalls when individual countries experienced these shortfalls.

Unfortunately, the world is far from realizing this idealized Nirvana. Trade barriers cause commodity markets to be more unstable than they otherwise would be. And in periods of tight supplies, these barriers become even more extensive.

What is probably needed to deal with the food-security problem that emerges as a consequence of these barriers is an international reserve designed specifically for the less-developed countries. If the advanced countries were to put up the initial capital endowment of grain, such a reserve could be managed as an insurance scheme. Participating countries would have access to the reserve supplies only when their domestic production fell below trend line by a predetermined amount. They would be responsible for paying this reserve back when their production was above trend. If there should be a problem in abusing the system, renewed access to the reserve could be precluded until the original trade was repaid.

Previous studies suggest that a modest reserve of 4-8 million metric tons could deal with most of the shortfalls for all the less-developed countries. This reserve would involve modest costs, and with the advantge to all countries that it would be mildly stabilizing to international commodity markets. Such a program could be developed on a regional basis rather than for the international economy as a whole.

Participants in the conference argued that strategic security issues should be separated from food-security issues. Most countries do integrate these two issues, but new efforts should be developed to separate the two.

Concluding Comments

The international economy has experienced dramatic changes in the post–World War II period, with these changes accelerating in the last decade. Trade patterns have changed significantly, major institutional developments have occurred—such as the emergence of a well-integrated international market for capital and the shift from fixed to flexible exchange rates—and there have been major realignments of political and economic power. The established institutional arrangements have not kept up with these changes, nor have new institutional arrangements evolved at the rate they should. Foreign relations and international diplomacy have increasingly been dominated by economic issues, yet countries have only crude and blunt tools for dealing with these problems. Perhaps at no time in the post–World War II period has the international situation so cried out for intellectual creativity in designing new institutional arrangements and for political leadership to implement them. The opportunities for international cooperation and collaboration are great. The issue is whether the world community will seize the moment.

Participants in the conference reached a consensus on a number of conclusions and suggestions for future research. First, they noted that the papers and discussions tended to concentrate on the supply side of the food issue, addressing possibilities for increasing agricultural productivity and achieving food security through different combinations of self-sufficiency and trade strategies. At least one participant pointed out the need to address the demand side, or the problems of the major food importers, e.g., Japan, in future work and discussions.

Second, and related to the first issue, strong sentiments were expressed concerning the need to direct even more attention to the problem of distribution of the potentially abundant world food supply. Not only does international inequality of demand and resources need to be addressed, but also internal equity and distribution problems. Further, particular attention should be paid to the very poor—those countries without the resources to develop their own agricultural capacity or to import sufficient amounts of food.

Third, new models need to be created for analyzing these problems. As one ASEAN participant remarked, "We are prisoners of our own fantasies about how to solve our problems." There was no consensus among participants about the extent of the need for new institutions or the direction their design should take. However, there was general recognition of the need for innovation in institution-building to solve the problems of the contemporary world, for which the old institutions such as GATT are worn and outdated. One new approach suggested for this effort is to think of the new institutions in terms of process rather than structure.

Fourth, as a first step toward initiating some functional cooperative efforts in food and agriculture in the Pacific Basin, participants suggested the formation of regional or international consultative bodies somewhat more formalized and ongoing than the present workshops, yet not at the level of a committee of sovereign states. The involvement of governments was viewed as risky because of many hostilities, yet the forums could serve as an important educational function for high-level officials.

The goals for the present workshops and future efforts, it was suggested, would be to first identify the patterns of trade and distribution and assess the needs for change, then to put forth options for governments to choose from in devising their own national policies. Only after these steps are taken will it be fruitful to discuss the establishment of all-encompassing formal organizations within a "Pacific Community."

Notes

1. For the evidence on Brazil, see Mauro Lopes and G. Edward Schuh, *A Mobilização de Recursos na Agricultura: Uma Analise de Politica para o Brazil* (Brasilia, Brazil: CFP-Ministerio de Agricultura, Coleçao Analise e Pesquisa, vol. 8, 1979).

2. Finis Welch, "Education in Production," *Journal of Political Economy* 79(3), May/June 1971.

3. T. Schultz, *Transforming Traditional Agriculture* (New Haven: Yale University Press, 1964).

4. G. Edward Schuh, "Out-migration, Rural Productivity, and the Distribution of Income," in *Essays on Migration and the Labor Market*, ed. R. H. Sabat (Boulder, Colo: Westview Press, 1982).

5. Yujiro Hayami and Vernon W. Ruttan, *Agricultural Development: An International Perspective* (Baltimore: The Johns Hopkins Press, 1970).

6. D. Gale Johnson, *World Agriculture in Disarray* (Fontana Publishers, 1973).
7. This perspective is known as the Prebisch thesis.
8. Advanced countries that fix their producer prices above market levels can hardly be expected to let foreign producers put a drain on their treasury.
9. G. Edward Schuh, "Floating Exchange Rates, International Interdependence, and Adjustment Policy," paper presented at the meetings of the International Association of Agricultural Economists, Banff, Canada, 1979.
10. For an analytical framework for considering the economies of foreign relations, see G. Edward Schuh "Economics and International Relations," *American Journal of Agricultural Economics* 63(5), December 1981:767-778.
11. Membership of the boards of directors of the International Agricultural Research Centers has in recent years been significantly diversified, with ample presence of representatives from the developing countries.

About the Contributors

Byung-joon Ahn is professor of political science at Yonsei University in Seoul, Korea.
Kym Anderson is professor of economics at the University of Adelaide in Australia.
Alejandro Cruz-Serrano is director of international transactions at the Ministry of Energy and Mining in Mexico City, Mexico.
Robert E. Evenson is professor of economics at Yale University, New Haven, Connecticut.
Michael J. Greenwood is professor of economics and director of the Center for Economic Analysis, University of Colorado, Boulder.
Wallace E. Huffman is professor of economics at Iowa State University, Ames.
M. Ann Judd is a research associate at the Economic Growth Center at Yale University, New Haven, Connecticut.
Ralph Lattimore is professor of agricultural economics at Lincoln College, Canterbury, New Zealand.
Cassio Luiselli is deputy director for the United Nations Economic Commission for Latin America in Mexico City, Mexico.
Chung H. Lee is professor of economics at the University of Hawaii at Manoa, Honolulu.
Jennifer L. McCoy is assistant professor of political science at Georgia State University, Atlanta.
Martin E. Piñeiro is senior researcher at the Center of Social Research over the State and Administration, Buenos Aires, Argentina, and at the International Service for Agricultural Research, The Hague, Netherlands.
James Roumasset is professor of economics at the University of Hawaii at Manoa and research associate at the East-West Resource Systems Institute, Honolulu.
Vernon W. Ruttan is professor of agricultural economics at the University of Minnesota, St. Paul.
G. Edward Schuh is director of the Agriculture and Rural Development Department at the World Bank, Washington, D.C.

P. Lynn Stuart is assistant professor of economics at Williams College, Williamstown, Massachusetts.

E. J. Trigo is senior research officer at the International Service for Agricultural Research, The Hague, Netherlands.

Wu Daxin is research fellow and senior agricultural economist at the Academy of Agricultural Sciences, Beijing, People's Republic of China.

Index

AARD. *See* Agency for Agricultural Research and Development
Abaca, 214
Accounting system, 191, 192-194(table)
ADB. *See* Asian Development Bank
Ad valorem tax, 51
Africa, 13, 20, 46, 47, 234-235(table). *See also specific countries*
African Development Bank, 209
Agency for Agricultural Research and Development (AARD) (Indonesia), 212
Agency for International Development, U.S. (AID), 207, 210, 211, 220
Agricultural commercialization, 92-93, 95, 243
Agricultural inputs industry, 237-238, 242, 256
Agricultural price supports, 3, 4, 38, 53, 178. *See also under* South Korea
Agricultural production, 1, 2, 3, 17, 19, 26, 30-31(table), 46, 50, 57, 58, 68-69(table), 100, 161, 211, 216, 229, 231, 232, 233-235(tables), 236, 240, 242, 249, 250, 271
 capital-intensive, 243, 245, 249
 growth, 256-257, 265
 and industrial sector, 94
 and land, 19, 20, 161, 206, 256
 and prices, 49(fig.), 50, 87
 specialization, 46, 60, 242
 See also Research; Technology
Agricultural surplus, 257-258. *See also* Food-surplus countries
Agriculture. *See* Agricultural production; Economic growth; Food; Industry, -agriculture interaction; Research; Technology; *under* Pacific Basin; *individual countries*
Agriculture, U.S. Department of (USDA), 77, 217, 237
"Agriculture as the Foundation and Industry as the Leading Factor" (People's Republic of China), 93
Agrochemicals, 237
Ahn, Byung-joon, 4

AID. *See* Agency for International Development, U.S.
Alaouse, Chris M., 54
Ambary hemp, 106, 107(tables)
Andean zone research funding, 230-231(table)
Anderson, Kym, 2
Animal power, 161
Animal protein, 61
Aquaculture, 62, 64-67(table)
Ardila, Jorge, 217
Argentina
 agricultural trade, 28-29(table), 32-36(tables)
 agriculture, 97(table)
 cereal exports, 27, 32-35(table), 47
 Chilean workers in, 121
 corn production, 229, 236
 experiment station, 226
 exports, nonfood, 32-35(table)
 farmer organizations, 239
 fertilizers, 238(table)
 food exports, 47, 103
 GNP, 28-37(tables), 97(table)
 graduate training, 228, 231-232(tables)
 industrialization, 95
 industrial sector, 97(table)
 labor force, 30-31(table), 47
 land endowment per capita, 27, 28-29(table)
 livestock exports, 27, 36(table)
 manufacturing, 26, 30-35(table), 97(table)
 national research program, 217, 227, 228, 231(table), 236
 patents, 184-185(table), 190, 192-194(table)
 population, 28-29(table)
 production growth rate, 30-31(table)
 service sector, 97(table)
 technology, 225, 236, 239
 wheat exports, 47
 yield increases, 233(table)
Arizona, 125
ASEAN. *See* Association of Southeast Asian Nations
Asian Development Bank (ADB), 63, 209

277

Index

Asian-Pacific Triangle provisions (U.S. immigration policy), 146–147
ASOCAÑA. See Association of Sugarcane Producers
Association of Southeast Asian Nations (ASEAN), 45, 272
Association of Sugarcane Producers (ASOCAÑA), (Colombia), 239
Australia
 agricultural trade, 28–29(table), 32–36(tables), 64–67(table)
 agriculture, 23, 25, 30–31(table), 38, 64–69(tables), 93
 beef exports, 103
 bilateral assistance programs, 207
 calories, daily provision, 68–69(table)
 exports, nonfood, 32–36(tables)
 as food exporter, 3, 27, 47, 61, 75, 103
 food imports, 68–69(table)
 food security, 68–69(table)
 GNP, 28–31(tables)
 immigration to, 146
 income growth, 25, 28–29(table)
 industrialization, 93, 95
 labor force, 30–31(table), 68–69(table)
 and labor migration, 121
 land endowment per capita, 25, 27, 28–29(table)
 livestock exports, 27, 32–35(table)
 patents, 184–185(table), 196–197(table)
 population, 28–29(table)
 private sector, 178, 179(table)
 production growth rate, 30–31(table), 68–69(table)
 protectionism, 78(table)
 research, 164–166(table), 178, 179(table)
 rice exports, 75, 76(table), 78(table)
 and self-sufficiency, 45
 technology, 64–67(table), 223
 wheat exports, 47, 64–67(table)
Austria, 179(table), 184–185(table), 196–197(table)
Autarchic policies, 261
Authoritarian governments, 94
Aviculture, 64–67(table)

BAI. See Bureau of Animal Industry
Bal, H. K., 211
Balance-of-payments problems, 47, 156, 246
Balassa, Bela, 94
Bananas, 36(table), 64–67(table), 233(table)
Bangladesh, 215, 216
Bangladesh Rice Research Institute, 216
Bangladesh Sugarcane Research Institute, 215
Barichello, Richard R., 50
Barley, 64–67(table), 100(table), 103
Basic needs, 45
Beans, 64–67(table), 100(table), 216, 233–235(tables)
Beef, 27, 36–37(tables), 38, 64–67(table), 103, 192–194(table), 216, 234–235(table), 236
Belgium, 130, 179(table), 184–185(table), 196–197(table), 207

Benelux countries, 184–185(table)
Bilateral cooperation, 57, 62, 207
Biogenetic inventions, 190–195, 198
Biotechnology, 62, 190–191
Bogotá Experimental Farm (Colombia), 226
Bolivia, 227, 233(table), 238(table)
Bolivian Institute of Agricultural Technology (IBTA), 227
Border prices, 48, 49, 53, 79
BPI. See Bureau of Plant Industry
Bracero program (1942–1964), 122, 124
"Brain drain," 5
Brazil
 agricultural trade, 28–29(table), 32–36(tables)
 agriculture, 97(table)
 exports, nonfood, 32–35(table)
 fertilizers, 238(table)
 GNP, 28–31(tables), 97(table)
 incomes, 25
 industrialization, 95
 industrial sector, 97(table)
 labor force, 30–31(table)
 land endowment per capita, 28–29(table)
 manufacturing, 26, 30–35(tables), 97(table)
 national research programs, 218, 227, 230–231(table), 239, 267
 patents, 184–186(tables), 190, 192–194(table), 195, 201
 population, 28–29(table)
 production growth rate, 30–31(table)
 resource endowment, 30–31(table)
 service sector, 97(table)
 yield increases, 233(table)
Breeding technology, 191, 192–194(table), 203
Bretton-Woods convention (1944), 266
Bulgaria, 184–185(table), 196–197(table)
Bureau of Animal Industry (BAI) (Philippines), 215
Bureau of Plant Industry (BPI) (Philippines), 215
Burma, 76(table), 163

California, 124, 125
Calories, 68–69(table), 110
Cambodia, 25
Canada
 agricultural trade, 28–29(table), 32–36(tables), 64–67(table), 261
 agriculture, 38, 64–69(tables)
 bilateral assistance programs, 207
 calories, daily provision, 68–69(table)
 dairy price policy, 50–51
 emigrants, 12, 150–151
 exports, nonfood, 32–36(tables)
 as food exporter, 3, 27, 32–35(table), 47, 61
 food imports, 68–69(table), 75
 food security, 68–69(table)
 GNP, 28–31(tables)
 immigration policies, 146
 income growth, 25
 labor force, 30–31(table), 68–69(table), 150

and labor migration, 121, 149, 150-151, 153
land endowment per capita, 25, 28-29(table)
patents, 184-185(table), 188-189(table), 196-197(table)
population, 28-29(table)
production growth rate, 30-31(table), 68-69(table)
protectionism, 78(table)
research, 164-166(table)
rice imports, 75, 78(table)
and self-sufficiency, 45
technology, 64-67(table), 223
wheat exports, 47, 64-67(table)
Cañete Experimental Station (Peru), 226
Canned food, 36(table), 64-67(table)
Capital. *See* Financing and investment; Research, expenditures; Resource capital
Capital accumulation, 24
Capital flow, 5, 17
Capital goods, 7, 224
Capital markets, 261, 263-264, 268, 270, 271
Carabeef, 215
CARE program, 210
Caribbean research funding, 230-231(table)
Carlata Stock Farm (Philippines), 215
Cartels, 54
Cash crops, 27, 36(table), 109
Cassava, 86, 233(table)
Catholic Relief, 210
Cauca Valley (Colombia), 226
CENICAÑA. *See* Sugarcane Research Center
Central Agricultural Experimental Station (Ecuador), 226
Central American Institute of Agricultural Technology (ICTA) (Guatemala), 227
Central America research funding, 230-231(table)
Centrally planned economies, 13, 20, 25, 184-185(table), 261
Central Rice Research Station (Indonesia), 214
Cereal trade, 13, 16, 17, 26-27, 32-37(tables), 53-54, 57, 59, 63, 68-69(table), 73, 103
CETA. *See* Consortia of French Agricultural Technology Experimentation
CGIAR. *See* Consultative Group on International Agricultural Research
Chickens, 27, 37(table)
Chile
  agricultural trade, 28-29(table), 32-36(tables), 64-67(table)
  agriculture, 26, 64-69(tables), 97(table)
  calories, daily provision, 68-69(table)
  experiment station, 226
  exports, nonfood, 32-36(tables)
  farmer organizations, 239
  fertilizers, 238(table)

food deficit, 61
food imports, 68-69(table)
GNP, 28-31(tables), 97(table)
industrialization, 95
industry, 97(table)
labor force, 30-31(table), 68-69(table)
labor migration, 121, 153
land endowment per capita, 28-29(table)
manufacturing, 26, 30-35(tables), 97(table)
national research institute, 227
patents, 184-185(table), 188-189(table), 192-194(table), 196-197(table)
population, 28-29(table)
private sector, 179(table)
production growth rate, 30-31(table), 68-69(table)
research, 164-166(table), 179(table)
service sector, 97(table)
technology, 239
yield increases, 233(table)
China. *See* People's Republic of China
Chinese Academy of Agricultural Sciences, 108
Chisholm, A. H., 77
Chun, Doo-Hwan, 101
CIAT. *See* International Center for Tropical Agriculture
CIMMYT. *See* International Wheat and Maize Improvement Center
Circulars on Rural Work (Chinese Communist Party), 114, 116
Club of Rome, 11
Cocoa, 36(table), 64-67(table)
Coconut, 36(table), 64-67(table), 215
Coffee, 27, 36(table), 64-67(table), 233(table)
Collectivization, 92, 93, 95
Colombia
  agricultural trade, 28-29(table), 32-36(tables), 64-67(table)
  agriculture, 64-69(tables)
  calories, daily provision, 68-69(table)
  experiment stations, 226
  exports, nonfood, 32-36(tables)
  extension service, 236
  fertilizers, 238(table)
  food imports, 68-69(table)
  food security, 68-69(table)
  graduate training, 228-232(tables)
  industrialization, 95
  labor migration, 121, 153
  labor force, 30-31(table), 68-69(table)
  land endowment per capita, 28-29(table)
  manufacturing, 26, 30-35(tables)
  national research program, 217, 227, 228, 231-232(tables)
  patents, 184-185(table), 196-197(table)
  population, 28-29(table)
  private sector, 236, 237
  production growth rate, 30-31(table), 68-69(table)
  research, 164-166(table), 239
  rice production, 229, 236, 239
  sugar production, 232, 237, 239
  technology, 64-67(table), 236, 239

Index

yield increase, 233(table)
Colombian Institute for Agriculture (ICA), 227, 231-232(tables), 239
Colorado, 125
Colza, 64-67(table)
Commodity prices, 15-17, 19, 24
Commodity taxes, 86
Communications. See Infrastructure
Comparative advantage, 2, 4, 22, 23, 24, 25-26, 27, 38-39, 58, 59, 60, 77, 79, 90, 92, 99, 103, 260, 262, 263, 266
  revealed, 26, 32-35(table), 41(n6)
Computer program, 191, 192-194(table)
Consortia of French Agricultural Technology Experimentation (CETA), 239
Constant prices, 106
Consultative Group on International Agricultural Research (CGIAR), 209, 267
Consumer price index, 50, 126-129(tables)
Contracts, 39, 87, 113, 114, 115, 117, 118, 161, 178
Cooperatives. See under People's Republic of China; South Korea
Corn, 64-67(table)
  exports, 36(table)
  as feed, 61
  hybrid, 108, 192-194(table), 200, 202, 203
  imports, 47
  prices, 16, 50, 52, 61, 86
  production, 229, 234-235(table)
  publications, 175-176(tables), 177
  and self-sufficiency, 27, 37(table)
  technology, 236
  yields, 233-235(tables)
Corn Laws (Great Britain), 93
Costa Rica, 164-166(table), 184-185(table), 196-197(table), 233(table), 238(table)
Cotton, 36(table), 106, 107(tables), 108, 175-176(tables), 226, 233(table)
CREA. See Regional Consortia of Agricultural Experimentation
Credit, 3, 63, 85, 86, 87, 162, 240
Cruz-Serrano, Alejandro, 3
Cuba, 196-197(table), 238(table)
Czechoslovakia, 184-185(table), 196-197(table)

Daegu (S. Korea), 98
Dairy products, 36-37(tables), 38, 64-67(table)
  pricing, 45, 50, 53
"Decision on Some Questions Concerning the Acceleration of Agricultural Development, The" (Chinese Communist Party), 109
Deficiency payments, 52
Deforestation, 260-261
Democracy, 93
Denmark, 184-185(table), 196-197(table)
Dependency, 95
Developing countries, 14, 20, 27, 30-36(tables), 93-94, 180, 184-185(table), 198

Development assistance, 45, 207-209. See also International aid
Division of labor, 46, 103, 104, 113
Dollar (U.S.), 16, 17
Domestic market, 48-49, 50, 52-53, 77, 95, 240, 249, 270
Domestic price (DP), 49(fig.), 50, 52-53, 79, 84, 85, 86, 103, 270
Dominican Republic, 230-231(table), 233(table), 238(table)
DP. See Domestic price
Dual economy, 94
Dumping, 270

Eastern Europe, 168-171(table), 184-185(table)
East Germany, 184-185(table)
ECLA. See Economic Commission for Latin America
Economic Commission for Latin America (ECLA), 240
Economic development, 2, 3, 4-5, 7, 39, 59, 161, 240, 248, 256, 257, 258
  inward- and outward-oriented strategies, 94-96
  social aspects of, 4-5
Economic growth, 22, 24, 25, 38, 46, 162, 265
Economic interdependence, 45, 73, 90, 91, 103
Economic Support Fund (U.S.), 207
Economic warfare, 264
Economy of scale, 99
Ecuador
  agricultural trade, 28-29(table), 32-36(tables), 64-67(table)
  agriculture, 64-69(tables)
  calories, daily provision, 68-69(table)
  Colombian workers in, 121
  experiment station, 226
  exports, nonfood, 32-35(table)
  fertilizers, 238(table)
  food deficit, 61
  food imports, 68-69(table)
  food security, 68-69(table)
  GNP, 28-31(tables)
  incomes, 25
  labor force, 30-31(table), 68-69(table)
  labor migration, 153
  land endowment per capita, 28-29(table)
  milk production, 232, 236
  national research institute, 227, 239
  patents, 184-185(table)
  population, 28-29(table)
  private sector, 236
  production growth rate, 30-31(table), 68-69(table)
  research, 164-166(table)
  technology, 64-67(table), 236
  yield increases, 233(table)
Edquist, C. H., 224
Edqvist, O., 224
Education, 109, 122, 228, 231-232(tables), 263, 267-268. See also Rural development

EEC. *See* European Economic Community
Eggs, 27, 37(table), 110
Egypt, 184-185(table), 220
El Salvador, 68-69(table), 233(table), 238(table)
EMBRAPA. *See* Empresa Brasilera de Pesquizas Agropecuarias
Employment. *See* Labor, distribution; Unemployment
Empresa Brasilera de Pesquizas Agropecuarias (EMBRAPA), 218, 227
Enclosure, 92
Energy policies, 16-17
Energy transformation, 249
EP. *See* Equilibrium price
Equilibrium price (EP), 49(fig.), 50
Equity, 46
Estanzuela experiment station (Uruguay), 226
Europe, 13, 25, 130, 198. *See also* Eastern Europe; Western Europe
European Community, 13
European Economic Community (EEC), 53, 130
Evenson, Robert E., 6, 211
Exchange rates, 3, 15, 16, 17, 18(fig.), 19, 48, 49(fig.), 99, 263, 266, 269, 270, 271
floating, 264, 268
Experiment stations, 204, 205, 210, 226, 227-228, 237
Export-promoting strategies, 91, 95. *See also* South Korea, export-led growth
Export tax, 15, 24, 27, 51, 257, 262
Extension services, 79, 86, 109, 163, 172, 198, 209, 213, 221, 224, 228, 236, 241, 256, 268

Factor prices, 249
Falcon, W. P., 75, 77, 79
Family planning, 101
Famine, 264, 265
FAO. *See* Food and Agriculture Organization
Far East, 234-235(table)
Farmers
  income, 39, 41(n9)
  organizations, 237, 238-239
  political clout, 4, 24
  See also South Korea, and self-help programs
Farming systems research, 216
FEDEARROZ. *See* National Federation of Rice Growers
Federal Reserve, U.S., 17
Fertilizer Fund (S. Korea), 100
Fertilizers, 62, 98, 100, 101, 108, 161, 190, 192-194(table), 237, 238(table), 256
Financing and investments, 58, 59, 63, 85, 100, 161, 162, 163, 198, 211, 213, 218-220, 232, 247
Finland, 184-185(table), 196-197(table)
Fish products, 36(table), 57, 60, 61-62, 64-67(table)
Five-year development plans, 94, 96

Florida, 125
FONAIAP. *See* National Fund for Agricultural and Livestock Research
Food
  basic, 216
  consumption, 47, 61
  demand, 59, 272
  distribution, 1, 2, 3, 20, 46, 56, 57, 161, 255, 272
  exports, 23, 25, 27, 28-29(table), 32-36(tables), 47, 58, 64-67(table). *See also* Food-exporting nations
  imports, 3, 4, 5, 11, 13-15, 17, 20, 25, 27, 28-29(table), 36(table), 38, 39, 50, 58, 64-69(tables), 103. *See also* Food-importing countries
  "inferior," 86
  as political weapon, 3, 39-40, 47, 58, 220, 271
  prices, 2, 3-4, 15-17, 19, 48-49, 50-53, 77, 86, 265. *See also* Agricultural price supports; *under specific crops*
  reserves, 56, 57, 63, 68-69(table), 271
  share of, 14, 68-69(table)
  shortage, 1, 11. *See also* Food-deficit countries
  stockpiling, 263, 264. *See also* Storage policies
  supply, 1, 2, 20, 47, 50, 161, 265, 271
  trade, 1, 2-5, 11, 12-13, 17, 19, 20, 24, 47-48. *See also* Pacific Basin, agricultural trade
  world production, 47, 74(table)
  See also Food security; Self-sufficiency
Food aid, 55(n7), 57, 58, 68-69(table), 208(table)
Food and Agriculture Organization (FAO), 62, 207
Food-deficit countries, 45, 46, 47, 54, 61
Food-exporting nations, 3, 15, 39, 53, 54, 61, 63
Food-importing countries, 3-4, 15, 27, 53, 54, 272
Food processing, 62
Food security, 1, 20, 39, 40, 255, 264-265
  defined, 3, 45
  indicators, 68-69(table)
  policies, 45, 47-48, 50-54, 56, 58, 73, 86-87
  and self-sufficiency, 1, 3, 4, 24, 39, 45, 50, 265, 271
  systems, 57. *See also* Mexican Food System
  and trade, 2-3, 4, 45-54, 57, 270-271
Food stamp program (U.S.), 265, 266
Food-surplus countries, 46, 47, 61
Ford Foundation, 209, 210, 211
Foreign Agricultural Circular (USDA), 77
Foreign exchange, 15, 85, 87, 256, 264
  social opportunity cost, 50
  See also Exchange rates
Foreign goods and services, 14
Four Modernizations (People's Republic of China), 93

Index

France, 130, 179(table), 184-185(table), 188-189(table), 196-197(table), 207, 239
Free trade, 48, 50, 53, 91, 92, 103, 260, 261-264, 265
Fruits, 27, 36-37(tables), 60, 64-67(table)
FUSAGRI. *See* Shell Foundation for Agriculture, Venezuela
Futures markets, 39, 84

GATT. *See* General Agreement on Tariffs and Trade
GDP. *See* Gross domestic product
General Agreement on Tariffs and Trade (GATT), 134, 137, 266, 269-270, 272
General equilibrium immigration framework, 131-134
Geothermal energy, 108
Germany, 123(table), 130, 184-186(tables), 188-189(table), 196-197(table), 207, 210, 238(table). *See also* East Germany
Ghana, 184-185(table)
GNP. *See* Gross national product
Government policy. *See* Policy interventions
Graduate training programs, 228, 231-232(tables), 267-268
Grain
 availability, 61
 contracts, 87
 disease, 108
 embargoes, 3, 47, 264
 exports, 45, 58
 imports, 53, 60
 insurance, 87, 265, 271
 prices, 47, 56, 59, 61, 87
 production, 106, 107(tables), 109-112
 supplies, 63, 87
 See also Cereal trade; *specific grains*
Grain buffer stocks, 45, 87
Grain Management Fund (S. Korea), 100
Great Britain, 92, 93, 130, 146, 184-185(table), 188-189(table), 196-197(table), 207, 211
Great Depression (1930s), 16, 17
Great Leap Forward (People's Republic of China), 93
Greece, 179(table), 184-185(table)
Green revolution, 101
Greenwood, Michael J., 5
Griliches, Zvi, 203
Gross domestic product (GDP), 68-69(table), 96
Gross national product (GNP), 12, 30-31(table), 270
 per capita, 25, 28-29(table)
Guatemala, 164-166(table), 227, 233(table), 238(table)
Guest worker program, 130
Gur, 215

Hadwiger, Don, 217
Hai River, 108
Haiti, 238(table)
Hayami, Yujiro, 262

Health, 221, 256
Hechscher-Ohlin-Samuelson (HOS) model, 131, 132
Herbicides, 190, 192-194(table)
High-income countries, 3, 14(table), 22, 24, 25, 27
High-yielding food crops, 86
Hirschman, Albert O., 91
Hogs, 50, 106, 107(tables)
Honduras, 233(table), 238(table)
Hong Kong
 agricultural trade, 28-29(table), 32-36(tables), 64-67(table)
 agriculture, 25, 64-69(tables), 97(table)
 calories, daily provision, 68-69(table)
 exports, nonfood, 32-35(table)
 food imports, 20, 36(table), 64-69(tables), 75
 and food security, 59, 61, 68-69(table)
 GNP, 28-31(tables), 97(table)
 industrial development, 61, 96, 97(table)
 labor force, 30-31(table), 68-69(table)
 land endowment per capita, 28-29(table)
 manufacturing sector, 97(table)
 patents, 184-185(table)
 population, 28-29(table)
 production growth rate, 30-31(table), 68-69(table)
 rice imports, 75, 76(table), 78
 and self-sufficiency, 78
 service sector, 97(table)
 technology, 64-67(table)
HOS. *See* Hechscher-Ohlin-Samuelson model
Huai River, 108
Huffman, Wallace E., 5
Hunan province (People's Republic of China), 111
Hungary, 184-185(table), 191, 196-197(table)
Hunger, 20, 57, 255, 265-266
Hydroelectric power, 108, 208

IBTA. *See* Bolivian Institute of Agricultural Technology
ICA. *See* Colombian Institute for Agriculture
ICTA. *See* Central American Institute of Agricultural Technology
IDB. *See* Inter-American Development Bank
IFPRI. *See* International Food Policy Research Institute
IITA. *See* International Institute for Tropical Agriculture
Illegal aliens, 130. *See also* United States, and Mexican labor migration
IMF. *See* International Monetary Fund
Immigration and Naturalization Service (INS), U.S., 125
Import restrictions, 24, 262
Import-substitution, 4, 54, 60, 92, 95, 96, 98, 262
Import tax, 24
Income
 distribution, 2, 60, 102, 157, 243, 248, 250, 260, 270

Index   283

growth, 23, 24, 25, 30-31(table), 38, 59, 257
growth and food demand, 27
inequality, 1, 259, 270
and patents, 195, 197(table)
per capita, 12, 13, 14(table), 15, 19, 20, 25, 96, 255, 256, 265
rural, 4, 39, 41(n9), 59, 101, 116
urban, 39
India, 95, 162, 184-185(table), 188-189(table), 196-197(table), 205(n7), 211, 220, 262, 265, 267
Indiana, 203
Indonesia
　agricultural trade, 28-29(table), 32-36(tables), 64-67(table)
　agriculture, 26, 64-69(tables), 86, 216
　calories, daily provision, 68-69(table)
　cereal imports, 68-69(table), 75
　exports, nonfood, 32-36(tables)
　food aid, 68-69(table)
　food security, 68-69(table)
　GNP, 28-31(tables)
　labor force, 30-31(table), 68-69(table)
　and labor migration, 149, 151, 157
　national research programs, 212-213, 214-215
　patents, 184-185(table)
　as petroleum exporter, 15, 26
　population, 28-29(table)
　production growth rate, 30-31(table), 68-69(table)
　provisionist policy, 78(table), 85
　research, 164-166(table), 167, 212-213, 214-215
　rice imports, 75, 76(table), 78(table), 85, 89(n12)
　rice technology, 213
　and self-sufficiency, 45, 85
　technology, 64-67(table), 213
　universities, 212
Indonesian National Vegetable Research Center, 214
Industrialization, 91, 92, 93, 94, 95, 259
Industrialized countries. See Australia; Canada; Japan; New Zealand; United States
Industrial revolution, 92
Industry, 3, 4, 5, 26, 38, 60, 61, 260, 262
　-agriculture interaction, 90-104, 116, 134-135, 237-238, 256
　investment, 59
　patents, 188-189(table)
　See also Manufacturing
Inflation, 47, 100, 103, 156
Infrastructure, 63, 79, 86, 98, 100, 161, 208, 228, 240, 242, 263
INIA. See Institute of Agricultural Technology (Peru); National Agricultural Research Institute (Mexico); National Institute for Agricultural Research (Chile)
INIAP. See National Institute for Agricultural and Livestock Research

INS. See Immigration and Naturalization Service, U.S.
Insecticides, 190, 192-194(table)
Institute of Agricultural Technology (INIA) (Peru), 227
Institute of Agricultural Technology (INTA) (Nicaragua), 227
Institutional change, 241-243
Insurance. See under Grain
INTA. See Institute of Agricultural Technology (Nicaragua); National Institute for Agricultural Research (Argentina)
Inter-American Development Bank (IDB), 63, 209
Interest groups, 24, 39
Interest rates, 47, 63, 95, 99
International Adjustment Fund, 270
International aid, 266-271, 272
　decline, 6, 45
　research, 206, 207-209, 217-221, 240
International Center for Tropical Agriculture (CIAT), 209, 236, 239
International Central Bank, 269
International division of labor, 12
International Food Policy Research Institute (IFPRI), 14
International Institute for Tropical Agriculture (IITA), 209
International Labor Office, 149
International Monetary Fund (IMF), 39, 63, 68-69(table), 87, 93, 269
International research institutes, 6, 177, 203, 205, 206, 209-210, 228, 232, 248
International Rice Research Institute (IRRI) (Philippines), 177, 209, 212
International Service for National Agricultural Research (ISNAR), 267
International Wheat and Maize Improvement Center (CIMMYT) (Mexico), 177, 209
Inventions, 178, 179, 180, 181, 187, 190-191, 192-194(table), 198-200, 204
Iowa, 203
Iran, 75, 76(table)
Iraq, 75, 76(table), 184-185(table)
Ireland, 184-185(table), 196-197(table)
IRRI. See International Rice Research Institute
Irrigation, 86, 101, 108, 161, 261
ISNAR. See International Service for National Agricultural Research
Israel, 184-185(table), 196-197(table)
Italy, 179(table), 186(table), 196-197(table)

Jabara, Cathy, 51
Jamaica, 238(table)
Japan
　and agricultural technology, 62, 64-67(table)
　agricultural trade, 28-29(table), 32-36(tables), 64-67(table), 261
　agriculture, 25, 26, 37(table), 64-69(tables), 162, 258

bilateral assistance programs, 207
calories, daily provision, 68-69(table)
emigration and immigration, 145, 146, 151, 152
exports, 26, 32-36(tables), 85
feedgrain imports, 38
fertilizers, 238(table)
fisheries, 62
food imports, 20, 61, 64-69(tables), 75, 272
food security, 68-69(table)
GNP, 28-31(tables)
income, 41(n9)
labor force, 30-31(table), 68-69(table)
and labor migration, 121, 149, 152
land endowment per capita, 28-29(table)
land tax, 258
manufacturing, 26, 30-35(tables), 61, 85, 95
national research system, 210-211
patents, 184-186(tables), 198, 201
population, 28-29(table)
private sector, 178, 179(table)
production growth rate, 30-31(table), 68-69(table)
protectionism, 38(table), 77, 78(table), 85
research, 164-166(table), 167, 178, 179(table), 191, 210-211
rice exports and imports, 75, 77, 78(table)
rice yield, 101, 212
and SAM philosophy, 59
self-sufficiency, 37(table), 45, 85
and sugar prices, 16
wheat imports, 13, 38, 64-67(table)
Java, 162, 214
Jha, Dayanath, 211
Jiangsu province (People's Republic of China), 111
Johnson, D. Gale, 16, 87, 262
Johnston, Bruce, 258
Jones, Ronald, 131
Judd, M. Ann, 6
Jute, 106, 107(tables)

Kahlon, A. S., 211
Kenya, 179(table), 184-185(table), 188-189(table), 196-197(table)
Keynesian economics, 45
Korea, Democratic People's Republic of, 61, 64-69(tables)
Korea, Republic of. See South Korea
Korean War (1950-1953), 16, 96
Kossoudji, Sherrie, 124

LAARC. See "Latin American Agricultural Research Corporation"
Labor, 22, 23, 24, 25, 26, 38, 59, 256
and capital accumulation, 23
capital intensive, 232
costs, 263
distribution, 30-31(table), 68-69(table)
participation rate, 150-151, 152
skilled, 152-154, 155, 156, 259
transfer, 258-260

See also Labor migration
Labor certification, 149
Labor migration, 1, 5-6, 121-138, 148-149, 259-260
and economy, 154-156, 259
See also Pacific Basin, migration within
La Granja Agricultural Research Center (Philippines), 215
La Molina Agrarian University (Peru), 227, 231-232(tables)
La Molina Experimental Station (Peru), 226
Land, 19, 20, 22, 23
capital intensive, 232
endowment per capita, 25, 27, 28-29(table)
inputs per unit, 161, 162
-person ratio, 260
ratio to capital, 23, 25
reform, 94, 95, 96
taxes, 258
Land Grant Colleges (U.S.), 237
Laos, 25
Latin America, 7, 25
agriculture, 25, 26, 216
cash crops, 27
development strategy, 95
incomes, 25
labor migration, 152
land endowment per capita, 25
manufacturing, 26
patents, 187, 190
research, 217
and technological change, 224, 225-250
wheat imports, 13
See also individual countries
"Latin American Agricultural Research Corporation" (LAARC), 187, 190, 192-194(table)
Lattimore, Ralph, 2
LDCs. See Less-developed countries
Lee, Chung H., 4
Legal systems, 161, 163, 177, 178, 187, 195.
See also Inventions; Patents
Less-developed countries (LDCs), 262, 271
agricultural output, 19
and food security, 45-46, 87
grain imports, 13, 85
manufacturing sector, 87
trade policies, 91, 261
Liberalism, 93
Limits to Growth, The (Meadows et al.), 11
LIPI. See National Science Development Board
Livestock
breeding, 226
feed, 13, 15, 38, 47, 51, 61, 63
production, 57, 58, 60, 106, 107(tables), 109
products, 13, 15, 27, 32-36(tables), 47, 64-67(table)
and self-sufficiency, 27, 37(table), 45
Live virus vaccine, 191, 192-194(table)
Locusts, 108
Long-term contracts, 39

Low-income countries, 4, 13, 14, 15, 19, 26, 30-31(table), 64-67(table), 168-171(table), 181, 187, 188-189(table), 256
Luiselli, Cassio, 3

McCalla, Alex F., 54
McCoy, Jennifer L., 2
McIntire, John, 46
Maize. *See* Corn
Malawi, 196-197(table)
Malaysia
  agricultural trade, 28-29(table), 32-36(tables), 64-67(table)
  agriculture, 26, 64-69(tables)
  calories, daily provision, 68-69(table)
  exports, nonfood, 32-36(tables)
  food deficit, 61
  food imports, 68-69(table), 76(table)
  GNP, 28-31(tables)
  labor force, 30-31(table), 68-69(table)
  land endowment per capita, 28-29(table)
  manufacturing, 26, 30-31(table), 32-35(table)
  national research program, 213
  patents, 196-197(table), 198
  population, 28-29(table)
  private sector, 178, 179(table)
  production growth rate, 30-31(table), 68-69(table)
  protectionism, 78(table)
  research, 164-166(table), 172, 178, 179(table), 198, 213
  rice imports, 76(table), 78(table)
  rubber, 213
  technology, 64-67(table)
Malaysian Agricultural Research and Development Institute (MARDI), 213
Malnutrition, 20, 57, 255, 265-266
Malthus, Thomas, 162
Malthusian crisis, 11, 12, 13, 14, 20, 255
Manufacturing, 22, 23, 26, 38, 39, 97(table), 103
  capital-intensive, 23, 95
  exports, 17, 23, 32-35(table), 103
  imports, 23, 103
  labor, 23, 24, 30-31(table)
  labor-intensive, 23, 24, 26, 95, 96, 98, 260
  prices, 24, 95
  production, 30-31(table)
  protectionism, 87
  See also Industry
MARDI. *See* Malaysian Agricultural Research and Development Institute
Manioc, 64-67(table)
Mao Zedong, 93
Market information, 161
Market interventions, 161, 162
Marsh gas. *See* Methane
Maryland, 125
Mauritius, 196-197(table)
MDCs. *See* More-developed countries
Meat, 64-67(table), 107(tables), 110, 111
  exports, 36(table)

  See also Beef; Pork; Poultry
Medellin Experimental Farm (Colombia), 226
Medicinal herbs, 115
Mercantilism, 93
Metals, 26, 32-35(table)
Methane, 108
Mexican Food System (SAM), 3, 57, 70(n1)
  applications of, 60-63
  basis of, 56, 59-60
Mexico
  agricultural trade, 28-29(table), 32-36(tables), 64-67(table)
  agriculture, 27, 59, 64-69(tables), 97(table)
  calories, daily provision, 68-69(table)
  consumer price index, 128-129(table)
  fertilizers, 238(table)
  food deficit, 61
  food exports, 27, 32-36(tables), 60, 64-67(table)
  food imports, 5, 15, 60, 64-69(tables), 75
  food security, 68-69(table)
  and foreign investment, 140(n27)
  GNP, 28-31(tables), 97(table), 128-129(table)
  industrial exports, 5, 32-35(table)
  industry, 97(table)
  investment, 128-129(table)
  labor costs, 27
  labor force, 30-31(table), 68-69(table), 128-129(table), 134. *See also* United States, and Mexican labor migration
  land endowment per capita, 28-29(table)
  manufacturing, 97(table)
  national research program, 216, 227, 230-231(table)
  patents, 184-185(table), 192-194(table)
  as petroleum exporter, 15, 32-35(table)
  population, 28-29(table), 121, 128-129(table)
  production growth rate, 30-31(table), 68-69(table)
  and regional cooperation, 62
  research, 164-166(table), 167, 172, 216, 230-231(table)
  rice imports, 75
  service sector, 97(table)
  technology, 64-67(table)
  wages, 128-129(table)
  yield increase, 233(table)
  See also Mexican Food System
Michigan, 125
Middle East, 15, 75
Middle-income countries, 19, 64-67(table), 98, 263
  cereal imports, 13
  income growth, 25, 30-31(table)
  income per capita, 14(table)
  industry, 26
  patents, 195
  research expenditures, 164-166(table), 167, 168-171(table), 172, 173-176(tables)
Mildew, 226
Milk, 27, 37(table), 50, 52, 107(table), 232, 233-235(tables), 236

286 Index

Millet, 64-67(table)
Minerals, 23, 25, 26, 32-35(table), 46
Modernization. See Latin America, and technological change
Monke, E. A., 75, 77, 79
Monopoly, 178, 179, 199-201, 204, 237, 243
More-developed countries (MDCs), 87
Morocco, 184-185(table), 196-197(table)
Most-favored-nation, 39
Multilateral trade, 53, 57
  negotiations, 12, 269
Multinational firms. See Transnational firms
Multiple sourcing, 46
Myrdal, Gunnar, 95

National Agricultural Research Institute (INIA) (Mexico), 216, 227
National Agricultural Society (Chile), 226
National autonomy, 2, 3, 60, 134, 144, 207
National Federation of Rice Growers (FEDEARROZ) (Colombia), 239
National Fund for Agricultural and Livestock Research (FONAIAP) (Venezuela), 227
National Institute for Agricultural and Livestock Research (INIAP) (Ecuador), 227
National Institute for Agricultural Research (INIA) (Chile), 227
National Institute for Agricultural Research (INTA) (Argentina), 226, 231-232(tables), 236
National origins quota system (U.S.), 146-147, 148
National Research Institutes, 6, 7, 163, 203, 204, 206, 210-217, 218, 223, 224, 226-229, 236, 237, 239-243, 246-247, 249, 250
  funding, 228, 230-231(table), 240
  graduate training, 228, 231-232(tables)
National Science and Technology Councils, 247
National Science Development Board (LIPI) (Indonesia), 212
National Strategic security, 2, 3, 5, 271
Neoclassical trade theory, 22
Netherlands, 130, 179(table), 184-185(table), 196-197(table), 207
New Community Movement (S. Korea), 4, 91, 96, 99, 100-102
New International Economic Order, 45, 62, 269
Newly industrializing countries (NICs), 3, 4, 25, 26, 38, 92, 94, 103, 263
New Village Factory Program (S. Korea), 101
New York State, 125
New Zealand
  agricultural trade, 28-29(table), 32-36(tables), 64-67(table)
  beef exports, 103
  calories, daily provision, 68-69(table)
  exports, nonfood, 32-36(tables)
  as food exporter, 3, 32-35(table), 61, 103

food imports, 68-69(table)
food security, 68-69(table)
GNP, 28-31(tables)
immigration to, 146
industrialization, 93, 95
labor force, 30-31(table), 68-69(table)
  and labor migration, 121
land endowment per capita, 27, 28-29(table)
livestock exports, 27, 36(table), 64-67(table)
patents, 184-185(table)
population, 28-29(table)
private sector, 178, 179(table)
production growth rate, 30-31(table), 68-69(table)
research, 164-166(table), 178, 179(table)
technology, 64-67(table)
Nicaragua, 68-69(table), 164-166(table), 220, 227, 233(table), 238(table)
Nicholls, William H., 257
NICs. See Newly industrializing countries
Nigeria, 15, 179(table)
Nitrogen-fixing bacteria, 191, 192-194(table)
Nontariff barriers, 85, 137, 266
North America, 234-235(table). See also Canada; United States
North Korea, 25
North-South debate, 266, 269
Norway, 20, 179(table), 184-185(table), 196-197(table)
Nutrition, 256
Nuts, 64-67(table)

OAPI, 184-185(table)
Oats, 64-67(table)
Office of Rural Development (S. Korea), 212
Ohio, 125
Oil, 59
  crises (1973, 1979), 91
  exports, 32-35(table)
  prices, 11, 26, 47
Oil palm, 36(table), 64-67(table)
Oils and fats, 36(table), 64-67(table), 106, 107(tables)
Oligopolistic markets, 53, 54, 58, 59, 60
OPEC. See Organization of Petroleum Exporting Countries
Oregon, 125
Organization of Petroleum Exporting Countries (OPEC), 11, 15, 26, 46

Pacific Basin
  agricultural technology and research, 6-7, 58, 79, 86, 163-205, 206, 208. See also Latin America, and technological change
  agricultural trade, 25-27, 28-29(tables), 32-36(tables), 38-39, 58, 62, 75, 256, 261-268
  agriculture, 1, 2, 4, 12, 22-40, 46, 104, 162
  countries, 25, 28-29(table), 64-67(table), 88(n1). See also individual countries

crops, 27, 36(table), 64-67(table). *See also specific crops*
 and economic integration and cooperation, 22, 39-40, 46, 57-58, 62-63, 91, 103-104, 223, 257, 268, 272
 exports, 26, 32-36(tables), 57, 74(table)
 food strategies, 57, 62
 imports, 57
 migrant labor policy recommendations, 5, 137-138
 migration within, 144-157
 population, 28-29(table), 45, 58
 problem issues, 256-266
 See also Food; Food security; Industry; Manufacturing; Self-sufficiency; Service sector
Pacific Basin Project, 1, 59
"Pacific Council," 104
Pacific island economies, 25
Pakistan, 75, 76(table), 184-185(table), 218, 220
Pakistan Agricultural Research Council (PARC), 218
Palawija crops, 216
Palmira Experimental Farm (Colombia), 226
Panama, 164-166(table), 230-231(table), 233(table), 238(table)
Papua New Guinea, 64-69(tables)
Paraguay, 233(table), 238(table)
PARC. *See* Pakistan Agricultural Research Council
Paris Convention, 181
Park Chung Hee, 96
Patents, 180-187, 188-189(table), 190-198, 199, 200, 201, 202, 242, 247
PBA (Pacific Basin area). *See* Pacific Basin
PCARR. *See* Philippine Council of Agricultural Research and Resources
Peace Corps (U.S.), 221(n3)
Peanuts, 64-67(table)
Pennsylvania, 125
People's Republic of China
 agricultural construction program, 106, 108
 agricultural education, 109
 agricultural policy, 109, 112-118
 agricultural production, 5, 62, 68-69(table), 105-108, 109, 110-111, 112, 113, 114
 agricultural technology and research, 108-109, 118
 agricultural trade, 28-29(table), 32-35(table), 64-67(table)
 agriculture, 5, 64-67(table), 93, 105-112
 aquaculture, 62
 arable land, 115
 calories, daily provision, 68-69(table), 110
 Chinese Communist Party, 105, 109, 112, 114
 collectivization, 93, 95, 105, 114, 115, 117
 communes, 105, 113, 117
 cooperatives, 116, 117, 118
 cotton, 106, 107(tables)
 Cultural Revolution (1966-1976), 109, 216
 economy, 110
 electricity, 108
 exports, nonfood, 32-35(table), 136
 food aid, 68-69(table)
 food consumption, 110, 111
 food deficit, 61
 food security, 68-69(table)
 forests, 108, 115
 GNP, 28-31(tables)
 grain imports, 45, 61, 64-69(tables), 110, 111
 grain production, 106, 107(tables), 108, 109-112
 grassland, 111
 household economies, 105, 113, 114-115, 116
 income, 116
 industrialization, 95
 industry, 106, 116, 136
 irrigation, 108
 jute and hemp, 106, 107(tables)
 labor force, 30-31(table), 68-69(table), 116-117
 labor migration, 151
 land endowment per capita, 28-29(table), 110, 115, 116
 livestock, 106, 107(tables), 109, 111
 milk, 107(table)
 national research programs, 216
 oil-bearing crops, 106, 107(tables)
 population, 28-29(table), 110, 111, 112
 prices, 112
 production brigades, 105, 106, 113, 117
 production growth rate, 30-31(table), 68-69(table), 106
 production teams, 105, 106, 113, 114, 117
 provisionist policy, 78(table)
 research, 164-166(table), 167, 173(table), 216
 rice exports, 75, 76(table), 78(table)
 rivers, 109
 rural, 105, 108, 110, 112, 113-118
 self-management, 113
 self-sufficiency, 5, 110
 silkworm cocoons, 106, 107(tables)
 state farms, 105
 sugar, 106, 107(tables)
 taxes, 114, 115
 tea, 106, 107(tables)
 technology, 64-67(table), 108, 118
 tractors, 108
 trade fairs, 113
 urban, 110
Pergamino Experimental Station (Argentina), 226
Peru
 agricultural trade, 28-29(table), 32-36(tables), 64-67(table)
 agriculture, 68-69(table)
 calories, daily provision, 68-69(table)
 experimental stations, 226
 exports, nonfood, 32-35(table)
 fertilizers, 238(table)
 food deficit, 61

food imports, 68-69(table)
food security, 68-69(table)
GNP, 28-31(tables)
graduate training, 228, 231-232(tables)
labor force, 30-31(table), 68-69(table)
land endowment per capita, 28-29(table)
national research program, 217, 227, 228, 231-232(tables)
patents, 192-194(table)
population, 28-29(table)
production growth rate, 30-31(table), 68-69(table)
research, 164-166(table)
technology, 64-67(table)
university, 227
yield increase, 233(table)
Pesticides, 62, 256
Philippine Council of Agricultural Research and Resources (PCARR), 212, 214, 215, 218
Philippines
  agricultural trade, 28-29(table), 32-36(tables), 64-67(table)
  agriculture, 26, 64-67(tables)
  calories, daily provision, 68-69(table)
  College of Agriculture, 208, 214
  exports, nonfood, 32-36(tables)
  food deficit, 61
  food imports, 68-69(table)
  food security, 68-69(table)
  GNP, 28-31(tables)
  labor force, 30-31(table), 68-69(table)
  and labor migration, 121, 151, 154, 157
  land endowment per capita, 28-29(table)
  legal system, 178
  manufacturing, 26, 30-35(tables)
  national research program, 211, 212, 214, 215, 217, 218
  patents, 184-186(tables), 188-189(table), 195, 196-197(table), 201
  population, 28-29(table)
  private sector, 198
  production growth rate, 30-31(table), 68-69(table)
  provisionist policy, 78(table)
  research, 164-166(table), 198, 211, 212, 214, 215, 217
  rice exports and imports, 75, 78(table)
  rice research, 212
  technology, 64-67(table)
Philippine Sugar Institute (PHILSUGEN), 215
PHILSUGEN. See Philippine Sugar Institute
Pigs, 61, 64-67(table)
Piñeiro, Martin E., 7, 217
Plant variety patent conventions (PVPCs), 203
Plow, 190, 192-194(table), 195
Poland, 184-186(tables), 196-197(table)
Policy interventions, 3-4, 24, 39-40, 47-48, 99, 100-101, 136-137, 161, 162, 178, 229, 256-266
  and technology, 243-249

See also Food security, programs; People's Republic of China, agricultural policy; Rice, policies; Self-sufficiency, policy
Political independence, 45, 93
Political pluralism, 93
Political repression, 5
Population growth, 14, 19
Pork, 27, 37(table), 110
Portugal, 179(table), 184-186(tables), 196-197(table)
Potatoes, 233-235(tables)
Poultry, 15, 27, 64-67(table)
Poverty, 1, 2, 20, 206, 207, 255, 256, 257, 265
Prebisch, Raul, 95
Prebisch model, 24
Pre-industrial states, 95
Price stabilization, 232
Primary products. See Commodity prices; Food, trade; Pacific Basin, agriculture; individual countries, agriculture
Private sector, 6, 7, 94, 103
  research, 163, 177-181, 191, 198, 200, 201, 202, 203, 204, 209, 210, 237, 240, 241, 242
  and technology, 223, 224, 227, 236, 237, 241, 247, 250
Producer price, 77
Productive sectors, 22
Protectionism, 4, 38, 39, 40, 49(fig.), 58, 77-78, 79, 82, 84, 85, 86-87, 103, 135-136, 162, 261, 262
  defined, 79
Protein, 61, 62, 110
Provisionist policies, 4, 77, 78, 79, 82, 84, 85-86
Publications research data, 172, 175-176(tables), 177
Pump wells, 108
Punta del Este meeting, 240
Pusan (S. Korea), 98
PVPCs. See Plant variety patent conventions

Quotas, 51, 199

Ranney, Susan, 124
Reagan, Ronald, 17
Recessions, 47
Refugee Act (1980) (U.S.), 147, 148
Regional Consortia of Agricultural Experimentation (CREA) (Argentina), 239
Regional integration. See Pacific Basin, and economic integration and cooperation
Remittances, 156, 157
Rents, 20, 199, 201
Replacement hypothesis, 156
Research, 6-7, 19, 163-177, 201, 202-205, 206-221, 226, 256, 267
  activity types, 248
  expenditures, 164-166(table), 167-177, 198, 210, 250
  funding, 218-220, 230-231(table), 267

See also International research institutes; National Research Institutes; Pacific Basin, agricultural technology and research; Patents
Resource allocation, 4, 48, 51, 77, 79, 84, 86, 161, 162, 216, 244, 245
Resource capital, 22, 23, 25, 91, 99
Resource conservation, 260-261
Resource endowment, 22, 25-26, 62, 90, 91, 94, 102, 256, 262
Ricardo, David, 162
Rice, 64-69(tables)
  consumption, 74-75, 82, 84
  demand, 77, 79, 80, 81(figs.), 82, 83-84
  export embargo, 47
  exports, 36(table), 74(table), 75, 76(table), 77, 78(tables), 81, 82, 83
  imports, 38, 75, 76(table), 77, 78(tables), 79, 80, 82, 85
  policies, 75, 77-87
  price, 4, 73, 77, 78, 79-86, 87, 100, 102, 103
  production, 4, 74, 75, 77, 79, 86, 100(table), 209, 212, 229, 234-235(table)
  publications, 175-176(tables), 177
  research, 212, 213, 215, 239. See also International Rice Research Institute
  supply, 77, 79, 80-81, 82, 83-84, 86
  technology, 236, 239
  varieties, 101, 108, 216
  yields, 101, 216, 233-235(tables)
Rice Producers' Federation (Colombia), 236
Risk-management, 84
Rockefeller Foundation, 209, 210, 211
Romania, 184-185(table), 191
Rose, 192-194(table)
Roumasset, James, 4
RRIM. See Rubber Research Institute of Malaysia
Rubber, 27, 36(table), 213, 215
Rubber Research Institute of Malaysia, 213
Rubber Research Station (Indonesia), 215
Rural development, 162, 198, 207, 221, 228, 256, 259, 268
Rural-urban labor adjustment, 12, 24, 101-102, 257, 258, 259
Ruttan, Vernon W., 6, 7, 262, 267
Rwanda, 196-197(table)
Rye, 64-67(table)

Sábato, J. F., 249
Saemaul Movement. See New Community Movement
Sahel region (Africa), 46
SAM. See Mexican Food System
Saudi Arabia, 75, 76(table)
Savings, 99
Saxena, P. N., 211
Scarcity rents, 20
Schuh, G. Edward, 2, 7, 48
Schultz, T., 243, 259
Schumacher, E. F., 248
Scientist man-years (SMYs), 164-166(table), 167, 168-171(table), 172, 173-174(tables), 178, 179(table)

Scobie, Grant M., 14, 16, 17
Seeds, 237, 250
Segmentation hypothesis, 154
Self-sufficiency, 4, 39, 59, 62, 78, 79, 92
  and feedstuffs-livestock products ratio, 27, 37(table), 61
  policy, 79, 83-84, 85, 87, 96, 264
  pricing, 45
  See also under Food security
Semi-industrialized countries, 164-166(table), 167, 168-171(table), 172, 173-176(tables), 177, 180, 184-185(table), 195, 198
Seoul (S. Korea), 98, 101
  National University, 212
Service sector, 23, 24, 30-31(table), 38, 97(table)
Sheep and goats, 106, 107(tables)
Shell Foundation for Agriculture, Venezuela (FUSAGRI), 227
Siamwalla, Ammar, 45, 46, 47
Sierra Leone, 196-197(table)
Silkworm cocoons. See under People's Republic of China
Singapore
  agricultural trade, 28-29(table), 32-36(tables), 64-67(table)
  agriculture, 25, 64-69(tables), 97(table)
  calories, daily provision, 68-69(table)
  exports, nonfood, 32-35(table)
  food imports, 20, 36(table), 64-67(table)
  and food security, 59, 61, 68-69(table)
  GNP, 28-31(tables), 97(table)
  industrial development, 61, 96, 97(table)
  labor force, 30-31(table), 68-69(table)
  land endowment per capita, 28-29(table)
  manufacturing, 97(table)
  patents, 184-185(table)
  population, 28-29(table)
  production growth rate, 30-31(table), 68-69(table)
  rice imports, 76(table), 78
  service sector, 97(table)
SMYs. See Scientist man-years
Socialist agriculture, 105. See also Centrally planned economies; People's Republic of China
Social justice, 94
Social values, 48-49, 50, 200
Solar energy, 108
Sorghum, 64-67(table), 108, 233(table)
South Africa, 179(table), 196-197(table)
South Carolina, 125
Southern Cone, 226, 230-231(table)
South Korea
  agricultural price supports, 4, 99, 101, 103
  agricultural production, 100, 101, 102
  agricultural trade, 28-29(table), 32-36(tables), 64-67(table)
  agriculture, 4, 5, 25, 30-31(table), 37(table), 64-69(tables), 91, 96, 97(table), 98, 99, 100, 102
  arable land, 99
  balance-of-trade deficits, 96, 102, 103
  beef prices, 51

Index

calories, daily provision, 68-69(table)
cooperatives, 62
emigration and immigration, 145, 151, 154
export-led growth, 4, 5, 32-35(table), 91, 96, 98, 101, 103
exports, 98
family planning, 101
feed-grain imports, 51, 64-67(table)
five-year plans, 96, 98(table), 99, 101
food deficit, 61
food imports, 68-69(table), 75, 103
food security, 68-69(table), 102
foreign exchange, 96
GDP, 96
GNP, 28-31(tables), 97(table)
imports, 91, 96, 102, 103
income, 41(n9), 96, 101, 102
industrial sector, 4, 5, 30-35(tables), 61, 91, 96-99, 102
inflation, 100, 103
infrastructure, 98, 100
labor force, 30-31(table), 68-69(table), 91, 98, 99, 102, 103
labor migration, 154
land endowment per capita, 28-29(table)
land reform, 96
legal system, 178
manufacturing, 97(table), 98(table), 103
national research program, 211-212
patents, 184-186(tables), 188-189(table), 196-197(table)
population, 28-29(table), 99, 101
prices, 99, 100, 102-103
private sector, 103, 179(table), 198
production growth rate, 30-31(table), 68-69(table), 98
protectionism, 38(table), 78(table)
research, 164-166(table), 167, 172, 179(table), 198, 211-212
rice exports and imports, 75, 76(table), 78(table)
rice production, 100, 101, 102, 212
rural, 99, 100, 101, 102
savings, 99
self-help programs, 4. See also New Community Movement
and self-sufficiency, 37(table), 45, 51, 102
service sector, 97(table)
tax system, 99
technology, 64-67(table)
trading companies, 99
urban, 98, 99, 100, 101, 102
South-South cooperation, 268
Soviet Union
  collectivization, 93
  food imports, 11, 13, 76(table)
  industrialization, 93
  patents, 184-185(table), 196-197(table)
  and U.S. grain embargo, 47
  wheat imports, 13
Soybeans, 64-67(table)
  export embargo (U.S.), 11
  exports, 36(table)
  prices, 50

research, 192-194(table), 203
and self-sufficiency, 27, 37(table)
yields, 233(table)
Spain, 179(table), 184-186(tables), 196-197(table)
Special Drawing Rights, 68-69(table)
Specialization, 103, 114
Sri Lanka, 76(table), 136, 184-185(table), 196-197(table)
Starvation, 1
State, U.S. Department of, 220
State farms. See under People's Republic of China
Storage policies, 3, 45, 62, 63, 85
Streeten, Paul, 45, 48
Stuart, P. Lynn, 5
Subsidies, 3, 17, 39, 50, 51, 60, 79, 86, 94
  export, 24, 87
  import, 15, 262
Sugar, 64-67(table)
  consumption, 110
  exports, 27, 36(table)
  prices, 16, 53
  production, 106, 107(tables), 232, 234-235(table)
  publications, 175-176(tables)
  research, 177, 215, 226, 239
  technology, 237, 239
  yields, 233-235(tables)
Sugarcane Research Center (CENICAÑA) (Colombia), 239
Sukamandi rice station (Indonesia), 213, 215
Supply prices, 20, 53
Sweden, 179(table), 184-185(table), 196-197(table), 207
Sweet potatoes, 64-67(table)
Switzerland, 130, 184-185(table), 188-189(table), 196-197(table), 207
Syria, 196-197(table)

Taiwan
  agricultural trade, 28-29(table), 32-36(tables), 64-67(table)
  agriculture, 25, 37(table), 64-67(table)
  exports, nonfood, 32-35(table), 136
  GNP, 28-31(tables)
  industrial development, 61, 96
  industry, 136
  labor force, 30-31(table)
  and labor migration, 121
  land endowment per capita, 28-29(table)
  legal system, 178
  population, 28-29(table)
  private sector, 178, 179(table)
  production growth rate, 30-31(table)
  protectionism, 38(table), 78(table)
  research, 164-166(table)
  rice exports, 75
  self-sufficiency ratios, 37(table)
  technology, 64-67(table)
Tanguis cotton, 226
Tariffs, 16, 178, 199, 257, 260
Taxation, 19, 39, 86, 99, 114, 258, 261. See also Export tax

Tea, 64–67(table), 106, 107(tables)
Technology, 2, 3, 6, 7, 12, 19–20, 22, 23, 24, 57, 62, 64–67(table), 161, 163, 179, 223, 249, 256, 257, 265
  appropriate, 248
  chemical, 178, 188–189(table), 190, 191, 198, 210
  development, 256–257, 268
  diffusion, 223, 224, 225–226, 238
  markets, 180–181
  mechanical, 178, 182–183(table), 188–189(table), 190, 192–194(table), 195, 198, 203, 210
  social carriers of, 224, 225, 236
  as social issue, 239–241, 244, 250
  transfer, 6, 56, 58, 198, 201, 210, 213, 220, 223, 227, 228, 229, 236, 238, 239, 241
  See also Inventions; Patents; Research
Texas, 125
Textile industry, 136
Thailand
  agricultural trade, 28–29(table), 32–36(tables), 64–67(table)
  agriculture, 26, 64–67(table), 68–69(table)
  calories, daily provision, 68–69(table)
  cereal exports, 27, 32–36(tables), 64–67(table)
  cereal imports, 68–69(table)
  exports, nonfood, 32–35(table)
  food aid, 68–69(table)
  food imports, 68–69(table)
  GNP, 28–31(tables)
  labor force, 30–31(table), 68–69(table)
  land endowment per capita, 28–29(table)
  manufacturing, 26, 30–35(tables)
  population, 28–29(table)
  production growth rate, 30–31(table), 68–69(table)
  provisionist policy, 78(table)
  research, 164–166(table), 167
  rice export embargo (1973), 47
  rice exports, 75, 76(table), 78(table)
  technology, 64–67(table)
Thompson, Robert L., 51
Three-factor model (Jones), 131–135
Timber, 27, 36(table)
Tomato, 234–235(table)
  harvester, 124
Tokyo round, 269
Tongil rice, 101
Trade barriers, 3, 5, 12, 270–271
Trademarks, 184–185(table)
Trade secrecy laws, 178–179, 200
Trading companies, 99
Transaction costs, 163
Transnational firms, 7, 58, 60, 70, 178, 199, 224, 226, 237–238, 241
"Transpacific Community," 56
Transportation. *See* Infrastructure
Trigo, E. J., 7, 217
Trinidad and Tobago, 196–197(table), 238(table)
Tunisia, 196–197(table)

Turkey, 184–185(table)
Two-price systems, 52
Tyers, R., 77

Uganda, 196–197(table)
UNCTAD. *See* United Nations Conference on Trade and Development
Unemployment, 249
United Nations, 62, 206–207, 269
United Nations Conference on Trade and Development (UNCTAD), 269
United States
  agricultural prices, 11
  agricultural production, 11, 30–31(table), 211
  agricultural trade, 28–29(table), 32–36(tables), 61, 64–67(table), 261
  agriculture, 38, 64–69(tables), 93
  bilateral assistance programs, 207, 208(table), 220
  Blacks, 155
  calories, daily provision, 68–69(table)
  capital flow to, 17
  commodity prices, 17
  consumer price index, 126–127(table)
  education, 122, 263
  energy policies, 16–17
  exports, nonfood, 32–36(tables)
  export subsidies, 11
  federal deficit, 17
  fertilizers, 238(table)
  as food exporter, 3, 17, 18(fig.), 27, 32–35(table), 47, 61, 75, 103, 262, 263
  food imports, 27, 36(table), 64–69(tables)
  food security, 68–69(table)
  GNP, 28–31(tables), 126–127(table)
  grain embargo use, 3, 11, 47, 264
  grain exports, 61, 64–67(table), 75
  grain reserve stocks, 45
  Hispanics, 155
  immigration policy, 122, 124, 137, 141, 143, 146–148, 154
  immigration to, 6, 123(table), 145, 146, 147, 149, 150–151, 152, 153, 154, 155, 156
  import subsidies, 17
  income growth, 25
  industrialization, 93, 95
  industry, 136
  interest rates, 17
  investment, 126–127(table)
  labor force, 30–31(table), 68–69(table), 121, 126–127(table), 135, 155, 260, 263
  land endowment per capita, 25, 28–29(table)
  macroeconomic indicators, 126–127(table)
  manufacturing, 61, 260
  market forces, 258
  and Mexican labor migration, 5, 121–125, 131, 134–137, 140(n28), 149, 153
  monetary policy, 264, 268
  national research program, 217
  patents, 180, 182–185(tables), 188–189(table), 190, 191, 192–194(table), 196–197(table), 198

population, 28-29(table), 126-127(table)
private sector, 178, 179(table), 237
production growth rate, 30-31(table), 68-69(table)
protectionism, 78(table), 135-136
Puerto Ricans, 155
research, 164-166(table), 178, 179(table), 198, 202-203, 210, 211, 217, 237
rice exports, 75, 76(table), 78(table)
and self-sufficiency, 45
and sugar prices, 16
technology, 64-67(table), 182-183(table), 192-194(table)
as technology exporter, 223
unemployment rate, 124
wages, 126-127(table)
wheat exports, 47, 64-67(table)
See also Food stamp program
Universities, 6, 204-205, 208, 212, 215, 217, 226
UPLB. See University of the Philippines at Los Baños
University of the Philippines at Los Baños, 215
Urban sector, 240, 256, 262
Uruguay, 184-185(table), 196-197(table), 225, 226, 238(table), 239
USDA. See Agriculture, U.S. Department of

Valdés, Alberto, 45, 46, 47
Value added, 68-69(table)
Vegetables, 27, 36-37(tables), 60, 64-67(table)
Venezuela, 15
  agricultural trade, 28-29(table), 32-36(tables)
  agriculture, 26
  Colombian workers in, 121
  exports, nonfood, 32-35(table)
  fertilizers, 238(table)
  GNP, 28-31(tables)
  labor force, 30-31(table)
  land endowment per capita, 28-29(table)
  national research institute, 227
  oil, 26, 32-35(table)
  patents, 184-185(table), 188-189(table), 192-194(table), 196-197(table)
  population, 28-29(table)
  private sector, 227
  production growth rate, 30-31(table)
  yield increases, 233(table)
Veterinary products, 237
Vietnam, 25, 76(table), 95
Virginia, 125

Wages, 23, 99, 124, 126-129(tables), 134-135, 148, 204
Washington, 125
Water supply, 261
Welch, Finis, 259
Western Europe, 25, 234-235(table), 261, 262
West Indies, 122
West Virginia, 125
Wheat, 64-69(tables)
  exports, 36(table), 47
  flour, 86
  imports, 12-13, 38, 47
  midges, 108
  prices, 16, 52, 86, 103
  production, 100(table), 209, 225
  publications, 175-176(tables), 177
  and self-sufficiency, 27, 37(table)
  varieties, 108
  yields, 233(table)
Wind energy, 108
Wool, 36(table)
World Agriculture in Disarray (Johnson), 262
World Bank, 63, 93, 207-209, 213, 214, 219
World economy, 12, 17, 19-20, 32-35(table), 38
World Food Conference (1974), 56
World Food Council, 62, 63
Wu Daxin, 5

Yantze River, 108
Yellow River, 108
Yugoslavia, 184-185(table)

Zaire, 196-197(table)
Zambia, 184-185(table), 196-197(table)
Zhejiang province (People's Republic of China), 111
Zimbabwe, 196-197(table)